What Matters in Probation

What Matters in Probation

edited by

George Mair

WILLAN
PUBLISHING

Willan Publishing
Culmcott House
Mill Street, Uffculme
Cullompton, Devon
EX15 3AT, UK
Tel: +44(0)1884 840337
Fax: +44(0)1884 840251
e-mail: info@willanpublishing.co.uk

Published simultaneously in the USA and Canada by

Willan Publishing
c/o ISBS, 920 NE 58th Ave, Suite 300
Portland, Oregon 97213-3644, USA
Tel: +001(0)503 287 3093
Fax: +001(0)503 280 8832

First published 2004

ISBN 1-84392-052-2 (paperback)

British Library Cataloguing-in-Publication Data
A catalogue record for this book is available from the British Library

Project management by Deer Park Productions
Typeset by GCS, Leighton Buzzard, Beds
Printed and bound by T.J. International, Padstow, Cornwall

Contents

List of figures and tables

Preface

This book had a lengthy gestation process. I slowly began to realise that others, too, had doubts about the What Works initiative and the way it was sweeping all before it. And after a conversation with Judith Rumgay at some conference or other, I decided to go ahead. I am very grateful for the swift agreement by the various contributors to participate and for their forbearance in dealing with my editorial requests and with the (usual) delays with a collection of this kind. Brian Willan, too, deserves thanks – not just for publishing the book but for being patient and supportive beyond the call of duty. Two other individuals have provided invaluable help: Tim Newburn for being a voice of relative sanity in an increasingly chaotic world; and Paul Kelly who gave me the idea for the title in a conversation about the book.

I have promised various children that they would see their names in print, so to avoid being nagged – Ruth Mair, Ethan Mair, Aishling Foley, Sophie Flanagan and Thomas Flanagan – thanks, although for what I'm not always sure.

Finally, my heart-felt thanks to Carmel who has been so supportive in so many ways.

George Mair
Liverpool, January 2004

Notes on contributors

Roy Bailey is an Honorary Senior Research Fellow at DeMontfort University. Previously he was with the probation service as Chief Probation Officer in Devon and then as Director of the Central Probation Council. Work with other organisations includes a long period on the Executive Committee of NACRO, and two years as Honorary Consultant with Save the Children in Northern Ireland. Publications include *Authority in Social Casework* (with Robert Foren), *Probation Supervision: Attitudes to Formalised Helping* (with Dave Ward) and *Interagency Partnerships in Youth Justice* (with Brian Williams).

Gwyneth Boswell is Professor of Criminology and Criminal Justice at DeMontfort University, where she is also Principal Lecturer on the BA in Community and Criminal Justice/Diploma in Probation Studies and Programme Leader for the MA in Community and Criminal Justice. She is co-author, with Davies and Wright, of *Contemporary Probation Practice* (Avebury 1993), editor of *Violent Children and Adolescents: Asking the Question Why* (Whurr 2000) and co-author, with Wedge, of *Imprisoned Fathers and their Children* (Jessica Kingsley 2002).

Jo Deakin is a Lecturer in Criminal Justice at Manchester University. Her research interests include victimisation and fear of crime, offender perspectives on street robbery, and reintegration strategies for offenders on release from prison. She has recently published a paper on women and imprisonment in the *Howard Journal of Criminal Justice* with Jon Spencer.

Stephen Farrall is a Research Fellow in the Department of Criminology, Keele University. He has previously worked for the Universities of Sheffield and Oxford. He is the author or co-author of over 20 journal articles and has edited two books as well as contributing several book chapters. In 2003 he published his monograph *Re-thinking What Works with Offenders: Probation, Social Context and Desistance from Crime*. His main areas of research include why people stop offending, the fear of crime, the offending of 'ordinary people' and comparative criminology. He has held grants from the Scottish Executive, the Home Office, the Economic and Social Research Council and the Leverhulme Trust.

Loraine Gelsthorpe is a Senior University Lecturer at the Institute of Criminology and a Fellow of Pembroke College, University of Cambridge. She has carried out a number of research studies since the mid-1980s including work on social inquiry reports, pre-sentence reports, race and gender issues in sentencing and community penalties. Recent publications include *Understanding the Sentencing of Women* (edited with Carol Hedderman), *Community Penalties: Change and Challenges* (edited with A.E. Bottoms and S. Rex) and *Exercising Discretion: Decision-Making in the Criminal Justice System and Beyond* (edited with N. Padfield). She is currently directing the reconviction study phase of the evaluation of community service as an element of community punishment upon which the chapter in this book is based.

Kelly Hannah-Moffat is Assistant Professor in the Department of Sociology, University of Toronto. She worked as a researcher and policy adviser for the Commission of Inquiry into Certain Events at the Prison for Women in Kingston. Her publications include *Punishment in Disguise: The Governance of Canadian Women's Federal Imprisonment*, 'Prisons that empower: neoliberal governance in Canadian women's prisons' in the *British Journal of Criminology* (for which she received the Radzinowicz Memorial Prize) and *An Ideal Prison? Critical Essays on Women's Imprisonment in Canada* (co-edited with Margaret Shaw). Her current research interests include risk theory, parole, penal reform, gender and crime, social policy and the sociology of punishment.

Paul Holt has been a main-grade probation officer, a practice development assessor, academic tutor for trainees and, latterly, an operational Senior Probation Officer. He is currently implementation manager for case management with Merseyside Probation Area and on part-time secondment to HM Prison Liverpool where he is consulting on case management development. He is a visiting research fellow at

DeMontfort University, has participated in major research projects relevant to probation and has published both on effective practice and case management. He has led workshops and presented at numerous national conferences, and is currently researching a PhD on case management in probation.

Hazel Kemshall is currently Professor of Community and Criminal Justice at DeMontfort University. She has research interests in risk assessment and the management of offenders, effective work in multi-agency public protection and implementing effective practice with offenders. She is the author of the Home Office risk-training materials for probation officers and the Scottish Office materials for social workers, and has published widely on risk. She has recently completed a literature review on risk assessment tools for violent and dangerous offenders and an evaluation of multi-agency public protection panels for the Home Office and the Scottish Executive, an audit of risk tools in Scotland with Gill McIvor and work on dangerous young offenders for the Youth Justice Board (with Yates). She is currently investigating pathways into and out of crime for young people under the ESRC network (with Boeck and Fleming), and has recently completed work on attrition from accredited programmes for the National Probation Service.

Kathleen Kendall is a Lecturer in the Medical School at the University of Southampton. She previously worked as a researcher/evaluator and special adviser on female offenders for the Correctional Service of Canada. She has published a number of articles on correctional cognitive behaviouralism and is currently conducting research into human experimentation in Canadian prisons with Dorothy Proctor.

George Mair has been E. Rex Makin Professor of Criminal Justice at Liverpool John Moores University since 1995, and is a member of the Merseyside Probation Board. Previously he was Principal Research Officer in the Home Office Research and Planning Unit where he was responsible for research into community penalties. His current research interests (besides community penalties) are criminal justice responses to drug-misusing offenders and the criminal justice policy process. He has recently completed a major ESRC-funded study of chief probation officers and is currently involved in researching the Merseyside Street Crime Initiative. He is co-editor of *Criminal Justice: The International Journal of Policy and Practice.*

Carol Hedderman was appointed as Assistant Director of the Home Office Research, Development and Statistics Directorate in 2002. She leads on research and statistics relating to the criminal justice system and correctional services. She was previously Deputy Director of the Criminal Policy Research Unit, London South Bank University. Her research interests include the imposition and enforcement of community penalties, sentencing disparities, parole decision-making, female offending, the treatment of women in the criminal justice system and strategies for improving services for the victims of domestic violence. She was a member of the Parole Board from 2001–2002.

Professor Mike Hough is Director of the Institute for Criminal Policy Research (ICPR) at the School of Law, King's College, London. The ICPR has some 20 staff and carries out policy research for independent trusts and for central and local government. Professor Hough has extensive experience in quantitative research methods, especially large-scale sample surveys such as the British Crime Survey and the Policing for London survey. He has published extensively on topics including drugs and the links between drugs and crime, crime prevention and community safety, policing and probation.

Gill McIvor is Professor of Social Work and Director of the Social Work Research Centre at the University of Stirling. Her previous research has focused primarily upon community penalties, young people and crime, and women and crime. She is currently involved in the evaluation of pilot drug and youth courts in Scotland and in comparative research on drug courts. Her publications include *Sentenced to Serve*, *Working with Offenders*, *Understanding Offending among Young People* (with Janet Jamieson and Cathy Murray) and *Women Who Offend*.

Fergus McNeill has been Lecturer in Social Work at the University of Glasgow since 1998. Before assuming this post, he worked as a criminal justice social worker in the East End of Glasgow for five years. His previous research and publications have addressed a variety of issues in probation and youth justice. His current projects include an exploration of front-line probation ideologies (on which his co-authored chapter in this volume draws), an ESRC-funded study of social inquiry and sentencing in the Scottish Sheriff Courts and an evaluation of the Pathfinder Provider initiative in Scotland for the Scottish Executive.

Sue Rex is a Senior Research Associate at the Institute of Criminology, University of Cambridge, with research interests in the areas of penal theory, sentencing principles and practice in the supervision of offenders in the community. She currently holds a fellowship with the Economic and Social Research Council to conduct a research programme to develop community penalties in theory and practice. As well as the evaluation of the Community Service Pathfinder projects, she has recently completed an evaluation of the Correctional Services Accreditation Panel. She is at present undertaking a major piece of research looking at processes of communication in sentencing and punishment and their application to community penalties.

Gwen Robinson is a Lecturer in Criminology at the University of Sheffield. Since 2002 she has been a member of a research team based at the university which is conducting a Home Office-funded evaluation of restorative justice schemes. She has been – and continues to be – involved in a number of research projects focusing on probation practice. She completed her PhD on risk assessment and management in probation at the University of Wales, Swansea, in 2001. Prior to this she was a researcher in the Probation Studies Unit at the University of Oxford. In 1996 she obtained a Diploma in Social Work, specialising in social work with offenders.

Judith Rumgay is Senior Lecturer in the Department of Social Policy, London School of Economics. She was a probation officer prior to her appointment at LSE, where she was initially responsible for the Home Office-sponsored probation stream on the postgraduate social work programme. Her teaching currently focuses on psychology and crime, rehabilitation of offenders and criminal justice policy. Her research interests include alcohol and drug-related offending, the probation service, female offenders and voluntary sector involvement in offender rehabilitation. She is the author of *Crime, Punishment and the Drinking Offender* and *The Addicted Offender: Developments in British Policy and Practice*.

Margaret Shaw, PhD, is Director of Analysis and Exchange at the International Centre for the Prevention of Crime (ICPC) in Montreal. She is a sociologist and criminologist who has worked as a research and policy analyst in the Home Office and for the federal and provincial governments in Canada. She taught in the Department of Sociology and Anthropology at Concordia University, Montreal, for the past ten years. Among other work, she has a longstanding interest in prisons and prison reform, women's involvement in law-breaking and treatment and programme evaluation. Her recent published work includes a number of studies on women's imprisonment including (with Kelly Hannah-Moffat) *Taking Risks: Incorporating Gender and Culture into the Classification and Assessment of Federally Sentenced Women in Canada*, an edited volume *An Ideal Prison? Critical Essay on Women's Imprisonment in Canada* and 'The meaning of risk in women's prisons: a critique' in *Gendered Justice* (edited by B. Bloom).

David Smith is Professor of Criminology at Lancaster University, where he has worked since 1976. A former probation officer, he has recently been involved in research on black and Asian men's experiences of probation, and on Irish people's views of probation and the criminal justice system. Other recent research has been on racist violence in Greater Manchester and the probation service's response to it, and – in Scotland – on support for witnesses, electronic monitoring and projects for serious juvenile offenders.

Jon Spencer is Senior Lecturer in Criminal Justice at the University of Manchester, Department of Applied Social Studies. He has undertaken a number of research studies concerning the probation service, evaluation of programmes and evaluation of service delivery strategies, and is especially interested in the process of how a person is considered to be 'rehabilitated'. He has written, with Jo Deakin, about women's imprisonment and the relationship between risk assessment and prison sentences for women. He has also undertaken research into criminal justice strategies in transitional societies, especially the Baltic States, and has worked closely with the Estonian Ministry of Justice. He has recently completed, with Jo Deakin, a study of street robbery.

Anne Worrall is Professor of Criminology at Keele University, having previously been a probation officer in Staffordshire and lecturer in social work at Manchester University. She has an extensive publications record, including *Offending Women* and *Punishment in the Community*. She has been involved in the evaluation of two joint police–probation projects for prolific offenders. She is a visiting research fellow at the Crime Research Centre, University of Western Australia, where she worked full time for a year in 2002/3 and where she reviewed cognitive skills programmes in prisons in Western Australia for the Office of the Inspector of Custodial Services. She is a member of the Parole Board of England and Wales.

Chapter 1

Introduction: What Works and what matters

George Mair

In June 1998 *Probation Circular* 35/1998 with the title *Effective Practice Initiative: National Implementation Plan for the Supervision of Offenders* was published by the Home Office, heralding the beginning of what is now known as the What Works initiative. Essentially, the initiative involved the development and implementation on a national basis of a demonstrably 'effective' set of core programmes of supervision for offenders. Most of these programmes are heavily dependent upon a cognitive behavioural approach. A Joint Prison/Probation Accreditation Panel (JPPAP; now the Correctional Services Accreditation Panel) was set up in 1999 to accredit programmes for national use (see JPPAP 2000, 2001 for details of the panel's work) and, while the panel does not rule out any 'effective' method, there is no doubt that its preference is for cognitive behavioural approaches.

There may be some uncertainty about the precise significance of the What Works initiative – is it simply the most important thing to hit the probation service in England and Wales in its history, or is it just another significant development thrust upon the service by a government that refuses to acknowledge the real strengths of probation – but there can be no doubt that it is a key aspect of current probation practice. Indeed, What Works is not only implicated in practice; the reorganisation of probation that took place on 1 April 2001 whereby a National Probation Service (NPS) was created is – in a sense – a result of What Works and the need to ensure that it could be rolled out consistently on a national basis. What Works, then, is having a profound impact upon the probation service – one might even go so far as to claim it as the new orthodoxy.

Perhaps surprisingly, however, the status of What Works is vague, to say the least. Is it an agenda, an initiative, a project, an idea, a model, a strategy, a vision, a movement, a set of principles? While these terms denote different things they can roughly be categorised as falling into one of two groups – either aspirational (a vision, a model, an idea) or prescriptive (an agenda, an initiative, a project). While What Works may have begun as – and should continue to be – a worthy aspiration, it has become much more a set of prescriptions that have delimited the scope and content of probation work (and in relation to this distinction it is worth noting that sometimes What Works comes with a question mark and sometimes not). Such vagueness – given the significance of What Works – is surely disturbing.

In the rush to embrace the tenets of What Works there has been surprisingly little academic or professional debate about the risks associated with it. What Works has been sold as the answer to all the problems of probation: it will prove its effectiveness as a credible sentence, it will lead to more funding, it will secure its future as a powerful organisation within the criminal justice system. The message emanating from the National Probation Directorate has been that What Works is beyond criticism; there is no alternative to it. To question What Works is seen to be casting doubt on the very foundations of probation work at a time when the service is trying to build up confidence among its stakeholders that it can be trusted. Those individuals who dare to question What Works are accused by its supporters of a 'desire to recreate the past' (Raynor forthcoming) or are mocked as working within a 'professional ideology of "knowledge destruction"' (Cullen and Gendreau 2001: 325) or relying on 'BAD common sense' (Gendreau *et al.* 2002: 362).

Despite the juggernaut nature of What Works for the NPS in England and Wales and the official discouragement to voice any scepticism about it or the way it has been developed and implemented, some voices have been raised expressing doubts – among them many of those who have contributed to this book. Others, too, have brought up issues that require a response. Kevin Gorman has argued that

> There can also be little doubt that the present fashion for cognitive behavioural interventions owes much to the charisma of Canadian researchers and entrepreneurs such as Robert Ross; and to the increasing aptitude of some indigenous academics and commentators for re-packaging what may be generally unimpressive research outcomes and presenting them in a more favourable light. (2001: 6)

Simon Merrington and Steve Stanley (2000) have questioned the strength of the evidence upon which the What Works initiative is based. Mark Oldfield (2002) has set out

> to contest the notion that 'What Works' represents some epistemological unity which can be delivered in neat packages if only the right managerial structures are put in place ... I have provided examples of how the 'principles' of effectiveness are contestable and how their combination as guarantors of effectiveness is not an unassailable piece of received wisdom. This is not to take a 'Nothing Works' attitude but to raise questions about the inflexibility and precipitate nature of the transitions probation has undergone. (2002: 70–1)

And the Underdown report, *Strategies for Effective Offender Supervision* (Underdown 1998), which could be argued to have kick started What Works in England and Wales, has recently been subjected to questioning by the (now ex-) member of the Home Office Research and Statistics Directorate who contributed to work on the evaluation survey that formed the core of the report (Ellis and Winstone 2002).

In the NPS there may be some signs of doubt with regard to What Works and the way in which it has been implemented. The targets for completions on accredited programmes set out in the first three-year integrated strategy for the NPS (2001) have – rather quietly – been halved, which at least indicates that they were set far too ambitiously in the first place. There are also signs that the evidence base is beginning to be challenged from within the Home Office. A recent evaluation of cognitive skills programmes for adult male prisoners 'found no difference between the two-year reconviction rates for a sample of adult male prisoners who had participated in a programme during the evaluation period of 1996 to 1998 and a matched group of offenders who had not' (Falshaw *et al.* 2003: 1). It is particularly interesting that this result contradicts findings from an earlier study (Friendship *et al.* 2002), which underlines the instability and inconsistency of research findings.

The What Works initiative is not just a policy/practice development for probation in England and Wales. It has wider implications, too, which are worth noting briefly here.

What Works in its probation incarnation, with its reliance on cognitive behaviouralism as the keystone for work with offenders, implies a return to the medical model of deviance. And we should not forget that this model was discredited in the 1970s and has yet to be officially rehabilitated. Cognitive behaviouralism, with its emphasis that

3

offenders are different from non-offenders and that their cognitive deficits can be treated, deals with offenders as 'others'. Such an approach – with its echoes of exclusion – sits uncomfortably with New Labour's commitment to social inclusion.

Rather similarly, an educative model is used in accredited programmes to remedy the cognitive deficits from which offenders suffer. Probation staff 'teach' offenders correct models of thinking from manuals which have to be followed with no deviations. This model, which seems to rely heavily on teaching by rote, is not calculated to appeal to offenders who – almost certainly – have not been successful at school and who may indeed have fallen out of education early. It may also lead to a lack of interest and therefore motivation – and motivation is a key factor in desistance from crime. Moreover, if an offender is sentenced for a second time to an accredited programme, what happens then – has he or she to sit through the same lessons taught in the same way? Or is the individual moved up tariff and imprisoned?

The What Works initiative discussed here is, of course, only part of a more general drive towards evidence-based policy and practice in the UK (and also in the USA) that has formed a key part of New Labour's approach to governance. And What Works throws light on some of the limitations of the emphasis on 'evidence'. First, and most crucially, what counts as evidence? This question has lain behind the whole nothing works/what works debate for 30 years since the publication of Robert Martinson's notorious article 'What works? Questions and answers about prison reform' (1974). It now looms behind the arguments between those who adhere to cognitive behaviouralism and those who stress the need to take account of structural factors. At the moment, psychologists are dominant in designing probation programmes and – as might be expected – are sceptical about whatever sociologists and others might offer. The struggle to 'control' the evidence that governments might use can be seen in the work of the Campbell Collaboration which, it would appear, seeks to become solely responsible for judging the quality of research. The Campbell Crime and Justice Co-ordinating Group sees its mission as 'to oversee the preparation, maintenance, and accessibility of systematic reviews of research on the effects of criminological and criminal justice interventions' (Farrington and Petrosino 2001: 39; for more details of the activities of this group, see the essays in the *Annals of the American Academy of Political and Social Science* 2001). Such an approach seems to be antithetical to the (somewhat battered) ideals of academic work and to the never-failing ability of research to throw up inconsistent findings.

Secondly, there is a naïve and taken-for-granted belief – even if we could be certain about what evidence counts and what does not – that such evidence will simply be taken on board by politicians, policy-makers and practitioners (and we should not forget that evidence-based policy and evidence-based practice are not the same). On the contrary, the policy process is complex and does not proceed on purely rational grounds: policy is driven by various factors but probably most of all by politics which can scarcely be said to be a rationally grounded activity. And getting evidence to influence practice is also no simple matter. Evidence needs to be distilled from academic work into a form which can be understood by practitioners and then disseminated to these practitioners who may have various reasons for failing to take the new practice on board fully (see Davies *et al.* 1999; Leicester 1999; Nutley *et al.* 2000, for some discussion of the difficulties of getting research into policy and practice).

Outline of the book

While it is important to subject What Works to rigorous examination, there is a tendency in such debates for standpoints to become polarised, as people yield to a compulsion to assert their position in the strongest terms. This book, however, is aimed at providing a reasoned critical overview of What Works. It is hoped that by offering a searching analysis of the background and claims of What Works and its place within the NPS, a more balanced debate can take place. The chapters which make up this book have not been written by dyed-in-the-wool sceptics and opponents of progress in probation; on the contrary, the contributors are respected commentators on probation; they have extensive records in research and writing (and, in some cases, in practice) on probation matters, and would see themselves as wanting a vigorous and effective probation service.

In Chapter 2, George Mair sets out the policy background to the What Works initiative and examines the context in which it has been implemented. He argues that the foundations upon which What Works has been constructed are flimsy, and that the circumstances in which it is being implemented are not especially conducive to success. Preliminary results from research are not promising, and even those who might be called adherents of What Works make cautionary noises at times. As an example of evidence-based policy-making, the What Works initiative is not inspiring.

The next three chapters look behind What Works. In Chapter 3 David Smith examines the ways in which research has been uncritically taken up by policy-makers. Politicians, policy-makers and practitioners all too often have been encouraged to rely upon a naïve positivism and thereby accept generalisations that gloss over the unpredicability, uncertainty and general 'messiness' of social life. The What Works initiative has relied on this model, which, by its nature is appealing to bureaucrats. Unfortunately, as Smith argues, this kind of approach to evidence is 'based on a misconception of the nature of the social sciences' (this volume). There are alternative traditions to positivism and, while evidence based on these may be less easy to assimilate into policy and/ or practice, it may prove to be more robust and reliable in the long run.

Kathy Kendall (Chapter 4) provides a history of the origins of cognitive behaviouralism, which has become accepted as *the* approach for the treatment of offenders. She points to the ways in which psychology has underpinned much of the work with offenders that went on in the twentieth century and notes how cognitive behaviouralism developed from this. Cognitive behaviouralism perfectly mirrors the political climate in which we live and, as a result of this 'fit', it is not surprising that it has been accepted so widely. It has brought responsibility back to the individual – which, of course, means that failure is due to the individual's faults rather than any failings of cognitive behaviouralism.

A common complaint about the cognitive behavioural approach upon which What Works is founded is that it has been built entirely on work with white male offenders. It is assumed that cognitive behavioural programmes that have been developed on such a population will work equally well with women and members of ethnic minority groups. In Chapter 5 Margaret Shaw and Kelly Hannah-Moffat argue that gender and diversity were left out of the development of risk/need assessment tools and of cognitive skills programmes in Canada. And Canada is, of course, the main source for What Works evidence and programmes in England and Wales. Worryingly, in response to criticisms about the marginalisation of gender and diversity, the Canadian response has simply been to 'add on' women and race to their work – which suggests that such criticisms are still not being taken seriously.

The following four chapters examine aspects of probation work in relation to What Works. Partnership has been a significant theme in probation for more than a decade (Home Office 1990), and Judith Rumgay (Chapter 6) discusses how the partnership approach offers an alternative model to that offered by What Works; a model which, according to her analysis, is more suited to the traditons of the probation service. While partnership may have been 'forced' on to the probation agenda, it offers a wealth of possibilities for fruitful and exciting work with offenders – possibilities that may not be realised given the present focus on cognitive behavioural therapies. Enforcement has been a key battlefield as it has been assumed that this is the key to credibility with sentencers and, as a result of retaining offenders in supervision programmes, is a critical factor in successful completions and thus lower reconviction rates. Carol Hedderman and Mike Hough in Chapter 7 look at the evidence regarding enforcement and especially some recent studies that suggest that tougher enforcement does not lead to high retention rates. This has important implications for the What Works initiative as one of its key measures of success is the number of completions of accredited programmes. The current emphasis on enforcement creates a tension with the objective of ensuring a high rate of programme completions, and Hedderman and Hough point to other, more appropriate, approaches to compliance that might be followed by probation officers.

What Works has been all too often associated with accredited programmes for offenders with little consideration being given to the infrastructure necessary to deliver such programmes effectively. In Chapter 8 Hazel Kemshall and her colleagues discuss the ways in which What Works, with its programme-driven approach, has paid little attention to implementation issues. Using data from a research project carried out in the North West Region, Kemshall and her colleagues show that probation areas were poorly equipped to deal with the organi-sational and cultural changes required to implement What Works. While this situation may have changed since the time of the research, it does suggest a degree of poor forward planning for such a significant initiative. And it may well have consequences in terms of high attrition rates for What Works programmes and thus low completion rates. As well as the organisational and cultural context within which What Works has been implemented, scant regard has been taken of the reasons why offenders on probation supervision desist from crime. The assumption is that faulty thinking lies behind offending and therefore learning how to think 'straight' will lead to a cessation from offending. Stephen Farrall (Chapter 9) demonstrates that the matter is rather more complicated, in that desistance seems to be intimately associated with the social and personal circumstances of offenders and their motivation – factors What Works has not focused upon. Farrall's offenders show very few cases where faulty thinking skills are evident, and the implications of this for What Works and its focus upon cognitive behavioural programmes are considerable.

The next two chapters take reintegration as their theme. In Chapter 10 Jon Spencer and Jo Deakin argue that, despite the lip-service paid to the idea that community reintegration is a key principle in What Works, in fact little attention has been paid to just how community reintegration 'fits' into the What Works project. Indeed, What Works tools such as risk assessment and classification, and cognitive behavioural therapy, are not part of the landscape of community reintegration. They argue for bringing community reintegration back into mainstream work with offenders and make suggestions about how this might be done. Loraine Gelsthorpe and Sue Rex (Chapter 11) also discuss reintegration, but in the context of community service. Their evaluation of the Community Service Pathfinder projects noted some implementation problems but a high completion rate by offenders. Projects that focused on skills accreditation seemed to have the most positive outcomes. Traditionally, women have been perceived by sentencers as not suitable for community service, but Gelsthorpe and Rex argue that this assumption needs to be investigated further. Community service does not fit with the traditional What Works model but, by showing encouraging signs of effectiveness (although reconviction studies have yet to be completed), it does suggest that reliance upon teaching cognitive skills is not the only approach. Further, community service may offer a way round the claims that the What Works emphasis on cognitive behaviouralism is based upon male experiences.

The views and attitudes of those involved in delivering new initiatives are rarely examined in any detail, yet if staff are not enthusiastic and committed to a new project then the likelihood of success is diminished. In Chapter 12 George Mair discusses the views of Chief Probation Officers (CPOs) about What Works and finds a public/private dichotomy. On the one hand, CPOs are publicly committed to What Works (indeed, it is hard to see how they could be anything else), but they have private doubts about it. What Works may have benefits for the NPS in terms of increased public credibility, helping to bring about major cultural change and greater consistency, but it has been rushed through with inadequate resourcing and planning, and it carries high risks for the future of the NPS. As such, CPOs publicly expressed confidence but privately demonstrated a rather weary determination to make the best of it.

Gwen Robinson and Fergus McNeill (Chapter 13) discuss the purpose of probation using both official documents and the results from two research studies, one carried out in England and Wales and the other in Scotland. Public protection appears to be emerging as the core purpose of probation, but this – it is argued – creates problems as well as offering solutions. If What Works is seen to have failed in terms of reducing reoffending, then probation's claims to offer public protection will be called into question. Moreover, the ways in which probation staff interpret their roles and the ways in which they work in practice suggest that the requirements of the What Works initiative may not be taken on board as straightforwardly as its designers expect.

What Works has not been limited to England and Wales; Scotland, too, has been influenced by its 'principles' but, as Gill McIvor shows in Chapter 14, the approach followed in Scotland has not paralleled that taken in England and Wales. Developments in Scotland have been less programme centred than those south of the border and more concerned with issues of social inclusion. Interventions with offenders have been more personalised and more concerned with the wider context of offending than those developed in England and Wales. While What Works in England and Wales is claimed to be evidence based, similar claims can be made for the Scottish model – which raises interesting questions about the nature of evidence and how it is interpreted.

What Works is a global brand and in the final chapter Anne Worrall examines some of the implications of this, with particular regard to working with Aboriginal offenders in Western Australia. As might be expected, Worrall argues that the What Works approach is problematic when applied to Aboriginal communities; levels of poverty, poor education and housing, high unemployment, ill-health and high morbidity rates make an emphasis on cognitive deficits as a response to offending laughable. What Works must be capable of adapting to different circumstances if it is to survive, and Worrall poses three questions that need to be addressed if this is to happen.

Taken together, the essays that make up this book suggest that the What Works initiative as it has been marketed and sold in England and Wales is not the only remedy for the ills of the probation service. What Works is not the evidence-based policy we have been led to believe; cognitive behaviouralism is not the objective, scientific method that its proponents claim, but is deeply implicated in neoliberal politics and has been constructed on offenders who are white and male; there are significant aspects of probation work that What Works has failed to address adequately; CPOs are not wholly convinced by it; and the claims made for universalism by What Works supporters cannot be sustained as in other jurisdictions different approaches have emerged.

It is to be hoped that this book will supply an injection of much-needed critical analysis to the What Works initiative. Even if it 'works' (whatever that might mean, and assuming that outright failure is inconceivable), a searching examination of how the initiative has been planned, developed, implemented and practised should help to ensure that these things are managed more effectively in the future. At the very least, the contributions to this book demonstrate that the current narrow focus on What Works is misconceived; we should be much more concerned with the wider question of what matters.

References

Annals of the American Academy of Political and Social Science (2001) 'Special issue – what works in preventing crime? Systematic reviews of experimental and quasi-experimental research', 578.

Cullen, F.T. and Gendreau, P. (2001) 'From nothing works to What Works: changing professional ideology in the 21st century', *Prison Journal*, 81 (3): 313–38.

Davies, H.T.O., Nutley, S.M. and Smith, P.C. (1999) 'Editorial: What Works? The role of evidence in public sector policy and practice', *Public Money and Management*, January–March: 3–5.

Ellis, T. and Winstone, J. (2002) 'The policy impact of a survey of programme evaluations in England and Wales: towards a new corrections-industrial complex?', in J. McGuire (ed.) *Offender Rehabilitation and Treatment: Effective Programmes and Policies to Reduce Re-offending.* Chichester: Wiley, 333–58.

Falshaw, L., Friendship, C., Travers, R. and Nugent, F. (2003) *Searching for 'What Works': An Evaluation of Cognitive Skills Programmes.* Home Office Research Findings 206. London: Home Office.

Farrington, D.P. and Petrosino, A. (2001) 'The Campbell Collaboration Crime and Justice Group', *The Annals of the American Academy of Political and Social Science*, 578: 35–49.

Friendship, C., Blud, L., Erikson, M. and Travers, R. (2002) *An Evaluation of Cognitive Behavioural Treatment for Prisoners.* Home Office Research Findings 161. London: Home Office.

Gendreau, P., Goggin, C., Cullen, F.T. and Paparozzi, M. (2002) 'The common-sense revolution and correctional policy', in J. McGuire (ed.) *Offender Rehabilitation and Treatment: Effective Programmes and Policies to Reduce Re-offending.* Chichester: Wiley, 359–86.

Gorman, K. (2001) 'Cognitive behaviouralism and the Holy Grail: the quest for a universal means of managing offender risk', *Probation Journal*, 48 (1): 3–9.

Home Office (1990) *Partnership in Dealing with Offenders in the Community: A Discussion Paper.* London: Home Office.

Home Office (1998) *Effective Practice Initiative: National Implementation Plan for the Supervision of Offenders.* Probation Circular 35/1998. London: Home Office.

Joint Prison/Probation Accreditation Panel (2000) *What Works: First Report from the Joint Prison Probation Accreditation Panel 1999–2000.* London: Home Office.

Joint Prison/Probation Accreditation Panel (2001) *What Works: Second Report from the Joint Prison Probation Accreditation Panel 2000–2001.* London: Home Office.

Leicester, G. (1999) 'The seven enemies of evidence-based policy', *Public Money and Management*, January–March, 5–7.

Martinson, R. (1974) 'What Works? Questions and answers about prison reform', *The Public Interest*, 35: 22–54.

Merrington, S. and Stanley, S. (2000) 'Doubts about the What Works initiative', *Probation Journal*, 47 (4): 272–75.

National Probation Service (2001) *A New Choreography: An Integrated Strategy for the National Probation Service for England and Wales*. London: Home Office.

Nutley, S., Davies, H.T.O. and Tilley, N. (2000) 'Editorial: getting research into practice', *Public Money and Management*, October–December: 3–6.

Oldfield, M. (2002) *From Welfare to Risk: Discourse, Power and Politics in the Probation Service*. Issues in Community and Criminal Justice Monograph 1. London: NAPO.

Raynor, P. (forthcoming) 'Seven ways to misunderstand evidence-based probation', in D. Smith (ed.) *Social Work and Evidence Based Practice*. London: Jessica Kingsley.

Underdown, A. (1998) *Strategies for Effective Offender Supervision: Report of the HMIP What Works Project*. London: Home Office.

Chapter 2

The origins of What Works in England and Wales: a house built on sand?

George Mair

This is the most important foreword I have ever written. The evidence drawn on in this report, states at its simplest that 'certain community programmes involving the same population significantly outperform custodial sentences in reducing offending. Further, we now know or at least have a beginning understanding of what makes these programmes so successful'.

The movement to achieve this is known as What Works. (Smith, in Underdown 1998: iii)

Introduction

In 1998, the late Sir Graham Smith, then Her Majesty's Chief Inspector of Probation, wrote the words quoted at the head of this chapter. They are proud and confidently assertive words but, on closer consideration, they reveal a degree of uncertainty: there is a slightly strained grammar – what does the 'this' in the final sentence refer to; there is an apparent hesitation in the penultimate sentence that qualifies its impact – 'we now know *or at least have a beginning understanding of* what makes those programmes so successful'; and, perhaps most importantly, no evidence is presented in the body of the report to back up the claim that certain community programmes significantly outperform custodial sentences. But whatever one might think about this statement when examined in detail, its rhetorical and political impact is unequivocal, and the report, which is prefaced by the Chief Inspector's words – *Strategies for effective supervision* (Underdown 1998) – has certainly been a profoundly significant document for the probation service.

The Underdown Report signals clearly the introduction of the What Works agenda to the probation service. What Works is now the foundation stone for the National Probation Service (NPS), the rock upon which the new church has been constructed. It is very much an orthodoxy which has strict commandments, and one deviates from these at one's peril. Like Protestantism in its more fundamental forms, if you adhere to the tenets of the What Works doctrine you are guaranteed – perhaps not salvation – but certainly reduced reoffending (and the benefits that go with it for the NPS – increased funding, political approval, greater power).

Like motherhood and apple pie, reduced levels of offending are something that we would all be in favour of – but, despite this renewed optimism, we should not forget that less than ten years ago it looked as if the probation service was in serious trouble. Its effectiveness was being questioned and its very existence was thought to be under consideration by Home Office ministers. Yet today there has been a remarkable turnaround in the fortunes of the service; there is increased confidence by government, there has been a radical reorganisation, staff levels have grown – and all these are grounded in What Works. So one might assume that this is a powerful foundation upon which to build – especially given the government's commitment to evidence-based policy which implies a rational aproach to policy formulation.

But is it a powerful foundation? Is it an example of rational policy development? In this chapter I propose to examine the origins of What Works in England and Wales and the current conditions under which it is being practised. To continue the religious imagery which has been running through this introduction, I hope that what I intend to do is not seen as heresy – traditionally the punishments for this particular sin have been especially painful – but as one of the tasks of an academic, which should be to examine critically and question issues of significance. And this is particularly important in the case of What Works as it is rapidly assuming the status of an orthodoxy which cannot be challenged.

The origins of What Works

So what are the origins of What Works? What are the factors that lie behind its emergence? A number of key factors can be identified, with varying degrees of overlap among them. In what follows there is no attempt to prioritise these factors, but they will discussed in roughly chronological order.

'Nothing works'

It would be possible to argue that the origins of What Works lie deep in the history of the probation service where there was an almost legendary lack of interest in measuring effectiveness. However, the immediate environment in which What Works originated was in relation to 'Nothing works', the now-notorious claim wrongly attributed to Robert Martinson as a result of his 1974 article 'What Works? Questions and answers about prison reform' (Martinson 1974, reprinted in Gardiner and Mulkey 1975). Martinson nowhere stated unequivocally that nothing worked; instead his summation of the evidence was that 'With few and isolated exceptions, the rehabilitative efforts that have been reported so far have had no appreciable effect on recidivism'(Martinson 1975: 157). Now this statement cannot easily be reduced to the flat and definite claim that 'nothing works' as there are far too many vague qualifiers in the sentence. Indeed, a reading of Martinson's article shows that it is littered with such words as 'impossible to interpret', 'no clear evidence', 'difficult to interpret', 'ambiguous results', 'suggestive', 'equivocal', 'problem in interpreting' and 'important caveat'.

The abundance of such words in the article should certainly have signalled caution in relation to claims about what Martinson meant. So too should the fact that Martinson relied on recidivism as his sole outcome criterion for judging the success or failure of a sentence. Recidivism, which is usually measured by reconviction rates, is a complex and limited measure (see, e.g., Maltz 1984; Lloyd *et al.* 1994), which is treated in a taken-for-granted manner by Martinson. And so too should the fact that Martinson's analysis took no account of the operation and organisation of sentences – the factors that led to the recidivism rate (although this is not surprising as the primary sources utilised for the study generally failed to address such issues). By failing to address these process factors, it is impossible to understand why the sentences examined had little effect upon reconvictions (e.g. it may have been to do with poor resourcing, ineffective staff, inappropriate targeting of offenders, inadequate organisational structures or bad management rather than programme failure per se).

It is interesting to consider the impact of 'nothing works' on probation staff. It is taken for granted that when probation officers became aware of this message in the mid-1970s there was a serious loss of morale and feelings of disempowerment. However, there was no research carried out around this time investigating probation officers' views of 'nothing works' – indeed, there is little evidence that they were particularly aware of its existence. On an anecdotal level, whenever I have talked about the topic with probation officers their response has always been the same: 'nothing works' made no difference whatsoever to what they were doing and how they were doing it, it was simply not an issue for them. Now this is at least a comment upon the significance of academic work for practitioners, but if 'nothing works' was not impacting upon probation work (except in the minds of academics) then what was its significance?

What Works is a reaction to 'nothing works' but, ironically, 'nothing works' was a paper tiger and its immediate significance for probation practitioners was minimal.

The Canadian connection

While a few commentators attacked the idea of 'nothing works' almost immediately (Palmer 1978; Gendreau and Ross 1979), it was difficult to combat successfully its neat simplicity. Sporadic attacks continued throughout the years, but sustained work to grapple with the meanings of 'nothing works' was not carried out – except in Canada. There, a small group of individuals who seemed to rotate between academic posts, civil service positions and as practitioners worked together in various permutations and took their work with them as they moved around. The names will be familiar to those who have followed the renaissance of What Works: Don Andrews, James Bonta, Paul Gendreau, Frank Porporino. Together and separately they have argued against the idea that 'nothing works', they have developed cognitive behavioural programmes with prisoners that seemed to be successful in reducing reconviction rates and they have published meta-analyses (of which more below) to prove that what works is cognitive behaviouralism.

The Canadians were the star turns at the various What Works conferences organised in the early 1990s by Greater Manchester and Hereford and Worcester probation services. They proclaimed the effectiveness of their programmes and convinced their audiences. I attended several of these conferences and can confirm that their presentations were a refreshing change to the prevailing culture of probation officers – which can be characterised as a weary resignation that despite doing the best they could with them offenders are liable to reoffend. Unfortunately, what I did not see at these conferences were any significant data to back up the claims that were made. If Canadian programmes were as popular and as successful as they seemed to be, why were the numbers presented as evidence of success only running to a few hundred? And why were more questions not asked about the fact that the Canadians were working in prisons – working with offenders in the community presented a different range of challenges that tended to be forgotten.

In a sense, the early What Works conferences seemed to me to be akin to an evangelical revivalist movement with the charismatic leaders being the Canadians (despite similar work being done by James Maguire and Philip Priestley their contributions remained in the background). But – and again to use religious imagery – we were being asked to buy into cognitive behaviouralism as an article of faith. This may well be appropriate for a religious movement but may not be an ideal basis upon which to construct a completely new foundation for probation work with offenders.

In the Hollywood version of What Works we already have an enemy ('nothing works') and an intrepid band of North American academics who dared to struggle aginst the enemy. The next sequence in the movie is the discovery of a new and deadly weapon that can be utilised against the enemy.

Meta-analysis

Meta-analysis – 'the statistical analysis of a large collection of analysis results from individual studies for the purpose of integrating the findings' (Glass 1976: 3) – has been widely used in medical research but only began to be carried out into community penalties from the mid-1980s (Garrett 1985). Meta-analysis is claimed to offer a 'rigorous alternative to the casual, narrative discussions of research studies which typify our attempts to make sense of the rapidly expanding research literature' (Glass 1976: 3). Such a claim may be sustainable to a certain extent, but meta-analysis still involves human beings making choices about which studies to include (assuming that all relevant studies are available, and if this is not the case there is the possibility of bias), and how to code the variables involved bearing in mind that 'Converting many varied research studies to a manageable set of coded variables is a process that potentially loses important meaning' (Bullock and Svyantek 1985: 114). And, of course, no matter how much one might argue for the hard objective facts of statistical analysis these are then subjected to interpretation by fallible humans. It is interesting to note, for example, that one of the early meta-analyses of rehabilitative treatment claimed that 'correctional treatment has little effect on recidivism' (Whitehead and Lab 1989: 291), but the authors did not calculate an overall effect size.[1] Subsequently, Losel (1993) did carry out such a calculation for this meta-analysis and found the effect size to be positive, thus changing the original authors' interpretation of the findings.

In any event, even if a positive effect size was to be found – and so far the relevant meta-analyses have indeed confirmed that 'treatment' works – the problem is how to translate that finding into practice. Meta-analysis may well point to certain kinds of treatment being effective, but it does not tell you how to put that treatment into practice. There has been a welcome interest in process evaluations in criminal justice in the past decade, but not enough of these have yet been carried out in enough detail to begin to delineate how to go about organising the context for putting, for example, a cognitive behavioural programme for violent offenders into practice. And the primary studies upon which meta-analyses have been based have, on the whole, had very little to say about the organisation and context of the 'treatments' evaluated.

Thus, while meta-analysis cannot be ignored, the claims made for its being a peculiarly privileged form of statistical technique do not stand up to scrutiny and the inferences that are drawn from meta-analytic studies are by no means as cast iron as they might appear to be (Copas 1995).

Probation under threat

The three factors discussed so far were necessary for the emergence of What Works but not sufficient. They were too rooted in academic debates and too distant from the mundane realities of probation work to have any immediate impact. However, with the arrival of Michael Howard as Home Secretary in 1993 everything changed.

While the probation service initially escaped remarkably lightly under the successive Conservative governments since 1979, this had not meant that probation staff were optimistic. The publication of the *Statement of National Objectives and Priorities* (Home Office 1984), the advent of computerisation (and who now remembers PROBIS?), the introduction of National Standards in 1989 and 1992, all these as well as a host of other initiatives (see Mair 1996) led to probation being in a state of constant anxiety about the future of the service. These initiatives, however, were successfully taken on board and at the beginning of the 1990s probation was publicly acknowledged to be moving 'centre stage', to use John Patten's phrase – the future looked promising. Perhaps inevitably, this honeymoon phase was brief. As Downes and Morgan (1997: 118) note: 'Since 1993 and the advent of Michael Howard as Home Secretary, criminal justice policy-making has become dominated, to quite an unprecedented extent, by the politics of law and order.' And the probation service bore the brunt of the onslaught.

It very quickly became possible to envisage no future for probation. Partnerships were encouraged more than ever; various organisations were mentioned as offering alternatives to the probation service; training arrangements for new probation officers were scrapped with no new system of training to replace them; resources were cut back; the use of electronic monitoring was expanded; and 'prison works' became the mantra of the moment.

It is difficult to judge just how serious the threat to the existence of probation was, but there is little doubt that it was seen to be significant. And matters were exacerbated by the lack of a distinct voice to argue probation's corner in the Home Office; the then head of C6 (the probation policy unit) was disliked by many probation staff and seen to be uninterested in the service. Chief Probation Officers felt cut off from the Home Office and their fears were magnified by the decision not to involve the Association of Chief Officers of Probation (ACOP) in seeing early drafts of the green paper *Strengthening Punishment in the Community* (Home Office 1995), a somewhat unusual step.

Two knights in shining armour

Absolutely vital in this inchoate, highly politicised situation was the coincidence of two individuals in the Home Office at this particular time. Policies are often talked of as if they were made by some abstract bloodless process, but policies are about choices and these choices are made by individuals who always have personal stakes in the situation, even if it is only to be seen to do a satisfactory job as this would help your career. Civil servants are often portrayed as cold, calculating individuals who care little about the impact of the policies they develop; having spent 16 years in the Home Office this is not a picture I recognise. Without the presence of Chris Nuttall, Head of Research and Statistics, and Graham Smith (later Sir Graham), Her Majesty's Chief Inspector of Probation, the What Works initiative is almost inconceivable – they acted as key entrepreneurs by 'selling' the idea of What Works, and they were in positions of considerable power and authority which meant that their marketing of What Works could not be brushed aside easily.

Crucially, Chris Nuttall had spent the previous 15 years or so before his return to the Home Office in Canada where he knew the Canadians discussed earlier and heard their ideas and the results of their work. Back in the Home Office, where usually American ideas and work were the only outside influences taken seriously, Nuttall encouraged

Canadian ideas and various Canadian academics visited the Home Office. What Works was something that Nuttall was strongly committed to and he pushed its claims at every opportunity.

Graham Smith had been Chief Probation Officer of the Inner London Probation Service prior to becoming Chief Inspector and, as such, he was a highly experienced and respected figure who believed strongly in probation. There is little doubt that Smith took seriously the potential threat to the probation service discussed above and also saw the hole at the heart of probation policy. As someone who had spent almost 30 years as a member of the probation service, it should not be surprising if Smith wished to defend the service and the most effective way was to occupy the vacuum in probation policy and argue for the effectiveness of probation work. Smith was aware of developments in Canada and utilised these as the basis for his defence of probation. It should be emphasised that he did not originate the What Works agenda in England and Wales: as already noted, a series of conferences on the subject had been organised; a report by Andrew Underdown was published in 1995, *Effectiveness of Community Supervision;* and the STOP project in Mid-Glamorgan was underway. But Smith picked up What Works, recognised its potential, and ran with it. Like Nuttall, he was a powerful figure and his voice could not be ignored.

Some feel that Smith saved the probation service from extinction but this is arguable (see Chapter 12 in this volume for some views on this). He may well have held the line (along with Nuttall) against the final attacks by the Conservative government, but the 1997 General Election opened the doors for Smith and Nuttall's ideas. This is not to suggest that the incoming Labour administration was about to return to some mythical past where probation was unquestioningly viewed as a good thing. The new government's interest in evidence-based practice and the What Works agenda chimed perfectly. Smith sponsored two significant reports, *Strategies for Effective Offender Supervision* (Underdown 1998) and *Evidence Based Practice* (Chapman and Hough 1998), for which great claims were made (see the quotation at the beginning of this chapter). As a basis for re-equipping the probation service for effective work with offenders both these reports were surprisingly flimsy; in neither was there the detailed, empirical evidence that one might have expected to see and in the former only four programmes were assessed as providing '*some* evidence of success' (Underdown 1998: 108, emphasis added) and each of these had limitations.

Nuttall too found a newly appreciative audience. In 1998 a Home Office research study was published that purported to summarise the research evidence on ways of dealing with offender behaviour

(Goldblatt and Lewis 1998; the original workshop was attended by a member of the Prime Minister's Office). Despite the certainty implied in the title *Reducing Offending* there was remarkably little in the chapter by Julie Vennard and Carol Hedderman on 'Effective interventions with offenders' that could lead one to be confident about basing a national programme for probation intervention on it, and the report itself noted that 'evidence on effectiveness, and more particularly cost effectiveness, is currently limited' (Goldblatt and Lewis 1998: 136). Similarly, a report a year earlier investigating cognitive behavioural approaches in the probation service found inconclusive messages from research and a situation in the probation service of badly delivered programmes, poor training and limited attention given to risk/need principles (Hedderman *et al*. 1997). It is rather ironic that in the struggle to overturn Martinson, the details of these reports have been ignored in the same way that Martinson's original message was lost.

Whatever one's apprehensions might be about the quantity and validity of the evidence base produced by the Home Office Research and Statistics Directorate and the Probation Inspectorate, these publications caught the political tide. The combination of Chris Nuttall and Graham Smith with a new government was irresistible.

The modernisation programme

What Works is intimately related to the project to modernise the probation service – it is both cause and effect. Since the introduction of the *Statement of National Objectives and Priorities* (SNOP) in 1984 (Home Office 1984), the probation service has been facing increasing pressure to prove itself effective and to demonstrate accountability. National standards were introduced and made more stringent. Performance indicators also appeared (and now with a financial penalty attached to failure to meet specific targets). Cash limits were introduced to put an end to the open-ended commitment that government would meet 80 per cent of probation expenditure (and the service is now 100 per cent government funded). Three-year plans were produced by the Home Office to direct the work of the service. The Probation Inspectorate carried out more rigorous and demanding inspections. At the same time, crime became an increasingly significant topic for political and media debate – and a crucial aspect of that debate focused upon failures to deal with offenders, which implicated the probation service.

All these developments pointed, more or less directly, to a national probation service. A major difficulty in holding probation accountable lay in the fact that there were 54 probation services, run almost as personal fiefdoms by chief probation officers. Within these services probation officers could (within fairly wide limits) deal with offenders as they saw fit, which meant that measuring effectiveness was not a simple matter. With the election of the Labour government in 1997, modernisation became an explicit part of the agenda – 'At the heart of New Labour's approach to governance and national renewal is the relentless quest for "modernization"' (McLaughlin *et al.* 2001: 305) – and evidence-based practice or What Works is a key aspect of modernisation.

Perhaps the clearest indication of modernisation for probation came with the reorganisation that took place on 1 April 2001 when a National Probation Service (NPS) with 42 areas replaced the 54 individual probation services. Each area is run by a board with paid members and the chief officer (previously chief probation officer) is a member of the board. While there is some confusion about lines of accountability (is the chief accountable to the board or the national director?), without the existence of a national service the What Works initiative could not have occurred; Robinson (2001: 248) has argued cogently that 'the "what works" agenda can be understood as a powerful catalyst to the creation of a national service'. When SNOP was introduced in 1984, all services responded to it but they did not all follow its prescriptions; services put their own spin on SNOP producing statements of local objectives and priorities (SLOPs) and even statements of team objectives and priorities (STOPs; see Lloyd 1986). If What Works had been introduced to 54 separate probation services, it is likely that implementation would have been partial, inconsistent, fragmented and resisted. While a national service was vital for What Works, the reorganisation that was entailed meant that the What Works initiative was being implemented at the same time that probation was in the midst of radical structural changes – not perhaps the most propitious time to launch an initiative of this nature.

Overall, and in spite of the rhetoric, the foundations of What Works in England and Wales cannot be said to be neat, evidence based, carefully considered and well planned. Instead we are faced with a messy, unco-ordinated, coincidental set of factors that lie behind this highly significant initiative. While we may imagine policy-making to be the result of a detailed, rational sifting of options and decision-making based upon clear evidence, this is certainly not the case for What Works. Instead we are faced with the kind of situation depicted by David Garland (2001: 26) when he discusses how new developments are selected for action:

the choices that cumulatively compose the selection process are made, more often than not, in a fashion that is blind to some of its consequences, and driven by value commitments rather than in-formed instrumental calculation. Socially situated, imperfectly knowledgeable actors stumble upon ways of doing things that seem to work, and seem to fit with their concerns. Authorities patch together workable solutions to problems that they see and can get to grips with. Agencies struggle to cope with their workload, please their political masters, and do the best job they can in the cir-cumstances. There is no omnipotent strategist, no abstract system, no all-seeing actor with perfect knowledge and unlimited powers.

The foundations of What Works look shaky.

The current situation

Whatever apprehensions one might have about the foundations of What Works, it is possible that current conditions are such that it will be effectively implemented nationally and prove successful in achieving the targets that have been set for it. I have already noted that What Works is being implemented at the same time as probation staff are having to come to terms with major structural reorganisation of the service – a development that could have implications for the success of What Works. In this part of the chapter I will consider various other issues that are part of the environment within which What Works is operating, and that serve as pointers to how the initiative is faring.

The NPS environment

Within the last few years the probation service has had to take on board a plethora of new responsibilities and, with the government-led emphasis on performance, these responsibilities have to be monitored and targets have to be met. The Crime and Disorder Act 1998 requires probation to participate in the new partnership arrangements, but it seems that increasingly probation staff are finding it difficult to find the time to attend partnership meetings. New court orders have been introduced (drug treatment and testing orders, drug abstinence orders, new uses of electronic monitoring) and probation staff have to work hard to organise these. Probation staff are members of youth offending teams. New initiatives continue to pour out from the Home Office, and the National Probation Directorate (NPD) – for obvious reasons – wishes to be seen to be willing to take these on board. The problem for What Works is that while it may be the most significant of the new initiatives it is not the only one – all of them have to be dealt with and with so much else going on it is possible that the focus required for something so important as What Works is lacking.

It is not surprising that alongside the added responsibilities there has been an increase in sickness absence rates. The latest data from the NPD show that only a handful of probation areas were below the 2002/03 target for sickness absence – and these were predominantly small areas (NPD 2002). A considerable amount of effort is going on in the NPS to try to cut sickness absence as programmes cannot be run effectively if staff are absent, but the problem is a significant one and its possible impact upon the What Works initiative cannot be underestimated. And this is especially so as sickness absence tends to be concentrated in probation officer and probation service officer grades – both of whom are heavily involved in the delivery of What Works programmes.

Allied to this issue are two more general matters about staffing. First – and impressionistically – it seems that in many cases accredited programmes are run by probation service officers (PSOs) who are, by definition, not qualified probation officers (and this is certainly not to question the commitment or abilities of PSOs). Now given the significance of What Works it would surely be wise to have fully qualified staff running programmes as this would be a better guarantee of success. Secondly, and to some extent the reason for the use of PSOs on these programmes, is the shortage of qualified staff across the NPS. Recruitment targets nationally have been increased but the effect of this will only be felt in a couple of years when the new staff begin full-time work. So, on the whole, the levels and types of staff who run What Works programmes appear to be somewhat minimal and unqualified.

Trends in the use of community penalties do not make encouraging reading. Between 1990 and 2000 the use of community rehabilitation orders (CROs) for summary offences has risen from 28 to 36 per cent; for community punishment orders (CPOs) the rise has been from 31 to 40 per cent; and for community punishment and rehabilitation orders (CPROs) the rise has been from 30 per cent (in 1992) to 43 per cent. It is scarcely an exaggeration to say that almost half community penalties are now made for summary offences. Added to this are changes in the criminal histories of those starting supervision: between 1995 and 2000 for CROs there was a decrease in those with experience of custody from 41 to 35 per cent, and a corresponding increase in those with no previous convictions from 16 to 25 per cent; for CPOs the picture was the same – a decrease in those with custodial experience from 27 to 19 per cent and an increase in those with no previous convictions from 28 to 47 per cent; in the case of CPROs the decrease in those who had served a custodial sentence was from 42 to 34 per cent, and the increase in those with no previous convictions was from 15 to 27 per cent. Finally, it is worth noting that the proportion of those receiving a CRO with an additional requirement has increased from around one quarter in 1991 to one third in 2000 – and this trend is likely to continue as accredited programmes come on stream (all the data in this paragraph are taken from Home Office 2002).

These trends suggest that community penalties are increasingly being used for less serious offenders who are being given more punishment (Morgan 2003 also comments on these trends) and this, in turn, may have consequences for the What Works initiative. It certainly raises important questions about the assessment criteria being used to decide which offenders are appropriate for programmes and how categories of risk are decided. It is also possible that too much may be expected of offenders who may, as a result, fail to complete a programme. And, more generally, there is surely an issue about increasing levels of punitiveness in a society which is already very fearful of crime.

There are currently two serious tensions in probation practice that threaten the What Works initiative. First, there is the tension between the need for rigorous assessment of offenders for accredited programmes and the need to ensure that targets in terms of numbers on such programmes are met. If not enough offenders are being referred and accepted on to programmes there may be pressure to tinker with the assessment criteria. Conversely, if this occurs, the integrity of the programme may be threatened as What Works programmes generally tend to be focused upon specific types of offenders. There is also a tension between the need to get offenders to complete programmes and the need to enforce rigorously the conditions of orders. One of the Stretch Objectives of the NPD – indeed its 'highest priority' (NPS 2001: 29) – is to improve the overall rate of enforcement of orders. However, if there is also a requirement to ensure that targets are met with regard to programme completions, then there may be situations where the need to enforce and the desire to ensure completion conflict. How such a conflict would be resolved is an interesting question as action on either side could have negative consequences.

I have already noted the need for accurate and reliable assessment tools in order to ensure that appropriate offenders are matched to relevant programmes. This is seen as especially necessary for What

Works programmes as these are finely calibrated so that effectiveness is dependent upon treating offenders who have specific needs or demonstrate certain types of risk. If the 'wrong' type of offender is placed upon a What Works programme he or she is more likely to fail – either in terms of failure to complete or by being reconvicted. So far, a single assessment tool is not available to the NPS so that consistency is threatened. Indeed, *A New Choreography* itself points to a worrying situation with regard to asessment: 'Current evidence suggests that some areas are not adequately matching offenders to the right programmes' (NPS 2001: 25). The reasons for this need to be examined as different action will be necessary depending upon whether this is, for example, a failure of staff, a failure of certain assessment tools or a failure of training.

The Accreditation Panel

I have discussed in a previous article the purpose, make-up and approach of the Accreditation Panel (Mair 2000) and my apprehensions about it, concluding that

> [The Panel] is dominated by narrow, sectarian interests; its relationship with HMIP is ambiguous; its methods of working do not seem to be focused on the substance of probation work – it is more interested in rhetoric than reality; it is much too prescriptive; and it is being asked to move far more quickly than such a critically important venture should be … instead of encouraging exciting, innovative work it could all too easily lead to such initiatives being suffocated. (2000: 271)

But it is worth reiterating that the panel is heavily biased in favour of cognitive behavioural approaches, which seems a somewhat blinkered way of going about what is supposed to be an evidence-based initiative. And it is also the case that the context within which an accredited programme is organised and run does not seem to be adequately covered by the documentation required by the panel for accreditation.

Progress by the panel has been slow: the second report of the panel's work notes that seven programmes were fully accredited for use by the NPS, four for general offending and the remainder for sex offenders and drunk drivers (Joint Prison/Probation Accreditation Panel 2001). This may sound like a reasonable number, but it is important to bear in mind that the earliest date at which some of these programmes received accreditation was September 2000 which (at the time of writing) left two years for national roll-out – not a particularly long time for such a complex process. It is one thing to devise a programme that is theoretically coherent, with committed staff and adequate levels of staffing, that fits into the structure of the organisation and that shows early signs of effectiveness in one probation area. It is an entirely different matter to then move to implement such a programme on a national basis; the potential problems are considerable, even if we ignore that fact that those who are responsible for formulating policy rarely have any interest or ability in implementation.

Early indicators

It will be some time before we get the reconviction rates associated with accredited programmes, and the rates for the first few years should be treated with considerable caution as the possible positive impact of a new programme delivered by committed, enthusiastic staff who choose carefully those who are accepted on to the programme needs to be borne in mind (it is worth remembering that the evaluation of the STOP programme in Mid-Glamorgan showed less success in terms of reconviction rates as time went on – see Raynor and Vanstone 1997). There are, however, a couple of pieces of work that give some indications of how the What Works initiative is going.

NAPO published some material in September 2001 that suggests that while staff were not unhappy about the initiative as a whole, they did have anxieties about the intensive assessment necessary before they could be allowed to deliver a programme, and about the levels of support they received in the transition period prior to working on an accredited programme. Perhaps most worrying was NAPO's data on the completion rate for programmes:

> The initial figures suggest that anywhere between 25% and 70% of offenders are successful in negotiating their way through the programme. It is highly probable that significant numbers of offenders do not have the initial literacy, numeracy and social skills in order to succeed (*NAPO News* 2001: 3).

The article points out (with some understandable scare-mongering) that if the national completion rate was in fact to be 25 per cent (which is very low indeed) almost a quarter of a million offenders would have to be referred in order to meet the national completion targets – a figure that 'exceeds the total probation caseload' (*NAPO News* 2001: 2).

The other study is an interim report examining how seven Pathfinder programmes were introduced into probation areas (Hollin *et al.* 2002). The conclusions to the report are by no means as positive as they might be:

> There did not seem to be a considerable problem with insufficient referrals for any of these programmes, but securing appropriate referrals for a particular programme was a concern felt by many ... there were high drop-out rates from programmes, particularly either before the start or in the early stages ... The provision of administrative staff emerged as a significant issue ... Most of those interviewed expressed dissatisfaction with the levels of administrative staff provided ... The concept of programme integrity and need for monitoring was well understood by staff in all these programmes, although lack of resources sometimes made this difficult to achieve ... It is clear that services require clearer central guidelines to facilitate the implementation and delivery of the programmes to produce a more consistent method for referrals and targeting, programme delivery, staff training and support, accommodation and integrity and monitoring provisions. (Hollin *et al.* 2002: 41–4)

These findings are more robust than those from NAPO, but it is significant that both studies point in the same direction. It seems clear that there are problems with the implementation of accredited programmes – not surprisingly – and such problems will have a negative impact upon the chances of programmes being successful in terms of reducing reconviction rates.

Further, if such problems are being found in the Pathfinder programmes, how much more likely are they to be found in the national roll-out? Despite having implementation difficulties noted and effective practice guides produced as a result of the research (see Home Office Development and Practice Report 2002), it would take a remarkably optimistic individual to believe that probation areas taking on What Works programmes as part of the national roll-out would be able to bypass problems. The guidance offered is couched in vague terms and delivered as brief bullet points with no suggestions on possible approaches to following the advice. For example:

- All staff should subscribe fully to the model behind the programme and its methods
- Tutors should be given adequate administrative support to prepare for the programme sessions and to collect monitoring data

- There are explicit targeting criteria for the programmes that should be strictly adhered to (Home Office Development and Practice Report 2002: 1–2)

If such terse directives were an effective way of ensuring that individuals carried out plans as they were designed to be practised, life would be a great deal simpler for those who try to implement programmes.

Even more worrying are the data collected by NPD itself about how far accredited programme completions have been achieved. Only four probation areas had met their targets by March 2002, and for England and Wales as a whole only 55 per cent of completions had been achieved. The reasons for the most part related to breach (NPD 2002). Unless there is a considerable increase in programme completions in the next two years, NPS will fail to meet its target of 60,000 completions of accredited programmes – and the political consequences of failure could be serious.[2]

While it must be emphasised that the full results of evaluations of the What Works programmes have yet to appear, the indicators discussed here are not especially encouraging. In particular, it looks as if there are real problems with getting individuals to complete programmes. As I have argued earlier, if action is taken to try to improve the completion rate this could lead to inappropriate offenders being accepted on to programmes, or to the insistence on rigorous enforcement of breach (as required by National Standards) becoming less of a priority. And neither of these roads is without its consequences.

If this analysis is correct, then the current conditions do not appear to be very encouraging for the success of the What Works initiative.

Conclusions

While it may appear, as a result of aggressive marketing, that there is no alternative to What Works and that doubts about its efficacy cannot be entertained, it is notable that a variety of commentators – even some of those most closely associated with it – have at times made cautious noises.

Jane Furniss, who was Deputy Chief Inspector of Probation under Sir Graham Smith and a key figure in promulgating the What Works gospel, has been involved in two articles that have noted the potential and actual difficulties facing the implementation of What Works, and have acknowledged the limitations in the knowledge base of What Works

(Furniss and Nutley 2000; Furness *et al*. 2001). Peter Raynor, another supporter of What Works, has also noted the limited nature of the evidence upon which What Works is purported to be based – 'It is true that the evidence base in Britain is still fairly small' (Raynor and Vanstone 2002: 105) – and has pointed out the risks associated with the iniative (Raynor 2002). Andrew Underdown, author of one of the reports that kick started the What Works initiative (1998), has also recently argued that 'there are a host of management and implementation challenges' to be overcome (2001: 117), especially in relation to making sure that offenders actually attend and complete accredited programmes.

The three individuals just referred to are all firmly inside the What Works camp, yet they are aware that the façade of confidence perhaps hides something less substantial. Others too have pointed to problematic issues. Gwen Robinson has noted a variety of risks that are related to central ownership of What Works (2001). Hazel Kemshall (2002: 53) has argued cogently that 'The centrally driven effective practice national curriculum and the reconstitution of the probation service as a nationally managed organisation has given the service a key role in the moral engineering agenda of advanced liberal governance' – a development that she does not view positively. Simon Merrington and Steve Stanley in a review of the UK evidence base for accredited programmes have argued that 'Whilst the international evidence for the impact of cognitive behavioural programmes is compelling, the published evidence in the UK that these programmes make a substantial impact on re-offending is not yet very strong' (2000: 274). And the editors of a recent collection of essays on community penalties have also had reservations: 'in the search for effective community penalties, we should not restrict ourselves to just one approach (such as the cognitive behavioural approach, important and promising thought that clearly is), but rather we should be open to the possibilities offered by several different approaches' (Bottoms *et al*. 2001: 230) and one such approach should be a return to enagaging with 'the reality of the social lives of offenders, and the communities in which they live' (Bottoms *et al*. 2001: 238).

None of those who have been quoted could be said to be enemies of What Works, yet all have apprehensions about it. The struggle to achieve consistent effective outcomes from community penalties has been going on for some time in various guises. Despite the claims made by the NPD and the good news stories in its 'What Works' newsletter, the reality is that the What Works initiative – a massive undertaking in criminal justice experimentation and one which carries huge risks for the

National Probation Service – is not based on solid ground, is being implemented in not particularly conducive circumstances and shows what at best might be described as not very encouraging results (although it must be remembered that these are preliminary and partial).

While the virtually unlimited discretion previously permitted to probation officers in how they worked with offenders was indefensible, What Works could all too easily move probation work to the opposite extreme. Do we really wish to end up with a probation service whose work is completely controlled by the centre? Probation training has been moving in this direction and probation resources now come entirely from government. The existence of a national service means the mechanism for central control is present, although precisely how that will be exercised remains to be seen. If practice is to be dictated by the centre one can only envisage disasterous consequences: low staff morale, deprofessionalisation, poor commitment. And how would this fit with the current interest in pro-social modelling by probation staff?

Perhaps I am being too pessimistic. I want to see an effective, well resourced probation service and I know very well that research results are rarely so negative (or so positive) that clear directives can be drawn from them. Indeed, the pendulum may have begun to swing back – and ironically the source for this is HMIP where the new Chief Inspector (an ex-academic, not an ex-probation officer) recently wrote:

The implementation of the What Works agenda has, however, been accompanied by a degree of what can best be described as programme fetishism. The unintended impression has sometimes been given that activities not falling under the accredited programme umbrella are of less importance. Nothing could be further from the truth. Let us be clear. The essence of the What Works agenda is that probation practice should be evidence-based. The evidence indicates that so-called What Works programmes – generally, at present, cognitive behavioural group work programmes – will not work unless delivered in the context of effective case management, based on a full risk and needs assessment which tackles the multiple criminogenic factors – drug abuse, accommodation problems, lack of educational and vocational skills, unemployment, debt, and so on – which characterise most supervised offenders. Offenders' motivation to change has to be identified and nurtured. Participation in programmes has to be encouraged and supported. Their practical, socially excluding problems have to be tackled. This emphatically means that traditional probation officer case management skills, grounded on more precise risk and needs assessment, must not be marginalised: they are vital. (HMIP 2002: 8)

Let us hope that the kind of balanced, reflective work which uses traditional skills but is not afraid to try out new methods characterises the probation service of the twenty-first century. Practice based around such precepts would have strong foundations.

Note

1   It is worth noting that the negative findings of the Whitehead and Lab meta-analysis were, to some extent, the stimulus for a highly influential meta-analysis by Don Andrews and his colleagues, thus highlighting again the importance of the Canadian connection (Andrews *et al*. 1990).
2   These targets have recently been cut.

References

Andrews, D.A., Zinger, I., Hoge, R.D., Bonta, J., Gendreau, P. and Cullen, F.T. (1990) 'Does correctional treatment work? A clinically relevant and psychologically informed meta-analysis', *Criminology*, 28: 369–404.

Bottoms, A., Gelsthorpe, L. and Rex, S. (2001) 'Concluding reflections', in A. Bottoms *et al*. (eds) *Community Penalties: Change and Challenges*. Cullompton: Willan, 226–40.

Bullock, R.J. and Svyantek, D.J. (1985) 'Analyzing meta-analysis: potential problems, an unsuccessful replication, and evaluation criteria', *Journal of Applied Psychology*, 70: 108–15.

Chapman, T. and Hough, M. (1998) *Evidence Based Practice: A Guide to Effective Practice*. London: HMIP.

Copas, J. (1995) *Some Comments on Meta-analysis*. Warwick: Department of Statistics, University of Warwick.

Downes, D. and Morgan, R. (1997) 'Dumping the "hostages to fortune"? The politics of law and order in post-war Britain', in M. Maguire *et al*. (eds) *The Oxford Handbook of Criminology* (2nd edn). Oxford: Clarendon Press, 87–134.

Furniss, J., Flaxington, F. and MacDonald, A. (2001) 'The role of audit in the holistic assessment of programme effectiveness', *Probation Journal*, 48: 171–8.

Furniss, J. and Nutley, S. (2000) 'Implementing What Works with offenders – the effective practice initiative', *Public Money and Management*, October–November: 23–8.

Garland, D. (2001) *The Culture of Control: Crime and Social Order in Contemporary Society*. Oxford: Oxford University Press.

Garrett, C. (1985) 'Effects of residential treatment on adjudicated delinquents', *Journal of Research in Crime and Delinquency*, 22: 287–308.

Gendreau, P. and Ross, R.R. (1979) 'Effectiveness of correctional treatment: bibliotherapy for cynics', *Crime and Delinquency*, 25: 463–9.

Glass, G. (1976) 'Primary, secondary and meta-analysis of research', *Educational Researcher*, 5: 3–8.

Goldblatt, P. and Lewis, C. (1998) *Reducing Offending: An Assessment of Research Evidence on Ways of Dealing with Offending Behaviour*. Home Office Research Study 187. London: Home Office.

Hedderman, C., Sugg, D. and Vennard, J. (1997) *Changing Offenders' Attitudes and Behaviour: What Works?* Home Office Research Study 171. London: Home Office.

Her Majesty's Inspectorate of Probation (2002) *Annual Report 2001–2002*. London: HMIP.

Hollin, C., McGuire, J., Palmer, E., Bilby, C., Hatcher, R. and Holmes, A. (2002) *Introducing Pathfinder Programmes into the Probation Service: An Interim Report*. Home Office Research Study 247. London: Home Office.

Home Office (1984) *Probation Service in England and Wales: Statement of National Objectives and Priorities*. London: Home Office.

Home Office (1995) *Strengthening Punishment in the Community: A Consultation Document* (Cm 2780). London: HMSO.

Home Office (2002) *Probation Statistics England and Wales 2000*. London: Home Office.

Home Office Development and Practice Report (2002) *Probation Offending Behaviour Programmes – Effective Practice Guide*. London: Home Office.

Joint Prison/Probation Accreditation Panel 2000–2001 (2001) *Second Report from the Joint Prison/Probation Accreditation Panel*. London: JPPAP.

Kemshall, H. (2002) 'Effective practice in probation: an example of "advanced liberal" responsibilisation?', *Howard Journal*, 41: 41–58.

Lloyd, C. (1986) *Response to SNOP*. Cambridge: Institute of Criminology.

Lloyd, C., Mair, G. and Hough, M. (1994) *Explaining Reconviction Rates: A Critical Analysis*. Home Office Research Study 136. London: HMSO.

Losel, F. (1993) 'The effectiveness of treatment in institutional and community settings', *Criminal Behaviour and Mental Health*, 3: 416–37.

Mair, G. (2000) 'Credible accreditation?', *Probation Journal*, 47: 268–71.

Maltz, M. (1984) *Recidivism*. London: Academic Press.

Martinson, R. (1975) 'What works? Questions and answers about prison reform', in J.A. Gardiner and M.A. Mulkey (eds) *Crime and Criminal Justice: Issues in Public Policy Analysis*. Lexington, MA: Heath, 155–87.

McLaughlin, E., Muncie, J. and Hughes, G. (2001) 'New Labour, new public management and the modernization of criminal justice', *Criminal Justice*, 1: 301–18.

Merrington, S. and Stanley, S. (2000) 'Doubts about the What Works initiative', *Probation Journal*, 47: 272–5.

Morgan, R. (2003) 'Thinking about the demand for probation services', *Probation Journal*, 50: 7–19.

NAPO News (2001) 'Accredited programmes – early indicators', Issue 132: 2–3.

National Probation Directorate (2002) *Performance Report 4 – Year Ending 2001–2002*. London: NPD.

National Probation Service (2001) *A New Choreography: An Integrated Strategy for the National Probation Service for England and Wales*. London: NPS.

Palmer, T. (1978) *Correctional Intervention and Research: Current Issues and Future Prospects*. Lexington, MA: Heath.

Raynor, P. (2002) 'What Works: have we moved on?' in D. Ward *et al.* (eds) *Probation: Working for Justice* (2nd edn). Oxford: Oxford University Press, 166–84.

Raynor, P. and Vanstone, M. (1997) *Straight Thinking on Probation (STOP): The Mid-Glamorgan Experiment*. Probation Studies Report 4. Oxford: Centre for Criminological Research.

Raynor, P. and Vanstone. M. (2002) *Understanding Community Penalties*. Buckingham: Open University Press.

Robinson, G. (2001) 'Power, knowledge and "What Works" in probation', *Howard Journal*, 40: 235–54.

Underdown, A. (1995) *Effectiveness of Community Supervision: Performance and Potential*. Manchester: Greater Manchester Probation Service.

Underdown, A. (1998) *Strategies for Effective Offender Supervision: Report of the HMIP What Works Project*. London: HMIP.

Underdown, A. (2001) 'Making "What Works" work: challenges in the delivery of community penalties', in A. Bottoms *et al.* (eds) *Community Penalties: Change and Challenges*. Cullompton: Willan, 117–25.

Whitehead, J.T. and Lab, S.P. (1989) 'A meta-analysis of juvenile correctional treatment', *Journal of Research in Crime Delinquency*, 26: 276–95.

Chapter 3

The uses and abuses of positivism

David Smith

Introduction

In the years since 1945, probation officers in England and Wales have given different answers to the question: 'Does what you are doing work?' – 'working' here being defined as reducing the rate of offending among the client population. Schematically, one can identify three distinct periods, defined by the answer typically given to this question. From 1945 to about 1975, the usual answer was along the lines of 'Of course it works'; between 1975 and around 1990, it was 'We all know it doesn't work, but there are other useful things we can do'; since 1990, it has been – at its most modest – along the lines of 'There are grounds for thinking that some things work better than other things, and we can more or less tell what these are'. The attitudes behind these answers might be described, in sequence, as naïve optimism, naïve pessimism and – at its best – cautious and rational optimism. They arose respectively from a general confidence in the feasibility of rational social engineering, characteristic of the period of postwar reconstruction and the development of the welfare state; from the dramatic loss of such confidence, in the context of a new political agenda and research findings that notoriously were summarised as 'nothing works'; and from a revival of faith following the appearance of more encouraging research findings and a sudden restoration of the status of psychology as a source of prescriptions for practice. The principal aim of this chapter – as of the book as a whole – is to explore how far the new optimism can be rationally justified. First, however, it is important to provide some context for the assertions above about the death and resurrection of rehabilitative optimism.

The context

The first position, of naïve optimism, could be justified on various grounds: that probation practitioners were known to be hard working, dedicated and conscientious; that the probation service enjoyed the support of successive governments (as shown by the expansion of its numbers and its functions, to encompass penal innovations such as parole and community service); and that it was the subject of an ambitious research programme, funded by the Home Office, that would soon demonstrate its effectiveness; in any case, as everyone knew, prison was not just ineffective but damaging. When the results of the key element in the research programme, the IMPACT experiment, were published (Folkard *et al.* 1976), this position, already weakened by the 'nothing works' interpretation of the American overview of research summarised by Martinson (1974), became extremely difficult to defend. IMPACT appeared to show that intensive probation produced worse results than normal probation, and that smaller caseloads would do worse than larger ones. In more politically favourable times, a defence of rehabilitation might have been possible; but in the mid-1970s the postwar consensus on state welfare was collapsing, and the influence of neoliberalism (soon to come to power in Reagan's USA and Thatcher's Britain) was becoming apparent in social and penal policy debates (the failure fully to implement the strongly welfare-oriented Children and Young Persons Act 1969 is symbolic of this loss of confidence in social engineering). So probation practitioners and, crucially, policy-makers sought another kind of justification for the service's continued existence, and among the answers they found was diversion from prison. Inspired by emerging trends in juvenile justice, Home Office policy recast the probation service as the main vehicle for delivering a reduction of the prison population (or at least a reduction in its rate of growth) (Home Office 1984). This meant that programmes for offenders in the community needed to be sufficiently demanding and rigorous to gain credibility with sentencers as alternatives to custody; and, since the aim was to change the workings of the criminal justice system, not the behaviour of individuals, pre-sentence advice to courts was to concentrate on cases in which there was a risk of custody.

The probation service could claim some success in pursuit of its new aim, and by the end of the 1990s it was – briefly – placed at 'centre stage' of the government's criminal justice policies. It had no sooner reached this position of prominence than it was removed from it – if not 'backstage' (Mair 1997: 1195) then at least into the wings. The Criminal Justice Act 1991, strongly anti-custodial in intent, was amended almost beyond recognition within months of its implementation, and by 1993 it was clear that the policy agenda of the previous ten years had been abandoned. The reduction – or even the control – of the size of the prison population was no longer a policy aim; there was therefore no longer any need for a probation service conceived in terms of its capacity to divert offenders from custody. Paradoxically, this marginalisation of the service occurred at exactly the time when probation officers were beginning to recover some rehabilitative optimism. Instead of believing that nothing worked, they were coming to believe that something might. The evidence seemed at last to be on their side. Studies of individual projects by Raynor (1988) and Roberts (1989), and McIvor's (1990) reanalysis of the findings of effectiveness research, were among the earliest British contributions to this revival of faith. By the mid-1990s these tentative stirrings of hope had been transformed into a powerful orthodoxy that was strongly supported by probation managers and increasingly came to inform policy and practice. By the turn of the century the revived optimism had become an all-embracing, highly prescriptive doctrine (Worrall 2000) that defined what probation officers should and should not attempt to do when they intervened in the lives of offenders.

The new orthodoxy

The broad outlines of this new doctrine are well known (see, e.g., Chapman and Hough 1998; Underdown 1998) and need not be rehearsed here. It has been embraced as the one best way of working by probation managers, nationally and locally, and by many practitioners. While there have been sceptical voices, within the service as well as in the academic community (e.g. Mair 2000; Merrington and Stanley 2000; Worrall 2000; Gorman 2001; Oldfield 2002), there is no doubt that new recruits to the probation service, their training separated from that of social workers since 1998, are firmly socialised within the service into the belief that their practice must be 'evidence based', and that the evidence points in one clear direction (cognitive-behavioural groupwork pro-grammes with a strong focus on offending behaviour). This confidence places university teachers of probation trainees in a dilemma because it is hardly fair to tell them that the 'what works' message that seems to provide them with a helpful guide to the do's and don'ts of practice is being oversold.

Yet there are good grounds for a more sceptical view of what we really know about effectiveness than that taken by enthusiasts for evidence-based practice, as is recognised in some analyses from the Home Office itself (e.g. Vennard *et al.* 1997: 33, who caution that research 'does not demonstrate that cognitive-behavioural approaches, or, indeed, any other type of approach, routinely produce major reductions in offending among a mixed population of offenders'). This is partly because of the nature of the evidence itself. The Home Office has commendably commissioned evaluative research on a range of probation programmes as part of its Crime Reduction Programme evaluation, but no firm results are available at the time of writing. As Merrington and Stanley (2000) – both authors actively involved in probation research – note, there is actually very little British evidence about the effectiveness of the programmes that make up the probation service's national curriculum. The one exception is Raynor and Vanstone's (1996, 1997) evaluation of the Mid-Glamorgan adaptation of the Canadian Reasoning and Rehabilitation programme, which was a pioneering effort – known as STOP – to act seriously upon the revised interpretation of the effectiveness research. While the one-year results for those who completed the programme were encouraging, the two-year results were less so: the reconviction rate was similar to that for other community sentences. The authors suggest that this may reflect a failure to follow up the learning achieved during the programme in subsequent supervision. This research is reasonably regarded as the most rigorous evaluation of a probation programme based on What Works principles yet published in Britain, and it is clear that the STOP programme was well resourced, carefully implemented and well supported by the local management. The results, while promising in some respects (the group who completed the programme reported fewer potentially crime-related problems, for instance), are hardly clear cut enough to justify the elevation of the cognitive-behavioural approach to a position of unquestioned superiority over all others. But this is exactly the position it has been given in the What Works initiative.

The durability of positivism

The argument of this chapter does not depend on the shortcomings of the existing evidence, however – important as these are; rather, it starts with what is arguably a misunderstanding on the part of probation managers and the relevant civil servants of the nature of evidence itself. Much of the relevant discussion about how evidence might be used to inform practice has been not in probation or criminal justice studies but in the related field of social work. For over 20 years, the best known and most persistent British advocate of evidence-based social work has been Brian Sheldon, currently Director of the Centre for Evidence-based Social Services at the University of Exeter. In a number of articles (for example, Macdonald and Sheldon 1992; Sheldon 1978, 1986, 2001) he has argued that social work practice ought to be more evidence based, that positivist, preferably experimental, approaches are the best means of obtaining evidence and determining what works and what does not, and that the evidence thus obtained demonstrates the superiority of behaviourist (and cognitive-behaviourist) forms of intervention over others. Sheldon claims (with some reason; see Sheldon and Chilvers 2000) that social workers (in this supposedly unlike other professional groups) tend to be unaware of effectiveness research, to lack the skills needed to read research critically, and to react defensively in the face of mainly negative results. The same charge of defensiveness is levelled against critics of a purely positivist methodology (Sheldon 1984; see also Cheetham *et al.* 1992). As for more radical, postmodern critiques of positivist rationality (e.g. Webb 2001), these are more appropriately termed 'post-rational' (Sheldon 2001: 801).

In 1987 the *British Journal of Social Work* published a much less radical, more 'modernist', attempt of mine (following the work of Raynor (1984) and Sheldon's (1984) dismissive response to it) to suggest some problems with positivism in social work research. This (Smith 1987) argued that Sheldon's traditional version of positivism, and his rejection of other research approaches, were epistemologically limited and limiting, and that if we were to take his advice a number of useful research approaches would be lost to the social work community. It also suggested that Sheldon was wrong to argue that social work's neglect of research distinguished it from other professions, since if this were true much of the evaluation research literature, which was full of complaints about practitioners' failures to attend to research findings (notably in education), would be incomprehensible. The article argued for attention to processes as well as to outcomes, on the grounds that measuring and counting outcomes were of little use unless one knew what had produced them (a naïve version of the 'realistic evaluation' more recently and thoroughly advocated by Pawson and Tilley (1997)). This was probably the part of the article that received most attention and gave it whatever influence it had (Cheetham *et al.* 1992). Since positivist outcome-oriented evaluation has made a dramatic comeback in the field of probation, and is the basis for the claim that we know what evidence-based practice ought to look like, and for managerial and political demands that practice should be based on What Works and on nothing else, it may be useful to try to develop some of the arguments of the 1987 paper and explore what should count as evidence and what it can and cannot tell us about effective practice.

Knowledge in the social sciences

Unlike postmodern critics of the whole principle of rationality in social work (or any) practice, management and research (e.g. Webb 2001), I do not have a problem with the basic proposition that practice should be 'evidence based'. Most of us, for example, are likely to be reassured to be told that evidence exists for the efficacy of the drugs our doctor prescribes, and – while the analogy with medicine is liable to be misleading – evidence also sounds a preferable basis to the alternatives, such as habit, whim, intuition, gut conviction and obsession, for practice in social work or probation. But it is still arguable that in the language of politicians and probation managers the demand that practice should be based on already-available evidence reveals an over-confident and oversimplified view of what evidence does or might consist of, and of how it should be interpreted and used. In trying to justify this claim and to suggest a more modest and nuanced (but perhaps more helpful) approach to thinking about evidence for effective probation practice I shall move from the general to the particular, arguing first that the managerial view of evidence and its implications rests on a mis-conception about the nature of empirically based theories in the social sciences, and then drawing on personal experience and the work of other evaluation researchers to propose that knowing what counts as evidence, what it is evidence of, and how we should use it rationally is more complicated than probation managers and politicians require it to be.

One problem is that the version of positivism that the probation service in England and Wales (along with comparable criminal justice services in Scotland) has been encouraged to adopt since about 1990 is a most uncritical one, and it is worth noting that this movement has taken place just as the most closely related academic disciplines have, in general, been trying to move in the opposite direction. It is not necessary to be a postmodernist thinker to wonder about the wisdom of putting all one's eggs into an old-fashioned positivist basket that seems to many apparently sane commentators to be in need of major repair. 'Positivism' means here, as it does for Sheldon, the assumption that the social sciences can and should proceed on the model of the natural sciences, and the closer they can get to this model the better – more rigorous, valid, useful and so on – they will be. The probation service, having had no (or very little) evidence on which to base its practice until the mid-1970s, and having then carried on its work in the shadow of the 'nothing works' slogan, understandably welcomed the news that the evidence was now on its side and developed a novel commitment to evidence-based practice. It is also understandable that the service's managers should adopt a view of the nature of evidence and its relevance for practice that holds out the promise of helping them to achieve control over their workforce and to produce standardised, predictable forms of practice; this is inherently what bureaucrats try to do; it is also what the government demands. Unfortunately, this bureaucratic view of evidence is based on a misconception of the nature of the social sciences.

The moral philosopher Alasdair MacIntyre, writing of the 'character of generalisations in the social sciences', explains the bureaucratic view thus: 'What managerial expertise requires for its vindication is a justified conception of social science as providing a stock of law-like generalizations with strong predictive power' (1985: 90). This, according to MacIntyre, is the image of social science that has been dominant for the past 200 years – since the late eighteenth-century Enlightenment – and it is a product of the positivist aspiration to render the social world knowable and predictable. But this aspiration, MacIntyre argues, is based on a misunderstanding of the nature of the social sciences and the kinds of generalisation they can produce. One of the examples he gives is Oscar Newman's (1973) theory of defensible space. Based on extensive research, this predicts, among other things, that crime rates will rise with the height of residential buildings up to a height of 13 storeys, and then level off. This is a risky prediction because it is refutable, and positivist criminologists hastened to try to refute it. Naturally, they found disconfirming instances as well as supportive ones. But this does not mean, as it would for a theory in the natural sciences, that the theory has to be abandoned or even radically modified: few large building projects of the past 20 years do not incorporate some version of defensible space. In practice, social science theories that are found useful can survive instances in which their predictions fail to be confirmed, because their usefulness does not reside primarily in their predictive power. It cannot do so because of the inevitable unpredictability of human life, which means that the logic of theory in the social sciences is necessarily different from that of theories in the natural sciences.

Within criminology, John Braithwaite (1993) has also discussed the limits of positivist approaches as guides to policy formation in a way which is close to the position I want to argue for in respect of the proper use of evidence in probation practice. Braithwaite (1993: 386–8) argues that the contribution of criminology should be to 'develop a range of

theories that are sometimes useful', and that for problem-solving purposes 'it is contextualized usefulness that counts, not decontextualized
statistical power'. Theories should be considered by practitioners as
metaphors, as sources of images and ideas that may or may not be useful
in particular problem-solving contexts. Positivist criminology 'can rule
out certain theories as making consistently unsupportable claims', but
we should not expect it to 'deliver us a unified explanatory edifice' that
will answer all the questions of practitioners and policy-makers.
Braithwaite (1993: 394) advised his original audience of members of the
American Society of Criminology (who, for the most part, do not seem to
have attended closely to his suggestions) as follows:

> Put positivist criminology in its place. Reject the prescriptions of
> the critical theorists and postmodernists who want to write off
> positivist criminology … But reject the view that the ultimate value
> in science is discovering that single unified set of law-like
> statements that offers the best explanation of the phenomenon.

In the gap in the quotation above, Braithwaite stresses the value of the
most rigorous positivist research, and MacIntyre too (1985: 104)
emphasises that the 'best available stock of generalizations about social
life' will 'be based on a good deal of research'. But such generalisations
will never achieve anything approaching the status of universal laws,
and even the best of them are likely to be confronted with 'counter-
examples' (empirical findings contrary to the predictions of the
generalisation) because 'the constant creation of counter-examples is a
feature of human life'. Thus any claim for the predictive power of any
social science theory should be (and, by most empirically oriented social
scientists, in fact is) preceded by some qualifying phrase such as
'Characteristically and for the most part' (MacIntyre 1985: 104–5), rather
than being offered as a universal truth. Positivist social scientists who
offer no such qualification, and present their theories to politicians,
managers, bureaucrats and practitioners as if they had the status of
universal laws, may satisfy the yearnings of their audience for a social
world from which all uncertainty has been removed, and which has thus
become predictable and controllable; but in doing so they misrepresent
the nature of generalisation in the social sciences – and politicians and
bureaucrats in search of simple unqualified solutions are only too ready
to accept the misrepresentation. In reality, the certainty and predict-
ability which the bureaucrat seeks cannot be found within social life, nor
within theories that are rooted in the forms of social life. Untidiness and
unpredictability – what Machiavelli, invoked by MacIntyre, called

'Fortuna' – are inherent in human life, and there is no need to rely on chaos theory or other postmodern fashions to explain why. They are also inherent in theories that try to explain it: MacIntyre's main examples of the failure of social science predictions are from two disciplines that have not been shy of predictions – demography and economics.

The importance of context and process

Braithwaite's (1993) paper on the limits of positivism stressed the need to think contextually rather than abstractly in designing potentially effective, problem-solving interventions, and context is among the unpredictable and uncontrollable factors that make universal, 'one best way' answers impossible (and mean that 'replication' of a successful intervention can never be precisely achieved (Tilley 1996)). The importance of context, changing over space and time, is crucial for the main alternative to positivism in evaluation research – the realist approach (Pawson and Tilley 1997). Pawson and Tilley stress that the context in which an intervention is delivered must be understood if evaluation is to be able to specify the conditions under which change was, or was not, achieved. Equally, they emphasise the need to attend to the processes or 'mechanisms' involved. 'Mechanisms' refers to the choices or capacities made available to participants in the programme, and their operation is dependent on the context in which they are experienced: 'subjects will only act upon the resources and choices offered by a program if they are in conducive settings' (1997: 216). Thus the focus of evaluation cannot be solely upon outcomes but needs to cover also the context that enables, or fails to enable, the mechanisms for change to work. Pawson and Tilley write of 'context-mechanism-out-come configurations', which are propositions stating what it is about programmes that 'works' – at least for some people in some circum-stances. With changes in context, what is ostensibly the 'same' pro-gramme will work differently, or may not work at all. (The same programme, for example the widely used and accredited 'Think First' programme in probation, can look very different, and is presumably experienced differently, depending on who delivers it and how they do it – with enthusiasm, commitment and optimism, for example, or mechanically, tediously and despairingly. Both styles are readily observable.) It follows that rather than trying to 'replicate' programmes which seem to have worked at a particular place and time, which is the model implied by the accreditation process criticised by Mair (2000), we should try to generalise about programmes by developing middle-range theories about context–mechanism–outcome configurations that will allow us to interpret (characteristically and for the most part) differences and similarities among groups of programmes. This is the realist alternative to traditional positivism, which, as a matter of empirical fact, has been much less helpful than its advocates claim in producing reliable findings on effectiveness (see the discussion above of the limits of the evidence for the 'new orthodoxy', and Braithwaite (1993) on the problems of purely positivist approaches in criminology more generally). The realist approach stands a much better chance of telling us something helpful about the questions that matter: what is it about this programme that works for whom in what specifiable conditions and given what contextual features?

This is because positivist approaches to evaluation tend to ignore contexts and, despite some protestations to the contrary, they generally also neglect processes, or mechanisms in Pawson and Tilley's terms. The decontextualised preoccupation with outcomes of much positivist evaluation means that most of its results are inconclusive or contradictory, because the theories that it is supposed to be testing depend crucially on the context and process of their implementation. Russell Keat (1981) provided a clear discussion of the problems of attributing outcomes to a particular aspect of the process of intervention in his account of the relationship between the truth or falsehood of psychoanalytic theory and the success or failure of psychoanalytic practice. In doing so he both illustrated the complexity of the relationship between theoretical claims and concrete predictions in the social sciences, and indicated the ground that realistic evaluation might occupy. Keat (1981: 159) argues that the failure of a therapeutic intervention is compatible with the truth of the theory informing the intervention (whether this is psychoanalysis or anything else), and the success of the intervention is compatible with the falsehood of the theory because 'in deriving predictions about therapeutic outcomes from psychoanalytic theory, a number of auxiliary statements must typically be assumed, whose own truth or falsity may display various degrees of independence from the explanatory claims made within this theory'. Such auxiliary statements make up a 'theory of technique', which aims to describe and explain the effects on the patient of various aspects of the therapeutic process. So even when predicted success is achieved, this does not necessarily count as support either for the version of psychoanalytic theory espoused by the analyst or for the theory of technique associated with it, since the success might be better explained by another theory of technique. The relationships between the theory underpinning an intervention and the intervention itself, and between the intervention and its outcomes, are therefore nothing like as linear and straightforward as positivist evaluators claim, or as managers and bureaucrats in search of a single right answer want to hear and believe.

These considerations may seem abstract but they have quite practical implications both for probation practice and for the evaluation of probation interventions. I suggested above that, contrary to the simple image of unproblematic and exact 'replication' entailed by the accreditation process and the idea of 'rolling out' experimental or 'pathfinding' programmes nationally, there is in fact substantial variation in the way in which what professes to be the same programme is delivered at different times and places. It is not that the orthodoxy on effective practice lacks what might be called a 'theory of technique'; on the contrary, the orthodoxy is highly prescriptive about this and stresses the 'risk principle', the importance of understanding 'responsivity', the need for programmes to be 'multi-modal' and to focus on social skills, and the importance of 'programme integrity' – all in addition to the primary requirement that the underlying theory be drawn from cognitive-behavioural psychology (for a version of this kind of list see McGuire and Priestley 1995). There is indeed every reason to believe that programmes which have these characteristics are likely to be more successful, more of the time and with more people, than programmes which do not. The problem is not what such lists contain but what they leave out.

Thus, while the prescriptions for effective practice typically mention the need for properly trained and supported staff, and for adequate resources, they are silent on questions of what sort of staff these should be and what kind of relationship they should have with those on the receiving end of the programme. But research as well as intuition suggest that the quality of the relationship between helper and helped (or supervisor and supervisee) matters, perhaps as much as the content of the intervention, as a predictor of success or failure of efforts to help people change. Early and now often disregarded research on the effectiveness of counselling and psychotherapy (Truax and Carkhuff 1967) suggested that the quality of the therapeutic relationship, and the personal qualities that the therapist was perceived as having, were more important influences on therapeutic outcomes than the theory and methods the therapist employed. Truax and Carkhuff tried to specify what these qualitative factors were, and suggested acceptance, accurate empathy and 'non-possessive warmth'. In trying to describe the elements of the working style of a successful project for persistent juvenile offenders in central Scotland, my colleagues and I concluded (Lobley *et al.* 2001) that it was hard to improve on Truax and Carkhuff's terms, even though the context of the work was quite different from that of counselling or psychotherapy, and required the workers to convey firmly that the young people's offending was unacceptable. The same is of course true of work in probation, and Rex (1999: 377) suggests that people on probation are prepared to accept, and even to welcome, a firmly directive style on the part of their supervisors as long as it is accompanied by 'a demonstration of concern and respect for the person'. There is every reason to believe that the quality of the relationship matters as much in groupwork programmes as in one-to-one supervision, but the managerial interpretation of the research evidence has nothing to say on this topic, beyond (sometimes) a perfunctory recognition of the need to treat offenders with respect.

But there is a problem over what this recognition can actually mean. It is difficult, but demonstrably not impossible, to follow the injunction to love the sinner and hate the sin, in its influential criminological form of reintegrative shaming (Braithwaite 1989), in a context in which there is room for the expression of concern, care and respect for the 'sinner' as a person. It may become impossible in a context where workers are discouraged from seeing those with whom they work as anything other than offenders, carriers of risks to be managed and controlled rather than of problems and troubles to be solved and assuaged, and subject to orders whose purpose is punishment, not the provision of support and advice. Many commentators have argued (for example, Kemshall 1998; Garland 2001) that the key shift in probation's focus during the 1990s was in its basis for intervention, from clients' needs and problems to offenders' riskiness and dangerousness; and this was accompanied by a redefinition of probation itself as a compulsory and non-negotiable form of punishment, instead of a measure in place of punishment, to which the offender's consent was logically required. It seems unlikely that the rhetoric of risk control and the delivery and enforcement of punishment has been, or could be, fully translated into practice; but such rhetoric has its own effects and the message it sends to probation staff is that they should hate the sinner as well as the sin – or, at the very least, that they should regard the sinner with distrust and suspicion and be ready to take the prescribed punitive action in the event of failures of compliance. In such a context, it is not obvious what room is left for the expression of concern and respect. The political and managerial interpretation of the findings of research on effectiveness, translated into practice, risks producing interventions that are much less effective than they could be, because they ignore the nature and quality of relationships that can help people change.

Some problems of evaluation research

I noted near the beginning that some sceptical commentators have called attention to the relative lack of good evidence to underpin the developments in practice at present under way; Merrington and Stanley (2000: 274), for example, remark that 'the published evidence in the UK that these [cognitive-behavioural] programmes make a substantial impact on re-offending is not yet very strong'. It is not only in respect of such programmes that supposedly evidence-based practice is being promoted on the basis of less evidence than one might hope for (and less than one would think exists, from the claims of politicians). The Sure Start programme for disadvantaged parents of young children, for example, while a positive example of willingness to invest crime reduction resources in work that cannot possibly produce quick results, rests largely on two, and only two, pieces of research on the effectiveness of early intervention – the Perry preschool programme and the Elmira perinatal and early intervention project. Indeed, a team from the RAND corporation (Karoly *et al.* 1998) concluded that these two projects were the only early years interventions on which convincing longitudinal data existed: the follow-up period was 28 years for the Perry programme and 15 years for the Elmira project which, in British terms, consisted of intensive targeted health visiting for poor single mothers. The research on these projects was also, and unusually, convincing because comparison groups were also followed up. Now it is true that these projects were exceptionally difficult to evaluate because of the inherently long-term nature of their potential impacts, and it is perhaps not surprising that a rigorous evaluation exists for only two such projects. It is, however, worth stressing that a good reason for the relative lack of good evaluation is that it is very difficult; among other good reasons are that it is expensive, time-consuming and liable to produce politically inconvenient results.

Reconviction rates, for instance, are often considered as being as hard a measure of the impact of intervention as it is possible to get; they are routinely the principal means of estimating success or failure. Cheetham *et al.* (1992) treat reconviction rates as a harder, more persuasive measure than is available for social work intervention in fields such as mental health or child care but, as Mair *et al.* (1997) among others have pointed out, the hardness of reconviction rates tends to become less impressive the more closely they are examined. Among the questions to be answered in using reconviction rates for evaluative purposes are what to count (court appearances at which a conviction is recorded, convictions or all offences), when to start counting (custodial and community penalties are usually assessed according to two different conventions), how to deal with false positives and false negatives arising from the time lag between the commission of an offence and conviction for it, and how to account (if at all) for geographical variations in police and prosecution practice. Above all, reconviction is not the same thing as reoffending, a fact usually acknowledged near the start of evaluation reports and then quietly forgotten.

Sometimes, however, it is impossible to forget: in the evaluation of the Freagarrach project mentioned above (Lobley *et al*. 2001), and in an earlier evaluation in Scotland (Lobley and Smith 1999) my colleagues and I had access both to Scottish Criminal Records Office (SCRO) data on convictions and pending court hearings, and to data held on local police information systems on the number and nature of charges brought against the young people up until their sixteenth birthday (the information systems were specifically for juvenile offenders). Comparison of the two sets of data showed that the SCRO gave a very attenuated account of the volume and rate of offending compared with the local information systems; it also showed that the time lag between charge and conviction, or at least the appearance of the conviction in the official record, is often very long (the source of the false negative problem). The local systems of course did not provide a 'true' record of offending any more than the SCRO records since they covered only alleged offences that had led to a charge; the young people may have been innocent of some of these and may have committed other offences with which they were never charged. But the local systems suggested a far higher rate of offending than the SCRO records, which created problems in estimating changes in the rate of offending by the young people after they started to attend the projects. We concluded that the Freagarrach project had a substantial positive effect on the offending rate of the majority of the young people it worked with, but the extent of the reduction could only be estimated as somewhere between 20 and 50 per cent (comparing the total number of offences estimated to have been committed by these young people in the year before they started at Freagarrach with the comparable figure for the year after).

In trying to account for Freagarrach's success, as we judged it to be even though very few young people were not known to have committed any offences when we had two or more years' follow-up data, we identified two factors that barely appear in the standard What Works literature (Lobley *et al*. 2001). Freagarrach did, on the whole, work in a way that was informed by and compatible with What Works recommendations, but the crucial elements of its success were judged to be, first, the quality of the relationships staff were able to establish with the young people, as mentioned above; and, secondly, the fact that, unlike many specialist projects, Freagarrach was the product of a coherent interagency strategy for young people in trouble in central Scotland, which brought benefits to Freagarrach such as access to police information, specialist educational resources and the absence of pressure to dilute its criteria for acceptance (that young people's offending should be not only persistent but relatively serious). Thus, as Pawson and Tilley (1997) would lead us to expect, it was essential to understand and specify the relevant mechanisms and the important contextual features of Freagarrach to make sense of the outcomes that it could reasonably be regarded as having helped to produce. The mechanisms and the context are also what make Freagarrach impossible to replicate, though it is understandable and desirable that practitioners and policy-makers should try to learn from its example.

Since evaluation is difficult, even (especially?) when dealing with supposedly 'hard', fact-like outcomes like reconvictions, it is not surprising that there is relatively little of it (to date), and that Underdown (1998) should have found that while cognitive-behavioural programmes were everywhere in probation practice few of them were being evaluated, and hardly any were being evaluated well. The essential reason why evaluation is difficult is that it is, in MacIntyre's (1985: 105) terms, 'rooted in the form – or lack of it – of human life', like the theoretical predictions it implicitly or explicitly sets out to test. A sense of the difficulty of evaluation, of the complexity of what is evaluated and of the provisional, tentative character of any conclusions and recommendations that can be drawn from its results ought therefore to inform the response to evaluative research of policy-makers and practitioners. In the conclusion I suggest how this kind of understanding of evaluative research could be translated into a more modest but also more helpful relationship between policy-makers, practitioners and researchers than prevails at present.

Conclusions

The claims of positivist social science to be capable of producing law-like universal statements have encouraged politicians, bureaucrats and (some) practitioners to believe that the social world is predictable and therefore controllable, and that it is therefore possible and desirable to use research findings as the justification for managerial prescriptions of particular kinds of practice, to the exclusion of others. The process of accreditation of programmes for the probation (and prison) service exemplifies the managerial faith that research can be used to identify effective programmes that can then be formulaically 'rolled out' and implemented in the same way, and with the same results, in different places and contexts, and at different times.

The argument of this chapter has been that this managerial faith is misplaced, since it rests on a misunderstanding of the nature of evidence in the social sciences. This is fundamentally because of the ineliminable unpredictability of human life; it is in the nature of bureaucracy to strive to eliminate it, and to fail. There is no evidence, nor can there be, that justifies the belief that, for example, an accredited programme for offenders that was judged to be effective in one place, at one time, will be similarly effective in different contexts. More specifically, the universalist assumptions of the accreditation model are ill-founded because, like most research in the positivist tradition, they pay insufficient attention to contexts and processes, and treat as unproblematic the question of what contextual and processual features may have produced a worthwhile difference, supposing this to have been identified.

There are alternative traditions, but the messages they bring are less easily assimilated by bureaucratic modes of thought, and less straightforwardly adaptable to prescriptions for practice. The stress in the realist tradition on context and the 'mechanisms' that produce changes implies more disconcertingly that there cannot be 'one best way', and that the crucial elements of any intervention are necessarily local and specific. This will not satisfy those who yearn for certainty, but it is a message that points the way to a more helpful conception of the uses of theory and research for practice. McNeill (2000) has sketched what the practice–theory connection might look like in respect of criminological theory in his suggestions for 'localising' criminology and for a mutual interrogation of theory and practice informed by local and contextual knowledge. His position is similar to that of Braithwaite (1993: 395), who argued for the development of 'contextual, integrated strategies' for crime prevention, in which practitioners combine those elements of competing theories which look useful for practical problem-solving in a specific context. The position argues for theoretical pluralism and tolerance of uncertainty, within limits set by positivist achievements in identifying nonsense. It asserts the importance of context and of the realist stress on what it is that has made the difference, and accepts the implication that simple conceptions of replication are doomed to disappointment. It suggests that much evidence will only emerge over a longer term, and after more careful analysis, than impatient policy-makers and managers might like, but that when it comes such evidence will be more reliable and useful than most that the positivist tradition has produced. And it encourages evaluation researchers to become more modest in the claims they make for their results, and to resist the demands of bureaucrats for single, universal answers.

References

Braithwaite, J. (1989) *Crime, Shame and Reintegration*. Cambridge: Cambridge University Press.

Braithwaite, J. (1993) 'Beyond positivism: learning from contextual integrated strategies', *Journal of Research in Crime and Delinquency*, 30 (4): 383–99.

Chapman, T. and Hough, M. (1998) *Evidence-based Practice*. London: Home Office.

Cheetham, J., Fuller, R., McIvor, G. and Petch, A. (1992) *Evaluating Social Work Effectiveness*. Buckingham: Open University Press.

Folkard, M.S., Smith, D.E. and Smith, D.E. (1976) *IMPACT Vol. II. The Results of the Experiment*. London: HMSO.

Garland, D. (2001) *The Culture of Control: Crime and Social Order in Contemporary Society*. Oxford: Oxford University Press.

Gorman, K. (2001) 'Cognitive behaviourism and the Holy Grail: the quest for a universal means of managing offender risk', *Probation Journal*, 48 (1): 3–9.

Home Office (1984) *Probation Service in England and Wales: Statement of National Objectives and Priorities*. London: Home Office.

Karoly, L.A., Greenwood, P.W., Everingham, S.S., Houb, J., Kilburn, M.R., Rydell, C.P., Sanders, M. and Chiesa, J. (1998) *What we Know and Don't Know about the Costs and Benefits of Early Childhood Interventions*. Santa Monica, CA: RAND Corporation.

Keat, R. (1981) *The Politics of Social Theory*. Oxford: Blackwell.

Kemshall, H. (1998) *Risk in Probation Practice*. Aldershot: Ashgate.

Lobley, D. and Smith, D. (1999) *Working with Persistent Juvenile Offenders: An Evaluation of the Apex CueTen Project*. Edinburgh: Scottish Office.

Lobley, D., Smith, D. and Stern, C. (2001) *Freagarrach: An Evaluation of a Project for Persistent Juvenile Offenders*. Edinburgh: Scottish Executive.

Macdonald, G. and Sheldon, B. (1992) 'Contemporary studies of the effectiveness of social work', *British Journal of Social Work*, 22 (6): 615–43.

MacIntyre, A. (1985) *After Virtue: A Study in Moral Theory*. London: Duckworth.

Mair, G. (1997) 'Community penalties and the probation service', in M. Maguire *et al.* (eds) *The Oxford Handbook of Criminology* (2nd edn). Oxford: Clarendon Press, 1195–1232.

Mair, G. (2000) 'Credible accreditation?', *Probation Journal*, 47 (4): 268–71.

Mair, G., Lloyd, C. and Hough, M. (1997) 'The limitations of reconviction rates', in G. Mair (ed.) *Evaluating the Effectiveness of Community Penalties*. Aldershot: Avebury, 34–46.

Martinson, R. (1974) 'What works? Questions and answers about prison reform', *The Public Interest*, 35: 22–54.

McGuire, J. and Priestley, P. (1995) 'Reviewing "What Works": past, present and future', in J. McGuire (ed.) *What Works: Reducing Offending*. Chichester: John Wiley and Sons, 3–34.

McIvor, G. (1990) *Sanctions for Serious or Persistent Offenders: A Review of the Literature*. Stirling: Social Work Research Centre, University of Stirling.

McNeill, F. (2000) 'Making criminology work: theory and practice in local context', *Probation Journal*, 47 (2): 108–18.

Merrington, S. and Stanley, S. (2000) 'Doubts about the What Works initiative', *Probation Journal*, 47 (4): 272–5.

Newman, O. (1973) *Defensible Space: Crime Prevention through Urban Design*. London: Architectural Press.

Oldfield, M. (2002) 'What Works and the conjunctural politics of probation: effectiveness, managerialism and neo-liberalism', *British Journal of Community Justice*, 1 (1): 79–97.

Pawson. R. and Tilley, N. (1997) *Realistic Evaluation*. London: Sage.

Raynor, P. (1984) 'Evaluation with one eye closed: the empiricist agenda in social work research', *British Journal of Social Work*, 14 (1): 1–14.

Raynor, P. (1988) *Probation as an Alternative to Custody*. Aldershot: Avebury.

Raynor, P. and Vanstone, M. (1996) 'Reasoning and rehabilitation in Britain: the results of the Straight Thinking on Probation (STOP) programme', *International Journal of Offender Therapy and Comparative Criminology*, 40: 279-91.

Raynor, P. and Vanstone, M. (1997) *Straight Thinking on Probation (STOP): The Mid-Glamorgan Experiment*. Oxford: Centre for Criminological Research.

Rex, S. (1999) 'Desistance from offending: experiences of probation', *Howard Journal of Criminal Justice*, 38 (4): 366-83.

Roberts, C. (1989) *First Evaluation Report: Young Offenders Project*. Worcester: Hereford and Worcester Probation Service.

Sheldon, B. (1978) 'Theory and practice in social work', *British Journal of Social Work*, 8 (1): 1–22.

Sheldon, B. (1984) 'Evaluation with one eye closed: the empiricist agenda in social work research – a reply to Peter Raynor', *British Journal of Social Work*, 14 (6): 635–7.

Sheldon, B. (1986) 'Social work effectiveness experiments: review and implications', *British Journal of Social Work*, 16 (2): 223–42.

Sheldon, B. (2001) 'The validity of evidence-based practice in social work: a reply to Stephen Webb', *British Journal of Social Work*, 31 (5): 801–9.

Sheldon, B. and Chilvers, R. (2001) *Evidence-based Social Care: A Study of Prospects and Problems*. Lyme Regis: Russell House.

Smith, D. (1987) 'The limits of positivism in social work research', *British Journal of Social Work*, 17: 401–16.

Tilley, N. (1996) 'Demonstration, exemplification, duplication and replication in evaluation research', *Evaluation*, 2 (1): 35–50.

Truax, C.B. and Carkhuff, R.R. (1967) *Towards Effective Counselling and Psychotherapy*. Chicago, IL: Aldine.

Underdown. A. (1998) *Strategies for Effective Offender Supervision*. London: Home Office.

Vennard, J., Sugg, D. and Hedderman, C. (1997) *Changing Offenders' Attitudes and Behaviour: What Works?* London: Home Office.

Webb, S.A. (2001) 'Some considerations on the value of evidence-based practice in social work', *British Journal of Social Work*, 31 (1): 57–79.

Worrall, A. (2000) 'What works at One Arm Point? A study of the transportation of a penal concept', *Probation Journal*, 47 (4): 243–9.

Chapter 4

Dangerous thinking: a critical history of correctional cognitive behaviouralism

Kathleen Kendall

'The biggest experiment in social engineering this country has ever seen'

On 5 May 2002, *The Observer* newspaper confidently reported that 'prison does work after all' (Rose, D. 2002a: 1). Noting a 'radical transformation in philosophy and practice now sweeping the British prison system', the article focused upon offending behaviour programmes. In making 'bad people' better the programmes are credited for much of this revolution in penal policy. One senior probation officer was quoted as describing these programmes as 'the biggest experiment in social engineering this country has ever seen'. This bold claim rests, in part, on the fact that offending behaviour programmes extend beyond prisons into the National Probation Service. Indeed, in 1999 the Home Office established a Joint Prison/Probation Accreditation Panel (now the Correctional Services Accreditation Panel) whose remit is officially to approve for national implementation only those programmes which have been proven to reduce reoffending. A target for probation was set for 60,000 offenders completing accredited programmes during the period 2003/4; it is anticipated that 30,000 of these will come from community service. This is expected to result in a minimum 4 per cent reduction in the reconviction rate of offenders subject to supervision (What Works Strategy Group 2000: 9).

This chapter provides a historical and critical overview of a key element of the offending behaviour programme experiment – correctional cognitive behaviouralism. It will be argued here that offending behaviour programmes, central to the What Works strategy, are emblematic of neoliberal crime policies (Pratt 1999; Hannah-Moffat 1999, 2000; Carlen 2002; Kemshall 2002). As such, they can be seen as a governmental technique, or way of regulating people's conduct, commensurate with the larger political climate. Within 'free' societies, populations are typically controlled, not through repressive measures but by self-management via the inculcation of moral codes (Foucault 1977; Rose 1999a, 1999b). Offending behaviour programmes rest on the notion that offenders have failed to internalise these codes because they are either lacking key thinking skills or have distorted thinking.

Cognitive behaviouralism – a fairly recent psychological approach – underlies this logic. In sum, cognitive behaviouralism assumes that a person's thinking or cognition affects his or her emotions and behaviour. It is therefore posited that behaviour can be altered by changing one's thinking. A variety of methods are used to achieve this end, such as the use of diaries, daily logs, role-playing, guided imagery, self-talk and self-disclosure (Dobson 1988). When applied to corrections, a cognitive behaviouralist approach (correctional cognitive behaviouralism) works on the assumption that offenders have faulty or deficient thinking which causes them to engage in immoral or criminal behaviour. Programmes, therefore, aim to 'remoralise' or 'ethically reconstruct' offenders by teaching them how to think 'pro-socially'. This is achieved through a variety of tools or techniques enabling offenders to monitor continually their own thoughts, thus ensuring that their conduct falls in line with the dominant ethos.

Nikolas Rose (1996, 1999b) argues that psychology and the related 'psy' disciplines (including psychiatry, psychotherapy and social work) have made it possible for people to be governed in ways that are compatible with liberal and neoliberal ideals. Specifically, the psy disciplines claim expert knowledge over the human mind. In purportedly having unique access to, and understanding of, human thoughts and emotions, they assert the ability to manipulate subjectivity and thus behaviour. The interference of 'experts of the soul' into the lives of people is legitimated on the grounds that their practices are benevolent and backed by a rational, empirical, objective science. Psychological methods, it is claimed, are designed to help people gain control over their own lives and thus empower individuals rather than restrain them. In equipping people with self-understanding and self-mastery, these methods are said to facilitate successful, independent lives. Moreover, because cognitive behaviouralism necessitates the active involvement of people in their own reformation, it works through agency rather than crushes it. In fact, cognitive behaviouralism insists that people take responsibility for their own lives. This deflects earlier criticisms that psychological practices, particularly those with offenders, encouraged passivity and dependency. It also signals broader shifts in government policy. Whereas welfare strategies of rehabilitation held the state accountable for offender reformation, cognitive behaviouralism insists that individuals are responsible for their own transformation. 'Responsibilisation techniques' such as this are paradigmatic of regulation within neoliberal societies (Garland 1996; Hannah-Moffat 1999, 2000; Rose 1996, 2000a). Rose (1999a: 140) uses the term 'advanced liberal' when referring to the most recent forms of governance employing such techniques.

Underpinning this form of governance is an assumption that individuals within 'free' societies are all equally socially positioned and are furthermore rational, responsible, prudent, moral and self-disciplined. Citizenship is thus conditional upon conduct that reflects this construction of an ethical subjectivity. Individuals who fail to meet this expectation are either reintegrated through programmes designed to reconstruct their morality or, if deemed un-assimilable, are managed through methods established to contain the dangers they purportedly pose. In either case, the failure to achieve citizenship is seen as the sole responsibility of the individual who has not met his or her responsibilities within an otherwise ethical community (Rose 2000a).

Rose (1999a, 2000a) refers to this obligation to think ethically as 'ethico-politics'. He suggests that it is becoming increasingly reflected within neoliberal criminal justice systems. More and more, offenders are being split into two groups: those who can be remoralised through programmes and those who are irredeemably immoral and therefore deserving of punitive containment and isolation. Correctional cognitive behaviouralism has been central to this development. Not only has it aided in the construction of classification tools used to distinguish between the two types of offenders but it has also helped to legitimate correctional policy in two ways: by promising a method that works to reform offenders; and by justifying the exclusion and punishment of those supposedly dangerous or immoral thinkers whose minds cannot be reformed (Pratt 1999; Robinson 1999; Kemshall 2002).

This chapter is intended as a contribution towards a critical history of psychology. Rose (2000b) suggests that there are three ways of writing the history of psychology. 'Recurrent history', adopted by most textbooks and authoritative works, presents a story of progress. Here, tales of successes and errors, individual sacrifice and prejudice have culminated in a true understanding of the human mind. 'History as critique' suggests that the discipline of psychology, while fundamentally honourable, has been subverted and/or distorted by various incursions.

Knowledge and understanding of where 'things went wrong' are used to help guide psychology in meeting its full potential. A stronger variant of this regards psychology to be an instrument of domination, its changing character merely reflecting the interests of those in power at any particular time. A 'critical history', on the other hand, investigates the past in order that we can think differently about the present and challenge our current knowledge. This type of history suggests that psychology is much more than a mere reflection of power relations. It has helped to shape how we think about other people, society and even ourselves. In this sense it fabricates and transforms the social and the subjective. Critical history asks 'how kinds of people come into being' and how 'systems of knowledge about kinds of people interact with the people who are known about' (Hacking 1995: 6).

In what follows I begin by briefly exploring the early development of psychology within Western liberal democracies. It will be demonstrated that psychology and its related disciplines helped make it possible to govern people initially in ways commensurate with liberal democracy and currently in ways compatible with neoliberalism. This is followed by a closer examination of various psychological models and practices used to govern criminals, focusing upon their use within the UK, Canada and USA. Although psychology has not been introduced into corrections consistently across these nations, some broad generalisations can be made. It will be argued that cognitive behaviouralism has become dominant within corrections, not because it works to reduce offending but because it provides a method of governance commensurate with neoliberal political rationalities. This helps partially to account for the wide and swift implementation of offending behaviour programmes despite the lack of evidence that they actually work to reduce reoffending. I consider how cognitive behaviouralism has encouraged us to think about people in a particular way and how this method of 'making people up' relates to authority, ethics and power.[1] It is intended that, by demonstrating the conditions which shaped current truth claims about the rehabilitations of offenders, this historical overview will allow us to think differently about the present as well as the future. This is not to suggest that cognitive behaviouralism offers no benefit to offenders or to imply that offenders are simply passive recipients. Rather, it is to warn about the limitations and potential harms which follow in the adoption of cognitive behaviouralism as a panacea in the treatment of offenders.

Revealing the criminal mind: the early development of psychology

This section provides a very brief examination of the emergence of the psychological sciences in the nineteenth century. Drawing heavily upon the work of Nikolas Rose (1988, 1996, 1999a, 1999b, 2000a, 2000b), it will be argued that the psy sciences, dedicated to the scientific study of the soul, psyche or mind, have made it possible to regulate individual conduct in ways compatible with liberal democracy. That is, they have provided the conditions for governance through freedom. Furthermore, it will be suggested that the founding of the psy sciences occurred through attempts to manage populations deemed problematic, most especially criminals and the insane. As such, the psy sciences are founded upon, and inextricably part of, governance.

Liberalism here denotes a particular style of government, originating in the Renaissance, gaining a stronger foothold through the Enlightenment and finally establishing itself within nineteenth-century Western democracies. Liberalism sought to avoid either governing too much or too little and envisioned a society comprising free individuals, valuing liberty above all else. In part, this emphasis on individual freedom evolved through economic relations under capitalism which necessitated the freedom to labour, produce and consume. It was contended that a free market was best achieved through non-interference with natural laws. None the less, limited government was recognised as necessary to ensure order, civility and productivity (Rose 1999a).

This assumption was embedded in the 'doctrine of the social contract' which maintained that society was held together by a bond between citizens and government. To ensure that the contract remain intact, some degree of governmental authority was necessary to ensure the protection of all citizens. At the same time, citizens had to surrender some of their individuality so that laws could be created, administered and enforced for the common good. The natural rights, freedoms and liberties of individuals would therefore be protected through the 'rule of law' (Goff 1999).

A related liberal assumption was the 'doctrine of free will'. This notion maintained that all humans had the ability to control their actions and therefore could freely and rationally choose to absorb the social contract and the rule of law. In this way, individuals who broke the law and breached the social contract were seen to deserve punishment. Embedded within the doctrine of the social contract and the doctrine of free will is the belief that all citizens are similarly situated upon a level playing-field, thus denying social inequalities (Goff 1999).

Nineteenth-century social changes, including urbanisation and industrialisation, created anxiety and disorder among the populations of Western Europe and North America. In response, social reformers argued that scientific methods used to understand, predict and control the natural world could also be applied to the social world. Informed by the eighteenth-century Enlightenment philosophy which questioned tradition and authority, attempted to replace superstition with reason and believed in human progress, it was thought that observation, calculation and classification would help discover general laws under-pinning society. Once these laws were known, social life could be predicted, controlled and contained and social order re-established economically and efficiently. Since scientific investigation claimed to discover objective facts through empirical means unimpeded by bias, policies which emanated from social research were professed to be in the best interests of everyone in society (Foucault 1977, 1991; Douglas 1992; Rose 1996, 1999a, 1999b).

An early application of the scientific method to social problems was the division of deviant populations into different categories and institutions. This involved, for example, the removal of lunatics, paupers and criminals from the gaols housing them all together into separate institutions: almshouses, asylums and penitentiaries. Soon, however, reformers and administrators demanded further categorisation and division as a means to achieve even better efficiency, order and control. Institutional populations were thus closely monitored and classified into increasingly precise categories of difference. The psy sciences emerged, in part, from these procedures. Methods of observation and calculation were also carried out in other institutions such as workplaces, hospitals and schools (Foucault 1977, 1991; Rose 1996, 1999a, 1999b).

The knowledge which emerged was used not only to manage insti-tutionalised populations but also people more generally. This was achieved as information gathered from various calculations was used to establish averages or norms. People were then compared to the characteristics of the 'ideal citizen' and, where found wanting, en-couraged to reconstruct themselves, often with the advice or assistance of experts. Foucault (1977) argues that this method of 'disciplinary power' increasingly replaced 'sovereign power' which exercised a more overt, physical and repressive means of regulation or control. This does not mean that more coercive measures disappeared. Rather, the success of disciplinary power meant that individuals largely internalised norms so that repressive tactics typically needed only to be applied against those who either would not or could not embrace established standards.

However, rather than being neutral and objective, the scientific knowledge producing these norms reflected power relations in society (Habermas 1987; Kuhn 1996). Therefore, people were governed in ways which reproduced the interests of the dominant social, political and cultural groups: white, Western, middle-class males. The further removed a person was from this elite cluster, the greater was his or her perceived difference and deviance. Criminals have historically comprised the most marginalised groups within society. When measured against the dominant standard, they can rarely be 'normal'.

Rose (1988, 1999b) argues that nascent psychology, and its related psy disciplines, emerged from these attempts to deal with perceived social problems, thus enabling the regulation of conduct through disciplinary power. This did not occur in a conspiratorial fashion at the bequest of the dominant elite but, rather, arose idiosyncratically and pragmatically as scientific techniques were applied to human beings. Specifically, the psy sciences developed through efforts to observe, calibrate and classify individual human beings. Through this process, individual capacities and subjectivities were transformed into something concrete – charts, diagrams and pictures (Rose 1988: 189). In rendering the human soul visible, the psy sciences also made it possible for new things to be done to it. Not only could these 'engineers of the soul' claim unique and scientific knowledge about individuals and their behaviour, but their expertise could also be used to think about and manage human problems in new ways.

As Rose (1988), drawing on Foucault, argues, this marked the expansion of individualisation whereby ordinary individuality became discernible. Prior to this time, only the socially privileged were generally regarded as worthy of observation and detailed study. The shift in attention from elite individuality to everyday individuality brought with it the objectification and subjectification of persons rather than their heroisation. The processes used to capture individuality did not simply report back a true representation. Rather, since people are complex and always shifting, studies of them can only ever access certain aspects. Furthermore, as discussed above, because knowledge is always informed and constrained by power relations, the products of psy sciences will always reflect these. Thus the psy sciences did not discover the true inner workings of the human mind or soul but, rather, invented an authoritative means of claiming to do so. As such, they made it possible to think about individuals and their behaviour in ways that rendered them governable in a manner consistent with notions of liberalism and democracy which were gaining greater coherence in the nineteenth century.

Rose (1988) suggests that the initial application of the scientific method to human subjectivity occurred through examinations of the body's surfaces. That is, various bodily contours and features were claimed to signify an individual's inner mental state. Thus, the nineteenth-century science of phrenology, followed by Joseph Gall, Johann Gaspar Spurzheim and Cesare Lombroso, produced volumes of visual images which were purportedly systematic mappings of hidden mental traits. Criminals, the insane and paupers were the key subjects of these depictions. In creating a means through which an individual's mental processes could ostensibly be made tangible, phrenology opened up the possibility that other hidden facets could be exposed.

Intelligence testing was the next significant scientific means of revealing secreted aspects of the psyche. Rose (1988, 1999a) argues that the first real contribution of psychology towards individualisation was through psychological tests of intelligence. These provided a method of expressing individual subjectivity which did not depend upon bodily surfaces, made possible by a new form of normalisation – the normal curve. The intellect became knowable and manageable as intellectual abilities came to be 'construed as a single dimension whose variation across the population was distributed according to precise statistical laws; the capacity of any given individual could be established in terms of his or her position within this distribution' (Rose 1988: 192). Those individuals lying outside the normal distribution could be identified and dealt with appropriately.

Following the invention of intelligence testing, psychology created numerous methods for accessing subjectivity, making it visible and modifiable. Personality assessments, developmental scales and diagnostic measures all attempted to quantify aspects of the human soul or mind. Each result was compared to a standard and, where people fell short of the norm, they were encouraged or required to change themselves. Here, individuals were assisted in their transformation through a variety of psychological methods such as behaviour modification and psychotherapy. Increasingly over the twentieth century citizens were encouraged to monitor their own subjectivity in their everyday lives in order that they lived up to expected behavioural norms. They willingly exercised self-awareness and self-control so as to be accepted by others and themselves as good citizens. When failing to achieve this satisfactorily, people were expected to seek expert help. Those individuals found unwilling or unable to do so were regarded as having broken the social contract and therefore deserving of punishment. In this way, populations were governed through their freedom in ways commensurate with liberal democracy (Rose 1996, 1999a, 1999b).

The psychological sciences thus made it possible to think about others and ourselves in new ways and, in so doing, helped to create novel ways of being, individually and socially. They did this by creating the conditions through which intimate knowledge of citizens, necessary for their regulation in ways commensurate with liberal democracy, could be obtained. With this knowledge, the object of governance became the soul or mind rather than the body. Furthermore, this 'conduct of conduct' was legitimated by claims to scientific neutrality, objectivity and rationality. In this way power and knowledge are inexorably linked: psychological knowledge has been used to exercise power, and power itself created new objects of knowledge while generating fresh kinds of information (Foucault 1977; Cohen 1985).

Treating the criminal mind: the rehabilitative ideal

Gorman (2001: 7) argues that a 'cult-like environment' has surrounded the implementation of the What Works strategy within probation. This strategy comprises various evidence-based schemes purportedly proven to reduce reoffending. The Probation Service (now the National Probation Service) has become so obsessed with cognitive behavioural programmes, Gorman claims, that it regards them as the 'definitive universal modality' for rehabilitating offenders. Furthermore, he suggests that although they have not yet actually been proven to work, any scepticism towards them is rejected as 'near-heretical'. Despite the polemical nature of Gorman's argument, I would agree with his main conclusions – cognitive behavioural programmes lack an adequate evidence base but none the less have been quickly adopted as a cure-all for the problem of offending. Lofty claims for correctional 'magic bullets' have been made before. As Glaser argues, the highway of corrections is paved with punctured panaceas (cited in Finckenauer and Gavin 1999: 13). Since panaceas reduce complex phenomena to simple explanations and solutions, this is unsurprising. Yet we do not appear to have learnt from the failure of earlier promises to 'fix' offenders. Rather, the success of cognitive behaviouralism is at least partially accounted for by its apparent ability to address the weaknesses of previous failures and to absorb earlier critiques in ways commensurate with current political rationalities. It is therefore useful to examine earlier attempts to reform criminals and the context surrounding their demise.

Prior to the eighteenth century, the treatment of offenders was typically informed by religious doctrine which comprehended criminality as sin or submission to temptation. Punishment was thus legitimated as a means through which individuals could be restored to a state of grace (Gamberg and Thomson 1984). Furthermore, the divine right of the monarchy depended upon sovereign power as the means of maintaining social control. This was established through physical, overt and repressive measures meant to deter criminals by terror. 'Recurrent histories' suggest that the shift from a religious to a scientific model of criminality was introduced for humanitarian reasons, marking the beginning of an ever-progressive approach to crime control. Thus the Enlightenment replaced superstition with science and challenged the authority of rulers. As stated earlier, however, it also inspired the application of scientific methods to human conduct, in the hope of discovering laws which governed social behaviour analogous to those associated with chemistry and physics. In this sense, one technique of social control was replaced with another seemingly less brutal and covert one.

Prisons, as means of dealing with crime and punishment, are relatively recent developments. Although prisons were alternatives to more public methods of control such as floggings, mutilations, and executions, early conditions were none the less harsh and repressive. As discussed above, some of the earliest attempts to apply the scientific method to social problems occurred in prisons. It was believed that classification and categorisation would not only help to manage prisoners but also expose the causes of crime and provide answers to the most effective means of dealing with individual offenders (Sim 1990). During the late nineteenth century, interventions modelled on medical practice were beginning to be championed as appropriate means of dealing with offenders. The application of medicine to criminals was most apparent in the treatment of criminal lunatics where alienists (nascent psychiatrists) eventually established themselves as experts with specialised knowledge (Foucault 1978; Menzies 1991).

At this time, however, the 'doctrine of free will' dominated and it was believed that most criminals rationally chose to act unlawfully. As such, they breached the social order and committed a moral offence against the community. Imprisonment was therefore deemed to be an appropriate response, since it purportedly combined punishment, deterrence and reform with humanitarianism (Gamberg and Thomson 1984).

Throughout the twentieth century, the psy sciences held increasingly important roles both within prisons and, later, probation. During the mid-1930s a rehabilitative model, drawing upon the expertise of psychiatrists, psychologists, physicians and other scientific experts, was proposed. However, the start of the Second World War prevented the immediate implementation of this approach. None the less, the psy sciences gained in power and prestige during the war as they were called into service as a means of establishing a more efficient and economic force of soldiers. The techniques developed by the psy sciences here were later applied to offenders and others (Rose 1999a).

The establishment of welfare provisions following the war gradually provided the necessary resources needed for implementing the rehabilitative philosophy with offenders. As Rose (1999a) states, while the degree to which different Western liberal nations established a welfare state is debatable, an array of social methods was implemented in the UK, USA and Canada during the twentieth century ostensibly to insure against individual and collective risks. A combination of postwar concern with the economy, social reform and political activism produced the beginnings of welfare measures. Governments thus intervened in the economy as well as the public and private lives of individuals through various means including unemployment benefits, old-age pension, public housing and medical insurance. It was believed that such social engineering could produce an ideal society. In return for the security these policies and practices promised, people were expected to act responsibly, meet their social obligations and welcome intervention if it was deemed necessary by representatives of the welfare state. Interference was legitimated on the grounds of benevolence. That is, it was said to be in the interest of doing good, both for individuals and society more generally. It was also expected that the provision of assistance would eventually allow individuals to become self-reliant.

The various welfare strategies were also an important means through which populations were governed. Thus the creation of complex webs of welfare apparatus ushered in new and expanding roles for an array of experts and non-experts whose role was to ensure that people conducted themselves appropriately as productive and law-abiding citizens. This was particularly true for psychologists and other psy-related practitioners who became central to the operation of various welfare strategies – including those established for offenders.

A 'soft machine' consisting of psychiatrists, psychologists, social workers, therapists and probation officers evolved to diagnose and treat offenders both in prisons and in the community. Initially, these 'helping professionals' spent much of their time engaged in classification procedures which became contingent upon the history taking and psychological testing of offenders (Jolliffe 1984; Watkins 1992). However, around the late 1950s and early 1960s the rehabilitative model became officially adopted by various correctional authorities, thus providing the psy-experts with ever greater opportunities to establish themselves within prisons and probation. This was especially the case because the rehabilitative philosophy rested upon and was implemented through the medical model.

The medical model generally assumes that people do not choose to become sick since ailments originate in causes beyond their control. As such, it is maintained that individuals should not be blamed or held accountable for their illnesses. Similarly, it is assumed that people cannot make themselves better through acts of will or fear of punishment since they have no control over the causes of their disease. The diseased or damaged parts of the body need to be repaired by medical experts who have the requisite skills and knowledge (Johnstone 1996).

When applied to offenders, the medical model implies that criminals do not willingly choose to offend and, therefore, they should not be held responsible for their criminal behaviour. It also suggests that offenders be treated rather than punished and that such treatment should be delivered by experts who have the necessary knowledge and abilities to understand and cure criminality. Furthermore, because they are sick, criminals deserve sympathy, understanding and compassion (Johnstone 1996).

Johnstone (1996) argues that these characteristics are true only of the medical model as an abstract ideal. In actual practice, the medical model as applied to crime has taken different forms and unfolded unevenly. Furthermore, Johnstone emphasises that medicine is not a monolith but, rather, comprises various philosophies and practices. Within corrections, psychiatry has been the most influential medical subdiscipline. Here he identifies two unique approaches: medical-somatic and social-psychological. The first assumes the existence of an organically rooted disorder typically located in the brain. Treatment closely mirrors physical medicine: surgery is performed and/or drugs are administered. Experts must be medically trained and they are highly active. On the other hand, patients are typically passive: 'Treatment is something done *to* the patient *by* medical professions' (Johnstone 1996: 20, emphasis in original).

Conversely, the psycho-social approach assumes that individuals are physically healthy, becoming ill only in response to their environment. As such, deviant behaviour is typically perceived to be the consequence of psychological or emotional damage caused by neglect, abuse or some other trauma. However, the focus is not on the environmental or situational causes but the psychological injuries they inflicted. Because the disorder is manifested 'subjectively' or within a person's psyche, he or she is expected to take an active part in his or her treatment. Medical expertise is not mandatory and treatment is therefore provided by a range of experts and even non-experts, including psychiatrists, psychologists, social workers, psychotherapists, occupational therapists, religious instructors, reformers and prison guards. It is here where psychologists as opposed to psychiatrists were able to strengthen their foothold within corrections (Johnstone 1996; Hannah-Moffat 2001).

Both the medical-somatic and social-psychological approaches individualise crime. Whether the cause of crime is located in the mind or the body the focus is on changing the individual rather than the social structure. Therefore the two reinforce one another. As such, it is unsurprising that they coexisted under the rehabilitation model. In practical terms, this meant that the rehabilitative model introduced a range of treatment practices, including plastic surgery, drug therapy, electroconvulsive treatment, psychosurgery, gas, antabuse, psychotherapy, group counselling, individual counselling, therapeutic communities, aversion therapy, operant conditioning and token economies (Cohen 1985; Sim 1990; Kendall 2000).

During the mid-1960s a series of strong criticisms were directed towards the medical model of crime and the treatment practices they introduced. While Johnstone (1996) importantly reminds us that many of these criticisms are targeted towards the ideal of the medical model rather than its actual implementation with offenders, they will be briefly outlined here. First, it is maintained that physical illnesses are fundamentally different from offending behaviour in that they exist independently of judgements made by others. Criminality, on the other hand, exists only within judgements made by other people. Secondly, it is argued that while illness is not the result of a rational, deliberate choice, crime is. The medical model of crime fails to consider the inner, subjective meanings of offenders and thus fails to address their motivations. Thirdly, illness and crime have different causes; while the former has a physical aetiology, the latter does not. The search for physical causes of crime is thus a pointless exercise which further serves to obscure the social causes of crime (Johnstone 1996).

Fourthly, and perhaps most importantly, many critics claimed that the introduction of the medical model created harm, both in deflecting attention away from social structural issues and through the invasive treatments it inspired. In viewing offenders as 'sick', they were also regarded as irrational, helpless and pitiful. They became stripped of agency and dehumanised. This pathologisation of offenders contributed to the fact that numerous harmful and invasive practices were carried out on them, including various therapeutic and non-therapeutic experimentations (Mitford 1973a, 1973b; Hornblum 1998). Often, such treatment was compulsory and indeterminate sentencing was invoked on rehabilitative grounds (Johnstone 1996). A final attack, coming from a different ideological position, maintained that the medical model of rehabilitation was 'soft on criminals'.

As these critiques were increasingly voiced they were reinforced by litigation, the civil rights movement, intellectual developments (including critical theory, postmodernism, poststructuralism and feminism) and the questioning of authority they provoked. Furthermore, research undertaken to determine the effectiveness of various programmes and treatments raised grave concern. In essence, it was increasingly believed that very few interventions had any impact upon reoffending. Most famously, Martinson's (1974) examination of 231 studies led to the broad conclusion that 'nothing worked' to reduce offending. While the claims associated with Martinson have since been deemed to be overstated, and challenged on various grounds, they none the less created a climate of doubt that offenders could be rehabilitated.

Taken together, these criticisms of rehabilitation contributed to a strong feeling of pessimism that offenders could not be successfully treated. The effect of all this arguably fell hardest upon the USA which has increasingly adopted a hard-line law-and-order approach towards crime. Vanstone (2000) maintains that in Britain the impact was greater at the policy level than in actual practice, but Crow (2001) contends that both levels were considerably influenced. Mair (1997) suggests that the election of Margaret Thatcher in 1979 was a more important factor in the decline of rehabilitation. The Conservative government she ushered in marked a transition away from the welfare state to 'neoliberalism'.

During the late 1970s welfare provision came under growing attack in the UK, USA and Canada. On one level it was posited that welfare was repressive and that recipients became dependent upon the state and therefore deprived of the opportunity to become responsible citizens. On another level, it was argued that welfare programmes and other public expenditures eroded the economy. Therefore, Western liberal governments increasingly came to insist that both individual citizens and the economy would be better served by dismantling welfare services and prioritising the market economy. Competition and entrepreneurialism, it was argued, would ensure a thriving economy and the well-being of citizens. Thus, managerial, market-driven models emphasising centralisation, economic efficiency and effectiveness have increasingly penetrated the social fabric. Endless audits to measure need, performance and change have become common place. Social provision, therefore, is now extended only to those determined to have genuine need as measured by means-testing, auditing and surveillance.

As this neoliberal philosophy has become implemented, the state provides less and less insurance against risk, except in the most extreme circumstances. Along with an erosion of services, neoliberal policies have created economic hardship, a growth in unemployment and poverty (Carrabine *et al.* 2000; Drakeford and Vanstone 2000; Hudson 2001, 2002; Kemshall 2002). Consequently, individual citizens are forced to adopt a prudent attitude – calculating and assessing each decision and action. Responsibility for governance has thus shifted from the state to individuals and conduct is regulated through an *obligation* to be 'free'. That is, we are each thought of as autonomous agents unimpeded by state interference. The choices that we make thus signify the kind of person we are. As such, we are obligated to make responsible choices and negotiate risks wisely. Since a level playing-field and an ethical community are assumed, disadvantage rooted within structural in-equalities and power relations is reframed as the outcome of wilful poor choice and unethical conduct. Failure to succeed is seen as *our* failure (Garland 1996, 1997; Rose 1999a, 1999b, 2000a, 2000b). Garland (1996) and Rose (2000a) call this form of governance *responsibilisation*.

Those people deemed to have made poor choices and acted unethically are further excluded as the survival strategies they employ – such as petty theft, begging, sleeping rough and substance use – are increasingly the focus of crime control agencies. Thus individuals are cycled 'from probation to prison because of probation violations, from prison to parole, and back to prison because of parole violations' (Rose 2000a: 336). In this way social exclusion has effectively become criminalised. Offenders are dealt with either by attempts to reintegrate them through moral reconstruction or with punitive measures which exclude them even further.

While correctional ideologies and their corresponding policies and practices have continually changed, certain key assumptions have remained. Specifically, understandings of crime have ultimately remained at the level of the individual. That is, the source of crime is regarded as lying within individual offenders rather than the social structure and inequalities embedded within it. As such, criminals are seen to be somehow very different from the majority of the population who purportedly remain law-abiding. Their perceived 'otherness' serves to legitimate both punitive and rehabilitative correctional treat-ment. While the problem of crime has remained located within individuals, *responsibility* for it has shifted across time. In particular, in conceptualising crime as a disease the medical model confronted the doctrine of free will by removing responsibility from offenders. In contrast, neoliberal policies hold individual offenders entirely respon-sible. The next section considers how the psychological sciences have informed responsibilisation techniques of governing offenders under neoliberalism.

Programming the criminal mind: cognitive behaviouralism

The critique of correctional rehabilitation and the shifting political climate led to the official end of the rehabilitative model during the late 1970s. In the USA, this helped to inform an increasingly punitive law-and-order regime emphasising incapacitation, retribution and deterrence alongside an alarming escalation in the prison population (Cayley 1998; Garland 2001). In both Britain and Canada the consequences were arguably less dramatic but none the less problematic. In Britain, no overall model replaced the rehabilitative ideal although there were several different attempts to develop new ones (Crow 2001). Most notable was the 'non-treatment paradigm' developed by Bottoms and McWilliams (1979). They recommended an approach which focused upon practical help rather than treatment and the diversion of offenders from custody into alternative sentences wherever possible. While this model informed probation in many areas, its influence was not uniform. Furthermore, research soon suggested that the prison population was increasing and that policy changes stemming from an 'alternatives to custody' approach actually contributed to net-widening and harsher sanctions. In response the government turned to a 'just deserts' model, formalised through the Criminal Justice Act of 1991. This Act introduced a new sentencing framework where punishments were to fit the crime as reflected in progressive restrictions on liberty. A range of community sentences, referred to as 'punishments in the community', were introduced and the probation order, which was legally an alternative to sentencing, became a sentence itself. Like the opportunities model, discussed next, these changes placed the onus of responsibility upon offenders themselves (Worrall 1997; Crow 2001; Raynor and Vanstone 2002).

In Canada, an opportunities model officially replaced the rehabilitation model. This approach, which encompassed an emphasis upon reintegration and community-based corrections, argued that the responsibility of corrections was to provide offenders with appropriate opportunities and inducements, but that ultimate responsibility for reformation rested with individual offenders. In contrast to the medical model, the opportunities framework asserted that offenders were accountable for their actions. If offenders failed to take up the opportunities offered to them or recidivated following their programme involvement, they alone were responsible. In this way the opportunities model did not negate rehabilitation; it more precisely defined it in such a way that responsibility was removed from corrections and placed almost entirely upon offenders (Gamberg and Thomson 1984; Duguid 2000). This development was part of the broader shift towards governance through responsibilisation.

It was in Canada, too, where the next big thing in corrections – the What Works strategy – was being most seriously pursued. While critiques of the medical model and the claim that nothing worked to reduce reoffending contributed towards changes in official policy and practice, they did not cause a complete end to rehabilitative programmes nor to the belief that something could work to reform offenders. Thus programmes continued to run and some yielded positive results most evidently in the UK (for example, Raynor 1988; Roberts 1989; McIvor 1990; McGuire and Priestley 1995) and Canada (for example, Ross and Fabiano 1985; Ross, Fabiano and Ewles 1988; Ross, Fabiano and Ross 1986, 1988). What distinguished the programmes in Canada was the fact that they soon gained institutional support from the centre, the Correctional Service of Canada (CSC). Official endorsement of these pro-grammes was aided by the appointment of a new Commissioner of Corrections who formalised a stronger managerial model into CSC through the creation of a mission statement and a correctional strategy in 1991. The strategy insisted that all programming was to be driven by offender needs directly related to their criminal behaviour and adopted the cognitive behavioural model for programme development.

Cognitive behaviouralism represents a synthesis of apparently competing psychological approaches: behaviourism (focused upon observable behaviour) and cognitivism (focused upon cognitions or subjectivity). In the mid-1970s these two separate traditions came together to produce a 'family' of approaches which can broadly be defined as cognitive behaviouralism. They share an assumption that 'thoughts, feelings and behaviour all interact with each other to produce observable behaviours' (Towl and Crighton 1996: 112).

In short, thinking or cognition is conceptualised as a complex developmental process, with many dangers along the way. A person's ability to think can be damaged or impaired throughout maturation in a number of ways including, for example, environmental stress, abuse or neglect. Such circumstances result in underdeveloped, unlearnt, unhealthy or distorted cognitive skills. This, in turn, creates problematic emotions and behaviours. However, because cognitive abilities are learnt rather than innate, there is the possibility of development, repair and replacement (Duguid 2000). Like the social psychological form of the medical model, the focus is on the individual rather than environment or the circumstances which supposedly impaired a person's thinking.

Two main types of techniques are used to help facilitate learning. The first, cognitive skills training, assumes that a person has not acquired particular thinking skills and therefore teaches these to him or her. Examples here include problem-solving and anger management. The second, cognitive restructuring, presupposes that a person's thinking is faulty and aims to replace defective cognitions with alternative ones. A common means of facilitating this is through 'thinking reports' in which people record their thinking and subsequent behaviours in order to be dissected and challenged (Dobson 1988; Curwen *et al.* 2000). Self-surveillance is central to both these general techniques since they require people continually to monitor and reflect upon their own thoughts and behaviours. Cognitive behavioural practices are now used not only for mental health problems such as depression and anxiety but also as means of self-actualising, attaining 'personal power' and achieving business success. They are advocated by television talk shows, magazines and management courses. Like their psychological precursors they are a potential means through which one can achieve successful citizenship (Rose 1999a).

While psychology textbooks tell a progressive history of cognitive behaviouralism resulting from the culmination of refined knowledge, they tend to neglect the fact that it was established when behaviourism, the dominant psychological model, was being widely and harshly criticised for being intrusive, dehumanising and failing to take account of human subjectivity. More importantly, most historical accounts do not contextualise the development and popularity of cognitive behaviouralism within the broader shift towards neoliberalism. Cognitive behaviouralism has become widespread, to a large degree, because it is compatible with neoliberal rationalities. That is, it relies upon methods of self-blame, self-surveillance and self-control. In framing difficulties we encounter as the consequence of our poor thinking it individualises social problems. However, it does this in ways which appear to empower us. Thus we gladly adopt methods of cognitive behaviouralism, not only so that we can be good citizens but in order to reach our full potential. In this sense we are governed through our freedom. Cognitive behaviouralism then is a responsibilisation technique which helps allow governance to occur in a way commensurate with neoliberalism.

There are a number of historical accounts outlining the development of correctional cognitive behaviouralism (see, for example, McGuire

1995; Ross and Ross 1995; Vanstone 2000; Crow 2001; Raynor and Vanstone 2002). Taken together, they cite Canadian psychologist Robert Ross as the 'founding father' of cognitive correctional behavioralism. In particular, his work with young female offenders[2] (Ross and McKay 1979) and literature reviews conducted with colleagues (Gendreau and Ross 1979; Ross and Gendreau 1980) led Ross to conclude that a considerable number of programmes were successful in rehabilitating offenders. Such programmes included a component which attempted to impact upon offenders' thinking. This in turn informed his assumption that criminal behaviour was associated with deficiencies in cognitive functioning. Ross's work fostered an optimism that offenders could be rehabilitated and informed the development of his own programme – Reasoning and Rehabilitation (R & R). Designed as a 'cognitive skills training package,' R & R was first implemented in the Ontario probation service and later adopted by the CSC in a number of prisons (Ross et al. 1988). The R & R programme was eventually transformed into a series of 'cognitive living skills' or 'cog skills' programmes. Duguid (2000) writes that cognitive behavioural models were first introduced into the CSC through education and training programmes. However, because the focus here was more educational than psychological and correctional they were soon abolished in favour of the preferred cognitive skills model.

Cognitive skills were designed as prepackaged modules to be delivered by prison staff. They emphasised the teaching of thinking skills. Following the establishment of the Correctional Strategy in 1991 cognitive skills encompassed four areas of core programming: cognitive skills training, personal and interpersonal development, prerelease programming and substance abuse (Duguid 2000). Since then the name 'cognitive skills' has been changed to 'living skills' but none the less remains the cornerstone of CSC policy and practice. The dismal failure of the medical model was soon forgotten and the gospel began to be spread globally. For example, the R & R course manual has been translated into at least five different languages and the programme delivered globally, including in the following places: Canada, England, Scotland, Wales, the USA, New Zealand, Australia, Estonia, Venezuela, Spain, Denmark and Sweden (Ross and Ross 1995). Cognitive skills had become an industry with some psychologists even setting up their own private consulting firm to sell it.[3] As Vanstone (2000) suggests, a What Works enterprise of research and programming in England, Scotland and Wales predated the R & R influence within the UK but it had not yet become insti-tutionalised.

The perceived success of correctional cognitive behaviourism in

Canada, as well as its aggressive marketing abroad, influenced the establishment of British programmes such as R & R and Straight Thinking On Probation (STOP) as well as a series of What Works conferences during the 1990s (McGuire 1995). However, the What Works project in England and Wales has flourished largely because of the shifting political climate and consequent changes to the prison and probation services (Vanstone 2000).

In May 1997 the election of a Labour government under Tony Blair cemented the realisation of neoliberal assumptions into correctional policy and practice. In July of the same year the Home Office published a report entitled *Changing Offenders' Attitudes and Behaviour: What Works?*. The first part of the report reviewed research on What Works and concluded that cognitive behavioural methods are the most successful in rehabilitating offenders (Vennard *et al.* 1997). The second part of the report presented the results of a national survey of probation service programmes assessing the degree to which they incorporated cognitive behavioural methods (Hedderman and Sugg 1997). The results indicated that although a majority of probation areas had established or bought programmes with a cognitive behavioural element, they did not know whether these programmes worked nor did they appear to be committed to the philosophy of What Works.

This was followed by a flurry of activity in 1998 intended to remedy the situation. In February, a report written by Andrew Underdown (1998) was launched at an HM Inspectorate of Probation (HMIP) conference. It was the culmination of a What Works project undertaken by HMIP in 1996. The project and its consequent report identified effective practice in area probation services. Five months later an effective practice guide appeared, also part of the HMIP's What Works project (Chapman and Hough 1998). Between these two publications, a national implementation strategy for the supervision of offenders was launched jointly by HMIP, the Home Office Probation Unit and the Association of Chief Officers of Probation in a probation circular (Home Office 1998). Initially entitled the 'Effective Practice Initiative' (EPI), it later became known as the What Works initiative. Essentially, it signalled the appropriation of the What Works movement by the political centre by ensuring that all probation services supervise offenders according to the principles shown to reduce offending (Kemshall 2002).

Shortly after the EPI was established, the Home Secretary published a report entitled *Reducing Offending* undertaken at the bequest of the new Labour government as part of a major review of the criminal justice system in order to identify what works to reduce crime. The enthusiasm with which the government met the report provided further support for the EPI. The What Works initiative has since become increasingly institutionalised through various developments, including the following: the Home Office Crime Reduction Programme introduced in April 1999 to establish and implement an evidence-based crime reduction strategy; the establishment of the Joint Prison and Probation Accreditation Panel in 1999 (now the Correctional Services Accreditation Panel); the release of the 'What Works strategy for the probation service' in 2000 (What Works Strategy Group 2000); and the replacement in 2001 of separate area probation services by a National Probation Service.

As discussed at the outset of this chapter, the implementation of What Works has become regarded as 'the biggest experiment in social engineering this country has ever seen'. Even Paul Gendreau, a leading Canadian champion of What Works was reportedly stunned by the large-scale and sudden adoption of the initiative (Rose, D. 2002b). All five of the core curriculum programmes are based upon cognitive behavioural techniques (Kemshall 2002). Yet what is the evidence that cognitive behavioural programmes and the broader What Works initiative actually work? The next section considers this question by, first, considering the knowledge claims made by the proponents of What Works and, secondly, by examining the evidence upon which these claims are based.

Does What Works really work?

Cognitive behaviouralism essentially regards offending behaviour to be a consequence of distorted or deficit thinking. Programmes, therefore, either aim to inculcate thinking skills or restructure cognitions (Home Office 2000a). Crucially, offenders are expected persistently to monitor their thinking in order to ensure that they practise their new skills as well as keep in check distorted or dangerous thoughts.[4] At the centre of correctional cognitive behaviouralism is the notion of a 'criminal mind'.[5] This assumption is perhaps most evident in the work of two leading Canadian psychologists in the field, Don Andrews and James Bonta (1998).[6] They claim to have developed a 'psychology of criminal conduct' (PCC) which rests on the notion that there is a criminal personality typifying offenders, regardless of their gender, race, ethnicity or class. This personality type is characterised by cognitive inadequacies or thinking deficits. Andrews and Bonta (1998: 363) warn that it is a waste of time to address social structural and systemic issues: 'Do not get trapped in arguments with primary prevention advocates who believe that a society-wide focus on unemployment, sexism or racism will eliminate crime.' Dissenters from PCC are accused of engaging in 'knowledge destruction'. Andrews and Bonta challenge criticisms of their own work by claiming that such evaluations merely reflect personal, professional and/or ideological bias. In contrast, they claim that their own work is empirical, objective, neutral and rational.

Since they claim that offenders engage in criminal behaviour because of their thinking it is unsurprising that Andrews and Bonta assert that programmes which target thinking work best to reduce reoffending. Indeed, this assumption is at the heart of the What Works movement. While What Works initiatives are broader than cognitive behavioural programming, they are none the less rooted in the notion that offending behaviour is essentially the consequence of faulty or deficient thinking and that successful programming must address this.

These knowledge claims are said to be supported by three main types of sources: individual evaluations, literature reviews of treatment research and meta-analyses. Research falling into the last category has been the most influential. Meta-analysis is essentially a statistical technique which codes various programmatic features and compares them according to their impact upon recidivism. A great deal of this work has been undertaken by Bonta and Andrews along with their colleagues at Carleton University, the University of Ottawa and the CSC (see, for example, Gendreau and Ross 1979, 1987; Andrews 1989; Andrews, Bonta and Hoge 1990; Andrews, Zinger *et al.* 1990; Gendreau, Goggin and Little 1996; Gendreau, Little and Goggin 1996; Bonta 1997). Taken as a whole, meta-analytic research has identified four key principles necessary for correctional programming to be effective:

1 *Risk*: programme intensity should be matched to the risk of reoffending. Those at greater risk require more intensive programmes, while programmes delivered to those least at risk may actually increase recidivism. Therefore it is essential that reliable risk assessments are undertaken.

2 *Need*: programmes should focus upon only those characteristics which are statistically associated with recidivism and relatively stable but nevertheless changeable. These predictors of future criminal conduct are called *criminogenic needs* or *dynamic risk factors*.[7] Most are linked to deficit or faulty thinking such as pro-criminal attitudes, interpersonal problem-solving, impulsivity, rigid thinking, a tendency to blame others and an external locus of control. Others include substance use and criminal associates. *Static risk factors* are unchangeable characteristics statistically associated with reoffending

and include gender, age, criminal history and early family factors such as little or no affection, supervision or discipline from parents. *Non-criminogenic factors* are said to include social class, personal distress variables (such as self-esteem, anxiety and depression), feelings of alienation, psychological discomfort and group cohesion. The need principle therefore recommends that only programmes which address criminogenic needs/dynamic risks should be offered to offenders.

3 *Responsivity*: the delivery approach should match the learning styles of offenders. It is claimed that offenders are most responsive to cognitive behavioural programmes which employ a skills-oriented approach to delivery.[8]

4 *Integrity*: treatment should be conducted in a structured way with strict adherence to the programme manual, and delivered by enthusiastic and dedicated staff according to the principles outlined above.

In sum, the principles recommend highly structured, prepackaged interventions which are rooted in a cognitive behavioural model addressing criminogenic needs/dynamic risks. The research furthermore suggests that although such programmes work effectively in prisons they work even better with offenders in the community. It is argued that programmes which follow these principles can reduce recidivism by more than 70 per cent (McGuire 2001: 35), although claims regarding the effect size are typically much more modest, at around 10–15 per cent.

The research upon which these bold assertions rest has been challenged by different scholars upon numerous grounds. The following are some of the key concerns raised about the meta-analytical studies used to legitimate What Works initiatives:

1 Different meta-analyses have produced inconsistent and contradictory findings (Gottschalk *et al*. 1987; Lab and Whitehead 1990; Logan and Gaes 1993; Palmer 1994).

2 There is a reliance upon primary studies which use only quantitative methods unable to take into account the context within which programmes operate and the dynamics or mechanisms which operate inside them (Pawson and Tilley 1997). As such, we cannot know definitively why and how interventions succeed or fail (Farrall 2002).

3   There is a publication bias in favour of primary studies which are large scale and produce positive results (Mair 1995, 1997; Hannah-Moffat and Shaw 2000).

4   The follow-up period in most primary studies is very short (Mair 1995, 1997).

5   Because crude categories are used to classify often rather dissimilar primary studies, distortions are introduced (Mair 1995, 1997).

6   Because not all primary studies use the same variables some findings may actually be reliant upon quite a small sample size (Raynor and Vanstone 2002).

7   The studies incorporated into meta-analysis rely heavily upon samples which largely include young American males. It cannot be assumed that the findings are transferable to women, other ethnic and racial groups, older populations and members of other nations. When gender, 'race', ethnicity and class are recognised, they are treated simply as variables capable of measurement like all the others (Bloom 2000; Hannah-Moffat and Shaw 2000; McMahon 2000; Shaw and Hannah-Moffat 2000; Worrall 2000; Kendall 1998, 2002; Kendall and Pollack 2003).

8   There are numerous problems in reliance upon recidivism as the indicator of programme success. For example, is recidivism determined by actual offence, arrest or conviction? It is likely the case that some people reoffend but do not get caught and despite their further reoffending would be counted as instances of programme success. Additionally, there are other factors which are not taken into account but which could be considered examples of programme success: compliance with supervision requirements, improved relationships and a decrease in the frequency and seriousness of offending. Furthermore, despite no further arrests or convictions many ex-offenders live in conditions of economic and social marginalisation (Hudson 1987; Kendall 1998; Merrington and Stanley 2000).

In addition to concerns about meta-analysis, there are problems with individual evaluations of cognitive behavioural programmes. In 2000, for example, Merrington and Stanley noted that were very few published UK studies demonstrating the success of four programmes which had recently been granted accreditation (Think First, R & R, ETS and Priestley 1:1). They concluded that evidence from these four general offending programmes in the UK is 'either not available or far from conclusive' (2000: 274). Yet, evidence-based practice implies that the evidence should have been available prior to implementation.

Since then, Friendship *et al.* (2002) carried out a prison-based evaluation of men enrolled in either the R & R programme or the ETS programme. Using two-year reconviction rates as the measure of programme success, they found a 14 per cent reduction in recidivism among medium–low-risk offenders and an 11 per cent reduction among medium–high-risk offenders when compared to matched control groups. The authors concluded that the study 'provides strong evidence on the effectiveness of cognitive behavioural treatment for offenders' (2002: 4). However, the researchers may now wish to retract this confident statement. A later study carried out by members of the same team employing a similar method to evaluate the two programmes found no differences between the experimental and control groups (Falshaw *et al.* 2003).

A final point can be made about the risk principle. To reiterate, it states that offenders who pose the greatest risk of reoffending should receive the most intense programming and that programmes may actually increase recidivism among low-risk offenders. It is therefore surprising that the operationalisation of the What Works strategy in the UK has essentially resulted in all offenders receiving the same type and intensity of programming regardless of risk or criminal offence (Gorman 2001). This appears to contradict the risk principle. To make matters even more confusing, a study conducted by Canadian researchers found that the cognitive skills programme they evaluated had no effect on subjects deemed high risk, but had a significant effect on lower-risk participants (Robinson 1995). As Duguid (2000) states, the author of the report rationalised the unexpected finding by claiming that all the subjects were actually 'high risk' regardless of what the classification procedure determined them to be! Furthermore, in their study attempting to examine the validity of broad conclusions reached by the What Works literature, Antonowicz and Ross (1994) found no support for the risk principle.

This brief overview suggests that the knowledge base upon which the What Works initiative rests is rather weak and problematic. Even Peter Raynor (2002), a member of the Corrections Accreditation Panel, notes that there is a limited body of evidence upon which to base effective probation programmes in Britain. It would appear that the implementers have been overconfident in the knowledge base. Unfortunately the risk of failing to meet expectations is incredibly high in a political climate which so strongly values outcome measurements (Robinson 2001). As Rex (2002: 69) states, 'in the long term, we will not do probation staff managing and implementing these programmes any favours if we disregard the inconclusive nature of the evidence upon which effective practice principles are actually based'. The danger is, as history has shown, that we will simply move on to the 'next big thing' rather than take stock and learn from our failures.

The following, and final, section of this chapter considers why the What Works strategy has been implemented with such zealous enthusiasm despite the lack of a solid evidence base and the harm it poses.

Concluding thoughts

The Home Office study published in 1997 noted that, although cognitive behavioural methods were the most successful in rehabilitating offenders, the research did not demonstrate that 'cognitive-behavioural approaches, or indeed any other type of approach, routinely produce major reductions in reoffending among a mixed population of offenders' (Vennard *et al.* 1997: 33). Even the original creators of correctional cognitive behaviouralism have been cautious in claims for its success, warning that there is no simple panacea (see, for example, Ross *et al.* 1995: 3). None the less, and contrary to evidence-based practice, the implementation of offending behaviour programmes in England and Wales is more ambitious than anywhere else in the world (Merrington and Stanley 2000). How can this be explained?

This chapter suggests that psychology has played a key role in the success of offending behaviour programmes and the larger What Works movement. In claiming the ability to render the mind visible in a scientific manner the psy sciences helped to create the conditions for governance under liberal democracy. Rather than controlling populations through their bodies, psychology provided a means by which people could be regulated through their subjectivities. This type of governance typically occurs in a covert fashion whereby citizens willingly govern themselves. However, when this disciplinary power appears to fail, people are dealt with in more visible and repressive ways. Their treatment is legitimated on the grounds that it is scientifically and therefore objectively necessary. Furthermore, because the psy sciences remove people from the social context, problems become individualised. This makes it easier to demonise or pathologise those who fall by the wayside because their control is justified as being for their own protection and/or public safety. Offenders are typical of those who are subjected to such practices.

The psy sciences have informed correctional policy and practice. Initially emerging, at least in part, through attempts to control institutional populations, the psy sciences continued to provide the rationalisations and technologies for regulating their conduct. From classification to rehabilitation, the psy sciences have allowed liberal democracies to deal with their 'failures' in ways that do not appear to compromise the political rationalities upon which they rest. This is because they frame 'failures' as individual aberrations rather than as manifestations of the social structure. The scientific status of psychology, furthermore, masks the power relations informing the criminalisation of certain behaviour and certain types of people. The treatment of criminals thus appears fair and just.

As the twentieth century progressed psychology became more important in the governance of deviant populations. Welfare reforms provided the necessary resources needed to establish the medical model within corrections. Through the social-psychological variant of the medical model, psychology was able to strengthen its grip. Crucially, it claimed to offer scientific evidence that offenders could be reformed. However, the often invasive practices which it inspired came under attack for a variety of reasons and from different political quarters. Its knowledge claims were further weakened by studies demonstrating the failure of interventions to prevent reoffending. As the rehabilitative model came under attack, broader political shifts were also informing correctional policy and practice.

While the welfare state took responsibility in providing individuals with insurance against risks, the emerging neoliberal regime insisted that individuals take responsibility for themselves. As such, buffers against misfortune which were established under welfarism began to be dismantled. Consequently, economic hardship, unemployment and poverty have intensified – thus creating ever-increasing numbers of socially marginalised people. Those coming under the jurisdiction of the criminal justice system are no longer seen to be sick. However, different countries adopted different correctional models, the most punitive in the USA.

In Canada, and to a lesser degree in Britain, the rehabilitative model remained important, at least in practice, to the treatment of offenders. However, it became transformed in such a way as to address its critics and reflect shifting political rationalities. Psychologists were able to reinvigorate the rehabilitative ideal by introducing a technique which allowed for offenders to be governed in ways commensurate with neo-liberalism. Specifically, correctional cognitive behaviouralism offered a method which not only held individuals responsible for their

79

circumstances but also claimed to have a strong evidence base for doing so. While the medical model implied that individuals were not to be blamed for their offences, the notion of faulty or deficit thinking placed responsibility squarely upon their shoulders. Furthermore, the 'risk principle' legitimated and provided technologies, such as risk assessments, for the rationing of resources. These risk assessments have bifurcated offenders into those who are deemed capable of altering their thinking and those who are not. While the former are enrolled in programmes designed to rehabilitate their faulty or deficient thinking, the latter are contained because of the serious danger their thinking is deemed to pose. Both groups, however, are demonised since they are stripped from their social context. For example, in boasting about the success of cognitive skills training, Lucie McClung, current Canadian Commissioner of Corrections, is quoted as saying: 'The criminal mind does not operate like yours and mine. What would work for you in terms of deterrence will not work for the offender' (Stewart 2001: 38).

While many proponents of correctional cognitive behaviouralism acknowledge the social context it is usually in a superficial way, such as the role social factors play in misshaping cognition. Because these are not usually considered dynamic criminogenic needs or risks they are not believed to be important. At the same time it is maintained that damaged cognitions cause offenders to misinterpret social processes. While recognising subjectivity, a criticism made of the medical model, cognitive behaviouralism reifies it to the exclusion of objective, material conditions. A Home Office report detailing a new strategy for women offenders is an example of this:

> This Government promised to be tough on crime and its causes. There is no excuse for crime, whatever a person's background or experience. However, the characteristics of women prisoners suggest that experiences such as poverty, abuse and drug addiction lead some women to *believe* that their options are limited. Many offending behaviour programmes are designed to help offenders *see* that there are always positive choices open to them that do not involve crime. At the same time, across Government, we are tackling the aspects of social exclusion that make some women *believe* their options are limited. (2000b: 7, emphasis added)

A recent report by the Social Exclusion Unit (2002), entitled *Reducing Reoffending by Ex-prisoners*, also appears less interested in addressing the material conditions of exclusion than in providing offenders with the human capital necessary for their operation as productive citizens. As

Farrall (2002) states, it is all very well teaching offenders cognitive skills that will help in selling themselves on the job market but it is another thing to ensure that jobs are out there to be had. The report further recommends a 'going straight contract':

> This should include rewards for participation and sanctions for non-participation [in programmes] ... prisoners should be required to follow their agreed programme, and make payments from their prison pay, both to make reparation to victims and to help finance the support the case manager would provide on release. (Social Exclusion Unit 2002: 11)

A critical history of correctional cognitive skills suggests that this neglect of the social structure should not be surprising. For allowing the social context to be fully recognised would undermine the agencies charged with managing human conduct (Fox 1999b). Even more importantly, it would threaten the belief in a level playing-field and non-constrained abundant choice, crucial for the operation of liberal democracies and neoliberalism. The psy sciences have helped to maintain this belief by providing a means of governance commensurate with liberal and neoliberal political rationalities. They offer the knowledge and technology through which to exercise power. Therefore we should not expect the psy sciences to address power relations and social inequalities in a challenging way. Cognitive behaviouralism is simply the current dominant operationalisation of governance within corrections. As the political climate shifts, its legitimacy will become easier to question. Like the practices preceding it, cognitive behaviouralism will fall out of favour and other techniques will be experimented with. This does not mean that it will entirely disappear, since remnants from earlier methods remain subsumed within their successors, including cognitive behaviouralism.

Cohen (1985: 249), drawing on Jacoby, argues that corrections is plagued with 'social amnesia'. That is, each time a new policy is adopted we repress the reasons why we implemented the last one. Nellis (2002: 34) suggests that the Probation Service (now the National Probation Service) is blighted by 'forced forgetting' since 'there is little in official rhetoric which suggests an appreciation of the Service's past' as well as little in the curricula of new probation training programmes. This, too, should not surprise us. In critically analysing links between the past and present we are in a better position to interrogate current truth claims and to think differently about the future. This really is 'dangerous thinking'!

Notes

1 This approach is very much influenced by the work of Karl Danziger (1990); Ian Hacking (1986, 1995); Nikolas Rose (1988, 1996, 1999a, 1999b, 2000a, 2000b); Kelly Hannah-Moffat (1999, 2000, 2001); Hazel Kemshall (2002); and John Pratt (1999, 2002).

2 The Grandview Training School for Girls where Robert Ross formulated his ideas about correctional cognitive behaviouralism was recently at the centre of abuse allegations. In 1976 investigations into abuse led to the school's closure. Eight former employees, including Ross, were since accused of physical, sexual and psychological abuse against former inmates. While Ross was acquitted of some of the charges and others were withdrawn, 11 remain stayed. Two guards were convicted and in 1999 the Ontario government issued a formal apology to former inmates as part of a compensation package (Grandview Agreement between the Grandview Survivors Support Group and the Government of Ontario 1994; Laframboise 1997; Globe and Mail 1999). The story was turned into a play entitled *The Girls of Grandview* written collectively by Toronto's Friendly Spike Theatre Band and members of the Grandview Survivors Group.

3 For example, a UK private consulting firm called the Association for Psychological Therapies runs a series of What Works courses (see www.whatworkswithoffenders.co.uk).

4 For excellent accounts of this process see Fox (1999a, 1999b, 2001) who studied the Cognitive Self-change Treatment Programme for Violent Offenders in an American prison. See also Kendall and Pollack (2003) for a description of similar methods used in dialectical behavioural therapy, a cognitive behavioural programme designed for women offenders.

5 I recognise that different supporters of correctional cognitive behaviouralism, such as McGuire (2000) and Ross and Fabiano (1985, 1981), dismiss the notion of a criminal personality as reductionist. Nevertheless, such an assumption has become embedded within correctional discourse since at least Hans Eysenck's seminal 1962 publication, *Crime and Personality*.

6 See also Yochelson and Samenow (1976, 1977), Samenow (1984, 1998) and Sharp (2000), who champion correctional cognitive behaviouralism and similarly maintain the existence of a criminal personality.

7 See Hannah-Moffat (1999) and Shaw and Hannah-Moffat (2000) for critical discussions on the slippage which has occurred between the concepts of need and risk. One of the concerns they identify is that risk assessment tools are increasingly incorporating adverse social circumstances and irrelevant factors (for example, dependency upon financial aid) in such a way as to criminalise people for their social disadvantage.

8 Gender, race and class have recently been adopted as responsivity factors on the grounds that programmes which take them into account will encourage offenders to be more receptive (Bonta 1997). Their conceptualisation remains at a superficial level of understanding.

References

Andrews, D. (1989) 'Recidivism is predictable and can be influenced: using risk assessments to reduce recidivism', *Forum on Corrections Research*, 1 (2): 11–18.

Andrews, D.A. and Bonta, J. (1998) *The Psychology of Criminal Conduct* (revised edn). Cincinnati, OH: Anderson.

Andrews, D., Bonta, J. and Hoge, R. (1990) 'Classification for effective rehabiliation', *Criminal Justice and Behaviour*, 17 (1): 19–52.

Andrews, D., Zinger, I., Hoge, R., Bonta, J., Gendreau, P. and Cullen, F. (1990) 'Does correctional treatment work? A clinically relevant and psychologically informed meta-analysis', *Criminology*, 28 (3): 369–494.

Antonowicz, D. and Ross, R. (1994) 'Essential components of successful rehabilitation programs for offenders', *International Journal of Offender Therapy and Comparative Criminology*, 38: 97–104.

Bloom, B. (2000) 'Beyond recidivism: perspectives on evaluation of programs for female offenders in community corrections', in M. McMahon (ed.) *Assessment to Assistance: Programs for Women in Community Corrections.* Lanham, MD: American Correctional Association, 107–38.

Bonta, J. (1997) *Offender Rehabilitation: From Research to Practice.* Research Report 1997–01. Ottawa: Ministry of the Solicitor General of Canada.

Bottoms, A.E and McWilliams, W. (1979) 'A non-treatment paradigm for probation practice', *British Journal of Social Work*, 9 (2): 159–202.

Carlen, P. (2002) 'New discourses of justification and reform for women's imprisonment in England', in P. Carlen (ed.) *Women and Punishment. The Struggle for Justice.* Cullompton: Willan, 220–36.

Carrabine, E., Lee, M. and South, N. (2000) 'Social wrongs and human rights in late modern Britain: social exclusion, crime control, and prospects for a public criminology', *Social Justice*, 27 (2): 193–251.

Cayley, D. (1998) *The Expanding Prison. The Crisis in Crime and Punishment and the Search for Alternatives.* Toronto: Anansi.

Chapman, T. and Hough, M. (1998) *Evidence Based Practice.* London: Home Office.

Cohen, S. (1985) *Visions of Social Control: Crime, Punishment and Classification.* Cambridge: Polity Press.

Crow, I. (2001) *The Treatment and Rehabilitation of Offenders.* London: Sage.

Curwen, B., Palmer, S. and Ruddell, P. (2000) *Brief Cognitive Therapy.* London: Sage.

Danziger, K. (1990) *Constructing the Subject.* Cambridge: Cambridge University Press.

Dobson, K. (1988) *Handbook of Cognitive-behavioral Therapies.* London: The Guilford Press.

Douglas, M. (1992) *Risk Acceptability to the Social Sciences.* London: Routledge and Kegan Paul.

Drakeford, M. and Vanstone, M. (2000) 'Social exclusion and the politics of criminal justice: a tale of two administrations', *The Howard Journal*, 3 (4): 369–81.

Duguid, S. (2000) *Can Prisons Work? The Prisoner as Object and Subject in Modern Corrections*. Toronto: University of Toronto Press.

Eysenck, H.J. (1964) *Crime and Personality*. London: Routledge and Kegan Paul.

Falshaw, L., Friendship, C. and Nugent, F. (2003) *Searching for 'What Works': An Evaluation of Cognitive Skills Programmes*. Findings 206. London: Home Office Research, Development and Statistics Directorate.

Farrall, S. (2002) *Rethinking What Works with Offenders. Probation, Social Context and Desistance from Crime*. Cullompton: Willan.

Finckenauer, J. and Gavin, P. (1999) *Scared Straight. The Panacea Phenomenon Revisted*. Prospect Heights, IL: Waveland Press.

Foucault, M. (1977) *Discipline and Punish: The Birth of the Prison*. London: Allen Lane.

Foucault, M. (1978) 'About the concept of the "dangerous individual" in 19th century legal psychiatry', *International Journal of Law and Psychiatry*, 1: 1–18.

Foucault, M. (1991) 'Governmentality', in C. Gordon and P. Miller (eds) *The Foucault Effect: Studies in Governmentality*. Chicago, IL: University of Chicago Press, 87–104.

Fox, K. (1999a) 'Changing violent minds: discursive correction and resistance in the cognitive treatment of violent offenders in prison', *Social Problems*, 46 (1): 88–103.

Fox, K. (1999b) 'Reproducing criminal types: cognitive treatment for violent offenders in prison', *The Sociological Quarterly*, 40: 435–53.

Fox, K. (2001) 'Self-change and resistance in prison', in J. Gubrium and J. Holstein (eds) *Institutional Selves. Troubled Identities in a Postmodern World*. Oxford: Oxford University Press, 176–92.

Friendship, C., Blud, L., Erikson, M. and Travers, R. (2002) *An Evaluation of Cognitive Behavioural Treatment for Offenders*. Findings 161. London: Home Office Research, Development and Statistics Directorate.

Gamberg, H. and Thomson, A. (1984) *The Illusion of Prison Reform. Corrections in Canada*. New York, NY: Peter Lang.

Garland, D. (1996) 'The limits of the sovereign state: strategies of crime control in contemporary society', *British Journal of Criminology*, 36 (1): 445–71.

Garland, D. (1997) '"Governmentality" and the problem of crime', *Theoretical Criminology*, 1 (2): 173–215.

Garland, D. (ed.) (2001) *Mass Imprisonment. Social Causes and Consequences*. London: Sage.

Gendreau, P., Goggin, C. and Little, T. (1996) *Adult Recidivism: What Works!* Research Report 1996–01. Ottawa: Ministry of the Solicitor General of Canada.

Gendreau, P., Little, T. and Goggin, C. (1996) 'A meta-analysis of the predictors of adult offender recidivism: what works!', *Criminology*, 34: 575–607.

Gendreau, P. and Ross, R. (1979) 'Effective correctional treatment: bibliotherapy for cynics', *Crime and Delinquency*, 25: 463–89.

Gendreau, P. and Ross, R. (1987) 'Revivification of rehabilitation: evidence from the 1980s', *Justice Quarterly*, 4: 349–408.

Globe and Mail (1999) 'Ontario apologises for Grandview abuse', 17 November: 3.

Goff, C. (1999) *Corrections in Canada*. Cincinnati, OH: Anderson.

Gorman, K. (2001) 'Cognitive behaviouralism and the Holy Grail: the quest for a universal means of managing offender risk', *Probation Journal*, 48 (1): 3–9.

Gottschalk, R., Davidson, W., Gensheimer, L. and Mayer, J. (1987) 'Community-based interventions', in H.C. Quay (ed.) *Handbook of Juvenile Delinquency*. New York: Wiley, 266–89.

Grandview Agreement between the Grandview Survivors Support Group and the Government of Ontario, 30 June 1994 (available at http://www.grandviewsurvivors.on.ca/ga1.html, accessed 8 July 2002).

Habermas, J. (1987) *The Philosophical Discourse on Modernity: Twelve Lectures.* Cambridge, MA: MIT Press.

Hacking, I. (1986) 'Making up people', in T. Heller *et al.* (eds) *Reconstructing Individualism. Autonomy, Individuality and the Self in Western Thought.* Standford, CA: Standford University Press, 222–36.

Hacking, I. (1995) *Rewriting the Soul: Multiple Personality and the Sciences of Memory.* Princeton, NJ: Princeton University Press.

Hannah-Moffat, K. (1999) 'Moral agent or actuarial subject: risk and Canadian women's imprisonment', *Theoretical Criminology*, 3 (1): 71–94.

Hannah-Moffat, K. (2000) 'Prisons that empower: neoliberal governance in Canadian women's prisons', *British Journal of Criminology*, 40 (3): 510–31.

Hannah-Moffat, K. (2001) *Punishment in Disguise. Penal Governance and Federal Imprisonment of Women in Canada.* Toronto: University of Toronto Press.

Hannah-Moffat, K. and Shaw, M. (2000) 'Thinking about cognitive skills? Think again!', *Criminal Justice Matters*, 39: 8–9.

Hedderman, C. and Sugg, D. (1997) 'Part II. The influence of cognitive approaches: a survey of probation programmes', in *Changing Offenders' Attitudes and Behavior: What Works?* Home Office Research Study 171. London: Home Office Research and Statistics Directorate, 37–52.

Home Office (1998) *Effective Practice Initiative: A National Implementation Plan for the Effective Supervision of Offenders.* Probation Circular 35/1998, June. London: Home Office.

Home Office (2000a) *What Works? Reducing Re-offending: Evidence-based Practice.* London: Home Office.

Home Office (2000b) *The Government's Strategy for Women Offenders.* London: Home Office.

Hornblum, A. (1998) *Acres of Skin. Human Experimentation at Holmesburg Prison.* London: Routledge.

Hudson, B. (1987) *Justice through Punishment. A Critique of the 'Justice' Model of Corrections.* Basingstoke: Macmillan.

Hudson, B. (2001) 'Human rights, public safety and the probation service: defending justice in the risk society', *The Howard Journal*, 40 (2): 103–13.

Hudson, B. (2002) 'Gender issues in penal policy and penal theory', in P. Carlen (ed.) *Women and Punishment*. Cullompton: Willan, 21–46.

Johnstone, G. (1996) *Medical Concept and Penal Policy*. London: Cavendish Publishing.

Joliffe, I. (1984) *Penitentiary Medical Services, 1835–1982*. Report 1984–19. Ottawa: Solicitor General Canada.

Kemshall, H. (2002) 'Effective practice in probation: an example of "advanced liberal" responsibilisation', *The Howard Journal*, 41 (1): 41–58.

Kendall, K. (1998) 'Evaluation of programs for female offenders', in R. Zaplin (ed.) *Female Offenders: Critical Perspectives and Effective Interventions*. Gaithersburg, MD: Aspen, 361–79.

Kendall, K. (2000) 'Psy-ence fiction: governing female prisoners through the psychological sciences', in K. Hannah-Moffat and M. Shaw (eds) *An Ideal Prison? Critical Essays on Women's Imprisonment in Canada*. Halifax: Fernwood Publishing, 82–93.

Kendall, K. (2002) 'Time to think again about cognitive behavioural programmes', in P. Carlen (ed.) *Women and Punishment. The Struggle for Justice*. Cullompton: Willan, 182–198.

Kendall, K. and Pollack, S. (2003) 'Cognitive behavioralism in women's prisons: a critical analysis of therapeutic assumptions and practices', in B. Bloom (ed.) *Gendered Justice. Addressing Female Offenders*. Durham, NC: Carolina Academic Press, 69–96.

Kuhn, T. (1996) *The Structure of Scientific Revolutions* (3rd edn). Chicago, IL: University of Chicago Press.

Lab, S. and Whitehead, J. (1990) 'From "nothing works" to "the appropriate works": the latest stop on the search for the secular grail', *Criminology*, 28: 405–17.

Laframboise, D. (1997) 'Who's the victim now?', *Globe and Mail*, 8 November: D3.

Logan, C. and G. Gaes (1993) 'Meta-analysis and the Rehabilitation of Punishment', *Justice Quarterly*, 10(2): 245–63.

Mair, G. (1995) 'Evaluating the impact of community penalties', *The University of Chicago Law School Roundtable*, 2 (2): 455–74.

Mair, G. (1997) 'Community penalties and probation', in M. Maguire *et al.* (eds) *The Oxford Handbook of Criminology* (2nd edn). Oxford: Oxford University Press.

Mair, G. (2000) 'Credible accreditation?', *Probation Journal*, 47 (4): 268–71.

Martinson, R. (1974) 'What works? Questions and answers about penal reform', *Public Interest*, 35: 22–45.

McGuire, J. (1995) *What Works: Reducing Offending*. Chichester: Wiley.

McGuire, J. (2000) *Cognitive-behavioural Approaches. An Introduction to Theory and Research*. London: HM Chief Inspector of Probation.

McGuire, J. (2001) 'What works in correctional interventions? Evidence and practical implications', in G.A. Bernfeld *et al.* (eds) *Offender Rehabilitation in Practice*. Chichester: Wiley, 25–43.

McGuire, J. and Priestly, P. (1985) *Offending Behaviour: Skills and Strategems for Going Straight*. London: Bristol.

McIvor, G. (1990) *Sanctions for Serious and Persistent Offenders: A Review of Literature*. Stirling: Social Work Research Centre.

McMahon, M. (2000) 'Assisting female offenders: art or science? Chairperson's commentary', in M. McMahon (ed.) *Assessment to Assistance: Programs for Women in Community Corrections*. Lanham, MD: American Correctional Association, 279–328.

Menzies, R. (1991) 'Psychiatry, dangerousness and legal control', in N. Boyd (ed.) *The Social Dimensions of Law*. Scarborough, Ontario: Prentice-Hall.

Merrington, S. and Stanley, S. (2000) 'Doubts about the what works initiative', *Probation Journal*, 47 (4): 272–75.

Mitford, J. (1973a) 'Experiments behind bars', *Atlantic Monthly*, 231 (1): 64–173.

Mitford, J. (1973b) *Kind and Unusual Punishment*. New York: Random House.

Nellis, M. (2002) 'Community penalties in historical perspective', in A. Bottoms *et al.* (eds) *Community Penalties: Change and Challenges*. Cullompton: Willan, 16–40.

Palmer, T. (1994) *A Profile of Correctional Effectiveness and New Directions for Research*. New York, NY: SUNY Press.

Pawson, R. and Tilley, N. (1997) *Realistic Evaluation*. London: Sage.

Pratt, J. (1999) 'Governmentality, neo-liberalism and dangerousness', in R. Smandych (ed.) *Governable Places: Readings on Governmentality and Crime Control*. Aldershot: Ashgate, 133–61.

Pratt, J. (2002) *Punishment and Civilization*. London: Sage.

Raynor, P. (1988) *Probation as an Alternative to Custody*. Aldershot: Averbury.

Raynor, P. (2002) 'Community penalties and social integration: "community" as solution and as problem', in A. Bottoms *et al.* (eds) *Community Penalties: Change and Challenges*. Cullompton: Willan, 183–99.

Raynor, P. and Vanstone, M. (2002) *Understanding Community Penalties: Probation, Policy and Social Change*. Buckingham: Open University Press.

Rex, S. (2002) 'Beyond cognitive behaviouralism? Reflections on the effectiveness literature', in A. Bottoms *et al.* (eds) *Community Penalties: Change and Challenges*. Cullompton: Willan, 67–86.

Roberts, C. (1989) *Hereford and Worcester Probation Service Young Offender Project: First Evaluation Report*. Oxford: Department of Social and Administrative Studies.

Robinson, D. (1995) *The Impact of Cognitive Skills Training on Post-release Recidivism among Canadian Federal Offenders*. Ottawa: Correctional Service of Canada.

Robinson, G. (1999) 'Risk management and rehabilitation in the probation service: collision and collusion', *The Howard Journal*, 38 (4): 421–33.

Robinson, G. (2001) 'Power, knowledge and "what works" in probation', *The Howard Journal*, 40 (3): 235–54.

Rose, D. (2002a) 'It's official – prison does work after all', *The Observer*, 5 May (available at http://www.observer.co.uk/focus/story/0,6903,710137,00.html, accessed 17 January 2003).

Rose, D. (2002b) 'Evolution of Britain's jail revolution', *The Observer*, 5 May (available at http://www.observer.co.uk/focus/story/0,6903,710138,00.html, accessed 17 January 2003).

Rose, N. (1988) 'Calculable minds and manageable individuals', *History of the Human Sciences*, 1 (2): 179–200.

Rose, N. (1996) *Inventing Ourselves: Psychology, Power and Personhood*. Cambridge: Cambridge University Press.

Rose, N. (1999a) *Powers of Freedom: Reframing Political Thought*. Cambridge: Cambridge University Press.

Rose, N. (1999b) *Governing the Soul: The Shaping of the Private Self* (2nd edn). London: Free Association Books.

Rose, N. (2000a) 'Government and control', *British Journal of Criminology*, 40: 321–39.

Rose, N. (2000b) *'Power and Subjectivity': Critical History and Psychology*. Academy for the Study of the Psychoanalytic Arts (available at http://www.academyanalyticarts.org/rose1.html, accessed 10 June 2003).

Ross, R., Antonowicz, D. and Dhaliwal, G. (1995) 'Something works', in R. Ross *et al.* (eds) *Going Straight: Effective Delinquency Prevention and Offender Rehabilitation*. Ottawa: Air Training and Publications, 3–28.

Ross, R. and Fabiano, E. (1981) *Time to Think: Cognition and Crime: Link and Remediation*. Ottawa: Department of Criminology, University of Ottawa.

Ross, R. and Fabiano, E. (1985) *Time to Think: A Cognitive Model of Delinquency Prevention and Offender Rehabilitation*. Johnson City, TN: Tennessee: Institute of Social Sciences and Arts.

Ross, R., Fabiano, E. and Ewles, C. (1988) 'Reasoning and rehabilitation', *International Journal of Offender Therapy and Comparative Criminology*, 32: 29–35.

Ross, R., Fabiano, E. and Ross, R. (1986) *Reasoning and Rehabilitation: A Handbook for Teaching Cognitive Skills*. Ottawa: University of Ottawa.

Ross, R., Fabiano, E. and Ross, R. (1988) '(Re)habilitation through education: a cognitive model for corrections', *Journal of Correctional Education*, 39 (2): 45.

Ross, R. and Gendreau, P. (1980) *Effective Correctional Treatment*. Toronto: Butterworths.

Ross, R. and McKay, H.G. (1979) *Self Mutilation*. Lexington, MA: Heath.

Ross, R. and Ross, R. (1995) *Thinking Straight. The Reasoning and Rehabilitation Program for Delinquency Prevention and Offender Rehabilitation*. Ottawa: Air Training and Publications.

Samenow, S.E. (1984) *Inside the Criminal Mind*. New York, NY: Times Books.

Samenow, S.E. (1998) *Straight Talk about Criminals: Understanding and Treating Antisocial Individuals*. London: Aronson.

Sharp, B.D. (2000) *Changing Criminal Thinking: A Treatment Program*. Lanham, MD: American Correctional Association.

Shaw, M. and Hannah-Moffat, K. (2000) 'Gender, diversity and risk assessment in Canadian corrections', *Probation Journal*, 47 (3): 163–72.

Sim, J. (1990) *Medical Power in Prisons: The Prison Medical Service in England 1774–1989*. Milton Keynes: Open University Press.

Social Exclusion Unit (2002) *Reducing Re-offending by Ex-prisoners*. London: Office of the Deputy Prime Minister.

Stewart, B. (2001) 'Not a country club', *Macleans*, 9 April: 34–8.

Towl, G. and Crighton, D. (1996) *The Handbook of Psychology for Forensic Practitioners*. London: Routledge.

Underdown, A. (1998) *Strategies for Effective Offender Supervision: Report of the HMIP What Works Project*. London: Home Office.

Vanstone, M. (2000) 'Cognitive-behavioural work with offenders in the UK: a history of influential endeavour', *The Howard Journal*, 39 (2): 71–183.

Vennard, J., Sugg, D. and Hedderman, C. (1997) 'Part I. The use of cognitive-behavioral approaches with offenders – messages from the research', in *Changing Offenders' Attitudes and Behavior: What works?* Home Office Research Study 171. London: Home Office Research and Statistics Directorate, 1–35.

Watkins, R. (1992) *An Historical Review of the Role and Practice of Psychology in the Field of Corrections*. Report R-28. Ottawa: Correctional Service of Canada.

What Works Strategy Group (2000) 'What Works Strategy for the probation Service.' Unpublished, 18 August.

Worrall, A. (1997) *Punishment in the Community: The Future of Criminal Justice*. London: Longman.

Worrall, A. (2000) 'What works at One Arm Point? A study of the transportation of a penal concept', *Probation Journal*, 47 (4): 243–49.

Yochelson, S. and Samenow, S.E. (1976) *The Criminal Personality. Volume 1. A Profile for Change*. New York, NY: Jason Aronson.

Yochelson, S. and Samenow, S.E. (1977) *The Criminal Personality. Volume 2. The Change Process*. New York, NY: Jason Aronson.

Chapter 5

How cognitive skills forgot about gender and diversity

Margaret Shaw and Kelly Hannah-Moffat

Introduction[1]

Much of the discussion around evidence-based policies and effective programmes in criminal justice settings is persuasive, and apparently straightforward. It promises better decision-making, safer citizens and communities, and lower risk-taking on the part of prison, parole and probation staff than hitherto. It promotes actuarial or mechanical risk-based scales, talks about What Works and has been adopted in a number of countries. Yet most of the discussion around these developments is silent on the origins of the research on which it is based, on its theoretical and methodological weaknesses, and its applicability to minority populations: to issues of gender and diversity.

There is an intricate association with the recovered belief in re-habilitation, with the What Works debate in correctional treatment and with the development of a new generation of classification techniques to assess risk and need and targeted interventions. Over the past decade, rehabilitation and treatment effectiveness, based on psychological principles and the use of cognitive-behavioural programmes, as well as the systematic application of actuarial risk and need classification systems, have been actively promoted by a group of Canadian psychologists working in and with corrections (see Vanstone 2000 for a partial UK history).

This chapter argues that in general this work takes for granted a number of assumptions about the style and appropriateness of treatment programmes for different clients. It assumes that those which have been developed for men will be applicable to women, that aspects of their lives other than their thinking patterns and individual deficiencies are relatively unimportant in reducing offending (and risk), and that ethnic and cultural differences are irrelevant in the grand scheme of scale construction, predictive validity and programme delivery. The chapter is based in part on a study of the implications of this body of work for women prisoners in federal Canadian prisons, and raises questions about the current vogue for cognitive skills-based programmes.[2] It questions the theoretical, methodological, ethical and practical weaknesses of research and practice grounded in a particular academic discipline, which is based on meta-analytic studies of majority male populations. This literature and subsequent practices ignore and dismiss the effects of gender and diversity, or the social and economic constraints on offenders' lives.

Before such approaches and technologies are used with women the logic, assumptions and research that support it ought to be thoroughly examined and placed in a broader contextual understanding of the gendered and racialised characteristics of criminalised behaviours and our responses to it. We show how generic risk/need assessment practices and subsequent targeted interventions (i.e. cognitive pro-grammes) decontextualise, individualise and pathologise offending in accordance with gendered and racialised norms. Such hegemonic practices ultimately reproduce a 'criminology of the other' (Garland 2001) and silence alternative practices (Pollack forthcoming) and meaningful dialogues about gender and cultural differences. This type of gendered and racialised analysis is critical especially given recent developments in Canadian women's penality which have attempted to restructure correctional responses to be gender-specific and culturally appropriate (Hannah-Moffat 2001, 2002a).

Risk/need and correctional classification

The templates for understanding and interpreting criminal conduct, and defining state responses to that conduct, are the practices of assessment and classification. These practices rely on gendered, racialised subjective constructions of conduct, and predefined generic programmes. Such programmes are validated on the premise that they target deficits and the antecedents of criminal behaviour identified through quasi-actuarial practices of assessment and which are amenable to change. Both classification practices as well as the subsequent programmes in-adequately address alternative understandings and demonstrated differences between men and women, and between women.

The emphasis on risk/need assessment and targeted programme intervention is part of an escalating focus on managerialism, efficiency and accountability in correctional systems and a movement away from concern with individual cases (Feeley and Simon 1994; Garland 1996). It is argued that risk/need classification and assessment are seen to enhance individual decision-making, judgement or clinical decisions, and to reduce ad hoc decision-making and result in greater uniformity and fairness in decisions. They are more efficient in fitting individuals to appropriate institutional settings and in the delivery of services and programmes. They also satisfy accountability and management concerns for correctional staff. Concerns about risk assessment and risk management are most apparent in the debates and policies related to security classification, intake assessments, programming and release planning (public safety). Each of these practices involves a social construction of an offender's perceived risk either to the public, to him or herself or to the institutional order. Related to these constructions are interventions that in theory are meant to minimise and make manageable the offender's risk.

From the late 1970s in North America and elsewhere, there was a shift in correctional classification policies. The primary *purpose* of many prison classification systems shifted away from security to *risk* and its management (e.g. of escape, risk to the public, to other prisoners, to staff, to institutions, to themselves), mainly through the use of incapacitative strategies. The *methods* of assessing risk and predicting risky behaviours also changed.[3] Previously used clinical checklists and assessments were now seen as *subjective* and discretionary methods of classification, to be replaced by *objective* tools and *actuarial* measurements that created standardised responses and risk profiles derived from research on large population samples (Gottfredson and Tonry 1987; Dallao 1997). These tools are seen to eliminate arbitrary decision-making, bias and prejudice, leading to more efficient and impartial classification, and rational, just institutions. Thus it is argued that these tools are better at *predicting* risk and recidivism than earlier measures.

In the 1990s, with a renewed emphasis on treatment and rehabilitation, risk and rehabilitative policy approaches became integrated (Hannah-Moffat 2002b). Much of this work has been undertaken in Canada by psychologists working in the correctional field (Andrews, Bonta and Hoge 1990; Andrews, Zinger *et al.* 1990). Risk/need assessment tools play a central role in matching 'levels of treatment service to the risk level of the offender'(Andrews, Bonta and Hoge 1990). It is closely tied to their view that only specific types of treatment (based in cognitive psychology) can reduce reoffending, and when they are targeted to particular groups of offenders.

The analysis of risk factors was linked to the identification of *criminogenic* factors that have a role in preventing offending rather than simply predicting offending, and which can be changed.[4] Actuarial risk prediction is now being developed in many Western prison and parole systems apart from Canada and the USA, including England and Wales (Clark *et al.* 1993; Ditchfield 1997; Mair 1999) and Australia (Brown 1996; Daley and Lane 1999; Dawson 1999), and similar shifts are apparent in other social services (cf. Castel 1991).

Risk and need classification, therefore, results in a security classification as well as allocation of level of treatment or supervision. More recently, the terminology has changed with criminogenic risk being referred to as *static* unchangeable factors (such as age or offence history) and criminogenic need as *dynamic* factors, which are capable of being modified by treatment programmes. Criminogenic needs are explicitly defined as problems that influence the chances of recidivism, rather than a statement of entitlements (Hannah-Moffat 1999). In the Canadian literature, however, not all needs are seen as criminogenic. In the recent policy literature on classification in Canada (particularly for female offenders) the hybrid term *risk/need* is often used and certain offender characteristics are identified as both risks and needs. For example, some of the characteristics defined as criminogenic needs include dependency, low self-esteem, poor educational and vocational achievement, parental death at an early age, foster care placement, constant changes in the location of foster care, residential placement, living on the streets, prostitution, suicide attempts, self-injury, substance abuse and parental responsibilities (FSWP 1994: 5). More recently, an adult history of abuse, victimisation and self-injurious behaviours has been constructed as risk factors for female offenders (Bonta *et al.* 1995; Blanchette 1997a, 1997b).

Such reconstructions imply the individual is responsible for the management of risk rather than an entitlement to programmes and services, while simultaneously justifying and reaffirming the significance of rehabilitative programmes as strategies for minimising the risk of recidivism. Interestingly, the same Canadian researchers who advocate the modification of risk assessment to include needs have also been the foremost proponents of cognitive correctional interventions (i.e. cognitive skills training or living skills).[5] A similar pattern is evident in the UK (Robinson 2001; Kendall 2002).

Thus, notwithstanding the scepticism within criminology and other social sciences about our ability to make accurate and reliable predictions of dangerousness and recidivism, Canadian correctional researchers maintain that there is a consistent relationship between the type and number of needs offenders present and the likelihood of recidivism, and further that the combined assessment of both risk and needs will improve our ability to predict who is likely to reoffend and who is not (Motiuk 1993; Verbrugge and Blanchette 2002). Researchers' attempts to identify and quantify risk/need have resulted in the reconceptualisation of needs and certain social structural barriers as risk factors. This recent trend reflects a hybridisation of risk and rehabilitation (Hannah-Moffat 2002b). It is a 'mixed model of government',[6] wherein traditional rehabilitative strategies are reaffirmed and deployed to minimise and reduce risk. It is a model of penal government that re-establishes a place for rehabilitative regimes in correctional institutions. Some of the characteristics of the Canadian federal classification system are considered in the next section.

Subjective nature of risk: the current Canadian federal classification system

The Offender Intake Assessment (OIA) was launched in 1994 in eight penitentiaries in Canada, including at that time the only federal penitentiary for women, known as Prison for Women (Motiuk 1997).[7] The OIA was developed and validated on the federal male population which is predominantly non-Aboriginal and white. The Canadian federal population comprises some 14,000 prisoners of whom only around 2 per cent have traditionally been female, and some 15–17 per cent Aboriginal. Among the female prison population, up to 25 per cent may be Aboriginal. The OIA is presently used in all federal facilities during intake including the four new women's federal institutions and the Healing Lodge for Aboriginal women.[8]

The intake assessment process is described as a multidisciplinary, multi-method and multi-source approach to classification.[9] The risk portion of the assessment is used to determine security classifications, and the needs assessments (e.g. of education, employment or abuse history) are held to be independent of security classification but central to the development of an appropriate correctional plan. That correctional plan should define a series of programmes that, if taken, may aid in reducing the likelihood of recidivism. At the end of the assessment process, ideally, correctional officials should have a thorough understanding of the risk the offender poses to the community, the factors that led the offender into criminality, those areas that need to be addressed to reduce risk of reoffending and the most appropriate institution[10] in which the offender should be placed. The needs assessment component of the OIA contains seven areas or domains: employment, marriage/family, associates/social interaction, substance abuse, community functioning, personal/emotional orientation and attitude. Responses to some 250 questions that operationalise these variables provide information on each of these domains. These questions have not been modified to reflect gender or ethno-cultural concerns or social-economic contexts.

Thus the key purpose of this tool is to identify the areas of an offender's life (criminogenic risk/need factors) that require intervention to reduce his or her risk, and to devise a correctional plan that targets these high-risk areas. Consequently, the offender is governed according to his or her membership of certain specified risk categories, ascribed to the individual and constructed as having a causal relationship with probable future conduct. The legitimation of correctional programmes is in their ability to minimise future risks through individual reformation. Administrative decisions about the management of the offender's sentence are to a great extent contingent on the offender's willingness and ability to 'gain insight' into his or her criminogenic factors and positively to address these factors through programmes in a way that makes his or her risk manageable in lower-security institutions and ultimately the community. The failure to comply with the risk reduction/management strategy can result, for example, in being reclassified and rehoused in a medium or maximum-security institution, or being denied parole.

These scales require assessors to make a host of moral judgements about the offenders' past and probable future conduct. While training may be given, there are likely to be differences in interpretation and use between those who construct risk assessment scales and practitioners who apply their tools.[11] The use and interpretation of tools are fundamental to understanding the intricacies of risk-based governance. Tools like the OIA require assessors to evaluate subjectively the leisure habits (or lack of socially accepted leisure habits), the quality of relationships, the attitudes of the offender, as well as employment stability and educational levels.[12] These evaluative criteria represent white middle-class moral and social standards. The failure to conform to such standards implies an unacceptable deviation from the norm. For example, variables used to evaluate community functioning and social interactions respectively include 'participation in organised activities (sports teams, clubs and church groups)' and 'unattached to community groups (charitable, Big Brothers, athletic)'. Such categorisations entail normative evaluations of leisure habits, which even many law-abiding citizens would not fulfil.

The criteria used as indicators of an offender's 'personal and emotional orientation' also require subjective assessment of behaviour that may reflect social status, ethno-cultural or gender-based constructions of individual characteristics. For instance, indicators like 'ethnicity is problematic' or 'religion is problematic' may reflect racist experiences or negative religious experiences in the case of many Aboriginals. Likewise, indicators such as 'sexual identity viewed by the offender as problematic', 'inappropriate sexual preferences' (meaning sexual preferences do not conform to the social norms), 'sexual attitudes problematic' (meaning the offender's sexual attitudes do not conform to social norms) infer that heterosexuality is the norm and non-traditional sexual preferences are deviant.

Similar judgements are revealed in the narrow evaluations of marital and familial relationships, which imply a stable, heterosexual, nuclear family where mothers are primary care givers is the norm. There is little guidance on how to evaluate diverse ethno-cultural familial relationships that rely on extended families. The following are examples of the criteria used in the OIA to evaluate marital and familial relationships: 'childhood lacked family ties', 'mother or maternal figure absent during childhood', 'father or paternal figure absent during childhood'; while others include being single, parental responsibilities, ability 'appropriately' to handle and control behaviour, understanding of child development and completion of marital/family programmes. Such criteria are used to evaluate *all* offenders regardless of their gender or race, or their relevance to the offender's conviction.

Quasi-actuarial assessments of risk include not only categories previously constructed as needs but also a series of social structural variables over which the offender has little if any control. While the inclusion or exclusion of variables in a given scale is often the result of a complex process, the inclusion of some variables, the tendency to individualise, and the failure to contextualise and qualify risk assessments can reproduce wider social inequalities and unfairly disadvantage certain social groups. Exposure to certain social conditions, either willingly or unwittingly, is used in institutional determinations of an offender's level of risk and the future manageability and minimisation of that risk. Actuarial techniques assess risk on an individual level and thus wider social structural variables or behaviours (poverty, racism, police discretion) that indirectly affect risk of recidivism, or characteristics of the institution itself (institutional structure, access to programmes, attitude of staff, professional discretion), which are rarely addressed through programmes, are not considered or seen as valid predictors.

For example, many correctional assessments of risk include variables such as 'lives in a criminogenic area' or 'unstable accommodation' (meaning moves frequently – more than once per year). These are likely to be a consequence of poverty and an inability to secure affordable housing in urban locations rather than evidence of an unwillingness to adopt a less criminal lifestyle. Questions included in assessment tools such as the Offender Intake System (OIA) which require yes or no answers to the following: 'has no bank account', 'has no collateral', 'has no credit' as indications of 'community functioning', also fail to account for poverty and social position. While it is difficult if not impossible for risk-profiling tools to integrate social structural variables, it is critical to acknowledge that structural factors (age, race, social class and gender) and different social contexts influence risk logics. Another Canadian risk tool, the Custody Rating Scale (CRS), includes criteria such as 'history of involvement in institutional incidents' to evaluate institutional adjustment.[13] While the inclusion of such criteria may make intuitive sense, they are highly individualistic and decontextualising.

McHugh (1997) has similarly argued that the concept of 'risk' focuses on something within the individual, leading to oversimplified categorisation and overlooking wider systemic concerns, and that regime differences and specific institutional procedures will affect risk. Staff, for example, may contribute to 'high risk' by their reaction and treatment of 'risky' individuals. He argues that a focus on the climate of an institution and the support systems available are more important ways to reduce risk than relying on 'better tools' and computer-led programmes. He also suggests that risk prediction instruments, which incorporate risk and need, do not add greatly to predictive power and are difficult to collect and quantify.

Thus wider sociological understandings of social stratification, sexism, racism or discretionary applications of rules are rarely in-corporated into correctional knowledges and calculations of risk, which focus on a narrow range of individualised correlations. Dominant cultural and gender norms inform the views of practitioners, and even when they have received sensitivity training or have an awareness of gender or cultural differences this knowledge cannot easily be applied or integrated into their risk/need assessments. Evaluations of such criteria are clearly discretionary and rely heavily on clinical as well as non-clinical judgements about an offender. These discretionary evaluations occur not only with the kinds of 'soft' dynamic (need) variables mentioned above but also with many of the so-called static variables such as criminal history, age of 'first' offence or 'legal employment' (Haggerty 1999). In short, the calculative rationality of risk is discretionary and subjective, and it creates only an illusion of objectivity, consistency and efficiency. While risk *factors* may appear to be amoral, *neutral statistical realities* uncovered through rigorous scientific research also reflect highly moralistic views of the social world.

Current advances in risk assessment and risk management technologies as they relate to the management of prisoners may appear to be more objective and efficient methods of penal governance, but the claims of these technologies are often misrepresented. For example, in most risk-based research the definitions of risks are statistical and reflect characteristics of populations and not individuals. Risk factors, generated through correctional research, reflect statistical not causal relationships. Nevertheless, as O'Malley (1999: 5) has observed, individuals are often ascribed the characteristics of risk categories (e.g. Sue has a 30 per cent chance of recidivism) and variables identified as risk factors or statistically to predict risk (such as 'living in a criminogenic area' or 'unemployment' or 'history of self-injury') are interpreted by practitioners who assess risk as causal factors.

Thus this individualised misuse of risk assessment, whether intentional or unintentional, is used to support critical correctional decisions and interventions (including programme plans, institutional placement, transfers, conditional release, etc.). The ability to identify and quantify risk, however, is critical to its governance. Once risks are successfully identified (i.e. factors leading to recidivism) and constructed as preventable (through programmes and release planning) then the responsibility for the management of risk can be assigned to specific individuals or groups.

The relevance of gender, culture and social position

Many of the above problems are magnified when generic risk assessment tools are used to govern women and ethno-culturally diverse correctional populations. Such populations are often more acutely marginalised than mainstream male populations. With few exceptions, analyses of risk-based governance have not fully explored the class-specific, gendered and ethno-cultural aspects of the social construction of risk and practices of risk management. As a number of writers have argued, risk is gendered and racialised (Bhui 1999; Dawson 1999; Hannah-Moffat 1999; Lupton 1999b).

Tools such as the CRS and the OIA were not developed for women, and assessors do not consistently adjust their interpretation of criteria when applying them to women.[14] This is a critical observation if one accepts that most forms of risk governance are based on the identification of characteristics common to a particular population, and that the characteristics of female and ethno-cultural populations are different from a white male correctional population. Few studies of risk pay attention to individual or group differences in pathways to crime, or to how risk and protective factors may vary from group to group. This is of particular concern for women and minority ethnic groups, 'for whom the nature, meaning, and impact over the life course of risk protective factors may be quite different from the mainstream' (Homel *et al.* 1999: 183). However, rather than questioning the suitability of risk assessment, researchers often attempt to construct a culturally specific set of risk predictors that can be added to standard lists (see, for example, Bonta *et al.* 1997; Homel *et al.* 1999).[15]

Initially, and reflecting the original intentions of the 1990 report *Creating Choices* to develop a women-centred correctional system, a set of gender-specific guidelines for completing the OIA was produced in 1996 for federal women's prisons. It was based on the existing case management manual and 'input from staff working in the women's institutions' (CSC 1996). This document appears to incorporate information that *contextualises* women's circumstances. Sex-trade work, for example, was to be separated from illegal income sources and explanations given for lack of work history or for school dropout (e.g. pregnancy or physical/ sexual abuse).

However, those early guidelines never appear to have been systematically used or promoted. Very few correctional staff currently responsible for assessing women are aware of its existence. Several of the staff reported difficulties interpreting and applying the gender-neutral risk criteria contained in the OIA.[16]

Partly in response to these kinds of critiques, Canadian correctional researchers have been attempting to validate security classification and risk assessment models for women over the past few years. However, this work has not engaged with the literature on gendered differences and ethno-cultural populations. There is little discussion or analysis of how wider institutional responses and staff actions affect prisoners' behaviour or the structural variables of women's crime and recidivism (Coulson *et al.* 1996; Blanchette 1997a, 1997b, 1997c; Blanchette and Motiuk 1995, 1997; Motiuk 1997; Motiuk and Blanchett 1998; Loucks and Zamble 1999; Verbrugge and Blanchette 2002). While a willingness to acknowledge difference is welcomed, the general practice of 'validating' pre-existing risk and need assessment scales, based on research and theories about men's crime, for female offenders is theoretically and empirically problematic.

The problems of using gender-neutral categories for women have been examined in relation to violence (Campbell 1993; Dougherty 1993; Shaw and Dubois 1995; Comack 1996; Jackson 1999; Comack *et al.* 2000; Shaw 2000). These problems include the inconsistency of definitions of violence in the literature; the diverse range of behaviour that is seen as violent; the limitations of official categories that 'lump together' diverse behaviours; and the importance of the cultural context that shapes our understanding and definition of violence. The mainstream literature on mental health or violence, for example, relies on highly selected samples and very small numbers of women. Comparisons between men and women are also confounded by the differential treatment of men and women by the police and the courts. More significantly, most of the literature on treatment, as with classification, has been developed on the basis of studies of men, and generalised to, or even ignored women entirely. Thirdly, different disciplines tend to explain and interpret behaviour in different ways, with sociological explanations taking account of the broader influences on behaviour, and psychology placing an emphasis on individual development or pathology. The focus of correctional systems on individual pathology tends to restrict consideration of context.

Research on gender also suggests the need to go beyond simply adding another variable to a risk scale or needs assessment. Gender neutrality or gender blindness are not necessarily eliminated by the *adaptation* of male-derived actuarial measures. Simply adjusting risk and need assessment scales to include gendered criteria does not accurately reflect the extent of differences between men and women, or among women. It takes for granted that all but a few assessment criteria are the 'same' for men and women, without challenging the gendered and racialised components of empirical data on which the scales were originally constructed.

Presently, it is argued that to develop effective programme interventions that meet the needs of women offenders and ultimately reduce their risk of reoffending, the demographics and the history of the female population, as well as how various life factors impact on their offending, must be considered (Abbott and Kerr 1995; Bloom and Covington 1998).[17] The characteristics of female prison populations are relatively well established. Some of these are shared with men, others are not. For example, women offenders are often victims of physical, sexual or other forms of abuse at the hands of intimates or others known to them. They are often mothers and the primary caretakers of children, they have more limited education and are more often than men unemployed at the time of their offence,[18] and many are financially dependent. Many have addictions to drugs or alcohol as well as physical and mental health concerns.

The quantitative differences between the number and type of offences committed by women are also fairly well understood.[19] What is less understood are the substantive contextual and qualitative gender differences between offences and offenders. While there are few comprehensive studies of female offending (and even fewer Canadian ones), current evidence suggests that the nature of women's offending is qualitatively different from men's even if the charges are similar. The criminal activities in which women are involved, their pathways to crime, their institutional adjustment patterns and their escape risks are different. In short, recent research on female offending suggests that crime is a highly gendered activity and that the motivation for crime, the context of offending and access to criminal opportunities, as well as in-prison responses, are shaped by differences in men's and women's lives (cf. Steffensmeier and Allan 1998). Since very few studies have addressed these differences in Canada, our knowledge of the causes of women's offending is limited. It follows that given the absence of both qualitative and quantitative studies of patterns of women's offending, our assessment tools and our ability to develop programmes are also inherently limited. In terms of initial offences and recidivism, and given the wide variations in populations of women offenders as well as justice systems, research conducted in North America has not established a pattern of causation that yields consistent results.

This problem is magnified when cultural or ethnic differences are considered. If little is known about women offenders, even less is understood about the qualitative differences between white and non-white offenders. The research that critiques the concept of a 'universal woman' argues that racial oppression and cultural differences contribute to further qualitative and quantitative differences between women offenders.[20] Jackson (1999), for example, argues that the intersection of race, gender and class presents a special context of difference for Aboriginal women, grounded in a colonial legacy of assimilation policies. Further, while there is some information about the dynamics and contextual differences between the experiences and histories of Aboriginal women and non-Aboriginal women,[21] considerably less is known about the experiences of black and other minority women in the Canadian criminal justice system, and the contextual patterns of their offences. However, recent government reports such as those by the Commission on Systemic Racism in the Ontario Criminal Justice System (1994, 1995) and the Royal Commission on Aboriginal Peoples (1993, 1996) reveal that the particular needs of these groups are often overlooked and that they experience various forms of systemic and direct racism and discrimination.

The Arbour Report (1996), which reviewed the circumstances of a series of events at the women's federal penitentiary, reiterated the view that women and cultural minorities have needs and characteristics that are different from those of men and thus require a different approach. In relation to Aboriginal women, the report stressed six specific problems (1996: 218–19): their over-representation in the prison population; their cultural, linguistic and social distinctness from other women in the federal population; their personal and social histories were significantly different; their offending histories were significantly different; their geographic dispersion was a particular burden for them; and that their holistic approach to healing and reintegration was at odds with the conventional philosophy and culture of prison environments. The report argued that these problems have been embedded and hidden within a penal environment which is at odds with many Aboriginal cultures (1996: 220). The cumulative effect of their longer offence histories, with more violent offences and more previous incarcerations than non-Aboriginal women, is generally higher security classification and risk assessment, which 'is heightened by the tensions and misunderstandings between Aboriginal cultures and that of criminal justice and penal settings' (1996: 221). The report concluded that while women have some things in common with men offenders there are more differences: 'Their crimes are different, their criminogenic factors are different, and their correctional needs for programmes and services are different. Most importantly, the risk that they pose to the public, as a group, is minimal, and considerably different from the security risk posed by men' (1996: 228).

Other writers have in the past also been critical of the emphasis on risk and the use of actuarial measures. In the 1980s concerns were raised about their impact on minorities, particularly black American males, although at that time there was almost no discussion of gender issues. It was argued, for example, that rigid and mechanical applications of assessment tools could lead to inequitable and unjust classifications (Petersilia and Turner 1987). Others warned that they could institutionalise the disadvantages experienced by minority groups (Gottfredson 1987). In the Canadian context such disadvantages include racism, residential school experiences, high unemployment rates, illiteracy, alcoholism, conflicting cultural demands and differences in local conditions, histories and social structures of Aboriginal communities.

Other literature suggests that even such basic concepts as the nature and meaning of crime may be different in some Aboriginal communities. Monture (2000) sees risk scales as individualised instruments that fail to account for the significance of colonial oppression in the lives of Aboriginal men and women and on their communities and nations. She argues that the individualised nature of law obscures systemic and structural factors, and that this problem exists in both the court process and in justice decision-making processes such as security classification, risk assessment, penitentiary placement and parole (2000: 57). In spite of some increasing awareness and concern to develop classification systems suitable for women, many studies and discussions of classification and risk prediction throughout the 1990s have still failed to deal with women or diversity. Some do not distinguish women from men; others fail even to mention the gender of their (male) subjects (e.g. Dhaliwal *et al.* 1994; Clements 1996; Holt 1996; Aubrey and Hough 1997; Quinsey *et al.* 1998).

Thus quantitative and qualitative differences around gender and ethnicity are critical; they impact institutional interpretations of 'risk' and ultimately impact the risk management practices. Several theoretical, statistical and methodological problems emerge when gender is ignored. The risk/rehabilitation model of penal governance directly and indirectly contributes to the discriminatory practices of identifying and managing needs and all decisions based on such assessments. Embedded in *neutral* risk assessments are criteria that do not reflect the social reality of specific correctional populations, and that represent marginalisation and decontextualised social disadvantages. Our central concern is that current understandings and social constructions of risk and its management lack an awareness of the wider structural inequalities and systemic differences among such groups. Further analysis of how risk is understood in other sociocultural contexts and how these contexts shape risk discourses is required.

The current popularity of risk/need assessment is integrally associated with two other phenomena: the revival of the notion that treatment works and the development of new methods of assessment of the outcome of treatment programmes. The rejection of Martinson's (1974) bleak conclusion that treatment programmes are a waste of time and money, and the revival of claims that *rehabilitation* can *work*, took place from the late 1980s, part of a practitioners' research-driven agenda (see Nellis 1995; Vanstone 2000 for a partial UK history).

Cognitive skills, meta-analysis and the resurrection of rehabilitation

Efforts to streamline, and to allocate efficiently and appropriately scarce treatment resources to suitable and responsive offenders, have resulted in the emergence of many new technologies of deficit identification such as the risk and need assessment practices outlined above. As noted, these technologies identify criminogenic factors that can be changed through targeted interventions. A fundamental goal of national correctional assessment classification is to identify the needs that can be targeted for intervention to reduce risk of recidivism. Andrews (1989: 9) argues 'the needs principle asserts that if correctional treatment services are to reduce recidivism', then 'the criminogenic needs of offenders must be targeted'. For him, some 'promising targets of rehabilitative service' include changing anti-social attitudes, anti-social feelings, peer associations; promoting family ties and association with anti-criminal role models; increasing self-control, self-management and problem-solving skills; reducing chemical dependencies; and insuring that the client is able to recognise risky situations and has a concrete and well rehearsed plan for dealing with those situations. And the most effective and efficient treatments are seen as those grounded in cognitive psychology.

The term cognitive behaviouralism, as Kendall (2002: 187) indicates, is associated with 'a range of interventions derived from three psycho-logical theories: social learning, cognitive theory and behaviouralism'. Cognitive behavioural programmes have widespread appeal. Much of the credit for the revival of rehabilitation and the What Works phenomenon has been claimed by Canadian academic and practising psychologists working with offender populations (e.g. Gendreau and Ross 1987; Andrews 1989). They have worked in close association with each other and the correctional system, at both federal and provincial levels. Their work began to emerge at the end of the 1970s with critical reviews by three psychologists, Paul Gendreau, Robert Ross and Don Andrews, but much of it dates from the late 1980s and early 1990s. Their claims that treatment can be effective were based on the application of the techniques of meta-analysis to correctional treatment programmes. These replaced simple summary accounts of research findings that balance the number of studies showing positive results against those with negative findings. Meta-analysis has been defined, in the very neutral terms characteristic of its proponents, as 'the statistical analysis of the summary findings of several independent research studies' (see Pearson et al. 2002). The technique enables programme features to be coded in terms of the characteristics and size of the population treated, the content and style of treatment, and allows for much finer comparisons to be made in terms of reconviction outcomes or effect sizes.

Conducting meta-analyses of large numbers of treatment programmes conducted from the 1960s to the 1980s in North America, these authors claimed there was indeed evidence that certain types of treatment can reduce recidivism when targeted to particular offenders. They concluded that programmes grounded in cognitive psychology, and which targeted thinking and reasoning and used skill development techniques, were the most effective. Moreover, they rejected as particularly ineffective programmes providing individual counselling, what they term 'vague' groupwork or those based on psychoanalytic principles. The results of these meta-analyses were published in two papers in 1990 (Andrews *et al.* 1990; Andrews, Bonta and Hoge 1990) and have been followed by an increasingly prolific flow of studies laying out the principles of effective intervention. Gendreau (1996: 145) promoted cognitive skills programmes as much more effective than those available when he had entered the correctional field as a prison psychologist in 1961. The latter had consisted of 'individual counselling and occasional group work of an amorphous nature, menial work programmes, and extensive use of medication and ECT for psychiatrically disturbed inmates.'[22]

Over the past 12 years or so this group has actively promoted treatment effectiveness based on appropriate cognitive psychological principles, combined with the systematic classification of offender risk and need (e.g. Motiuk 1993; Blanchette and Motiuk 1995; Wormith 1995; Andrews and Bonta 1996; Hanson and Bussier 1996). In Canada in the 1990s, certainly at the federal level, their work began to influence correctional practice. Andrews (1996: 5), for example, claims that the ideas he put forward in 1989 on risk, need and responsivity have contributed to the revival of rehabilitation in correctional practice. To support his claim he cites evidence of a shift in core training programmes in Correctional Service Canada and the National Parole Board, the US Department of Justice consultation and training on What Works, research conferences of the International Community Corrections Association (Harland 1996), the American Probation and Parole Association's endorsement of an intensive treatment model (Fulton *et al.* 1995), special editions of journals devoted to offender treatment, and the publication of a number of books on offender assessment and treatment. This includes a book outlining their overall approach (*The Psychology of Criminal Conduct* – Andrews and Bonta 1998) and a guide for psychologists practising in corrections (*Forensic*

Psychology: Policy and Practice in Corrections – Leis *et al.* 1995). This body of work has continued to draw in more psychologists in the correctional field and to produce more 'evidence' supporting its position.[23] By the mid 1990s programmes inspired by their work had begun to gain a foothold in the UK, Australia and New Zealand (e.g. Logan and Gaes 1993; McGuire 1995; Brown 1996; Vanstone 2000; Pearson *et al.* 2002).

From the start this work was not without critics in Canada and elsewhere.[24] However, these critiques have faded from public discourse and the approach promoted by the What Works agenda now dominates correctional narratives and policy. As a whole, this group has also been curiously defensive, nevertheless. Gendreau (1996), for example, talked in the language of pique: of being 'derided', of 'the aforementioned cynics', of being 'ridiculed on moral and professional grounds', of needing a 'little more respect', even of 'knowledge destruction' which was defined as 'a deliberate and conscious attempt to ignore or dismiss competing findings'. Against this 'anti-rehabilitation rhetoric of mainstream criminology' it was suggested that the 'psychology of criminal conduct' provides, as they put it, 'a stimulating and facilitative home for the analysis and development of rehabilitation' (Andrews, Bonta and Hoge 1990: 20).

Overall, therefore, some distinguishing characteristics of the literature supporting cognitive intervention include the following:

- A dedication to the demonstration of the efficacy of treatment in corrections, to the predictive capacity of the human sciences (psychology) to help minimise risk and maximise successful outcomes, and to provide appropriate treatment based on psychological principles.

- An extensive use of, and promotion of the importance of, objective measurement. It is dismissive of all 'qualitative or phenomenological studies', regarding only quantitative work which employs objective measures of variables, evaluated by means of statistical tests of relationships, as reliable.

- Considerable use of meta-analysis to argue for the weight of evidence of 'effective' over 'ineffective' treatments in corrections.

- An emphasis on the development of indicators of risk and need and responsivity for treatment or release decision-making, using standardised scales and classification instruments.

- A privileging of behavioural and social learning approaches (interpersonal influence, skill enhancement and cognitive change) over other types of treatment programme, and an emphasis on tightly controlled programme delivery to specifically targeted populations.

- A self-reflexivity in the sense that much of the work cites and supports its propositions and arguments by reference to its own publications.[25]

Thus the focus on rehabilitation, and the promotion of cognitive skills programmes, is neatly combined with the renewed emphasis on risk and need assessment in corrections, offering a professional, scientific and apparently optimistic series of tools for the management of large groups of offenders, characterised as lacking many of the necessary skills in life for a non-criminal lifestyle. Successful rehabilitation is seen to depend on the delivery of 'clinically relevant and psychologically informed principles of treatment' (Andrews, Zinger *et al.* 1990: 377).

These programmes target the antecedents to crime and the choices made by the offender with the goal of transforming the offender into a prudent, normative subject who makes 'good choices'. They target the patterns of thinking seen to be associated with reoffending. They use carefully scripted and controlled group settings and set clear short-term goals. They are now used extensively in prison, probation and community interventions in many countries. They seem to offer great hope for practitioners and administrators alike. They claim to be more successful than other types of programmes in reducing reoffending and, when targeted at those offenders with the greatest risk of reoffending, appear to allow for the most efficient use of scarce programme resources. The manuals for cognitive behavioural programmes designed by Canadian researchers have been translated into five languages and programmes are being delivered globally in ten countries – it is an expanding industry (Kendall 2002: 191–2).

This logic and its supporting treatment models provide little if any space for social context and a discussion of the impact of marginalisation and/or oppression, which if evoked are viewed as denial or rationalisations for offending (Fox 2001; Gorman 2001; Kendall 2002; Pollack forthcoming). Offenders are simply constructed as different from the majority – they are the 'troublesome other' who failed to learn the requisite skills (Kendall 2002). The individual is the locus of the problem. This research alternatively ignores or dismisses the critical scholarship such as feminist and critical race studies as well as alternative social and psychological models that reject singular and pathologising models in favour of responses that understand and situate behaviours in broader social structural contexts of criminalisation, poverty, racism and sexual violence. Such critical frameworks avoid the construction of 'women as victim' and do not deny agency or the capacity for individual change. Instead, they argue, for example, for the integration of systemic and interpersonal factors in programmes addressing women's mental health and social needs for shelter, income and safety (see, for instance, Pollack forthcoming).

Cognitive skills, gender and ethnicity

What was again strikingly apparent from an early stage of the development of cognitive skills research was that, for all the apparent sophistication of the meta-analytic techniques, the extensiveness of the range of studies on which analysis was based and the significance of the results, the conclusions on the effectiveness of such programmes were based on studies of male correctional populations. Primarily, they involved studies on young males in the USA. Gender and ethnicity were absent. There was no discussion of the appropriateness or impact of programmes on minorities, no discussion of race, ethnic and cultural diversity, or women and girls. Many of the articles written in the 1990s are without any reference to the sex – what Klein (1995) refers to as 'the modifying adjective' – of their subjects.

In an article on response to treatment among native and non-native inmates, for example, Bonta (1989) makes no mention of the sex of the sample. Bonta and Gendreau (1990) provide an account of multiple (almost all male) treatment evaluations, but nowhere do they discuss gender issues. The two seminal articles reporting the results of their meta-analyses (Andrews, Bonta and Hoge 1990; Andrews, Zinger et al. 1990) are likewise almost totally without mention of gender or diversity, apart from a final note that the relationship between responsivity and race, gender and age should 'in the future' be examined (Andrews, Bonta and Hoge 1990). Clearly in most instances the problem of gender and diversity is seen as resolvable by 'tweaking the programme content' (Gorman 2001: 6). The logic of 'minor adjustments' is understandable, given that the assumptions underpinning both the technologies of risk/ need assessment and of cognitive programmes as defined by these scholars assume a general criminal personality that transcends gender, race, ethnicity and socioeconomic status.

There are some exceptions. Bonta (1989) compared risk and need issues for samples of native and non-native (presumably male) inmates, and some work has more recently explored the predictive utility of risk assessment measures on female offender populations (e.g. Bonta *et al.* 1995; Blanchette and Motiuk 1995; Blanchette 1997a, 1997b; Blanchette *et al.* 2002; Verbrugge and Blanchette 2002). Yet often, when data on female offenders are collated, along with males, the disparity of size in the samples makes any traditional comparison difficult. For instance, the assessment of employment needs among federally sentenced offenders used samples of 2,738 men and 31 women (Motiuk 1996); that on response to substance abuse programmes was conducted on samples of 315 men and 9 women (Weekes *et al.* 1995).

One of the most telling examples is a paper on the assessment of risk and need for female offenders (Motiuk and Blanchette 1998) which is to a large extent a reproduction of two earlier papers on the risk assessment of (male) offenders, with the addition of some results on women. While it claims to be about gender-specific classification, it is a clear example of 'adding women' to a male (paper and) model. It is written in the language of system improvement and error minimisation. Moreover, discussions of the failure to show that the male-based assessment instruments used on samples of women were predictive of reconviction are described as being 'hampered' by the fact that so few women (only 8 out of a sample of 219) were reconvicted.

More fundamentally, however, even when gender and race are considered, they are treated as categories capable of measurement in the same way as all other variables. They are treated as unproblematic in their application and use against assessment tools (such as standardised risk/need instruments) developed on the basis of the overwhelming white, male correctional population. How else could conclusions such as the following, based on a comparative study of native and non-native inmates in Ontario prisons, have been reached (Bonta 1989: 58): 'These findings lead us to conclude that the courts, by and large, assessed judicial penalties on the basis of legal and criminal factors and that race was inconsequential. The examination of the more "secret" world of the prison also failed to evidence any racial biases'?

The findings of the Commission on Systemic Racism in the Ontario Criminal Justice System (1994, 1995) provide ample evidence to the contrary, as do the extensive examinations of discrimination against Aboriginal peoples in Canada (e.g. Hamilton and Sinclair 1991; Linn 1992; Royal Commission on Aboriginal Peoples 1993, 1996; Monture-Angus 2001); specific accounts of the destruction of native communities (e.g. Shkilnyk 1985); and accounts of the differences between native and non-native concepts of the process of justice (e.g. Ross 1992). Thus not only is this un-gendered research and race-blind, but the narrowness of the definitions used also removes all trace of context.

There is a sense, too, in which the realities of the lives of minority groups as well as the dominant offender population are rendered not only unproblematic but also denigrated. They are seen as individuals with poor cognitive skills, intellectual ability or motivation to change. Outlining the rationale for the cognitive skills training programme developed for use in the federal prison system, it is argued that the main source of criminal behaviour is 'cognitive inadequacies':

> Offenders with cognitive inadequacies ... are likely to evidence major difficulties in social adjustment. They are impulsive, and tend to act before they think. When they do stop to think, they think poorly. They blame others, they fail to see their own impact on others. Their thought processes are narrow and variously described as 'simplistic and illogical' and 'exceptionally shallow, narrow and rigid'. (Fabiano *et al.* 1991 in Johnson 1996: 274)

While more recent work does now acknowledge the necessity of making race or gender-specific accommodation to 'needs' in terms of programming, this is *only* to be on the basis of their predictive power to reduce recidivism. In a discussion of the effects of in-prison programming on subsequent recidivism of native and non-native inmates, for example, Bonta (1989: 60) argued that since (lack of) post-release accommodation and finance appeared to be more important explanations of recidivism among non-native than native offenders, housing and financial counselling were more worth while for non-natives: 'inadequate accommodations and financial difficulties spell difficulties for non-natives but not particularly so for Natives.'

Again, in discussing the implication of the predictive power of risk and need scales on a sample of federally sentenced female offenders Bonta *et al.* (1995: 291) argued that prison programmes appeared to have had 'little or no association with criminal behaviour on release'. Thus they suggest that only those programmes that target 'criminogenic need' should, in future, be pursued. For example, counselling that focuses upon healing the hurt of past victimisations may help victims feel better about themselves and improve relationships with others but may not alter the factors that initiated and maintained their criminal behaviour. A budgeting course may help a single mother on welfare make ends meet but may not affect her views on the acceptability of crime for coping in life. Offenders present many needs but not all these needs are necessarily criminogenic.

One might ask what a single mother who does not see crime as acceptable must do if she is still unable to make ends meet. They also suggested that future programmes for women offenders developed at the new regional prisons should be carefully evaluated to test their effects on reconviction, and rejected if they fail to prove effective (Bonta *et al.* 1995) – an approach clearly at odds with the model of *Creating Choices* with its stress on giving women some choice in programmes they felt they needed. The implication is that unless a programme can be shown to reduce recidivism it should not be made available to a prison or post-release population, and programmes are expected to target specific sets of 'criminogenic needs'. Only those 'needs' which are statistically related to recidivism are seen as criminogenic and, therefore, worth targeting. The circle is complete. The tautological reasoning used in much of this work has been noticed by other critics (e.g. Lab and Whitehead 1990; Logan and Gaes 1993).

It must also be noted that the conclusions drawn about the ineffectiveness of programmes for women were based on a study which attempted to apply male-derived standardised measures to the small and heterogeneous federal female population in Canada, using interview data collected for a quite different purpose (Shaw *et al.* 1991).[26] The original interviews did not explore the real content or extent of programme involvement, and in correctional usage such a term tends to be used for everything from leisure pursuits and occasional attendance at AA meetings, to intensive counselling. At most, this mainstream work has, belatedly, accepted an 'add women' (and race) approach.

Conclusions

This chapter has mapped out how gender and diversity were left out of the development of two now very popular correctional and research-led movements in Canada – the development of risk/need assessment and classification, and the promotion of cognitive skills programmes, both of them associated with the re-emergence of rehabilitation. It has also begun to map out questions for further research and to consider the implications of these issues for penal policy. Clearly, more work is needed to understand these differences more fully, and their significance both theoretically and empirically. Failure to engage in and with such explorations may have adverse and discriminatory effects for minority penal populations. While there have been some recent attempts to respond to criticism, the assumption is that women and minority groups can be 'fitted in' to the dominant scales and assessments and the cognitive skills approach. The latter requires strict adherence to treatment delivery, rigorous testing, evaluation and programme accreditation to ensure that the master patterns are maintained.

It is our hope that this chapter will stimulate a thoughtful debate on practices of risk-based governance as they relate to What Works in corrections and in particular female and non-white correctional populations, and enhance the gender and ethno-cultural specificity of correctional research, policy and operations as they relate to security classification and risk/needs assessment. Links that are more concrete need to be made between theory and research, policy and correctional practice, and the relationship between these spheres in terms of how risk is operationalised and managed.

Gendered and racialised risk/need knowledges inform correctional practices. While risk factors are statistical artifacts that reflect certain population characteristics, these factors are often ascribed to individuals and used to legitimate a wide range of interventions, including the responsibilisation of offenders. The ascription of risk to individuals occurs through the development of assessment tools and through the administration and interpretation of these tools. Our observations of this process have revealed some disturbing trends that call for critical evaluation of the criteria used in risk assessment technologies and the proposed methods of risk reduction. Researchers and practitioners who advocate risk technologies often define risk from the standpoint of white middle-class morality. Social-structural disadvantages as well as gender and ethno-culturally based stereotypes are discretely institutionalised and reproduced. Risk and the enterprise of risk management appear on the surface to be amoral, efficient, objective and non-discriminatory, but they are not.

Notes

1 We would like to thank Status of Women Canada for funding the two-year research project on 'Gender, diversity, risk assessment and classification for federally sentenced women', and the participants at the workshop on risk held in Toronto in May 1999. The empirical data collected for this project have informed our theorisation and critique of current practices. This chapter extends and develops a paper published in French in *Criminologie*, 4 (1) 2001.
2 Hannah-Moffat and Shaw (2001).
3 These followed the development of parole and sentencing guidelines.
4 This construction of the criminogenic factor is similar to what O'Malley (1999) calls a protective factor.
5 The research on cognitive skills and crime in Canada appears to originate

with Gendreau and Ross (1979, 1987), Ross and Fabiano (1988) and subsequently Andrews *et al.* (1990) and Fabiano *et al.* (1991).

6 See O'Malley (1999) for a more elaborate discussion of the 'mixed models of governance' that occur through the blending of risk and punishment, risk and restorative justice and risk and rehabilitation.

7 In Canada, federal or provincial status is determined by length of sentence: those sentenced to two years or more are housed in federal prisons, those to under two years in provincial prisons.

8 These changes resulted from the *Report of the Task Force on Federally Sentenced Women* (Creating Choices), published in 1990. See Hannah-Moffat and Shaw (2000) for a history of the recent changes in women's federal corrections in Canada.

9 This information is from the CSC's (1994) *Offender Intake Assessment and Correctional Plan – User's Manual.*

10 Institutional placement options for women are restricted to multi-level regional prisons. The range of accommodation options that exist for men is not the same as for women.

11 Some degree of disjuncture between the intent of the developer of a tool and the use of those tools in practice is common. However, in spite of this gap, we maintain that the tools, even if correctly applied, impose certain normative standards.

12 See the *Offender Intake Assessment and Correctional Plan – User's Manual* developed by Correctional Service of Canada.

13 For a more complete description of the variable included in the Custody Rating Scale, see Grant and Luciani (1998).

14 In our research, which involved a detailed study of the process of classification in federally sentenced women's facilities across Canada, we found a great deal of regional variation in how women were assessed and in individual parole officers (case management officers) interpretations of OIA and CRS criteria. See Hannah-Moffat and Shaw (2000) for a detailed discussion of the findings.

15 Much of the research conducted in the research division of the Correctional Service of Canada attempts to fulfil this objective. For examples, see their periodical publication *Forum on Corrections Research.*

16 See Hannah-Moffat and Shaw (2000).

17 There is an extensive range of feminist scholarship that suggests learning is gendered and racialised because of differential socialisation on the basis of gender and race, ethnicity and culture (Morris 1987). It is also suggested that there are differences in how men and women learn and approach the social world and interact with others (Bloom and Covington 1998; also see Zaplin 1998).

18 In Canada, a substantially greater portion of female than male offenders are unemployed at the time of their admission to correctional facilities. The recent survey found that 64 per cent of female inmates in provincial/ territorial facilities and 80 per cent of females in federal facilities were

unemployed at the time of admission compared to 43 and 54 per cent respectively of male inmates (Finn *et al.* 1999: 5).

19   For detailed examples of such differences in Canada see Johnson (1996), Boritch (1997) and Finn *et al. (*1999).

20   For a detailed description of some of the Canadian research that critiques the concept of the universal women, see Bouchard *et al. (*1999).

21   Knowledge of these differences is critical given that Aboriginal women account for approximately 30 per cent of all female admissions to provincial and territorial facilities (Lipinski 1991), and approximately 19 per cent of the federally sentenced womens population (Arbour 1996). This is astonishing, given that Aboriginal people comprise only approximately 3 per cent of the entire population. Aboriginal women have different cultural and spiritual needs from white women, and they tend to have a higher incidence of single-parent homes, family difficulties and foster-home placements (Correctional Law Review 1988; Caswey *et al.* 1991; Royal Commission of Aboriginal Peoples 1996), as well as a higher incidence of economic and social deprivation combined with experiences of racism (Royal Commission of Aboriginal Peoples 1996).

22   Most of these measures, with the exception of ECT perhaps, are in fact still employed on a regular basis in many prisons in Canada and elsewhere.

23   See, for example, articles in *Forum on Corrections Research* published three times a year by the Research Division of Correctional Service Canada. This journal has become almost exclusively concerned with issues of risk prediction and treatment assessment and effectiveness.

24   A heated debate took place, for example, in the *Canadian Journal of Criminology* between Don Andrews (1990) and Jean-Paul Brodeur and Anthony Doob (1989) over the treatment of rehabilitation issues in the Report of the Canadian Sentencing Commission (1987). From the beginning, however, the groups were curiously defensive, attacking mainstream criminology (and 'the outrageous promotion of sociology') for its concerns about the resurrection of rehabilitation. They were sensitive to any criticism of their work. They saw themselves as reclaiming a discredited foothold within a mainstream (read sociological) criminology, which they felt was preoccupied with issues of structural inequality, and law and order. They talked about 'the outrageous promotion of sociology and the disregard for evidence so apparent in mainstream criminology' (Andrews and Bonta 1994: iv). They were very sensitive to criticism by criminologists who 'seem to *know* that the causes of crime are buried deep in political economy, culture, and social structure, just as they *know* intervention is mere tinkering' (Andrews, Bonta and Hoge, 1990: 45). By the mid-1990s Andrews (1996: 43) was suggesting that 'pockets of antipsychology bias may have increased in recent years'.

25   Of course other fields, such as feminist discourse, do this too, but they are usually much more open about their arguments, disputes and uncertainties.

26   In this sense the researchers acted as a Trojan Horse, providing a data set which was subsequently amended and augmented by prison disciplinary data to enable prediction studies on 'a female data set' to be carried out.

References

Abbott, B. and Kerr, D. (1995) *Substance Abuse Programme for Federally Sentenced Women*. Ottawa: Correctional Service of Canada.

Aboriginal Justice Inquiry of Manitoba (1991) *Report of the Aboriginal Justice Inquiry of Manitoba*. Winnipeg: Queen's Printer.

Andrews, D.A. (1989) 'Recidivism is predictable and can be influenced: using risk assessment to reduce recidivism', *Forum on Corrections Research*, 1 (2).

Andrews, D.A. (1990) 'Some criminological sources of anti-rehabilitation bias in the report of the Canadian Sentencing Commission', *Canadian Journal of Criminology*, 32 (3): 511–23.

Andrews, D.A. (1996) 'Criminal recidivism is predictable and can be influenced: an update', *Forum on Corrections Research*, 8 (3).

Andrews, D.A. and Bonta, J. (1998) *The Psychology of Criminal Conduct*. Cincinnati, OH: Anderson.

Andrews, D., Bonta, J. and Hoge, R.D. (1990) 'Classification for effective rehabilitation', *Criminal Justice And Behaviour*, 17: 19–52.

Andrews, D., Zinger, I., Hoge, R.D., Bonta, J., Gendreau, P. and Cullen, F.T. (1990) 'Does correctional treatment work? A clinically relevant and psychologically informed meta-analysis', *Criminology*, 28 (3): 369–404.

Arbour, Madame Justice Louise (1996) *Report of the Commission of Inquiry into Certain Events at the Prison for Women in Kingston*. Ottawa: Public Works and Government Services.

Aubrey, R. and Hough, M. (1997) *Assessing Offender's Needs: Assessment Scales for the Probation Service*. Home Office Research Study 166. London: Home Office.

Bhui, H.S. (1999) 'Racism and risk assessment: linking theory to practice with black mentally disordered offenders', *Probation Journal*, 46 (3): 171–81.

Blanchette, K. (1997a) 'Classifying female offenders for correctional interventions', *Forum on Corrections Research*, 9 (1).

Blanchette, K. (1997b) 'Comparing violent and non-violent offenders on risk and need', *Forum on Corrections Research*, 9 (2).

Blanchette, K. (1997c) *Risk and Need among Federally-sentenced Female Offenders: A Comparison of Minimum-, Medium- and Maximum-security Inmates*. Research Report R-58. Ottawa: Correctional Service Canada.

Blanchette, K. and Motiuk, L. (1995) 'Female offenders risk assessment: the case management strategies approach.' Paper presented at the Canadian Psychological Association Annual Convention, Charlottetown.

Blanchette, K. and Motiuk, L. (1997) 'Maximum security female and male federal offenders: a comparison', *Forum on Corrections Research* 9 (3).

Blanchette, K., Verbrugge, P. and Wichmann, C. (2002) *The Custody Rating Scale. Initial Security Level Placement and Women Offenders*. Research Branch Report R-127. Ottawa: Correctional Service Canada.

Bloom, B. and Covington, S. (1998) 'Gender-specific programming for female offenders: what is it and why is it important?' Paper presented at the American Society of Criminology Meeting, Washington, DC, November.

Bonta, J. (1989) 'Native inmates: institutional response, risk and needs', *Canadian Journal of Criminology*, 31 (1): 49–60.

Bonta, J. and Gendreau, P. (1990) 'Re-examining the cruel and unusual punishment of prison life', *Law and Human Behaviour*, 14 (4): 347–72.

Bonta, J., LaPrairie, C. and Wallace-Capretta, S. (1997) 'Risk predictors and re-offending: Aboriginals and non-Aboriginal offenders', *Canadian Journal of Criminology*, 39 (2): 127–44.

Bonta, J., Pang, B. and Wallace-Capretta, S. (1995) 'Predictors of recidivism among incarcerated females offenders', *The Prison Journal*, 75 (3): 227–93.

Boritch, H. (1997) *Fallen Women: Female Crime and Criminal Justice in Canada*. Toronto: I.T.P. Nelson.

Bouchard, J., Boyd, S. and Sheehy, L. (1999) 'Canadian feminist research on law: an annotated bibliography', *Canadian Journal of Women and the Law*, 11 (1 & 2).

Brodeur, J. and Doob, A. (1989) 'Rehabilitating the debate on rehabilitation', *Justice Quarterly*, 5 (4): 179–92.

Brown, M. (1996) 'Refining the risk concept: decision context as a factor mediating the relation between risk and programme effectiveness', *Crime and Delinquency*, 42 (3): 435–55.

Campbell, A. (1993) *Men, Women and Aggression*. New York, NY: Basic Books.

Castel, R. (1991) 'From dangerousness to risk', in G. Burchell *et al.* (eds) *The Foucault Effect: Studies in Governmentality*. Chicago, IL: University of Chicago Press.

Caswey, R. with Bear, L., Bertolin, C., Cooper, C., Frenklin, J., Galet, A. and Gallagher, M. (1991) *Justice on Trial: Report of the Task Force on the Criminal Justice System and its Impact on Indian, Metis People of Alberta*. Edmonton.

CCJA (1998) *Prison Overcrowding and the Reintegration of Offenders*. Ottawa.

Clark, D.A., Fisher, M.J. and McDougall, C. (1993) 'A new methodology for assessing level of risk in incarcerated offenders', *British Journal of Criminology*, 33 (3): 436–48.

Clements, C.B. (1996) 'Offender classification: two decades of progress', *Criminal Justice and Behaviour*, 23 (1): 121–43.

Comack, E. (1996) *Women in Trouble*. Halifax: Fernwood Publishing.

Comack, E., Chopyk, V. and Wood, L. (2000) *Mean Streets? The Social Locations, Gender Dynamics, and Patterns of Violent Crime in Winnepeg*. Ottawa: Canadian Centre for Policy Alternatives (available at www.policyalternatives.ca).

Commission on Systemic Racism in the Ontario Criminal Justice System (1994, 1995) *Racism behind Bars* (1994); *Main Report* (1995). Toronto: Queen's Printer for Ontario.

Correctional Law Review (1988) *Correctional Issues Affecting Native Peoples*. Ottawa: Ministry of the Solicitor General.

Correctional Service of Canada (CSC) (1994) *OIA – Offender Intake Assessment – Users' Manual*. Ottawa: Correctional Service of Canada.

Correctional Service of Canada (CSC) (1996) *FSW Facilities Offender Intake Assessment Content Guidelines*. Ottawa: Correctional Service of Canada.

✳✳Coulson, G., Ilacqua, G., Nutbrown, V., Giulekas, D. and Cudjoe, F. (1996) 'Predictive utility of the LSI for incarcerated female offenders,' *Criminal Justice and Behaviour*, 23 (3): 427–39.

Creating Choices (1990) *Report of the Task Force on Federally Sentenced Women*. Ottawa: Ministry of the Solicitor General.

Culpitt, I. (1999) *Social Policy and Risk*. London: Sage.

Daley, D. and Lane, R. (1999) 'Actuarially based "on line" risk assessment in Western Australia', *Probation Journal*, 46 (3): 164–70.

Dallao, M. (1997) 'Keeping classification current', *Corrections Today*, July: 86–8.

Dawson, D. (1999) 'Risk of violence assessment: Aboriginal offenders and assumption of homogeneity.' Paper presented at the 'Best practice interventions in corrections for indigenous people' conference, Adelaide, Australia.

Dean, M. (1999) *Governmentality: Power and Rule in Modern Society*. London: Sage.

Defert, D. (1991) 'Popular life and insurance technology', in G. Burchell *et al.* (eds) *The Foucault Effect: Studies in Governmentality*. Chicago, IL: University of Chicago Press, 211–34.

Dhaliwal, G.K., Porporino, F. and Ross, R.R. (1994) 'Assessment of criminogenic factors, program assignment, and recidivism', *Criminal Justice and Behaviour*, 21 (4): 454–67.

Ditchfield, J. (1997) 'Actuarial prediction and risk assessment', *Prison Service Journal*, 113: 8–13.

Dougherty, J. (1993) 'Women's violence against their children: a feminist perspective', *Women and Criminal Justice*, 4 (2): 91–114.

Ericson, R. and Haggerty, K. (1997) *Policing the Risk Society*. Toronto: University of Toronto Press.

Ewald, F. (1991) 'Insurance and risk', in G. Burchell *et al.* (eds) *The Foucault Effect: Studies in Governmentality*. Chicago, IL: University of Chicago Press.

Fabiano, E.A., Robinson, D. and Porporino, F. (1991) *A Preliminary Assessment of the Cogitive Skills Training Programme*. Ottawa: Correctional Service Canada.

Federally Sentenced Women's Program (FSWP) (1994) *Literature Review*. Ottawa: Correctional Services.

Feeley, M. and Simon, J. (1992) 'The new penology: notes on the emerging strategy of corrections and its implications.' *Criminology*, 30 (4): 49–74.

Feeley, M. and Simon, J. (1994) 'Actuarial justice: the emerging new criminal law', in D. Nelken (ed.) *The Futures of Criminology*. London: Sage.

Finn, A., Trevethan, S., Carrière, G. and Kowalski, M. (1999) 'Female inmates, Aboriginal inmates and inmates serving life sentences: a one day snapshot', *Juristat*, 19 (5): 1–5.

Fox, K. (2001) 'Self change and resistance in prison', in J. Gubrium and

J. Holstein (eds) *Institutional Selves: Troubled Identities in a Post Modern World*. Oxford: Oxford University Press.

Fulton, P., Gendreau, P. and Paparozzi, M. (1995) 'APPA's prototypical Intensive Supervision Program: as it was meant to be', *Perspectives*, 19: 25–42.

Garland, D. (1996) 'The limits of the sovereign state: strategies of crime control in contemporary society', *British Journal of Criminology*, 36 (4): 445–71.

Garland, D. (1997) 'Governmentality and the problem of crime: Foucault, criminology, sociology', *Theoretical Criminology*, 1 (2): 173–214.

Garland, D. (2001) *The Culture of Control*. Chicago, IL: University of Chicago Press.

Gendreau, P. (1996) 'Offender rehabilitation: what we know now and what needs to be done', *Criminal Justice and Behaviour*, 23 (1): 144–61.

Gendreau, P., Goggin, C. and Gray, G. (1998) 'Case need domain: "employment"', *Forum on Corrections Research*, 10 (3).

Gendreau, P. and Ross, R.R. (1979) 'Effective correctional treatment: bibliotheraphy for cynics', *Crime and Delinquency*, 24 (4): 463–89.

Gendreau, P. and Ross, R.R. (1987) 'Revivification of rehabilitation: evidence from the 1980s', *Justice Quarterly*, 4 (3): 349–407.

Gorman, K. (2001) 'Cognitive behaviouralism and the Holy Grail: the quest for a universal means of managing offender risk', *Probation Journal*, 48 (1): 3–9.

Gottfredson, S. (1987) 'Prediction: an overview of selected methodological issues', in D.M. Gottfredson and M. Tonry (eds) *Prediction and Classification. Crime and Justice Vol. 9*. Chicago, IL: University of Chicago Press.

Gottfredson, D.M. and Tonry, M. (eds) (1987) *Prediction and Classification. Crime and Justice Vol. 9*. Chicago, IL: University of Chicago Press.

Grant, B. and Luciani, F. (1998) *Security Classification Using the Custody Rating Scale*. Ottawa: Research Branch, Correctional Service of Canada.

Haggerty, K. (1999) 'Correctional risk classifications: pragmatic cautions and theoretical reflections.' Paper presented at the research workshop on 'Risk, gender and diversity', Toronto, May.

Hannah-Moffat, K. (1999) 'Moral agent or actuarial subject: risk and Canadian women's imprisonment', *Theoretical Criminology*, 3 (1): 71–94.

Hannah-Moffat, K. (2000) 'Re-forming the prison – rethinking our ideals', in K. Hannah-Moffat and M. Shaw (eds) *An Ideal Prison? Critical Essays on Women's Imprisonment in Canada*. Halifax: Fernwood.

Hannah-Moffat, K. (2001) *Punishment in Disguise: Governance in Canadian Women's Prisons*. Toronto: University of Toronto Press.

Hannah-Moffat, K. (2002a) 'Lessons learned: some reflections on federal women's prison re-form', in P. Carlen (ed.) *Women and Punishment: The Struggle for Justice*. Cullompton: Willan.

Hannah-Moffat, K. (2002b) 'Transformative risk subject: hybridization of risk and need.' Paper presented at the British criminology conference, Keele University, July.

Hannah-Moffat, K. and Shaw, M. (eds) (2000) *An Ideal Prison? Critical Essays on Women's Imprisonment in Canada*. Halifax: Fernwood.

Hannah-Moffat, K. and Shaw, M. (2001) *Taking Risks: Incorporating Gender and Culture into the Classification and Assessment of Federally Sentenced Women in Canada.* Ottawa: Status of Women Canada.

Harer, M.D. and Langan, N.P. (2001) 'Gender differences in predictors of prison violence: assessing the predictive validity of a risk classification system', *Crime and Delinquency,* 47 (4): 513–36.

Harland, A.T. (1996) *Choosing Correctional Options that Work: Defining the Demand and Evaluating the Supply.* Thousand Oaks, CA: Sage.

Holt, N. (1996) *Inmate Classification: A Validation Study of the California System.* California Department of Corrections.

✳ Homel, R., Lincoln, R. and Herd, B. (1999) 'Risk and resilience: crime and violence prevention in Aboriginal communities', *Australian and New Zealand Journal of Criminology,* 32 (2): 182–96.

Jackson, M. (1999) 'Canadian Aboriginal women and their "criminality": the cycle of violence in the context of difference', *Australian and New Zealand Journal of Criminology,* 32 (2): 197–208.

Johnson, H. (1996) *Dangerous Domains: Violence against Women in Canada.* Toronto: Nelson.

Johnson, R. (1996) *Hard Time: Understanding and Reforming the Prison* (2nd edn). Belmont, CA: Wadsworth.

Kendall, K. (2002) 'Time to think again about cognitive behavioural programmes', in P. Carlen (ed.) *Women and Punishment: The Struggle for Justice.* Cullompton: Willan.

Klein, D. (1995) 'Crime through gender's prism: feminist criminology in the United States', in N.H. Rafter and F. Heidensohn (eds) *International Feminist Perspectives in Criminology: Engendering a Discipline.* Buckingham: Open University Press.

Lab, S.P. and Whitehead, J.T. (1990) 'From "Nothing works" to "The appropriate works": the latest stop in the search for the secular grail', *Criminology,* 28 (3): 405–17.

Leis, T.A., Motiuk, L.L. and Ogloff, J.R.P. (1995) *Forensic Psychology: Policy and Practice in Corrections.* Ottawa: Corrections Service Canada.

Lipinski, S. (1991) 'Adult female offenders in provincial/territorial correctional systems 1989–90', *Juristat,* 11 (6).

Logan, C.H. and Gaes, G.G. (1993) 'Meta-analysis and the rehabilitation of punishment', *Justice Quarterly,* 10 (2): 245–63.

Loucks, A. and Zamble, E. (1999) 'Predictors of recidivism in serious female offenders – Canada searches for predictors common to both men and women', *Corrections Today,* February: 26–32.

Luhmann, N. (1993) *Risk: A Sociological Theory.* New York, NY: Aldine De Gruyter.

Lupton, D. (1999a) *Risk.* London: Routledge.

Lupton, D. (1999b) *Risk and Socio-cultural Theory: New Directions and Perspectives.* Cambridge: Cambridge University Press.

Mair, G. (1999) 'Its a man's man's man's world.' Paper presented at the workshop on 'Risk, gender and diversity.' Toronto, May.

Martinson, R. (1974) 'What works? Questions and answers about prison reform', *The Public Interest*, 35: 22–54.

McGuire, J. (ed.) (1995) *What Works: Reducing Reoffending*. Chichester: Wiley.

McHugh, M. (1997) 'Risk assessment and management of suicides in prison', *Prison Service Journal*, 113: 4–8.

Monture-Angus, P. (2001) 'Aboriginal women and correctional practice', in K. Hannah-Moffat and M. Shaw (eds) *An Ideal Prison? Critical Essays on Women's Imprisonment in Canada*. Halifax: Fernwood.

Morris, A. (1987) *Women, Crime and Criminal Justice*. New York, NY: Blackwell.

Motiuk, L. (1993) 'Where are we in our ability to assess risk?', *Forum on Corrections Research*, 5 (2).

Motiuk, L. (1996) 'Targeting employment patterns to reduce offender risk and need', *Forum on Corrections Research*, 8 (1): 22–4.

Motiuk, L. (1997) 'Classification for correctional programming: the Offender Intake Assessment (OIA) process', *Forum on Corrections Research*, 9 (1).

Motiuk, L. and Blanchette, K. (1998) 'What works in assessing female offender risk and need.' Paper presented at the sixth ICCA annual research conference, Arlington, VA.

Nellis, M. (1995) 'Probation values for the 1990s', *Howard Journal of Criminal Justice*, 34 (1): 19–44.

O'Malley, P. (1992) 'Risk, power and crime prevention', *Economy and Society*, 21 (3): 252–75.

O'Malley, P. (1998) *Crime and the Risk Society*. Sydney: Ashgate Dartmouth.

O'Malley. P. (1999) *The Risk Society: Implications for Justice and Beyond*. Report Commissioned for the Department of Justice, Victoria, Australia.

Parton, N. (1996) *Social Theory, Social Change and Social Work*. New York, NY: Routledge.

Pearson, F.S., Lipton, D.S., Cleveland, C.M. and Yee, D.S. (2002). 'The effects of behavioral/cognitive-behavioural programs on recidivism', *Crime and Delinquency*, 48 (3): 576–496.

Petersilia, J. and Turner, S. (1987) 'Prediction and racial minorities', in D.M. Gottfredson and M. Tonry (eds) *Prediction and Classification. Crime and Justice Vol. 9*. Chicago, IL: University of Chicago Press.

Pollack, S. (forthcoming) 'Anti-oppressive social work practice with women in prison: discursive reconstructions and alternative practices, *British Journal of Social Work*.

Pratt, J. (1993) 'Dangerousness, risk and technologies of power', *Australian and New Zealand Journal of Criminology*, 28 (3).

Pratt, J. (1997) *Governing the Dangerous*. Sydney: Federation Press.

Price, R. (1997) 'On the risks of risk prediction', *Journal of Forensic Psychiatry*, 8 (1): 1–4.

Quinsey, V., Harris, G.T., Rice, M.E. and Cormier, C.A. (1998) *Violent Offenders: Appraising and Managing Risk*. Washington, DC: American Psychological Association.

Report of the Canadian Sentencing Commission (1987) *Sentencing Reform: A Canadian Approach*. Ottawa: Supply and Services.

Robinson, G. (2001) 'Power, knowledge and "What Works" in probation', *Howard Journal*, 40 (3): 235–54.

Ross, R. (1992) *Dancing with a Ghost*. Markham: Octopus.

Ross, R.R. and Fabiano, E.A. (1985) *Correctional Afterthoughts: Programs for Female Offenders*. User Report 1985–18. Ottawa: Ministry of the Solicitor General of Canada.

Royal Commission on Aboriginal Peoples (1993, 1996) *Bridging the Cultural Divide. Report on Aboriginal Peoples in the Criminal Justice System*. Ottawa: Ministry of Supply and Service.

Shaw, M. (2000) 'Women, violence and disorder in prisons', in K. Hannah-Moffat and M. Shaw (eds) *An Ideal Prison? Critical Essays on Women's Imprisonment in Canada*. Halifax: Fernwood.

Shaw, M. and Dubois, S. (1995) *Understanding Violence by Women*. Ottawa: Correctional Service Canada.

Shaw, M., Rodgers, K., Blanchette, J., Hattem, T., Thomas, L.S. and Tamarak, L. (1991) *Survey of Federally Sentenced Women: Report to the Task Force on Federally Sentenced Women*. User Report 1991–4. Ottawa: Ministry of the Solicitor General.

Shkilnyk, A.M. (1985) *A Poison Stronger than Love: The Destruction of an Ojibwa Community*. New Haven, CT: Yale University Press.

Simon, J. (1987) 'The emergence of a risk society: insurance, law and the state', *Socialist Review*, 95 (1): 93–108.

Simon, J. (1988) 'The ideological effects of actuarial practices', *Law and Society Review*, 22 (4): 771–800.

Simon, J. and Feeley, M. (1995) 'True crime: the new penology and public discourses on crime', in T. Blomberg and S. Cohen (eds) *Punishment and Social Control*. New York, NY: Aldine De Gruyter.

Steffensmeier, D. and Allan, E. (1998) 'Nature of female offending: patterns and explanation', in R. Zaplin (ed.) *Female Offenders: Critical Perspectives and Effective Interventions*. Maryland: Aspen.

Vanstone, M. (2000) 'Cognitive-behavioural work with offenders in the UK: a history of influential endeavour', *Howard Journal*, 39 (2): 171–83.

Verbrugge, P. and Blanchette, K. (2002) 'The validity of the Custody Rating Scale for the initial security classification of Aboriginal women', *Forum On Corrections Research*, 14 (3).

Weekes, J.R., Millson, W.A. and Lightfoot, L.O. (1995) 'Factors influencing the outcome of offender substance abuse treatment', *Forum On Corrections Research*, 7 (3): 8–11.

Wormith, J.S. (1995) 'The Youth Management Assessment: assessment of young offenders at risk of serious offending.'

Zaplin, R.T. (ed.) (1998) *Female Offenders: Critical Perspectives And Effective Interventions*. Maryland: Aspen.

Chapter 6

The barking dog? Partnership and effective practice

Judith Rumgay

Introduction

The 'curious incident' of the dog that 'did nothing in the night-time' (Doyle 1894) has been a popular metaphor for our human fallibility in problem perception for many years. The failure of the dog in the Sherlock Holmes tale to bark, and thereby to rouse people from their slumbering insensitivity to a perilous intruder, told the mastermind of crime detection that the danger had in fact emanated from within the household. Outside that story, crime fiction has many times offered alternative reasons for the unlikely silence of dogs at crucial moments: perhaps the intruder was a trusted friend or the malign stranger fed the (oddly unsuspecting at this point) animal meat impregnated with tranquillisers.

The argument that I wish to develop here invokes a very different account of human failure to hear a warning. In this account, the players have not been and, indeed, still are not listening. Moreover, their deafness is not the result of physiological misfortune or environmental conditions beyond their power to resist or correct. Rather, it is rooted in a wilful disregard of obvious signals that all is not well. In this version of the legend, the members of the household simply do not want to hear the barking dog.

The household of this narrative is the probation service, currently caught up in a drama of challenge and change that is shaking the foundations of the family home, and placing its faith for salvation in the drive for effectiveness that has become commonly known as the What Works agenda. This agenda requires the household to invest in a massive mustering of its internal resources in the attempt to fight off the threat to its safety. Unlike so many accounts of the heroic battle for survival within turmoil and tribulation, however, this one looks beyond the household at centre-stage to consider the implications of its struggle for its neighbours, which in this case are those organisations with which the probation service is joined in partnership. The argument explores an alternative pathway to the household's survival: to call on the neighbours and seek their help.

The details of the background to, and content of, the What Works agenda for effective practice are not elaborated here (see Chapter 2 of this volume). Nor is this chapter a text on the practicalities of partnership (see, e.g., Mattessich *et al.* 2001). It moves directly to issues in partnership of relevance to its central theme: the scale of the probation service's partnership enterprise; alternative definitions of the crime problem that inform different routes to its resolution; and problems of exclusivity, effectiveness and accountability. Throughout, contrasts are drawn between the What Works approach and the partnership pathway through these challenges to securing its organisational mission and integrity.

The scale of the partnership enterprise

Throughout the 1990s, and continuing to the present day, the probation service has been enmeshed in an increasing and diversifying range of partnership activities. While the service has generally been keen to proclaim its traditions of interagency co-operation, the past decade of partnership expansion has derived more noticeably from central policy and legislative mandate than from any particular intrinsic driving enthusiasm for the enterprise. The service's tendency to react with – at best – ambivalence to initiatives which are not of its own making has contributed to its patchy progress along the path to fruitful partnership engagement, which is lined with examples of both excellent and poor-quality practice (Rumgay 2000; Mair and Jamel 2002).

The service's involvement in partnerships during this period of rapid, centrally mandated growth has been remarkable for the diversity of forms that it has taken. It has been required to develop mechanisms for contracting for elements of its provision for offenders; to participate in multi-agency collaborations for community crime prevention (crime and disorder reduction partnerships); to join multi-agency groups targeting specific groups of individuals involved in, or at risk of involvement in crime (drug action teams, youth offending teams and multi-agency public protection panels); and to contribute to interagency implementation of social policies for support of society's most vulnerable groups (see Rumgay 2003 for an account of these developments).

Interestingly, the last of these types of initiative has been lacking in prominence in discussions of the probation service's partnership enterprise compared to the attention that has been directed at the others. This imbalance is probably due to the overt focus of the first four categories on crime and criminals. The political sensitivity of issues concerning the management of crime and risk in contemporary society and the concomitant policy emphasis on the probation service as an agency of law enforcement mask the extent to which it is bound by ties to the systems of social welfare as much as those of criminal justice. Thus, for example, the Supporting People project for planning and delivery of social and supported housing commits the probation service to multi-agency collaboration in and, indeed, financial contribution to a major restructuring of the ways that such provision is developed and funded. Similarly, the probation service has been required since 1998 to negotiate multi-agency agreements aimed at improving offenders' access to employment and training opportunities (Fletcher 2001).

From the perspective of the argument developed in these pages, the neglect of these kinds of partnership activity is unfortunate for two reasons. First, it colludes with a political rhetoric that portrays offenders as individuals deserving punishment by exclusion from mainstream social provision, even while central policy explicitly – but more mutedly – targets them as a vulnerable group with special needs for supported access to those opportunities. Secondly, it disguises the unique nature of the probation service which, alone as an organisation, has successfully inhabited the two worlds of criminal justice and social welfare since its inception. That government has singled out the probation service to represent the needs of offenders within these fields of broad social endeavour is not an accident: there is no other agency with the experience, capability and motivation for such a difficult undertaking in the face of public hostility to offenders that has been fanned, in part, by the rhetoric of exclusion (Rumgay 2001).

Nevertheless, the partnership enterprise has extracted a significant toll on the probation service's resources and confused its priorities. It has deepened the service's connections to the voluntary sector by requiring it to form contractual relationships for supervision services, even while an emergent preoccupation with risk has weakened the acknowledgement of such partners and emphasised statutory organisational relationships in successive criminal and social policy documents (see, for example, Home Office 1998; Department of Health 1998, 1999). It has demanded active engagement with the agencies of criminal justice and social welfare while the service simultaneously struggles to adapt to its own newly centralised internal structure. It has required the service to look beyond its own organisational boundaries to develop alternative provision for surveillance and support of offenders, while it must accommodate a plethora of penal innovations in the forms of new types of supervision order and programme delivery requirements within its own in-house resources.

In the face of such upheaval, it can hardly surprise us to learn that the service's response to the demands of partnership has been often reluctant, uneven and based selectively on a mixture of perceived political imperatives and territorial preferences (Rumgay 2000; Mair and Jamel 2002). Nevertheless, as the mandates for partnerships to tackle a broad range of social problems increase, it is the argument of this chapter that the probation service should not squander the opportunity that partnerships present to assert the service's unique identity as keystone of the bridge between the criminal and social policy worlds. Since the probation service is obliged to enter into partnerships in diverse fields of policy and practice, it should turn the endeavour to the purpose that will best serve its future interests for the preservation of its mission and organisational integrity.

Defining the crime problem and its solution

The expanding demand for partnership activity reflects a growing appreciation of the complexity of a broad range of social problems, including crime, and the consequently poor prospects of resolving them through the typically unco-ordinated efforts of organisations working in comparative isolation (Johnson *et al.* 1990; Glisson 1994; Annie E. Casey Foundation 1995; Orians *et al.* 1995; Lowndes and Skelcher 1998; Mattessich *et al.* 2001; Rosenbaum 2002). Policy-makers' recognition of this, and of the inertia of organisations that continue to operate autonomously in the face of exhortations to do otherwise, is demonstrated in the extent to which they have been willing to subject collaborative participation to statutory mandate. Indeed, it is fair to remark that Mattessich *et al.* caution against '"collaboration mania" among some people who set policy and offer funding' (2001: 34), raising the prospect that we might achieve the denigration of a good idea through indiscriminate application that has been the fate of a number of penal innovations. Those who most welcome the collaborative mood that has characterised much contemporary criminal and social policy-making are also those who strongly counsel its judicious implementation (Annie E. Casey Foundation 1995; Huxham 1996; Mattessich *et al.* 2001).

Nevertheless, in the manner in which it has been interpreted and implemented, the effective practice initiative is curiously insensitive to this mood. Despite the broad, and somewhat ill-defined (Rumgay forthcoming), range of 'criminogenic needs' identified by key promoters of the effective practice drive (Andrews and Bonta 1994), programme development has largely been narrowly focused on cognitive be-havioural treatment. Yet such treatment answers only a small subset of the criminogenic needs described by these authorities (Rumgay forth-coming). Thus a problem which has been widely understood in criminological literature to comprise a complex and dynamic mix of multiple factors ranging from the biological and psychological to the social, cultural and economic (see Rosenbaum 2002 for a summary of this position and its implications for partnership) has been, effectively, reduced to a set of defects in the thinking patterns of offenders. For the probation service, with its long experience of the myriad complexities of dealing with offenders in their family and community contexts, to have bought this restrictive definition of the crime problem is so surprising as to defy any simple explanation, such as the persuasion of overwhelming scientific evidence. It smacks of desperation far more than of faith – a possibility that will be considered later.

The ways in which social problems become defined, and redefined over time, have been the object of much study. Moreover, that such definitions may reflect strategic, political and attitudinal positions more than the fruits of dispassionate research in empirical realities, and that their subsequent redefinitions do not always advance in the manner of progressive enlightenment has been observed many times. The resilience of definitions of social problems as the products of aberrant individuals is particularly notable in this regard. For example, Humphreys and Rappaport (1993) describe the decline in support for the progressive community mental health movement, alongside increasing emphasis on substance abuse programmes during the presidency of Ronald Reagan, remarking that it facilitated an expansion of social control based on the premise of individual fault in the causation of 'our most important social problem'. Similarly, the perception of, and response to, child abuse as a problem of individually deviant parents and incompetent professionals has proved extremely persistent and has distorted social work practice with families, despite the evidence of its relationship to multidimensional social factors (Garbarino and Kostelny 1992; Belsky 1993; Sanders *et al.* 1997). Acceptance of a particular definition of a social problem also has the consequence of directing funding for programmes and research towards those projects that support it, thus narrowing the scope for effective challenge (Humphreys and Rappaport 1993). Thus, control of the definition of an important public issue is a powerful instrument of social organisation (Dalton *et al.* 2001). Moreover, individuals and organisations will 'buy in' to research evidence on the nature of and solution to a particular social problem, notwithstanding its objective validity, in so far as they value the anticipated consequences of their acceptance (Hausman 2002).

Thus the evidence base on which policy-makers, practitioners and the lay public draw for their understanding of social problems such as crime tends to become selectively distorted and fragmented according to the needs, motivations and aspirations of different actors. While, as suggested above, this appears to have happened in the way in which the What Works initiative has been understood and implemented, the directives for practice that flow from it offer few clues as to how to cope with dissent from, or misunderstanding of, the central definition of the crime problem that it promulgates. Indeed, the guidance on implementation largely assumes both the validity and acceptance of the evidential claims.

From the perspective of partnership engagement, however, the variable relationships of individuals and organisations to research-based definitions of the problem which they are charged collectively to tackle are to be *expected*, *accommodated* and *used* to advance the collaborative enterprise. One reason for this integral flexibility derives from the frequently observed problems of communication and conflict that arise when different professions invoke specialised theories of, descriptive vocabularies for and intervention approaches to the problems with which they deal (Bennett and Lawson 1994; Armstrong 1997; Minicucci 1997; Rosenbaum 2002). Equally, not all partners are specialists in crime, experiencing it only as an occasional issue in their work: Morrison, similarly, observes that '(c)ollaboration takes place across groups whose investment in and knowledge base about child protection is so diverse as to appear at times mutually unrecognizable' (1996: 130). The fact that potential partners have been brought to the collaborating table by statutory mandate, the prospect of new funding or even altruism is no guarantee of rapid or sustained agreement between them on project objectives and strategies (Sutton and Cherney 2002). Indeed, Mackintosh describes partnerships as 'sites of *continuing* political and economic renegotiation' (1993: 211, emphasis added). Thus, where crime reduction policies are not understood by alternative agencies to complement other policies with which they are more directly concerned, partners may drift away from the table through loss of interest (Sutton and Cherney 2002). Moreover, power differentials between agencies may create resentments and conflicts that interfere with positive collaborative progress either through their destructive potential or through inappropriate strategies of suppression (Lowndes and Skelcher 1998; Crawford 1999; Rosenbaum 2002; Sutton and Cherney 2002).

Another reason for accommodating flexible – and not entirely accurate by research standards – definitions of the problems at stake stems from the trend for inclusion of lay members of the public in consultations and projects targeting crime prevention and offender management. There is, to my knowledge at least, scant evidence of communities (or partner organisations for that matter) demanding programmes for the correction of the cognitive deficits of their offending members as the preferred solution to such pervasive problems as poverty, disadvantage and social disorder. A number of studies have remarked on the disappointing failure of local community residents to appreciate either social scientific knowledge of crime problems or the priorities for their resolution that are set at central policy-making level. Of particular interest here is the tendency for community residents to conflate specific crime problems with broader quality-of-life concerns (Hausman 2002; Mair and Jamel 2002; Clear and Cadora 2003).

The wise collaborator is advised to adapt crime prevention planning to include these expectations of broader social opportunities and neighbourhood improvement in order to keep partners at the table and to retain local goodwill towards the project (Mackintosh 1993; Mattessich et al. 2001; Hausman 2002). Such accommodation of organisations and individuals with alternative perspectives on crime and its resolution appears as a distraction from the real task of crime prevention when viewed from the perspective of a restrictive definition of the problem, particularly one that is couched in offenders' unique deviance from normality. Yet we know that crime clusters with multiple social problems of poverty, environmental decay, unemployment and sickness (Social Exclusion Unit 1998). As Sanders et al. remark, when 'child abuse is simply one manifestation of the multiple deprivations suffered by children growing up in impoverished families and neighbourhoods' (1997: 153), it makes little sense to single out that problem for an intensification of resources that serves largely to impoverish broader family and community support services (also Munro 1999). Similarly, to treat criminal behaviour in isolation from the social and economic contexts in which it disproportionately arises wastes the potential resources of co-operative effort for community improvement, notwithstanding the compromises that may be necessary along the way

(Rumgay 2001). Thus, the inclusion of alternative perspectives is viewed, not merely as a necessary encumbrance of partnership, but as vital to ensuring that problem-solving strategies do not simply reflect the limited repertoires of a few dominant agencies (Rosenbaum 2002).

Thus the partnership perspective shifts the focus of attention in understanding crime problems from a restricted concern with unique attributes of offenders to the systemic relationships between the personal, social, health and economic problems of those neighbourhoods where crime proliferates. Consequently, the solution to crime problems is also viewed systemically, rather than individually, couched less in terms of specific treatment programmes for the correction of offenders' faults, and more in terms of the relationships between the agencies charged with tackling each of those broader problems. Indeed, as partnerships evolve, the requirements of *systemic* change are expected to lead to fundamental changes *within* the partners themselves, in terms of their organisational structures, operating methods and ethos (Mackintosh 1993; Annie E. Casey Foundation 1995; Rosenbaum 2002). Thus Mackintosh argues that 'partnerships are one, quite important, site where broader processes of social and economic change are fought out' (1993: 213).

This broad systemic perspective is not, as is commonly assumed, an evasion of personal responsibility in the lifestyles, motivations and decisions of offenders. Rather, it represents an approach that understands and tackles those aspects of criminality in the community contexts within which they develop, in which multiple problems, including crime, impoverish the opportunities of all residents. Such a contextual approach recognises the importance of the relationships between offenders and their communities in seeking partnership arrangements that protect the public, hold offenders accountable for their behaviour and offer them a pathway towards reintegration (Karp and Clear 2001). Moreover, it explains and justifies the probation service's resource expenditure in the partnership enterprise, and joins it to the contemporary mood for collaboration at central policy-making and local practice levels.

Implementing the solution

No writer in the field of partnerships pretends to underestimate the difficulty of the enterprise, for 'comprehensive system reform is the path of most resistance' (Annie E. Casey Foundation 1995: 9). The partnership focus on systems as the targets for change challenges the inertia of organisations that have been long accustomed to discrete, categorical, rather than integrated, cross-disciplinary approaches to the social problems that concern them. Literature of interest to those who contemplate the partnership route is replete with warnings about the level of commitment in time, effort and resources that will be required for their endeavour to bear fruit (Annie E. Casey Foundation 1995; Huxham 1996; Rumgay 2000; Rosenbaum 2002). Notwithstanding the level of statutory mandate for collaboration, therefore, it is understandable that the probation service might cautiously moderate its investment, with the uneven results already observed.

Nevertheless, the implementation of the What Works agenda has consumed enormous resources at central and local levels. The reasons for this have been predictable from the start. First, psychological programmes that show promising results in the controlled clinical environments in which they are developed are notoriously disappointing when transferred to community settings. A complex combination of factors can account for this, including, for example the costs of transition to an unfamiliar style of practice (Backer *et al.* 1986); professional responses ranging from bureaucratic inertia to outright hostility (Repucci and Saunders 1974; Backer *et al.* 1986; Bernfeld 2001; Dalton *et al.* 2001); failure of programme innovators to engage potential users' interest or to instigate rewards for their involvement (Backer *et al.* 1986; Dalton *et al.* 2001); external pressure from powerful groups such as funders, political representatives, oppositional professionals or client advocates (Repucci and Saunders 1974; Backer *et al.* 1986; Bernfeld 2001; Edwards *et al.* 2001); and the inability of the programme directors to control the contingencies of the natural setting (Repucci and Saunders 1974).

Secondly, the attempt to overcome such problems has appealed to the contemporary faith in centralised prescription, monitoring, audit and sanction of policy implementation for constraining the irritating tendency of professionals to diversify and moderate their practice in light of their perceptions of immediate opportunities, challenges and preferences (Boyne 1998; O'Neill 2002). In so doing, the What Works initiative has failed to appreciate the well established observation that '(p)sychological innovations are operator-dependent, not standardised' (Dalton *et al.* 2001: 316). The result, for the What Works experiment in piloting accredited programmes through 'pathfinder' initiatives in selected areas, is clearly spelt out in a recent report on their progress: administrative overload compounded by inadequate support staffing; unsystematic collection of vast quantities of monitoring data without prospect of their constructive utilisation (see O'Neill 2002 for commentary on this contemporary phenomenon); and, despite the pretensions of the enterprise to standardisation of practice, local variations in implementation based on professional perceptions of need (Hollin *et al.* 2002).

Thus, huge commitments of organisational resources and staff energies have been spent in the quest for standardised implementation of programmes narrowly targeted at those specific groups of offenders who meet their entry criteria. Yet that quest has thus far been thwarted in the context of a small set of pathfinder projects dedicated to the implementation endeavour, raising the prospect that national roll-out of these programmes will be characterised by wide-scale subversion of central policy intentions. Indeed, all the evidence of research on professional behaviour in public bureaucracies, including probation, tells us that this continuing re-emergence of discretion between the interstices of central control is entirely predictable (e.g. McCleary 1978; Lipsky 1980; Rumgay and Brewster 1996). Nevertheless, the report insists that 'programmes should be fixed once the Joint Accreditation Panel awards accreditation and the programmes are to be evaluated' (Hollin *et al.* 2002: 41), as if in anticipation that tablets of stone can be relied upon to act as effective determinants of human behaviour, despite compelling evidence to the contrary that has accumulated since the technique was first tried in biblical times.

The partnership enterprise offers a very different perspective on this battle for central control of local practice. The partnership approach *expects* projects to vary across locations, to change over time and to develop unique adaptations of 'model' programmes in light of local conditions. Thus, effective innovations in community provision actively attend to the history, culture and contemporary attributes of the specific neighbourhoods in which they are developed, as does the process of their successful transfer to alternative settings (Dalton *et al.* 2001). When supporting mechanisms of clear leadership, objective setting and lines of communication are in place to prevent project drift and 'collaborative inertia' (Huxham 1996), review and adaptation of specific goals and methods in light of progress and altered contingencies are regarded as positive and beneficial to the collaborative process and its outcomes (Annie E. Casey Foundation 1995; Dalton *et al.* 2001; Mattessich *et al.* 2001; Rosenbaum 2002). Moreover, such creativity, rather than standardised replication, is regarded as crucial to the local ownership, vitality and endurance of the enterprise (Dalton *et al.* 2001).

The most successful partnership ventures undertaken by the probation service exemplify creative adaptations to unique variations in constraints and opportunities and, moreover, would make little sense if they did not reflect local conditions in this way (Rumgay 2000). Moreover, it is arguably indefensible for community support services to be skewed towards special provision for offenders while their law-abiding neighbours suffer continuing disadvantage (Rumgay 2001). Thus recent explorations of the dimensions of partnership approaches to community safety and offender supervision emphasise 'place' as a determining influence, not only on the nature of the crime problems experienced within a neighbourhood but also on the formulation of locally relevant and valued responses (Karp and Clear 2002; Clear and Cadora 2003).

This observation does not imply a demand for a laissez-faire approach to practice development at central level, nor is it a licence for indiscriminate or atheoretical local innovation. Rather it points to the need to strike a balance between 'top down' direction and 'grass roots' initiative. Indeed, commentary on multi-agency collaborations reveals a strong consensus that the issue at stake is not a choice between one or other approach, but the means to establishing such a balance between central policy-making and implementation guidance and local flexibility (Provan and Milward 1995; Hassett and Austin 1997; O'Looney 1997; Dalton et al. 2001). If anything, top-down directions to develop multi-agency partnerships have been remiss, not in pursuing the advantages of the collaborative approach in principle but in their failure to provide the supportive infrastructure that is needed in terms of preparation time for the complex challenges of implementation, training in the skills needed for effectiveness and dissemination of good practice examples (Rumgay 2000; Mair and Jamel 2002).

Exclusivity and exclusion

The Home Office's interim evaluation of the pathfinder projects (Hollin et al. 2002) reveals worries on the part of probation staff as to the exclusivity of the programmes they were running. Programmes were alleged to be dominated by male referrals, strongly masculine in orientation and to require unrealistic literacy competence. The scope of programmes was challenged. For example, on the one hand staff complained that the cut-off points on the formal assessment instruments denied many offenders the opportunity of programmes from which they could benefit. On the other hand, substance misuse programmes, while recruiting broadly, appeared to target a particular stage in a drug-using career, thus inviting high drop-out rates among both chaotic users and those who had already achieved substantial stability.

The research team concludes: 'a lack of consensus about who is an appropriate referral is felt to be partly a reflection of the present state of knowledge with regard to treatment for individual offenders' (Hollin *et al*. 2002: 42). While this may be true it is a rather odd admission in the context of a drive for effective practice in which confidence – if not certainty – has been a hallmark. Perhaps more poignantly, these conflicts highlight the inadequacy of narrowly targeted programmes focused on specific behaviours to cater for the diversity of offenders' needs.

Drop-out rates on all but one pathfinder programme have been worryingly high, ranging upwards from 24 per cent and achieving 100 per cent at one programme. The research team repeatedly advises stronger screening processes, yet it is not clear what this is expected to achieve. In so far as it might increase completion rates, it seems that this can only be achieved by reducing still further the numbers of offenders entering the programmes, ensuring that only the 'best risks' are admitted. What, then, is to be the nature and quality of the service offered to the rest, who will be, by definition, the most vulnerable by virtue of their complex needs? This question becomes even more pertinent when the extent to which resources have been diverted to the programmes from which these offenders are excluded is taken into account. Yet the probation service, of all agencies, has no need to relearn the lessons of younger projects such as the New Deal for the un-employed, that the most vulnerable programme participants require intensive, individualised and extended support if they are to overcome their multiple barriers to social inclusion (Millar 2000; see also Fletcher 2001 on employment partnerships for offenders).

Drop-out rates are a sensitive issue in the effective practice initiative since offenders who fail to complete programmes appear to fare particularly badly in terms of reconviction (Raynor and Vanstone 1997; Probation Studies Unit 2000). (One programme manual recommends warning recruits about their poor prognosis in the event of dropping out of treatment in the context of its advice on lessening their anxiety! [Home Office undated].) This suggests that, while a programme may benefit those who are able both to enter and to complete it, a substantial number may be harmed by it. Add to this number the lack of any overt interest in service development for those who are excluded from the programmes, and one must begin to wonder whether the harms inflicted outweigh the good that is conferred.

Similar questions have begun to be asked in the field of child protection, with growing appreciation of the negative effects of inter-ventions: those that do not lead to positive identification of child maltreatment are not simply neutral but damaging to the families involved; and intensive investment in screening for abuse impoverishes the support available to families that do not pass that test for service delivery (Farmer and Owen 1995; Sanders *et al.* 1997; Munro 1999). Likewise, drugs services in the 1980s retreated from a brief flirtation with one-dimensional, confrontational programmes that damaged the prospects of recovery of the majority of addicts who were unable to rise to the challenge of rapid withdrawal and abstinence (Berridge 1993; Mitcheson 1994).

In line with the trend in drugs treatment, the partnership approach facilitates embracement of a harm minimisation perspective on offender rehabilitation (Rumgay 2000, 2001). The partnership perspective observes that offenders share in the problems of non-offending disadvantaged groups. From this point of view, provision of support services to those groups can be improved by integrated multi-agency practice. Thus, the partnership approach looks to inclusion of offenders in mainstream provision, alongside other disadvantaged groups, rather than exclusion from narrowly targeted programmes when they are expected to fail. In so far as offenders require special assistance, it is to enhance their access to, and ability to utilise, mainstream services. This is, in itself, an ambitious and demanding enterprise when considered in light of the, often mutual, avoidance and severance of contact between offenders and community support services (e.g. Lewis 1982; Kemp 1997; Burney 1999; Rumgay 2000; Abel 2001).

Effectiveness, evaluation and accountability

As stated earlier, this is not the place to rehearse critiques of the evidence base for the What Works initiative as it has been understood and implemented. In the light of the foregoing arguments, however, one particular observation is pertinent to discussion of the evaluation of partnership effectiveness. Hough, observing the current popularity of cognitive behavioural techniques, remarks that their apparent effectiveness may derive from their accord with contemporary cultural perspectives on social problems and their treatment: 'address(ing) questions about social responsibility in a technical, morally neutral way ... is probably very helpful at this precise point in our social and cultural history' (2000: 256). It is worth bearing in mind that the current reification of 'cognitive deficits' as 'objects' to be corrected by clinical programmes (as laser treatment corrects irregularities in the lens of the eye) belies their real status as conceptual constructs within a particular theoretical approach. Moreover, the assumption that programmes that have been frozen in time at the point of accreditation will always provide us with satisfying solutions to the problem of criminal behaviour contradicts everything we know about the dynamic nature both of social phenomena themselves and their cultural definitions.

Thus, our understanding of What Works is necessarily incomplete. The impact of scientific evidence on social programmes owes at least as much to the inverse, often self-serving relationship between empirical research and policy as to the strength of its conclusions (Berridge and Thom 1996; see also Chapters 2 and 3 of this volume). In short, then, there is not a contest between the empirical realities of the 'hard science' of What Works against the 'soft', abstract and value-laden aspirations of alternative approaches such as the partnership model. Nevertheless, without some attention to the evaluation of effectiveness within the partnership approach, this discussion would be open to allegations of ignoring the need for objective evidence of its worth.

As we have seen, the effective practice enterprise currently lacks a realistic, efficient approach to the monitoring of programme implementation. Tilley's trenchant critique of the 'recipe book' approach to delivery of programmes exposes the fault-line in this attempt to constrain practice within a standardised script: 'Enforcing the adequate is in effect to engage in mediocratisation. Evaluators steering us towards it belong to a new class of evidence-based mediocrats' (2001: 95). Tilley calls for practitioners 'to be (evidence-based) theory learners, users, refiners and developers, not mechanical deliverers of standard programmes implemented with integrity' (2001: 94).

The reflective practice called for by Tilley is precisely the type of informed professional discretion that, as we have seen, is assumed in the partnership approach. In this perspective, practitioners' refusal to be wholly bound by the 'recipe book' reflects their desire for fulfilment through ownership of the project and is a source of energy to be harnessed rather than eliminated (Dalton et al. 2001). Successful partnerships have repeatedly shown the enduring commitment to a project's future that comes from such ownership through creativity (Rumgay 2000). Indeed, Hausman (2002) suggests that enforced standardisation of practice not only fits poorly with the partnership goals of community empowerment but is also more likely to invite estrangement of potentially supportive agencies through the demise of existing, locally valued projects.

Preservation of local autonomy within common codes of practice need not inevitably lead to immeasurability and incomparability, if professional accountability rests on results rather than process (Murphy-Berman et al. 2000). Here the problem of establishing evaluation standards that are capable of accommodating local variation in design and evolutionary changes in individual projects is regarded as a problem for research methodology rather than, as it is commonly viewed by frustrated evaluators, implementation anarchy (Cook and Roehl 1993; Murphy-Berman *et al.* 2000; Berkowitz 2001). This is not a licence for indiscriminate practice but, rather, demands research guidance on those elements of programmes that are crucial to their success and those that may be optional (Armstrong 1997; Dalton *et al.* 2001; Reilly 2001; Hausmann 2002). Model programmes thus acquire the status of guides that permit local variations based on informed choice.

Evaluation of the partnership approach in action recognises that its effectiveness is likely to derive from interaction effects accruing from multidimensional programmes (Klitzner 1993; Provan and Milward 1995; Rosenbaum 2002; Sanderson 2002). Moreover, the partnership literature acknowledges, far more than the currently favoured effective practice evidence appears to, the difficulty of attributing cause for any changes that occur to the effects of a single intervention, when social welfare and criminal justice agencies are in constant states of flux and a range of community-wide programmes are being introduced over the same time period (Klitzner 1993; Martin and Sanderson 1999). Thus outcome evaluation of multifaceted partnership programmes would consider the summative impact of the different contributing projects on broad-level measures of community well-being (Murphy-Berman *et al.* 2000).

This does not mean that process is unimportant. Indeed, partnerships are known for their ability to flounder as preoccupation with internal interactions between partners obscures the progress towards goal achievement (Wolff 2001). A range of partnership literature now exists to guide the process of partnership development and activity towards project completion (e.g. Hassett and Austin 1997; Dalton *et al.* 2001; Mattessich *et al.* 2001; Wolff 2001).

Summary

The What Works initiative has been remarkable for the extent to which it has been driven from the top. Partnership, however, even when statutorily mandated, relies on grass-roots support for its accomplishments. Table 6.1 expresses some of the tensions between 'top down' and 'grass roots' approaches to community provision for offenders exposed by this comparison of the effective practice initiative, as it has been understood and implemented thus far, and a partnership perspective.

Table 6.1 Two models of integrated provision

	Top down	Grass roots
Policy	Crime reduction	Social exclusion
Direction	Central government	Local agreements
Funding	Secure	Insecure
Provision	Standardised	Diverse
Access	Equal	Uneven
Mandate	What works	What's needed
Partnership	Contractual	Collaborative
Programmes	Standardised Accredited Targeted Coerced	Local adaptations Inclusive Mixed voluntary/coerced
Success	Reduced reconvictions	Reduced need

While central policy tends to emanate from a specific primary objective such as crime reduction, local collaborations, as we have seen, thrive when there is a broader stated aim capable of accommodating diverse interests. It is precisely this accommodation that keeps partners at the 'negotiating table' (Mackintosh 1993; Hausmann 2002). Indeed, the whole point of partnership, in contrast to specialist isolation, is to pool diversity of expertise and resources (Chavis 2001). Thus collaborative grass-roots projects targeting social exclusion might more readily offer the flexibility of purpose required to sustain motivation and effort among partners with different perspectives and priorities. Top-down approaches take their direction from central policy-making level, while grass roots operate on the basis of local agreements that reflect unique conditions in terms of the particular set of statutory and voluntary sector partners, opportunities and constraints. Funding for an enterprise mandated by central authority is generally more secure, at least in the early stages of the project, while grass-roots initiatives often struggle to find funding from multiple and impermanent sources.

Where the top-down agenda strives for standardisation of provision, grass-roots partnerships embrace local diversity. In the partnership context, effective leadership may be seen in management of a fluid, and sometimes volatile, external environment to enhance staff capacity to cope, rather than control of the behaviour of front-line practitioners (Menefee 1997). A theoretical advantage of standardisation is equality of access to the service, while opportunities are notoriously unevenly distributed when left to the discretion of local areas. This would hopefully be true in terms of geographical availability although, as we have seen, access to programmes accredited through the What Works initiative is restricted to those who meet their entry criteria.

The mandate for service type in the top-down approach is what works in terms of its specific primary objective, while the broader remit of grass-roots initiatives requires a local perspective on what is needed to resolve a community's problems. Within the top-down What Works agenda there is little acknowledgement of, or scope for, interorganisational relationships other than those based on contracts for provision of elements of accredited programmes. A grass-roots approach aspires to a collaborative style of multi-agency relationships that will address issues in negotiation, power sharing and resource interdependence. Top-down practice development directs the implementation of programmes that are centrally accredited, targeted on specific offender populations and coerced. Collaborative grass-roots initiatives, however, will include intervention strategies that are adapted to local contingencies, are accessible to a broad range of community residents with common problems and thus capable of mixing voluntary and coerced clientele. Finally, while success in the top-down approach is measured narrowly in terms of reduced convictions, the broader remit of grass-roots collaborations will look to reduced levels of need in local communities.

In so far as the top-down approach yields an integrated structure of provision, it is a relatively limited form of integration in the sense of coherence between a focused policy objective and its implementation in respect of a narrow target group. The grass-roots approach aspires to integration of services across disciplines and client groups, which is altogether a broader, more multifaceted and more inclusive conceptualisation of a policy goal and the pathways to its achievement. While there is undoubtedly a place for the former approach, particularly for the most challenging groups of offenders with specific needs relating to their rehabilitation and community safety, it is the argument of this chapter that this limited project should not overwhelm the capacity of the probation service to invest vigorously in the latter enterprise. Moreover, while central guidance is needed for policy direction and good practice dissemination (O'Looney 1994; Foster-Fishman *et al.* 2001), it should not suppress the vitality of local flexibility and creativity.

Conclusion

Unlike the silent hound in the Sherlock Holmes tale, the partnership dog is barking furiously. Were we to listen, we would hear its message clearly: the probation service's commitment to mandatory partnerships is increasing in depth and breadth; the time, effort and resources being committed to partnerships demand a defensible return; and the partnership enterprise offers an alternative, more realistic and more palatable vision of the service's mission, grounded in its own traditions, than one founded on delivery of narrowly defined offending behaviour programmes. Yet few, if any, are listening to the valiant hound's attempts to attract attention.

How has the What Works agenda, with its heavy emphasis on discrete behavioural programmes, achieved such supremacy over the holistic – and altogether more wholesome – alternative of a partnership agenda? A possible answer lies in the nature of the perceived threat to the probation service that underpinned the transformative efforts of the What Works pioneers. Mair (see Chapter 2) describes that threat as striking at the probation service's very survival. The challenge to the probation service's existence, which – whatever its objective likelihood – was widely believed and feared, would not be answered by a claim to offer an effective pathway to offender reintegration through multi-agency networks linking them to opportunities in the mainstream of service delivery. Indeed, in Mair's analysis, partnerships were part of the problem in so far as they challenged the probation service's pretension to unique expertise in dealing with offenders. What the service needed was a plausible claim to be the sole agency capable of delivering the specialised types of response required to reduce the offending behaviour of its clientele. Cognitive behavioural psychology provided the theoretical base for the argument that offenders suffered from specific deficits, setting them apart from conventional people and thereby conventional therapies. Meta-analysis supplied the evidence on which to base the claim that particular types of specialised programmes were necessary for the correction of those deficits.

Effective multi-agency integration consumes time, effort, resources and expertise. Organisations do not embark upon such an enterprise unless they perceive the potential gains to outweigh these costs (Provan and Milward 1995; Finn 1996; Huxham 1996). Yet when organisational effectiveness is commonly measured by the performance of activities solely attributable to the agency under scrutiny, multi-agency effectiveness is unlikely to be a valued commodity since it looks to the network of partners as a whole for its impact (Provan and Milward 1995; Rosenbaum 2002).

Nevertheless, the claim that the probation service is uniquely equipped to provide cognitive behavioural therapies to offenders does not bear scrutiny for long. Yet the search for another organisation capable of 'brokerage' (Lowndes and Skelcher 1998) between the worlds of criminal justice and social welfare, with equal appreciation of both and without prejudice towards either, would be long, hard and certainly fruitless. The success of the contemporary partnership enterprise requires just such an organisation, with '(c)redibility and legitimacy ... to speak with authority and candor, to be taken seriously ... and to become a respected source of information' (Annie E. Casey Foundation 1995). Indeed, it has been remarked that examples of the probation service's practice excellence and strongest commitment derive from those projects in which it contributes collaboratively to the overall health of its local communities (Rumgay 2000). Thus the partnership approach, properly presented, holds the promise of securing professional support through its appeal to the service's established traditions (Dalton *et al.* 2001).

However, it has not been argued here that the probation service engages, or should engage, in partnership out of some altruistic sense of philanthropic mission and self-consciousness of its own social importance, although it would be gratifying to think that it operates on the basis of such lofty motives. While this argument does not reject ethical values as an important guide for the service's future choices, a more instrumental point is being made here. Just as the choice to move down the path of the What Works agenda was far more an instrumental decision than it was a response to certainties borne out of effectiveness research, so too might partnerships be used to further the service's own ends. In many respects the service has not chosen the partnership pathway for itself. Rather, policy and statutory mandate have thrust that path upon it. The expenditure of resources thus to be committed could be put to good use in securing the service's future role in the community. It is not an effort to be wasted, but an opportunity to be exploited.

References

Abel, E.M. (2001) 'Comparing the social service utilization, exposure to violence and trauma symptomology of domestic violence female "victims" and female "batterers"', *Journal of Family Violence*, 16 (4): 401–20.

Andrews, D. and Bonta, J. (1994) *The Psychology of Criminal Conduct*. Cincinnati, OH: Anderson.

Annie E. Casey Foundation (1995) *The Path of Most Resistance: Reflections on Lessons Learned from New Futures*. Baltimore, MD: Annie E. Casey Foundation.

Armstrong, K.L. (1997) 'Launching a family-centred, neighbourhood-based human services system: lessons from working the hallways and street corners', *Administration in Social Work*, 21 (3/4): 109–26.

Backer, T.E., Liberman, R.P. and Kuehnel, T.G. (1986) 'Dissemination and adoption of innovative psychosocial interventions', *Journal of Consulting and Clinical Psychology*, 54 (1): 111–18.

Belsky, J. (1993) 'Etiology of child maltreatment: a developmental-ecological analysis.' *Psychological Bulletin*, 114 (3): 413–34.

Bennett, L. and Lawson, M. (1994) 'Barriers to cooperation between domestic-violence and substance-abuse programs', *Families in Society: The Journal of Contemporary Human Services*, May: 277–86.

Berkowitz, B. (2001) 'Studying the outcomes of community-based coalitions', *American Journal of Community Psychology*, 29 (2): 213–27.

Bernfeld, G.A. (2001) 'The struggle for treatment integrity in a "dis-integrated" service delivery system', in G.A. Bernfeld *et al.* (eds) *Offender Rehabilitation in Practice: Implementing and Evaluating Effective Programs*. Chichester: Wiley, 167–88.

Berridge, V. (1993) 'AIDS and British drug policy: continuity or change?', in V. Berridge and P. Strong (eds) *AIDS and Contemporary History*. Cambridge: Cambridge University Press, 135–56.

Berridge, V. and Thom, B. (1996) 'Research and policy: what determines the relationship?', *Policy Studies*, 17 (1): 23–33.

Boyne, G.A. (1998) 'Competitive tendering in local government: a review of theory and evidence', *Public Administration*, 76 (Winter): 695–712.

Burney, E. (1999) *Crime and Banishment: Nuisance and Exclusion in Social Housing*. Winchester: Waterside Press.

Chavis, D.M. (2001) 'The paradoxes and promise of community coalitions', *American Journal of Community Psychology*, 29 (2): 309–20.

Clear, T.R. and Cadora, E. (2003) *Community Justice*. Belmont, CA: Wadsworth/Thompson Learning.

Cook, R.F. and Roehl, J.A. (1993) 'National evaluation of the Community Partnership Program: preliminary findings', in R.C. Davis *et al.* (eds) *Drugs and the Community: Involving Community Residents in Combatting the Sale of Illegal Drugs*. Springfield, IL: Charles C. Thomas, 225–48.

Crawford, A. (1999) *The Local Governance of Crime: Appeals to Community and Partnerships*. Oxford: Oxford University Press.

Dalton, J.H., Elias, M.J. and Wandersman, A. (2001) *Community Psychology: Linking Individuals and Communities*. Belmont, CA: Wadsworth/Thompson Learning.

Department of Health (1998) *Modernising Social Services: Promoting Independence, Improving Protection, Raising Standards* (Cm 4169). London: Department of Health.

Department of Health (1999) *Modernising Mental Health Services: Safe, Sound and Supportive*. London: Department of Health.

Doyle, A.C. (1894) 'The Memoirs of Sherlock Holmes: The Adventure of Silver Blaze'. Reprinted in Sir A.C. Doyle *Sherlock Holmes: The Complete Illustrated Short Stories*. London: Chancellor Press, 1985, pp. 235–56.

Edwards, D.L., Schoenwald, S.K., Henggeler, S.W. and Strother, K.B. (2001) 'A multilevel perspective on the implementation of multisystemic therapy (MST): attempting dissemination with fidelity', in G.A. Bernfeld *et al.* (eds) *Offender Rehabilitation in Practice: Implementing and Evaluating Effective Programs*. Chichester: Wiley, 97–119.

Farmer, E. and Owen, M. (1995) *Child Protection Practice: Private Risks and Public Remedies*. London: HMSO.

Finn, C.B. (1996) 'Utilizing stakeholder strategies for positive collaboration outcomes', in C. Huxham (ed.) *Creating Collaborative Advantage*. London: Sage, 152–64.

Fletcher, D.R. (2001) 'Ex-offenders, the labour market and the new public administration', *Public Administration*, 79 (4): 871–91.

Foster-Fishman, P.G., Salem, D.A., Allen, N.A. and Fahrbach, K. (2001) 'Facilitating interorganizational collaboration: the contributions of inter-organizational alliances', *American Journal of Psychology*, 29 (6): 875–905.

Garbarino, J. and Kostelny, K. (1992) 'Child maltreatment as a community problem.' *Child Abuse and Neglect*, 16: 455–64.

Glisson, C. (1994) 'The effect of services coordination teams on outcomes for children in state custody', *Administration in Social Work*, 18 (4): 1–23.

Hassett, S. and Austin, M.J. (1997) 'Service integration: something old and something new', *Administration in Social Work*, 21 (3/4): 9–29.

Hausman, A.J. (2002) 'Implications of evidence-based practice for community health', *American Journal of Community Psychology*, 30 (3): 453–67.

Hollin, C., McGuire, J., Palmer, E., Bilby, C., Hatcher, R. and Holmes, A. (2002) *Introducing Pathfinder Programmes into the Probation Service: An Interim Report*. Home Office Research Study 247. London: Home Office Research, Development and Statistics Directorate.

Home Office (1998) *Joining Forces to Protect the Public: Prisons–Probation. A Consultation Document*. London: Home Office.

Home Office (undated) *Think First Management Manual*. London: Home Office.

Hough, M. (2000) 'Evaluation: a "realistic" perspective', in J. Fountain *et al.* (eds) *Understanding and Responding to Drug Use: The Role of Qualitative Research*. EMCDDA Scientific Monograph Series 4. Luxembourg: Office for Official Publications of the European Communities, 253–7.

Humphreys, K. and Rappaport, J. (1993) 'From the community mental health movement to the war on drugs: a study in the definition of social problems', *American Psychologist*, 48 (8): 892–901.

Huxham, C. (1996) 'Collaboration and collaborative advantage', in C. Huxham (ed.) *Creating Collaborative Advantage*. London: Sage, 1–18.

Johnson, C.A., Pentz, M.A., Weber, M.D., Dwyer, J.H., Baer, N., MacKinnon, D.P., Hansen, W.B. and Flay, B.R. (1990) 'Relative effectiveness of comprehensive community programming for drug abuse prevention with high-risk and low-risk adolescents', *Journal of Consulting and Clinical Psychology*, 58 (4): 447–56.

Karp, D.R. and Clear, T.R. (2002) 'Preface. The community justice frontier: an introduction', in D.R. Karp and T.R. Clear (eds) *What is Community Justice? Case Studies of Restorative Justice and Community Supervision*. Thousand Oaks: CA, Sage, ix–xvi.

Kemp, P.A. (1997) 'The characteristics of single homeless people in England', in R. Burrows *et al.* (eds) *Homelessness and Social Policy*. London: Routledge, 69–87.

Klitzner, M. (1993) 'A public health/dynamic systems approach to community-wide alcohol and other drug initiatives', in R.C. Davis, A.J. Lurigio, D.P. Rosenbaum (eds) *Drugs and the Community: Involving Community Residents in Combatting the Sale of Illegal Drugs*. Springfield, IL: Charles C. Thomas, 201–24.

Lewis, D.K. (1982) 'Female ex-offenders and community programs: barriers to service', *Crime and Delinquency*, 28 (1): 40–51.

Lipsky, M. (1980) *Street-level Bureaucracy: Dilemmas of the Individual in Public Services*. New York, NY: Russell Sage.

Lowndes, V. and Skelcher, C. (1998) 'The dynamics of multi-organizational partnerships: an analysis of changing modes of governance', *Public Administration*, 76 (Summer): 313–33.

Mackintosh, M. (1993) 'Partnership: issues of policy and negotiation', *Local Economy*, 7 (3): 210–24.

Mair, G. and Jamel, J. (2002) 'Crime and disorder partnerships in Liverpool.' Paper presented at the European Society of Criminology Conference, Toledo, 5–7 September.

Martin, S. and Sanderson, I. (1999) 'Evaluating public policy experiments: measuring outcomes, monitoring processes or managing pilots?' *Evaluation*, 5 (3): 245–58.

Mattessich, P.W., Murray-Close, M. and Monsey, B.R. (2001) *Collaboration: What Makes it Work* (2nd edn). Saint Paul, MN: Amherst H. Wilder Foundation.

McCleary, R. (1978) *Dangerous Men: The Sociology of Parole*. Beverley Hills, CA: Sage.

Menefee, D. (1997) 'Strategic administration of nonprofit human service organizations: a model for executive success in turbulent times', *Administration in Social Work*, 21 (2): 1–19.

Millar, J. (2000) *Keeping Track of Welfare Reform: The New Deal Programmes*. York: Joseph Rowntree Foundation.

Minicucci, C. (1997) 'Assessing a family-centered neighbourhood service agency: the Del Paso Heights model', *Administration in Social Work*, 21 (3/4): 127–43.

Mitcheson, M. (1994) 'Drug clinics in the 1970s', in J. Strang and M. Gossop (eds) *Heroin Addiction and Drug Policy: The British System*. Oxford: Oxford University Press, 178–91.

Morrison, T. (1996) 'Partnership and collaboration: rhetoric and reality', *Child Abuse and Neglect*, 20 (2): 127–40.

Munro, E.M. (1999) 'Protecting children in an anxious society', *Health, Risk and Society*, 1 (1): 117–27.

Murphy-Berman, V., Schnoes, C. and Chambers, J.M. (2000) 'An early stage evaluation model for assessing the effectiveness of comprehensive community initiatives: three case studies in Nebraska', *Evaluation and Program Planning*, 23: 157–63.

O'Looney, J. (1997) 'Marking progress toward service integration: learning to use evaluation to overcome barriers', *Administration in Social Work*, 21 (3/4): 31–65.

O'Neill, O. (2002) *A Question of Trust. The BBC Reith Lectures 2002*. Cambridge: Cambridge University Press.

Orians, C.E., Liebow, E.B. and Branch, K.M. (1995) 'Community-based organizations and HIV prevention among Seattle's inner-city teens', *Urban Anthropology*, 24 (1–2): 36–58.

Probation Studies Unit (2000) *Report on the Retrospective Study of the Hereford and Worcester Probation Service Women's Programme*. Oxford: University of Oxford, Centre for Criminological Research, Probation Studies Unit.

Provan, K.G. and Milward, H.B. (1995) 'A preliminary theory of inter-organizational network effectiveness: a comparative study of four community mental health systems', *Administrative Science Quarterly*, 40: 1–33.

Raynor, P. and Vanstone, M. (1997) *Straight Thinking on Probation: The Mid Glamorgan Experiment*. Oxford: University of Oxford, Centre for Criminological Research.

Reilly, T. (2001) 'Collaboration in action: an uncertain process', *Administration in Social Work*, 25 (1): 53–74.

Reppucci, N.D. and Saunders, J.T. (1974) 'Social psychology of behaviour modification: problems of implementation in natural settings', *American Psychologist*, September: 649–60.

Rosenbaum, D.P. (2002) 'Evaluating multi-agency anti-crime partnerships: theory, design and measurement issues', in N. Tilley (ed.) *Evaluation for Crime Prevention*. Crime Prevention Studies Vol. 14. Monsey, NY: Criminal Justice Press, 171–225.

Rumgay, J. (2000) *The Addicted Offender: Developments in British Policy and Practice*. Basingstoke: Palgrave.

Rumgay, J. (2001) 'Accountability in the delivery of community penalties: to whom, for what and why?', in A. Bottoms *et al.* (eds) *Community Penalties: Change and Challenges*. Cullompton: Willan, 126–45.

Rumgay, J. (2003) 'Partnerships in the Probation Service', in M. Nellis and W.H. Chui (eds) *Moving Probation Forward: Evidence and Arguments*. Harlow: Longman/Pearson Education.

Rumgay, J. (forthcoming) 'Living with paradox: community supervision of women offenders', in G. McIvor (ed.) *Women who Offend: Research Highlights in Social Work 44.* London: Jessica Kingsley.

Rumgay, J. and Brewster, M. (1996) 'Restructuring probation in England and Wales: lessons from an American experience'. *The Prison Journal*, 76 (3): 331–47.

Sanders, R., Jackson, S. and Thomas, N. (1997) 'Policy priorities in child protection: perception of risk and agency strategy', *Policy Studies*, 18 (2): 139–58.

Sanderson, I. (2002) 'Evaluation, policy learning and evidence-based policy making', *Public Administration*, 80 (1): 1–22.

Social Exclusion Unit (1998) *Bringing Britain Together: A National Strategy for Neighbourhood Renewal* (Cm 4045). London: HMSO.

Sutton, A. and Cherney, A. (2002) 'Prevention without politics? The cyclical progress of crime prevention in an Australian state', *Criminal Justice*, 2 (3): 325–44.

Tilley, N. (2001) 'Evaluation and evidence-led crime reduction policy and practice', in R. Matthews and J. Pitts (eds) *Crime, Disorder and Community Safety: A New Agenda?* London: Routledge, 81–97.

Wolff, T. (2001) 'A practitioner's guide to successful coalitions', *American Journal of Community Psychology*, 29 (2): 173–91.

Chapter 7

Getting tough or being effective: what matters?[1]

Carol Hedderman and Mike Hough

The aim of this chapter is to examine some of the tensions in current What Works policy about maintaining offenders' compliance with conditions specified as part of probation supervision. How the probation service enforces these conditions is a key policy issue; we argue that a shift of emphasis in enforcement policy would increase the use of community penalties, help probation staff engage with offenders and make it clearer to offenders what is expected of them. We shall argue that a more coherent enforcement strategy would increase the chances of supervision 'working' and would thus strengthen the What Works initiative.

The chapter starts with a 'potted history' of probation since the 1970s. It focuses on enforcement, describing the policy context in which National Standards for supervision were introduced and the way in which legislation sought to re-badge probation and community service as proportionate responses to moderately serious offending rather than diversion from custody. The second part of the chapter summarises the results of three audits carried out under the direction of one of the authors, which demonstrate how enforcement standards became more rigorous through the introduction of successive National Standards. The third part of the chapter draws on empirical studies that shed some light on the degree to which these changes may have affected the effectiveness of probation work with offenders. We present the results of a reconviction study linked to one of the audits; this exploits the natural variation in enforcement regimes between probation areas to test whether offenders respond to these differences. We also examine completion rates and reconviction rates for offenders on Drug Treatment and Testing Orders. The reconviction studies in particular illustrate difficult dilemmas for those who want to maximise the effectiveness of probation in preventing reoffending, while ensuring that community penalties are rigorous and demanding.

The chapter concludes by laying out a new framework for thinking about how the government's enforcement strategies might be revised with a view to balancing the competing aims of maximising justice, reducing reoffending and enhancing sentencer and public confidence in community sentences.

A brief history of enforcement

Supervision in place of custody or following custody is inherently conditional. For example, the United Nations (1951: 4) describes probation as consisting of 'the conditional suspension of punishment while the offender is placed under supervision and is given individual guidance or "treatment"' (cited in Harris 1995). As Harris (1995) points out, providing similar services without sanction would not be probation, it would be social work. What differentiates probation from social work is that the former generally involves the possibility of coercion and the latter – with exceptions – does not.

This coercive feature of probation work has been apparent since the probation service was set up in England and Wales in 1907. The power to return non-compliant offenders to court was available to Police Court missionaries working in London as early as 1872 (King 1958; Dersley 2000). The Probation of Offenders Act 1907 made it clear that when offenders consented to probation supervision, unsatisfactory behaviour would result in a return to court. The court could then impose another penalty for the original offence or impose a fine while allowing supervision to continue.

Dersley (2000) reports that, by the end of the first year, less than 5 per cent of those on probation had been recalled. Part of the reason for this is to be found in the nature of offenders who traditionally formed the core of probation workloads; for most of the service's existence probation work has targeted low-risk offenders who posed very little threat to the community. However it was also true that the criteria for judging breach were poorly defined, and subsequent legislation and guidance through the first half of the twentieth century did little to clarify this. In fact the Probation Rules of 1949 positively encouraged supervisors to use their discretion about the frequency of appointments, taking account of individual offenders' circumstances and progress. Resorting to formal breach proceedings was generally seen as a last resort, although in a very few cases it was acknowledged that early breach might be used as a short sharp shock to get an offender to comply (King 1969). Dersley (2000) notes that this approach fitted well with prevailing concerns about reconciling probation officers' obligations to the court with the necessity of maintaining a positive relationship of trust with the offender.

Willis (1981), in one of the few studies carried out prior to the Criminal Justice Act 1991 and the introduction of National Standards, argued that both probation officers and offenders were more concerned with employment and financial and domestic problems than with control. Fielding (1984) also suggests that supervisors may have been reluctant to breach because it could be interpreted as a measure of their own inability to engage with and reform the offender.

'Nothing works' and diversion from custody

By the early 1980s the traditional optimism about the scope for rehabilitative work with offenders had begun to wane. Martinson's now notorious 'What Works' article (1974) was widely interpreted on both sides of the Atlantic as showing that 'Nothing Works' and 'nothing' here included probation as well as imprisonment. In Britain, a Home Office publication, *The Effectiveness of Sentencing* (Brody 1976), served to consolidate this view. It mattered little that the 'small print' in both publications offered substantial qualifications to their pessimistic tone. For example, Martinson actually concluded that the evidence base was too flawed to be able to draw conclusions about what was effective. As Vennard *et al.* (1997: 2) note these caveats 'tended, however, to be overlooked by those who saw in the article strong empirical support for the rejection of a treatment approach and for return to a just deserts perspective, in which the principle of appropriate and proportionate punishment is paramount in the sentencing decision'. The 'Nothing Works' scepticism was a product of its time. Critics of the rehabilitative enterprise ranged far wider than those retributivists who simply wanted to see tougher punishment. There was the liberal critique by deserts theorists who argued that, however well intentioned, attempts to rehabilitate offenders privileged prevention at the expense of justice. There were also critiques about the 'caring professions' from the radical left, resonant of counter-cultural values, about the damaging over-reach of the state into the lives of individuals;[2] the view was that the medical and social work professions crushed spontaneity and imposed conformity at considerable cost to individuals' well-being. Thus by the start of the 1980s probation could find few allies at any point along the political spectrum.

An important consequence of this, for our purposes, was a redefinition of the probation role, led by probation managers and supported by the Home Office, that carried profound implications for the way the service set about enforcing compliance. It was thought that if there was little to choose between prison and probation in terms of outcome, it would make sense for the probation service to target its efforts on those offenders most at risk of custody, and to woo sentencers by offering them attractive community penalties for this high-risk group. Actuarial scales measuring 'risk of custody', or ROC scales, were developed to help refine the targeting process.

The probation service achieved some success in this 'decarceral' enterprise in the second half of the 1980s, increasing its market share of sentences at the expense of custodial sentences (Home Office 1992). But it almost certainly had the consequence of reducing effort spent on enforcement to securing compliance. If the *raison d'être* of the service had evolved into diversion of offenders from custody at the point of sentence, there was little point in pursuing an enforcement regime that returned them to prison once they had started their orders. Arguably, the overall enterprise damaged relations between probation and sentencers; it probably reduced the latter's confidence in the former, as the probation service was aiming simultaneously to subvert and to support sentencers' intentions.

Punishment in the community and National Standards

There was another change of political direction towards the end of the 1980s. With Douglas Hurd as Home Secretary the Conservative administration continued to pursue a fairly determined decarceral policy. In support of this policy government started to place much more emphasis on probation – 'placing the probation service centre-stage' in the words of the then Minister of State, John Patten. The aim was to reshape probation as a more effective and more plausible alternative to custody than it had been – and been seen to be – in the 1980s. The probation service was no longer to 'assist, advise and befriend' petty and inadequate offenders; its new role was to provide 'punishment in the community', and this was to be 'tough and demanding'. Seen from this perspective, probation orders and community service orders should not be regarded as second-best alternatives to custody but as punishments in their own right. The decarceral policy survived into the early 1990s, as evidenced by the white paper *Crime, Justice and Protecting the Public*

(Home Office 1990) and key provisions in the subsequent Criminal Justice Act 1991.[3] The emphasis on tough and demanding community penalties continues to remain in place, as is discussed below.

It was never totally clear to what extent the policy of 'punishment in the community' was driven by the imperative to contain the prison population and prison expenditure, and to what extent by a commitment to rehabilitating offenders through probation work. Whatever the case, expectation of supervision style and content began to change.

Supervisors were encouraged to police attendance more rigorously. The aim was to bolster the public's and sentencers' confidence in noncustodial options and overcome their image as 'soft options'. Failing to breach for non-compliance was viewed as a sign that supervisors were siding with offenders rather than working in the broader public interest. The Home Office began to draft National Standards for a range of probation functions, starting with National Standards for Community Service in 1989.[4] The formalisation of National Standards continued, and a set covering probation orders, community service orders, combination orders, supervision orders and supervision on licence and pre-sentence reports was introduced in 1992.

Lloyd (1991) described the trend towards tougher enforcement after the introduction of National Standards for community service, with supervisors breaching after three rather than four absences. The number of orders terminated for breach also increased. As these changes were accompanied by an increase in the use of community service, it is reasonable to conclude there was a link. However, Lloyd also warned that overly tough enforcement might have the opposite effect to that intended as sentencers might be discouraged from using the orders if they were asked to deal with too many trivial breaches. He also expressed concern about the way an overzealous use of breach and revocation might affect the prison population.

In the run-up to these changes and shortly after they were introduced, commentators began to speculate how they would affect practice. Drakeford (1993: 299–300) advocated a 'minimalist approach' in which breach was to be treated as a response of last resort. He pointed to the way the Standards allowed room for professional judgement and argued that local guidance should encourage this to be used particularly for offenders with chaotic lifestyles. Broad (1991) was also concerned that the move towards standardisation might have unfortunate and unintended effects, warning that it might lead to officers failing to investigate adequately the reasons for non-attendance in their rush to breach. He also predicted that issuing local guidelines would promote these effects. In contrast, McWilliams and Pease (1990: 22) were concerned that, while seeking to limit the exercise of discretion, local codes of practice would actually serve to drive the use of discretion underground. Thus decision-making would become both more arbitrary and less easy to scrutinise. They argued that statutory control had always been part of the probation officers' role and that the officers 'who collude with the evasion of court-mandated control give the opposite communication to that required'.

Possibly the most important change brought in by the 1992 National Standards was the specification of the number of appointments which should be made ordinarily, and the minimum number which might be made where this could not be achieved. In other respects, the Standards were drafted in such a way as to regularise rather than eliminate the exercise of professional judgement in dealing with absences and other failures to comply. An examination of how probation and community service staff viewed the standards found that they were considered 'helpful in ensuring fair and consistent enforcement practice, and allowed them to use discretion where necessary. However, it was also clear from their replies that probation staff sometimes employed National Standards loosely' (Ellis *et al.* 1996: 54). Unusually, this study also considered how officers encouraged compliance, including setting more frequent appointments,[5] cancelling hours worked when an offender on community service had turned up but behaved badly, revoking early for good behaviour and setting appointments to coincide with other important regular events (usually signing on). Despite Drakeford's (1993) contention that the notion of constructive breach was a fallacy, all the 89 officers interviewed drew a distinction between breaches where the intention was to reinforce respect and encourage compliance and those with a recommendation to revoke. They described using the latter where the order had become unworkable due to repeatedly poor attendance or the offender had otherwise withdrawn his or her co-operation.[6] In either case the officers cautioned that whether breach actually served to discipline or punish was not entirely within their control: 'there is little point in the Probation Service reacting swiftly to breach proceedings if, when an offender fails to answer a summons, the police are slow to enforce the resulting warrant; or the case takes so long to come to court that the order has been completed' (Ellis *et al.* 1996: 52).

'Prison works' – but 'more of the same' for probation

The Conservative government's penal policy saw yet another shift in early 1993. The new year had seen several brutal murders, most notably that of two-year-old James Bulger. The press, led by the *Daily Mail*, made excoriating attacks on the reforms introduced by the 1991 Act, painting a picture of liberal do-gooders wrecking the criminal justice system while crime spiralled out of control. The prison population began to rise almost immediately. In the face of mounting criticism the government began to move away from its decarceral policy, amending the Criminal Justice Act to remove some of the new restrictions on sentencers' powers to pass prison sentences.[7] The amendments actually took effect in August 1993, but sentencers appear to have anticipated the legislation well before this. By October 1994 the government had largely abandoned its decarceral policies. The then Home Secretary, Michael Howard, announced a set of 27 'get tough' policies under the banner 'Prison Works'.

The shift of policy towards the use of custody left probation policy broadly unchanged, though there were increasingly intensive efforts to change the values and ideology of the service. The government continued to press for tougher and more credible community penalties, publishing *Strengthening Punishment in the Community* (Home Office 1995). As its name implies, this green paper discussed how community sentences might be used to deliver punishment and deterrence as well as rehabilitation (Hedderman *et al.* 1999). Changes were made to the system of probation training, breaking the long-standing link with social work training.[8] The year 1995 also saw the introduction of revised and tougher National Standards, which considerably curtailed supervisors' discretion about when to breach and how to respond to first and second failures to attend.

Enforcement under New Labour and What Works

A change of government in 1997 led to some changes in penal policy, but also some continuity. The new administration took a clear policy of non-intervention in relation to sentencing practice, at a time when the populist climate of opinion was continuing to fuel rises in the prison population (see Hough *et al.* 2003). There were some obvious continuities, too, in probation policy, with a continued emphasis on tighter management and tougher enforcement. National Standards were further toughened up in April 2000; as a result there are now very few circumstances in which an absence may be regarded as acceptable and virtually every case in which more than one unacceptable absence occurs will go to court for a breach hearing.

One of the main reasons for the revisions was that Probation Inspectorate 'Quality and Effectiveness' reports which scrutinised individual areas' performance on a common set of measures criticised one area after another during the 1990s for failing to offer appointments in line with National Standards, or to enforce them rigorously. In some cases chiefs were even said to have simply decided not to require staff to work to a particular requirement. By 1998 the service had been criticised by the Home Affairs Select Committee on Alternatives to Custody, who expressed concern about the laxity with which orders were being enforced (House of Commons 1998).

By that point the extent to which cases were breached on or before a third unacceptable absence had been made a key performance indicator (KPI), with a target of 90 per cent. However, there was a lack of clarity about how rates should be calculated when breach was initiated more than once in relation to a single order. This made it possible to generate breach rates of more than 100 per cent, making the results nonsensical. Making breach a KPI also implied that the government's concern with enforcement was purely managerial.

While Labour adopted some key features of the previous administration's penal and probation policy, there were some emerging differences. By the time National Standards 2000 were introduced, if not before, there were signs of a renewed and genuine interest in probation as a tool for reducing crime. Throughout the 1990s there had been a significant shift in thinking among probation professionals and researchers away from the 'nothing works' perspective that had characterised the late 1970s and 1980s. There was an increasing perception that the relevant evaluative research had been mis-represented and over-interpreted. A new What Works research literature was emerging,[9] supporting the more balanced view that 'some things work for some people some of the time'. The Labour administration embraced the principle of evidence-based policy and with it a renewed optimism about rehabilitation – though this included a commitment to rehabilitating offenders while in prison. One especially significant development was the establishment in 1999 of the Correctional Services Accreditation Panel, which 'quality-assured' probation and prison programmes for rehabilitating offenders.

A consistent finding from the What Works literature is that those who fail to complete programmes have worse reconviction results than those who complete and usually worse than control groups.[10] This difference is partly due to selection effects, in that those who are least likely to reoffend are also those who are most likely to complete. However, we also know that offenders can be persuaded, cajoled and coerced into a programme with beneficial effects (see Edmunds *et al.* 1999 for an example relating to drug offenders). To this extent National Standards might be seen as supporting effective practice. However, the idea that programme delivery should incorporate notions of 'pro-social modelling' was also being strongly advocated (HMI Probation 1998). Derived from the work of Trotter (1993), pro-social modelling assumes that positive reinforcement is more effective in securing not only offenders' attendance at programmes but also their active and willing participation. Thus supervisors are expected to praise and reward offenders displaying appropriate, non-criminal behaviour, rather than using negative sanctions to deter non-compliance. The then Chief Inspector suggested that, seen from this perspective, National Standards also: 'belong to offenders who should know what is expected of them and what action will be taken if they fail to comply with the requirements but also what they can expect from the probation service in the way they are being supervised' (Her Majesty's Chief Inspector of Probation 1996 cited in Chapman and Hough 1998). However, aside from offering advice about the number of appointments offenders will be offered, the standards say nothing about the standard of help an offender might reasonably expect or how compliance might be rewarded. They are also couched in terms that focus on prohibiting poor behaviour rather than reinforcing appropriate conduct.

Currently, then, National Standards are expected to promote a variety of objectives. They are expected to promote compliance while also serving to limit discretion, making decision-making more transparent and accountable, measuring officers' (and areas') performance, promoting confidence in community penalties to ensure that courts make use of them, setting probation apart from social work and discouraging collusion between supervisors and offenders. There is a natural tension between at least some of these. In particular, as discussed below, allowing fewer failures before breaching and reducing supervisors' discretion about when to breach may promote public and sentencer confidence, but at the same time it reduces the options and time a supervisor will have actively to encourage compliance. With very limited discretion supervisors may be able to wield a stick but have few positive inducements with which to promote compliance.

Auditing enforcement standards

In 1999, responding to then Home Secretary's complaints about poor enforcement, the Association of Chief Officers of Probation (ACOP)[11] moved to improve matters. Part of the action plan was to arrange for an independent audit of the way court orders and post-release licences were enforced throughout England and Wales. This was supervised by one of the current authors (Hedderman 1999). The audit set a baseline against which to measure subsequent changes in practice, following new guidance from ACOP on enforcement and recording enforcement action. Six months after the first audit, ACOP commissioned a second round of the audit. This showed improvements on most measures, including:

- more timely first appointments;

- a higher proportion of offenders on probation being offered 12 or more appointments; and

- an increase in the proportion of offenders on probation, community service (CS) and post-release licences being dealt with in line with or in excess of National Standards requirements at a first, second or third unacceptable absence.

Although there was still variation between areas, the extent of variation had narrowed on most measures and the trend towards tougher enforcement was a general one.

While the results were still some way short of meeting the KPI target of 90 per cent of appropriate cases being breached by a third unacceptable absence, they suggested that improvements could be made without further instruction or guidance from the inspectorate or the government.

The current National Standards (2000), which came into force on 1 April 2000, clarified some 1995 standards and made others more stringent. One of the most important changes was the requirement that, for offenders on court orders, breach should be instigated as a result of a second unacceptable failure to attend rather than a third, with the first failure being responded to by means of a final (red) warning letter.[12] Other changes included the following:

- Requiring that offenders be informed of the time of their first appointment before they leave court.

- Changing references to the first 'three months' of CRO and CPO supervision to '12 weeks'[13] and some clarification of the number of appointments to be made in licence cases.

- Distinguishing more clearly between a first CPO appointment for assessment, for which the deadline is five working days from sentence, and for first work placement, which should be made within ten working days.

- Making it clear that non-attendance at an appointment with a partner organisation should be dealt with in the same way as a failed probation appointment.[14]

- Providing more specific guidance about the limited range of circumstances in which absences may be considered acceptable.

- Regarding absences as unacceptable unless proved otherwise.

All the then 54 services took part in each round of the audit.[15] This involved providing details of appointments made and attended and responses to non-attendance over the first three months for probation and community service orders and post-release licences initiated in March 1999 ($n = 10{,}008$), the first half of September 1999 ($n = 4{,}386$) and September 2000 ($n = 8{,}924$), respectively. As the audits represent only a sample of cases active in each year, estimates are inevitably subject to some sampling error. As a cautious guide, differences of at least two percentage points in the results of the second and third audits may be considered statistically significant.

Cases sampled in all three rounds of the audit were found to be alike in terms of the offences for which offenders had been sentenced, age, sex, ethnicity and type and length of supervision. This makes comparisons between different rounds of the audit meaningful as they are not distorted by being based on very different mixes of cases. It also confirms that areas did not 'fix' their returns to generate more favourable results.

When compared to the results of the second audit, the results of the third audit show the following:

- The proportion of first appointments that were set in the time-frames required by National Standard rose from 82 to 90 per cent.

- Possibly as a consequence of the new requirement to notify offenders of first appointments before they leave court, attendance at first appointments went up from 81 to 85 per cent.

- The new requirement to offer a first placement session within 10 working days to those on CPOs was achieved in 74 per cent of all CPO cases and 85 per cent of cases where a first assessment appointment was made within 5 days.

- The proportion of probation cases in which offenders were offered 12 appointments was virtually unchanged at 75 per cent. However, the proportion of cases in which services offered more than 12 appointments went up from 50 per cent by 6 percentage points.[16]

- The newly clarified Standard of 9 appointments in the first 3 months was met or exceeded in about the same proportion (80 per cent) of licence cases.

- The percentage of offenders who attended all their appointments or had an acceptable reason for being absent rose from 46 to 53 per cent.

Under the 1995 National Standards, offenders were allowed up to two unacceptable absences before being breached. An overall compliance rate can be generated by adding together cases which had no unacceptable absences with those which involved less than three. This shows that the compliance rate for offenders in the second audit was 78 per cent. Judged by 1995 Standards, the compliance rate in the 2000 audit would have been 84 per cent.

The more stringent National Standards 2000 require that offenders on court orders are allowed only one acceptable absence before being breached, although those on licence may have two. Calculated on this basis 73 per cent of offenders in the third audit complied. The comparable figure for audit 2 (i.e. if National Standards 2000 had been in place) was 67 per cent.

The third audit showed that 71 per cent of offenders were dealt with at least as severely as National Standards 2000 require at a first unacceptable absence, whereas 77 per cent of those in the second audit were dealt with as the 1995 Standards required. The proportion of cases in which no action was taken remained at around 10 per cent while the use of measures which are less than National Standards require (e.g. a verbal or written reminder) rose from 7 to 15 per cent. This means that while performance may not have improved to the level required by the 2000 Standards, performance in relation to the 1995 Standards was maintained.

About two thirds of responses to a second unacceptable absence were at least as severe as the relevant set of Standards required in the second and third audits. However, the proportion of cases in which less severe action (as opposed to no action) was taken trebled (to 9 per cent). If cases in the third round were judged by 1995 Standards, this means that performance levels were either being maintained or improved on.

On the whole, the results of the third audit suggest that, while the stricter enforcement standards required by National Standards 2000 had not been achieved, performance had been maintained and in some instances improved in relation to 1995 Standards. In particular, compliance had gone up.

Does tough enforcement 'work'?

As we discussed at the start of this chapter, much of the impetus for toughening up enforcement practice came from the perceived need to build confidence in community penalties as tough and demanding penalties. We shall not address the question whether tougher enforcement has 'worked' in this way – except to note that in another study (Hough *et al.* 2003) we found that a sample of judges and magistrates were uniform in acknowledging and welcoming improvements in enforcement standards. Awareness of the work of the probation service is low among the general public, and it will take several years before any changes in working practice register.

Whether tough enforcement actually improves the effectiveness of community penalties in reducing reoffending is a separate, but equally complicated, issue, and one to which we now turn. It is a specific and narrow form of the more general dilemma facing those who want to influence other people's behaviour: is threat of punishment or promise of reward the more effective route to securing compliance?

The argument in favour of tough enforcement as a route to reducing reoffending is a deterrent one. If offenders are in no doubt that non-compliance will result in swift and certain punishment, the reasoning goes, they will make sure that they take their supervision seriously. To use a medical analogy, offenders are 'retained in treatment' by coercive threat for sufficient periods of time to receive sufficient dosage of treatment to benefit. The argument against tough enforcement is that it imposes a needlessly high drop-out (or throw-out) rate from treatment, and that a more pragmatic style of enforcement could result in higher retention rates, higher dosage and greater effectiveness. In other words, the benefits derived from the group retained in treatment are offset by the costs associated with the high drop-out rate.

In principle, questions about the relationship between enforcement, retention and effectiveness are empirical ones – although there are complex issues about offenders' shared perceptions of enforcement practice, which may or may not reflect reality. We have mounted two studies which make a start, at least, to fill in some pieces of the jigsaw.

The enforcement reconviction study

The 1999 ACOP audit, discussed above, provided us with an opportunity to exploit the natural variation between probation areas in their enforcement style. The idea was to compare reconviction rates between areas that pursued tough and lenient enforcement strategies, as defined by their breach rates. The findings summarised here are presented in more detail in Hearnden and Millie (2003, 2004 in press). At the time of the second audit, the 1995 National Standards were in operation. As discussed, these required that breach proceedings be initiated against all offenders no later than the third unacceptable absence; the 2000 National Standards allowed only one unacceptable absence before breach.

The audit generated a sample of 4,386 offenders under various forms of probation supervision across all probation areas. For the reconviction study complete enforcement records and reasons for termination were obtained from a sample of probation areas representing tough and lenient enforcers. A mix of large, medium and small areas was also selected, based on the number of cases included in the second audit. Treating the five original services in London as one area, eleven probation areas provided updated enforcement details. In all, data were gathered on 882 cases. Successful matches with OI data were made in 97 per cent (852) of this subsample, which otherwise appeared to be a fairly good reflection of the entire sample in the audit.

Complete details of each appointment made and attended were available for 89 per cent (782) of cases in the follow-up sample.[17] Of these, 70 per cent (545) either completed their order or had it terminated early for good behaviour. However, 12 per cent (68) of the 545 had breach proceedings initiated against them after three or more unacceptable absences that did not ultimately lead to the offender being breached at court.

The tough probation areas breached offenders at almost twice the rate of the lenient areas. Often initiation of a breach did not result in a breach at court because the supervision period had expired before a court date hearing was set. However, probation staff in several areas commented that in some cases where breach was initiated, this was used to alert the offender to the fact that he or she was were liable to end up in court. Some areas continued to offer appointments to all offenders after breach was initiated, while others did so only for CPO cases. Effectively this process functioned as an extra layer of warning after a final warning, to be applied to relatively motivated offenders whose record of reporting was generally good. Table 7.1 shows reconviction rates and order outcome for the tough and lenient areas.

In both types of area[18] the proportion reconvicted following breach at court was, unsurprisingly, much higher than for others. However, there was very little difference in the overall reconviction rates for high or low-

Table 7.1 Reconviction and order outcome for areas with high and low rates of breach at court

High breach rate areas ($n = 379$)		Low breach rate areas ($n = 418$)	
Breached 101 (27%) ↓	Not breached 278 (73%) ↓	Breached 62 (15%) ↓	Not breached 356 (85%) ↓
Reconvicted 76 (75% of breached)	Reconvicted 109 (39% of not breached)	Reconvicted 49 (79% of breached)	Reconvicted 148 (42% of not breached)
Overall reconviction rate 49%		Overall reconviction rate 47%	

breaching areas. Viewed purely in terms of whether an area has a high or low rate of breach at court, strictness of enforcement appears to have little impact on the overall reconviction rate. This suggests that offenders either disregard, or are oblivious to, strict probation enforcement strategies.

These results must be regarded as tentative, partly for methodological reasons. Differences in reconviction rates may result from differences in victims' willingness to report crimes, the police detection rate and the proportion of cases going to court resulting in a conviction, none of which we were able to control for. More information on offender characteristics and an understanding of the offender perspective on the impact of enforcement would also be useful. One can also interpret the findings in other ways. For example, one might question the assumption that areas with high breach rates had the toughest enforcement regimes. It is conceivable, at least, that these were actually areas which had been traditionally most lenient but were now 'toughening up'. Those with a long tradition of really tough enforcement might actually demonstrate rather low breach rates as a consequence – on the principle that people who make the most convincing threats achieve the highest levels of compliance.

Our own view is that offenders under probation supervision typically have a long history of insensitivity to deterrent threat – whether made in the home, the classroom, in the youth justice system or in the adult courts. One can explain the current findings most economically by suggesting that this group continues to be relatively inured to deterrent threats when these are made by probation officers. We find it un-convincing to suggest that probationers are responsive to different enforcement regimes, even when the differences are quite gross, as in the analysis presented here.

The Drug Treatment and Testing Order (DTTO) pilots

Our evaluation of the DTTO pilots sheds some further light on possible links between enforcement style and reconviction rates (fuller details are to be found in Hough *et al.* 2003). There were three pilot sites – in Croydon, Gloucestershire and Liverpool – and 210 offenders served DTTOs during the pilot period, which ran from October 1998 until March 2000. Overall, two-year reconviction rates were high at 80 per cent, as might be expected for a group of highly persistent offenders with serious problems of drug dependency. However, there were very substantial differences in reconviction rates between offenders who completed their orders and those who whose orders were revoked, as Table 7.2 shows.

Table 7.2 Two-year DTTO reconviction rates, by outcome of order ($n = 157$)

Reconvicted	%	Number
Completed	53	49
Revoked	91	108
Total	79	157

These findings are not especially surprising as reoffending is often a cause of breach and revocation, rather than vice versa. However they are at least suggestive of the possibility that retention of DTTO offenders on their orders leads to lower reconviction rates. It is also clear that the annual conviction rate of those retained on their orders drops from 6 per year in the year prior to the order to 2 per year in the two years from the start of the order. When one compares the three sites' revocation rates and reconviction rates, as in Table 7.3, the case strengthens for arguing that revocation rates affect reconviction rates as well as vice versa. The Gloucestershire scheme had very high revocation rates, associated both with its abstinence-based treatment philosophy and with implementation problems (see Turnbull *et al.* 2001).

Table 7.3 is not conclusive proof that high revocation rates yield high reconviction rates; the results could be explained by differences in assessment and selection – in that Croydon selected the 'safest bets' and

Table 7.3 Two-year reconviction and revocation rates ($n = 174$)

	% reconvicted	% revoked	n
Croydon	65	52	34
Liverpool	73	64	55
Gloucestershire	91	76	85
Total	80	67	174

Note:
Revocation rates based on 161 cases, due to missing data.

Gloucestershire went for offenders with a high risk of failure.[19] However, when the table is interpreted in the light of the implementation history of the three sites, it seems highly likely that a more flexible attitude on the part of the Gloucestershire team towards positive drug tests, coupled with shorter waiting times for assessment and treatment, could have reduced its revocation rate, and that this in turn could have reduced the reconviction rate from 91 per cent to something nearer 75 per cent.

One final comparison is illuminating. DTTOs were introduced in both England and Wales and in Scotland. There were two Scottish pilot schemes, evaluated separately from the English ones, in Glasgow and Fife. DTTO teams included social workers[20] and addiction workers; and the pilot covered 96 orders. In many ways the results of the Scottish pilot mirrored those from England (Eley *et al.* 2002). Most of the 96 offenders had long criminal histories and their average weekly spend on drugs before the order was comparable to the English sample. However, the pattern of enforcement was markedly different. By the end of the evaluation fieldwork, nine breach proceedings had been submitted and three orders had been revoked. The evaluation report does not provide the final revocation rate but the figure must be very much lower than the 67 per cent in the English pilots. These contrasting results are interesting in demonstrating that DTTOs established under the same legislation can be implemented in such radically different ways. The Scottish DTTO teams managed to retain their offenders in treatment to an impressive degree. What is not known at present is whether they did so at the cost of tolerating significant non-compliance. Nor do we know how the reconviction rates compare for the Scottish and English pilots.

Conclusions: forging a link between enforcement, compliance and effective practice

We have seen that enforcement practice has undoubtedly got tougher over the 1990s. This shift of practice has almost certainly improved sentencers' confidence in community penalties, and in time this confidence may trickle through to the general public. In this sense, at least, getting tough has probably 'worked'.

Whether tougher enforcement leads to lower reconviction rates remains an open question. The evidence that we have assembled in the latter part of the chapter offers no grounds for thinking that the deterrent effect of enforcement ensures fuller compliance, and some grounds for thinking that tough enforcement can lead to low retention rates in programmes, which in turn leads to high reconviction rates. While the evidence that we have presented is by itself far from conclusive, the body of criminological knowledge on deterrence supports the idea that the sort of persistent offender that now forms the staple of probation workloads is relatively inured to deterrent threat. Given that probationers typically have very long histories of non-compliance with parents, teachers, police and courts, it seems especially optimistic that probation officers will succeed in securing compliance where all others have failed.

This creates a policy dilemma of some intensity. It is essential that there should be judicial and public confidence in community penalties. This is unlikely to be achieved if the probation service routinely turns a Nelsonian blind-eye to non-compliance. On the other hand, we can be fairly certain that a zero-tolerant approach will result in poor retention rates and high reconviction rates.

Various principles can be identified to help reconcile the demands of public confidence and the need to retain offenders on programmes. First, in promoting compliance, there is obvious value in a graduated response running from reminding offenders of the terms of their orders through initial and final warnings. Punishing non-compliance by substituting a custodial sentence should be reserved for those who have shown themselves to be unwilling to comply despite efforts made to assist and encourage them to do so. Each revision of the national standards has reduced the number of failures an offender is permitted and sought to increase the chances of an order being terminated. However, the implications this may have for programme retention rates do not seem to have been thought through. Those offenders who are most in need of effective supervision may be breached and resentenced before they have a chance to be transformed into 'completers'.

Secondly, it makes sense to deploy the full range of strategies for promoting compliance, and to avoid over-focusing on coercive threat. Bottoms (2001) suggests that compliance may come about in response to constraint or coercion, because of habit, through a calculation of self-interest or because of a feeling of moral obligation. National standards are almost entirely geared to ensuring compliance through constraint or coercion. They make passing reference to encouraging attendance to become a habit; for example, by making appointments coincide with 'signing-on' days or making first appointments before the offender leaves court. But there is much more scope to 'design out' non-attendance employing ideas adapted from a situational crime prevention perspective (Clarke 1997). Examples might include sentencers stressing the consequences of non-attendance when pronouncing sentence and having agreed times and days of the week for first appointments so that its timing can be announced at the time of sentence (Hedderman *et al.* 1999).

Thirdly – building on Bottoms' perspective – rewarding compliance may prove as effective as punishing non-compliance. The standards are strikingly silent about encouraging compliance by rewarding it. Teesside's idea of providing breakfast to those attending a final programme session is one example, but Underdown (2001: 120) recommends that other stronger incentives might include 'reducing the restrictions or lessening the demands that the overall community penalty imposes'. He suggests that this might be accomplished by increasing the court's role in overseeing orders. There are also symbolic forms of reward that can be deployed, such as the praise bestowed by American drug courts on offenders who have made good progress.

Another option might be to move to a graduated system of positive rewards which could be incorporated into national standards (Hedderman and Hough 2000). These might range from awarding attendance certificates (the positive equivalent of a final warning letter) to early termination for good behaviour. What is novel about this suggestion is not the range of techniques – experienced practitioners will be able to think of many other options – but the idea that, like the breach system, routes to positive rewards should be spelt out and operated even-handedly and transparently. Any sign of arbitrary decision-making would bring the system into disrepute with offenders in much the same way that such decision making is said to undermine sentencers' confidence in enforcement. Encouraging offenders to appreciate 'what's in it for them' is another obvious strategy. Appealing at the outset to their self-interest by spelling out the help which can be accessed in relation to employment, education, accommodation, finances, childcare and transport may encourage attendance in a way that promising to work with them on their offending behaviour may not.

Encouraging compliance by making it normative is probably the most difficult to achieve given that, by definition, offenders are given to rule breaking. However, Underdown (2001: 120–1) suggests that 'Cognitive training programmes aim to improve cause–effect thinking and understanding of social obligation through values enhancement'. Recruiting the support of law-abiding family members as a sort of unofficial mentor might also be worth considering (Webster *et al.* 2001). Pro-social modelling techniques such as ensuring that sessions begin on time and that staff treat offenders with respect and courtesy may also encourage offenders into normative compliance; Trotter's work (1999) certainly suggests that it does so. This may also follow, as Underdown (2001) suggests, when attendance at cognitive behavioural programmes leads to a better understanding of social obligations and changes in the values to which participants subscribe.

Finally, it is essential to ensure that there are *organisational* rewards for securing compliance, as well as rewards for the individual offender. Those probation areas that participated in the DTTO pilots had to achieve a specified number of commencements. The National Probation Directorate continues to specify targets for DTTO commencements. There is a case for requiring a given number of completions instead – or at least for including completions in the battery of performance indicators used to assess how a particular type of order is faring. Although this risks having the perverse effect of skewing probation effort from the neediest and most intractable offenders to the more compliant, it would ensure that areas designed their enforcement strategy to prioritise relapse prevention and to minimise the risks of unecessary revocations.

Much more research is needed about the link between enforcement and reconviction before the tentative conclusions reached here can be firmed up. If the government's aim of putting 30,000 offenders through probation programmes by 2004 (Home Office 2001) is to be achieved, however, new research is needed which focuses on exactly how positive approaches to securing compliance 'work'.

Notes

1 This chapter develops ideas first published in a paper by Hedderman (2003).

2 See especially the 'anti-psychiatry' movement associated with Cooper (1967) and Laing (1985).

3 For example, that custody should be reserved for the most serious offences or to protect the public from serious (violent or sexual) harm.

4 These standards required offenders to be breached or warned in writing following a first incident of non-compliance. At a second failure, the case was to be referred to a senior probation officer for a decision about breach. The offender was to be breached after three failures in all cases.

5 Some officers thought this simply doubled an offender's opportunities to fail.

6 Respondents explained that offenders were rarely breached for anything other than failure to attend, partly because this was the most common form of non-compliance but also because it was easiest to prove.

7 The amendments in the Criminal Justice Act 1993 did little more than clarify the law about 'sentencing on record', reverting to the position prior to the 1991 Act; but they had a symbolic importance in signalling a move away from the philosophy of the 1991 Act.

8 Breaking the link between probation and social work training was especially symbolic; previously both probation officers and social workers were required to obtain a Certificate of Qualification in Social Work (CQSW), ensuring a degree of commonality of outlook between the two professions.

9 See Vennard et al. (1997) for a review.

10 See, for example, the National Probation Directorate's (2000) summary of results from an evaluation of the 'Think first' programme by the Probation Studies Unit.

11 ACOP was disbanded on 1 April 2001 when the new National Probation Service was established. The association was a Professional Association of Chief and Assistant Chiefs. It functioned as an informed pressure group and was frequently consulted on changes in legislation and practice by government and the media.

12 National Standards 2000 stated that the letter should be 'yellow', but this was amended to 'red' by Probation Circular 24/00.

13 Previously areas were free to interpret 'three' months as 12 weeks, a quarter of a year (13 weeks) or even calendar months.

14 Circular 24/00 amended this requirement to refer only to appointments that are of a similar frequency and duration to appointments with a supervising officer.

15 On 1 April 2001 the 54 services became 42 areas within the new National Probation Service.

16 These figures cannot be calculated for CS as the standards specify the number of hours to be worked rather than the number of appointments.

17 The 782 for which full enforcement details were available were compared to all the 882 cases in the follow-up sample. There were no differences in terms of average age, gender and ethnic breakdown.

18 There was no significant difference between high and low breach-rate areas.
19 The Croydon offenders had slightly lower OGRS scores than the other two sites; however, there was no significant difference between OGRS scores in the other two sites.
20 There is no separate probation service in Scotland. Criminal justice social workers operate within social services departments.

References

Bottoms, A. (2001) 'Compliance and community penalties', in A. Bottoms *et al.* (eds) *Community Penalties: Change and Challenges*. Cullompton: Willan.

Broad, B. (1991) *Punishment under Pressure: The Probaton Service in the Inner City.* London: Kingsley.

Brody, S. (1976) *The Effectiveness of Sentencing*. Home Office Research Study 76. London: HMSO.

Chapman, T. and Hough, M. (1998) *Evidence-based Practice: A Guide to Effective Practice*. London: HMI Probation.

Clarke, R.V. (1997) *Situational Crime Prevention: Successful Case Studies*. Albany, NY: Harrow & Heston.

Cooper, D. (1967) *Psychiatry and Anti-psychiatry*. London: Tavistock.

Dersley, I. (2000) 'Acceptable or unacceptable? Local probation service policy on non-complaince and enforcement.' Unpublished dissertation. Birmingham University School of Social Sciences.

Drakeford, M. (1993) 'The probation service, breach and the Criminal Justice Act 1991', *Howard Journal*, 32 (4): 291–302.

Edmunds, M., Hough, M. Turnbull, P.J. and May, T. (1999) *Doing Justice to Treatment: Referring Offenders to Drug Services*. London: Home Office.

Eley, S., Gallop, K., McIvor, G., Morgan, K. and Yates, R. (2002) *Drug Treatment and Testing Orders: Evaluation of the Scottish pilots*. Edinburgh: Scottish Executive Central Research Unit (available at http://2www.scotland.gov.uk/cru/kd01/green/dtts-09.asp).

Fielding, N. (1984) *Probation Practice: Client Support under Social Control*. Aldershot: Gower.

Harris, R. (1995) 'Studying Probation: a comparative approach', in K. Hamai *et al.* (eds) *Probation around the World*. London: Routledge.

Hearnden, I. and Millie, A. (2003) *Investigating the Link between Probation Enforcement and Reconviction*. Home Office Research Findings. London: Home Office Research, Development and Statistics Directorate.

Hearnden, I. and Millie, A. (2004 in press) 'Does tougher enforcement lead to lower reconviction?', *Probation Journal*.

Hedderman, C. (1999) *ACOP Enforcement Survey. Stage 1*. London: ACOP (available at www.sbu.ac.uk/cpru).

Hedderman, C. (2003) 'Enforcing supervision and encouraging compliance', in W.H. Chui and M. Nellis (eds), *Moving Probation Forward*. London: Pearson Longman.

Hedderman, C., Ellis, T. and Sugg, D. (1999) *Increasing Confidence in Community Sentences: The Results of Two Demonstration Projects*. Home Office Research Study 194. London: Home Office.

Hedderman, C. and Hearnden, I. (2000) *Improving Enforcement – the Second ACOP Enforcement Audit*. London: ACOP (available at www.sbu.ac.uk/cpru).

Hedderman, C. and Hough, M. (2000) 'Tightening up probation: a step too far?', *Criminal Justice Matters*, April.

HMI Probation (2000) *Making National Standards Work: A Study by HMIP of Enforcement Practice in Community Penalties*. London: HMI Probation.

Home Office (1991) *Crime, Justice and Protecting the Public* (Cm 965). London: HMSO.

Home Office (1992) *Criminal Statistics England and Wales 1990* (Cm 1935). London: HMSO.

Home Office (1995) *Strengthening Punishment in the Community* (Cm 2780). London: HMSO.

Home Office (2001) *Criminal Justice: The Way Ahead*. London: Home Office.

Hough, M., Clancy, A., McSweeney, T. and Turnbull, P. (2003) *The Impact of DTTOs on Offending: Two-year Reconviction Results*. Home Office Research Findings. London: Home Office.

Hough, M., Jacobson, A. and Milllie, A. (2003) *The Decision to Imprison*. London: Prison Reform Trust.

House of Commons (1998) *Home Affairs Committee Third Report: Alternatives to Prison Sentences. Volume 1*. London: HMSO.

King, J. (1958) *The Probation Service*. London: Butterworths.

King, J. (1969) *The Probation and Aftercare Service*. London: Butterworths.

Laing, R.D. (1985) *Wisdom, Madness and Folly*. London: Macmillan.

Lloyd, C. (1991) 'National standards for community service orders: the first two years of operation', *RPU Bulletin*, 31.

Lord Chief Justice (2001) Prison Reform Trust Annual Lecture.

Martinson, R. (1974) 'What works? Questions and answers about prison reforms', *Public Interest*, 35: 22–54.

McWilliams, W. and Pease, K. (1990) 'Probation practice and an end to punishment', *Howard Journal*, 29 (1): 14–24.

National Probation Directorate (2000) *What Works Newsletter*, edition 4, August.

Trotter, C. (1999) *Working with Involuntary Clients: A Guide to Practice*. London: Sage.

Turnbull, P.J., McSweeney, T., Webster, R., Edmunds, M. and Hough, M. (2000) *Drug Treatment and Testing Orders: Final Evaluation Report*. Home Office Research Study 212. London: Home Office.

Underdown, A. (2001) 'Making "What Works" work: challenges in the delivery of community penalties', in A. Bottoms *et al.* (eds) *Community Penalties: Changes and Challenges*. Cullompton: Willan.

United Nations (1951) *Probation and Related Measures* (Document E/CN.5/230). New York, NY: United Nations.

Vennard, J. and Hedderman, C. (1999) 'Learning lessons from serious incidents', *VISTA*, Spring.

Vennard, J., Sugg, D. and Hedderman, C. (1997) 'The use of cognitive behavioural approaches with offenders: messages from the research', in *Changing Offenders' Attitudes and Behaviour: What Works?* Home Office Research Study 171. London: Home Office.

Webster, R., Hedderman, C., Turnbull, P.J. and May, T. (2001) *Building Bridges to Employment for Prisoners*. Home Office Research Study 226. London: Home Office.

Willis, A. (1981) 'Social welfare and social control: a survey of young men on probation', *RPU Bulletin*, 8.

Chapter 8

Beyond programmes: organisational and cultural issues in the implementation of What Works

*Hazel Kemshall, Paul Holt, Roy Bailey
and Gwyneth Boswell*

Background

Recent Home Office initiatives have placed What Works and effective interventions with offenders on to the probation service's agenda. The pace of change both nationally and within areas has been swift,[1] leading to some criticism that implementation has been forced before there is sufficient evidence of effectiveness from the pilot Pathfinder programmes (Merrington and Stanley 2000). The Home Office Effective Practice initiative has placed unprecedented demand upon probation areas to implement a detailed curriculum of What Works programmes for offenders paralleled by increased attention to evidence-led work and consistent standards across the national service (Home Office 1998, 1999a, 1999b; Robinson 2001). During this period probation areas were also subjected to quality and effectiveness inspections, and performance inspections focused on performance standards and service delivery issues (commonly known as PIP inspections). The 'culture of individualism' in probation practice has also been criticised for its inconsistency and idiosyncracy (Burnett 1996), and a 'culture of evidence' has been promoted to replace its worst excesses (Nutley and Davies 1999).

Two influential documents in this process were *Strategies for Effective Offender Supervision* (Underdown 1998) and *Evidence-based Practice* (Chapman and Hough 1998), both produced for Her Majesty's Inspectorate of Probation. The work of Underdown in particular revealed the inconsistency of probation practice on What Works and highlighted the need for a centrally led initiative to ensure that the key principles were properly taken up. The inspectorate became a key driver of the What Works agenda (Raynor 2002), and a campaign of knowledge dissemination and Pathfinder programmes ensued.

Centralisation became a key plank in the implementation strategy, greatly assisted by the role taken by the inspectorate and the creation of a national service in 2001 followed by the publication of national targets in 2001 (National Probation Service 2001) 'incorporating "stretch objectives" designed to produce change' (Raynor 2002: 1189).

The above documents contributed to the dissemination of the What Works knowledge base but, more importantly, attempted to highlight the practice, management and organisational issues that were likely to arise from the implementation of the What Works agenda. In brief, the most significant are as follows:

Practice
- The challenge to individualised practice and the increased need for accountability, performance management and consistency.
- Greater attention to targeting offenders to the correct programmes.
- Greater attention to motivational issues, securing compliance and reducing programme attrition.
- Quality assuring programme integrity.

Management
- Increasing performance management and embedding an objective and outcome-led culture into organisational life.
- Managing resources towards desired ends in a more rational and accountable manner.
- Ensuring quality of service delivery and effective practice to reduce crime.
- Managing and using information to inform organisational decision-making and resource deployment.
- Effectively managing the change process.

Organisational
- To ensure that the logistics of service delivery are well managed.
- To ensure that the supporting processes for effective practice and the delivery of programmes are in place (e.g. case management, training of staff, assessment and targeting procedures, key structures and processes).
- Communication structures are in place and work well.
- Strategic planning and resource management.
- Leadership and change management strategies.

(See Chapman and Hough 1998: chs 1–5, 9; Underdown 1998: chs 5–10.)

This chapter will argue that the programme-driven approach to the delivery of effective practice has obscured attention to these broader issues of implementation, and that organisational and cultural challenges have been underestimated, resulting in low programme completion rates in some areas (NPD 2002) and broader difficulties in implementing effective practice (Kemshall *et al.* 2001).[2]

Methodology

The chapter draws on data collected some 15 months after the launch of the Home Office Effective Practice initiative and follows the im-plementation of effective practice in one region. The research was able to focus on the impact and demand of the Home Office roll-out and the challenges generated by the national curriculum of What Works programmes for offenders. In particular the research was commissioned to examine the first 12 weeks of supervision across the region, including both one-to-one supervision and programme provision. The key objective of the research was to establish the extent to which practice was 'evidence led' and based upon What Works principles. The research focus was upon the implementation and take-up of effective practice in the first 12 weeks of supervision and *not* upon the impact of individual programmes. In essence, the research examined the infrastructure and management processes required to make What Works work – in effect, the extent to which the region had met the 'Underdown template' (see below).

The following areas were examined:

- Assessment practices for both group and individual supervision.
- Content of supervision plans and group programmes.
- Referral and induction practices.
- The establishment of offender motivation and the maintenance of the change process.
- Measurements of programme impact used by services.
- Principles of resource allocation and actual use in the field.

The main methods used were:

- Analysis of documentary material, particularly material prepared for the performance inspections, statistical material and policy documents.

- Paper material on programmes currently running.
- Case-file assessment and supervision plan reading using an adaptation of the HMIP case-file reader from the 1999 inspection.
- Observation of key elements of practice.
- Focus groups with staff and managers supported by individual interviews.
- Interviews with offenders who had experienced the first 12 weeks of supervision.

A total of 9 assistant chief officers (ACOs), 25 senior probation officers (SPOs) and 61 main-grade staff (including probation service officers) were interviewed; 75 offenders were interviewed and 297 case files were read. The data were analysed using well established coding and categorising techniques for the analysis of qualitative data (Miles and Huberman 1994; Denscombe 1998). Validity and reliability were achieved through the well established technique of triangulation across methods, different data sets, grades of staff and settings (Denzin 1978; Silverman 1993).

The key challenges

In Chapter 10 of *Strategies for Effective Offender Supervision*, Andrew Underdown offers a template for organisational fitness to deliver effective practice. In his overview he presents these as follows:

- Roles and levels of leadership to promote practice and management changes.
- Principles to inform change strategy and organisational structure.
- Features of culture that support effectiveness developments.
- Challenges posed by resource constraints.
- Opportunities for improved planning and greater collaboration.
- Issues in achieving staff development – developing competence, building ownership and clarifying roles.
- Approaches to quality assurance and the value of a consistent and rigorous provision for programme audit (adapted from Underdown 1998: 127).

In effect, these can be understood as crucial requirements for the effective implementation of What Works. They require service attention to organisational issues; leadership, culture and change management; operational management and communication; staff development and training; practice issues and case management; and capacity planning and performance management.[3] However, in the rush to roll out the programme curriculum, it is these factors that have been overlooked (Kemshall *et al.* 2001; Link 2002). This leaves services with significant barriers to the adoption and implementation of effective practice as the *key principle of service delivery,* and locates effective practice within peripheral programmes that fail to meet completion targets (Kemshall 2002; NPD 2002). The rest of the chapter considers the implementation challenges under each of these headings using data from the regional study.

Organisational issues

While staff are familiar with the key principles and messages of What Works, it has yet to be routinely integrated into service activities. This lack of integration and embedding is exhibited by lack of staff ownership and commitment to What Works. Internal communication on effective practice had not always had the desired impact on practice and, as a consequence, the What Works message was known but not owned. This situation was exacerbated by a perceived lack of consultation between managers and staff, and a perception that the What Works agenda was both centrally driven and taking place too quickly within a climate of inadequate resource.

Culturally the traditional individualism of service delivery (Burnett 1996) also creates a significant tension against a more managed approach to targeting, resource allocation (most notably staff time and activities) and supervision content. Performance management in itself down-grades certain tasks, some of which provide staff with significant job satisfaction and professional value. In these circumstances organisational transformation to a new task and role agenda is bound to create tension, confusion and resentment. This transformation to one key organisational objective (that is, effective practice) is also undermined by the fragmented and functional nature of service delivery (discussed in more detail below). The offender's journey is not a 'seamless join' underpinned by one key message but, rather, a series of encounters with differing staff providing a range of messages on What Works (Kemshall *et al.* 2001: viii).

This has resulted in a somewhat piecemeal response to the effective practice agenda focusing on programme setup and roll-out. Acceptability of What Works is rarely an issue, but how it should be organised and delivered is, particularly where significant practice change is required or professional discretion and autonomy are reduced

174

(Kemshall *et al.* 2001; Kemshall 2002). Thus performance management and accountability for practice have become acute issues, resulting in disputes over professional control and workload management (*NAPO News*, 2002). The gap between what practitioners felt were the ideals of What Works and the reality of current practice was a source of both frustration and disappointment.

Organisationally, providing a 'joined up' service around effective practice is proving a key challenge, particularly the tendency of functional specialisms to compartmentalise and to create a fragmented journey through the service for the offender. While offenders prefer contact with a single officer, they do understand the principle of being referred elsewhere for particular services or groups. The key issues for them are consistency of message, fair treatment, problem-solving and reinforcement of programme learning (Bailey and Ward 1992; Bailey 1994; Merrington 1995; Rex 1995; Kemshall *et al.* 2001). For offenders the main criterion of effective practice is the extent to which probation supervision would stop them offending in the future, and the rigorous challenge to offending behaviour was seen as a key aspect of successful supervision. Offenders were able to recognise that this was about the outcomes of supervision rather than a process of supervision they might have preferred or enjoyed. The long waiting times for groups, currently ranging nationally from 5 weeks to 4–5 months with an average of 13 weeks (Kemshall *et al.* 2002), tended to reduce motivation, or events such as reoffending and rearrest overtook offenders. Routine reporting in the period before groups was described as 'dead time' and motivational opportunities and confidence in the group programme to change problematic behaviours were lost. Paradoxically, where the supervisory process was disjointed, the need for reinforcement of learning from group programmes was the greatest.

Leadership, culture and change management

The development agenda in the Underdown document outlines the extent of cultural and organisational change required to deliver What Works (1998: ch. 10). Lewis (1999) has used the notion of a learning culture and a positive emphasis upon management and pro-social modelling of effective practice as key mechanisms for achieving change (see also Rex and Matravers 1998; Gast and Taylor 1999), a view supported by the Association of Chief Officers of Probation (1997, 1998). At a time when staff will be experiencing uncertainty, loss of professional autonomy and discretion and workload pressure, the barriers to effective communication and consensus on change should not be underestimated (Schein 1992; Kotter 1995), and there is a risk of 'strategic drift' in the face of low morale and cynicism (Johnson and Scholes 1993). In the face of high attrition rates (NPD 2002) and increasing recognition that programmes are not the 'whole story', attention has recently turned to leadership and the role of strategic management in delivering the effective practice agenda (Murphy 2002). Udall (2001), in a recent consultancy for Lancashire Probation Service on the role of managers in the delivery of effective practice, has emphasised the important connection between effective people management and organisational success. Udall has argued that the 'effective supervision of offenders must be underpinned by effective supervision of staff' (2001: 134). She draws important connections between 'effective employment practice and effective probation practice' (p. 138) in which demonstrable coherence between the two systems would achieve business excellence. In essence, management must itself adhere to the key principles of evidence-led practice and create a seamless join between management objectives, staff practices and service delivery to offenders.

Kotter (1995), in a study of about one hundred companies and organisations in America, found that key steps must be undertaken for any major change initiative to be successful. In the probation context, these steps can be modified thus:

- Establishing a sense of urgency and building a case for change.
- Establishing a powerful guiding coalition to steer the change process.
- Creating and communicating a sense of vision.
- Removing obstacles to change and empowering people who can put the vision into action.
- Planning and establishing initial short-term gains to consolidate support.
- Anchoring changes into a new culture (as adapted by Bailey and Williams 2000).

In its most recent audit the inspectorate recognised the important roles of 'committed leadership and supportive management; programme management; quality of programme delivery; and case management' to the effective delivery of accredited programmes (2002: 49) and has set performance standards in these key areas, resulting in the award of an Implementation Quality Rating (IQR). While the inspectorate acknowledges that there is as yet no empirical evidence that probation areas with higher IQRs achieve higher rates of programme completion, it is assumed that higher IQRs do reflect higher-performing areas. Thus, IQRs and completions are linked so that 'if 100 offenders complete a programme with an IQR score of 50% only 50 completions are recorded against the area's targets' (HMIP 2002: 62). These are related to the government's Service Delivery Agreement targets for the NPD, and funding reflects how far these targets (for completions and quality ratings) are met, tying services to 'year on year improvements' (2002: 62).

The inspectorate identifies the 'characteristics of good performing areas' as 'effective liaison between case managers and programme staff; clear enforcement of attendance on accredited programmes', good communication between different units and integrated supervision (HMIP 2002: 59). This new practice of audit itself represents closer attention to the 'organisational context in which programmes are delivered' (p. 61).

Operational management and communication

While most operational managers acknowledged that What Works was now firmly recognised and on the agenda, integration of effective practice into the work of the service was seen as disappointingly slow. Significant barriers to the effective use of the middle manager role in achieving the effective practice agenda were identified. Effective face-to-face communication with staff was seen as crucial to embedding the message. However, effective communication was not always assisted by organisational structures and the growing isolationism of key functions (e.g courts and PSR writing). Functional divisions left operational managers with differing levels of knowledge and responsibility for effective practice, a situation that mitigated against integration of What Works. The sheer pressure of work was also seen as an obstacle to effective change management and cultural shift. Strategic leadership was seen as crucial, particularly about effective practice vision, priorities and, importantly, what staff were no longer required to do. Head-quarters staff were seen as overemphasising information giving (usually through emails or paper) with rather less emphasis upon leadership and face-to-face communication with staff. The consequence of this is knowledge without belief.

Communication with staff was seen as confined to 'bits of the jigsaw' like the Think First programme, with less emphasis upon a holistic message of effective practice and the key role of all staff in its delivery. The impact of communication strategies was doubted, particularly where key management messages had been communicated in training events rather than through the line management structure. Operational managers also wrestled daily with resource inadequacies, and none felt that effective practice had been appropriately costed. Resource allocation was hindered by inadequacies in information about unit costs and by resource allocation models driven by functional requirements rather than by effective practice and risk. Indeed, managers were unsure whether high-risk work and effective practice could both be resourced at an adequate level, and that the resource-hungry activities of What Works took resources required for public protection. In practice, this left operational managers in particular with difficult daily decisions on resource allocation, and probation officers straining to meet both the requirements of effective practice and the community risk management of high-risk offenders. Strategic managers talked of 'robbing Peter to pay Paul' and many programmes such as Think First were seen as distinct from risk management rather than integral to it.

Practice issues (including case management)

The challenges for practice arise from:

- the unexpected costs of effective practice, particularly the staff resource costs of programmes;
- the high demands upon all staff of centrally driven and time-limited change; and
- the organisational and cultural difficulties arising from any period of intensive change.

Staff were well aware of the effective practice agenda and saw the key elements as:

- appropriate targeting;
- using intervention methods that work;
- consistency in practice;
- increased accountability for practice; and
- to a large extent, vested in prescribed programmes.

The distinction made by staff between routine practice and accredited programmes was marked, although some staff saw this as 'unbalanced' and advocated a more holistic approach to What Works. However, during the period of the research What Works and programmes were becoming synonymous – resulting in a fragmentation of the effective practice message and a devaluing of the supervision role. This in itself raised confusion about role and responsibilities (particularly for case managers), and some negative perceptions around deskilling and over-emphasis upon enforcement.

Assessment and targeting produced particular problems, especially around the consistent and appropriate use of the targeting matrix, and the perceived strain between meeting service performance targets on eligibility (that is, meeting the risk score for programme eligibility) and assessments of offender unsuitability for group programmes.

Assessments of offender motivation can appear particularly perfunctory (based on case-file reading of 297 cases). The designation of too many cases as 'not group ready' or 'ungroupable' has serious knock-on effects for local resource management and meeting national accredited programme completion targets. 'Unsuitability' is presently functioning as an 'opt-out clause' rather than as an issue to be worked on through structured motivational work in the early stages of case management (Kemshall et al. 2002). The case-file reading revealed very few cases in which supervision plans specified how motivation was going to be 'enhanced and encouraged' (HMIP 1999). Supervision plans also lacked focus on objectives and outcomes, with staff confusing objectives with descriptions of the routes that would lead to their achievement. This led to activities such as liaison or referral being presented as case objectives. While attitudinal change and compliance were the most common examples of impact measures in supervision plans there was little evidence that they were actually used and measured. The use of SMART objectives in supervision planning has yet to be fully realised (Kemshall et al. 2001).[4]

This situation has been exacerbated by the failure of the service to specify role and responsibilities for case management and to gain ready acceptance for the role among staff. Case management currently lacks clarity and attraction (Holt 2000b). As Holt outlines there are three main models of case management:

- A minimal approach of simple brokerage and administrative tasks (Ross 1980).
- A co-ordinating model which encompasses assessment, planning, referral, some advocacy and direct casework, support and reassessment (Ross 1980; Huxley 1993).
- A comprehensive model which adds key tasks of advocacy for resource development, monitoring and quality issues, public education and crisis intervention to the tasks above (Ross 1980).

Holt has suggested that in probation work the key functions of case management will be assessment, planning, linking, monitoring and evaluation; underpinned by a commitment to consistency of service delivery; continuity of service delivery and appropriate management of sequencing; consolidation and reinforcement of learning; and commitment to the offender's change process (Holt 2000b: 57–72).

However, the role has largely been cast as minimalist (to some extent due to resource pressures) and has consequently lacked commitment from staff. What staff are actually expected to do has also received little attention, leaving staff uncertain and demotivated. In addition to the tasks outlined by Holt above, case managers are required to target and appropriately refer to programmes; motivate offenders to change and secure compliance; maintain offender compliance throughout the order; function as adult teachers and reinforce learning; act as consistent pro-social modellers; be solution focused; act as change managers; identify and implement relapse prevention techniques with the offender; and act as mentors. The term 'case management' is hardly adequate to capture the range of professional tasks required of staff.

Effective case management is the key to a 'joined up' service of effective practice. This requires a positive reframing of case management – in effect reframing from a mechanism for handling high caseloads in a climate of limited resource into a professional role incorporating motivational work, responsivity assessment, appropriate targeting, reinforcement and learning, support and relapse prevention.

Skill development and staff training

Skill development and staff training are seen as key requirements in the Underdown template for effective implementation of What Works (1998). Training has, however, been differentially delivered and experienced, and evaluation of its impact has not been routine. This has left staff with differing and inconsistent levels of knowledge of What Works, some of which has been confined to theory and key principles with less emphasis upon implementation issues. Some training has been confined to one programme (i.e. Think First), and staff have not readily transferred this learning to other aspects of effective practice. Training is rarely routinely reinforced 'on the job' and key issues have not been revisited during the period of effective practice implementation. In some services training has been used as a substitute for adequate management communication with staff and, where training events have had to cope with high levels of staff dissent or resistance, the effectiveness of the events has been compromised. Skills, competencies and practice tasks should be specified in advance of training, and the latter constructed and delivered in order to assist staff to acquire and achieve them. They are not the natural products of ill-defined training events, nor do they naturally follow training events without significant reinforcement and supervision.

Performance management and capacity planning

Increased accountability has resulted in higher levels of scrutiny on performance and requirements routinely to monitor key areas of activity (for example, for PIPs and the recent HMIP audit of accredited programmes – HMIP 2002). However, staff and operational managers are unable to use this information directly to improve their performance, and much of it is concerned with throughput and outputs rather than quality and outcomes. Accredited programmes are a key point. Completions are routinely monitored because they are directly linked to NPD targets and financial allocations. However, attrition (or failure to complete) is not. While the NPD has begun to monitor attrition (NPD 2002), local systems and figures are inadequate and the routine categories for attrition are failing to capture attrition causes (Kemshall *et al.* 2002; Stephens 2002). In this situation the service lacks the knowledge about attrition rates and its causes upon which to base corrective action (Kemshall *et al.* 2002). In essence, information must assist the service to identify and define the problem before it can solve it. The Underdown Report points out that sound information systems are crucial to the appropriate capacity planning of programmes and to avoid under-occupancy, and laments a 'reactive approach' based upon 'waiting for referrals before establishing programme start dates' (1998: 133). This has resulted in lengthy waiting times for groups (ranging from 5 weeks to 5 months) and has contributed to attrition rates as offenders lose commitment and motivation to attend (Kemshall *et al.* 2002).

Conclusion

Within the broader context of a nationally driven agenda to achieve effective practice a number of key considerations pertinent to the implementation agenda can be identified. Of these the pace of change, the level of central 'driving' and the unprecedented level of account-ability and scrutiny on the service have been the most significant. These have been paralleled by a degree of unpredictability (for example, the changes in risk assessment tools and the implications for targeting); the perceived lack of co-ordination centrally of the effective practice agenda (for example, its initiation before the completion and introduction of OASys); and the tensions between parts of the central agenda (for example, the rigorous enforcement agenda is seen to hinder effective practice with those offenders for whom securing and maintaining compliance may be more difficult). This first phase of programme roll-out has resulted in a degree of implementation fatigue, for both practitioners and managers. Practitioners perceive that What Works has been hijacked from front-line staff, and are disappointed with the gap between the ideal and reality. Managers are frustrated with the slow pace of implementation and levels of resistance still expressed by staff. All are concerned that resources are not keeping pace with demands. As the service enters phase two (that is, the effective integration of What Works into all aspects of service delivery), there is a growing realisation that implementing and doing effective practice well is a long haul. Ensuring that pro-social modelling is effectively integrated within all aspects of case management and programme delivery will require careful planning and effective training (see Kemshall *et al.* 2002).

The over-association of What Works with accredited programmes has also received criticism. For example, the NAPO annual general meeting of 2001 adopted a resolution rejecting accredited programmes (Raynor 2002: 1193) although, for Raynor, this also illustrates the misunder-standing of probation staff who too readily associate effective practice with prescriptive cognitive behavioural programmes. He argues that there is now sufficient evidence that pro-social approaches to super-vision are associated with better reconviction outcomes (see Rex and Matravers 1998; Trotter 1993, 2000), suggesting that pro-social modelling is a key task for case management requiring high levels of skill. There is also research suggesting that offenders value learning strategies to 'cope with problems or temptations to offend' (Raynor 2002: 1194; Raynor and Vanstone 1997).

Integration of What Works is now the key issue, and this requires effective practice to be embedded into the daily life of the agency. This will not happen without systems and processes to achieve it. Agency culture and identity do not change themselves, they have to be changed. The following are suggested as key mechanisms in achieving such change:

• Communicate clearly what is required *and* what is no longer required.
• Integrate effective practice into all appraisal objectives for all staff (regardless of role or function), such as 'All staff contact with offenders will exhibit pro-social modelling', 'All service delivery must contain SMART objectives'.
• Ensure quality assurance of key points of delivery in the effective practice journey of the offender.

• Promote, disseminate and actively reward good practice.

Programmes are not effective practice; they are a core component of effective practice. The appropriate implementation of effective practice requires a strategic and whole-system approach in which attention is given to the supporting processes, systems and infrastructure required to ensure its effective delivery. This requires a holistic and corporate response to effective practice, and not a 'mere programmes' approach (Link 2002). This will require senior management teams to ask the crucial question 'Are we fit for purpose?' – that is to say, 'are we fit to deliver effective practice?' This question could be answered by carrying out a self-assessment audit of the key points of effective practice delivery in any offender's journey through the service. What are the points of 'threat'? Where is the quality and consistency of service delivery compromised? Where does the service need to 'bridge and bond' fragmentation in the offender's journey? What key points require proactive quality assurance?

The probation service's performance on effective practice is set at the level of the least convinced and least committed member of staff. Organisations have to secure compliance from their staff just as staff have to secure compliance from offenders. To do so, the service must provide incentives for staff to perform; legitimate and validate its key goals; structure practice towards desirable ends; and routinise performance into daily practice so that it can confidently say: 'Effective practice – that's what we do.'

Notes

1 An overview of recent What Works history is provided in Holt (2000a).
2 The chapter draws on a research project into 'The implementation of effective practice in the Northwest Region', and thanks are extended to all in the region who participated in this research and to the Northwest Effective Practice Steering Group who commissioned the research. The research represents the region during 1999 and should not be taken as indicative of the state of effective practice implementation at the present time.
3 In practice there is considerable overlap between the factors and they have been differentiated here for heuristic purposes.
4 The SMART acronym stands for Specific, Measurable, Achievable, Realistic, Timely/Time limited.

References

Association of Chief Officers of Probation (ACOP) (1997) *The Strategic Place of Training and Staff Development to Create the Learning Organisation.* London: ACOP.

Association of Chief Officers of Probation (ACOP) (1998) *An Integrated Approach to Training and Development and Human Resource Management.* London: ACOP.

Bailey, R. (1994) 'Probation supervision: attitudes to formalised helping.' Unpublished PhD thesis, Nottingham University.

Bailey, R. and Ward, D. (1992) *Probation Supervision – Attitudes to Formalised Helping.* Belfast: Probation Board for Northern Ireland and Nottingham Centre for Social Action, Nottingham University.

Bailey, R. and Williams, B. (2000) *Inter-agency Partnerships in Youth Justice: Implementing the Crime and Disorder Act 1998.* Social Services Monographs Research in Practice. Sheffield: University of Sheffield/Community Care.

Burnett, R. (1996) *Fitting Supervision to Offenders: Assessment and Allocation Decisions in the Probation Service.* Home Office Research Study 169. London: Home Office.

Chapman, T. and Hough, M. (1998) *Evidence-based Practice.* London: Home Office/HMIP.

Denzin, N.K. (1978) *The Research Act in Sociology.* London: Butterworths.

Desncombe, M. (1998) *The Good Research Guide.* Buckingham: Open University Press.

Gast, L. and Taylor, P. (1999) *Influence and Integrity: A Practice Handbook for Pro-social Modelling.* Birmingham: Midlands Probation Training Consortium.

Her Majesty's Inspectorate of Probation (HMIP) (1999) Checklist from the performance inspections, adapted from the HMIP documentation *HMIP Quality and Effectiveness (Q and E) Inspection Programme.* Inspection of all 53 probation areas during 1994–8 (reports for individual areas are available at www.homeoffice.gov.uk/hmiprob/hmipip).

Her Majesty's Inspectorate of Probation (HMIP) (2002) *Annual Report.* London: Home Office.

Holt, P. (2000a) *Take up and Rollout: Contexts and Issues in the Implementation of Effective Practice in the Probation Service.* Community and Criminal Justice Monograph 1. Leicester: DeMontfort University.

Holt, P. (2000b) *Case Management: Context for Supervision. A Review of Research on Models of Case Management: Design Implications for Effective Practice.* Community and Criminal Justice Monograph 2. Leicester: DeMontfort University.

Home Office (1998) *Effective Practice Initiative: A National Implementation Plan for the Effective Supervision of Offenders.* Probation Circular 35/1998. London: Home Office.

Home Office (1999a) *'What Works'? Reducing Reoffending: Evidence Based Practice.* London: Home Office.

Home Office (1999b) *Probation Circular 86/1999: Better Quality Services and the European Excellence Model*. London: Home Office.

Huxley, P. (1993) 'Case management and care management in community care', *British Journal of Social Work*, 23: 365–81.

Johnson, G. and Scholes, K. (1993) *Exploring Corporate Strategy: Text and Cases*. Hemel Hempstead: Prentice Hall.

Kemshall, H. (2002) 'Reducing programme attrition.' Presentation to the 'What Works' conference, Notttingham, 1–3 October.

Kemshall, H., Canton, R., Dominey, J., with Bailey, R., Simpkin, B. and Yates, S. (2002) *The Effective Management of Programme Attrition*. Report for the National Probation Service (commissioned by the Welsh region). Leicester: DeMontfort University.

Kemshall, H., Holt, P., Boswell, G. and Bailey, R. (2001) *The Implementation of Effective Practice in the Northwest Region*. Leicester: DeMontfort University.

Kotter, J.P. (1995) 'Leading change: why transformation efforts fail', *Harvard Business Review*, March/April: 59–67.

Lewis, P. (1999) 'Evidence-based management: the challenge of effective practice', *VISTA*, 5 (1): 23–36.

Link, S. (2002) 'Improving performance on completion: an area perspective.' Presentation to the 'What Works' conference, Nottingham, 1–3 October.

Merrington, S. (1995) *Offenders on Probation – a Qualitative Study of Offenders' Views on their Probation Orders*. Cambridge: Cambridgeshire Probation Service.

Merrington, S. and Stanley, S. (2000) 'Doubts about the "What Works" initiative', *Probation Journal*, 47: 272–5.

Miles, M.B. and Huberman, A.M. (1994) *Qualitative Data Analysis*. London: Sage.

Murphy, S. (2002) '"What Works" implementation and performance.' Presentation to the 'What Works' conference, Nottingham 1–3 October.

NAPO News (2002) 'Action on workloads? AGM to decide', Issue 143, October: 1.

National Probation Directorate (2002) *Accredited Programmes Performance Report 2001–2002*. London: National Probation Service.

National Probation Service (2001) *The New Choreography*. London: National Probation Service.

Nutley, S. and Davies, H. (1999) 'The fall and rise of evidence in criminal justice', *Public Money and Management*, 19 (9): 47–54.

Raynor, P. (2002) 'Community penalties: probation, punishment and "What Works"', in M. Maguire *et al.* (eds) *The Oxford Handbook of Criminology* (3rd edn). Oxford: Oxford University Press, 1169–205.

Raynor, P. and Vanstone, M. (1997) *Straight Thinking on Probation (STOP): The Mid Glamorgan Experiment*. Probation Studies Unit Report 4. Oxford: University of Oxford Centre for Criminological Research.

Rex, S. (1995) *Offenders' and their Supervisors' Views of Probation – Help within a Restrictive Framework*. Cambridge: Cambridge University Institute of Criminology.

Rex, S. and Matravers, A. (1998) *Pro-social Modelling and Legitimacy*. Cambridge: Cambridge Institute of Criminology.

Robinson, G. (2001) 'Power, knowledge and "What Works" in probation', *Howard Journal*, 40 (3): 235-54.

Ross, H. (1980) *Proceedings of the Conference on the Evaluation of Case Management Programs (March 5–6 1979)*. Los Angeles, CA: Volunteers for Services to Older Persons.

Schein, E.H. (1992) *Organisational Culture and Leadership*. San Francisco, CA: Jossey-Bass.

Silverman, D. (1993) *Interpreting Qualitative Data*. London: Sage.

Stephens, K. (2002) *What is Programme Attrition? Towards an Action-oriented Typology*. National Probation Service, West Yorkshire (draft, September).

Trotter, C. (1993) *The Supervision of Offenders – 'What Works'? A Study Undertaken in Community Based Corrections*. Victoria: Social Work Department, Monash University and the Victoria Department of Justice, Melbourne.

Trotter, C. (2000) 'Social work education, pro-social modelling and effective probation practice', *Probation Journal*, 47: 256-61.

Udall, S. (2001) 'Seamless supervision: the role of managers in effective practice', *VISTA*, 6 (2): 132–42.

Underdown, A. (1998) *Strategies for Effective Offender Supervision: Report of the HMIP 'What Works' Project*. London: Home Office/HMIP.

Chapter 9

Supervision, motivation and social context: what matters most when probationers desist?

Stephen Farrall

Introduction: what works?

Initial investigations into the outcomes of probation supervision in the 1950s and 1960s were concerned chiefly with outlining the general patterns in the usage of probation, and devoted considerable attention to describing which offenders (in terms of their age, gender and criminal history) were made subject to probation supervision (Radzinowicz 1958; Barr and O'Leary 1966). As part of this initial period of investigation, trends in the rates of 'success' and 'failure' started to emerge. For example, Radzinowicz (1958: 2) reported that 79 per cent of adults, but slightly fewer juveniles (73 per cent), successfully completed their orders. As few of the studies during this initial period considered probationers outside the 17–21-year-old age range, the impact of age on rates of success and failure was rarely commented upon. However, later studies found age to be one of the best predictors of reconviction, especially for males. The gender of the probationer was, however, more commonly noted to be associated with probation outcomes (Radzinowicz 1958) as was the number of previous convictions. However, while the correlates of reconviction had been identified, there appeared to be little evidence that probation-based interventions could do very much to lower the possibility of offending once these variables had been taken into account (e.g. Martinson 1974; Folkard *et al.* 1974, 1976), and so the 1970s ended on a depressing note in this respect.

The more recent work in this field has placed a greater emphasis on assessing the outcomes of cognitive-behavioural interventions and (as a result of the development of day centres, groupwork programmes and other specified activities) has focused upon assessing the outcomes of specific interventions rather than 'generic' probation; for example, Mair and Nee (1992) studied day-centre reconviction rates, Brownlee (1995) evaluated intensive probation in Leeds and Wilkinson (1997) studied the Idlerton motor-car project run by Inner London Probation Service. These interventions often do not cover the whole period of probation and, as such, few have developed a picture of the *whole* probation order from beginning to end. In addition, few of the studies of probation outcomes had paid very much attention to social or personal factors – although Chris May's (1999) study has started to fill this gap.

The 1980s and 1990s saw a rise in rehabilitative efforts based around cognitive behaviouralist approaches. McGuire and Priestly argued that models of intervention based on cognitive and behavioural psychology emerged as 'offering the most encouraging approaches' (1995: 16), and suggested that teaching probationers new styles of thinking and acting will help them to avoid the situations and temptations which had previously led them to offend. These approaches include techniques such as reinforcement (Lawson 1983); covert punishment (Guidry 1975); mentoring (O'Donnell *et al.* 1979; Hughes 1997); behaviour modification (Bank *et al.* 1987); relaxation (Hazaleus and Deffenbacher 1986); social skills training (Priestly *et al.* 1984); and training in moral reasoning (McDougall *et al.* 1987). This line of thinking was echoed by Lösel (1995: 91) when he wrote that 'it is mostly cognitive-behavioural, skill-orientated and multi-modal programmes that yield the best effects'. Writing from a North American perspective, Gendreau also supported this line of thinking: 'behavioural strategies are essential to effective service delivery' (1996: 120). Palmer, too, found support for such approaches and concluded that vocational training and other interventions aimed at providing probationers with employment were found to have some impact on rates of recidivism (1996: 139). Educational training (academic programming, remedial education and/or individual tutoring) was also reported to have had positive effects (1996: 140), as were behavioural interventions, cognitive-behavioural approaches, life skills and multi-modal approaches (1996: 141–3).

It was against this backdrop of cognitive and behavioural approaches that Tracking Progress on Probation, the research project discussed here, was undertaken. The project aimed to understand the processes that occurred during probation orders which were either conducive to desistance from crime or which contributed to persistence (see Farrall 2002 for a full report of the study's findings). While it is true that the correlates of recidivism and desistance are well known, the mechanisms by which these correlates are produced – and in particular the role that criminal justice sanctions play in this – remain less well understood. In order better to understand the role of probation supervision in encouraging the processes associated with desistance, the project investigated the effects of probation supervision on the criminal careers and behaviour of 199 probationers. Six probation services (as they then were) in England were recruited into the study, and in these a number of probation offices (in all 22) were selected for fieldwork. All probationers aged 17–35 years and starting probation or combination orders of 6–24 months duration between the start of October 1997 and the end of March 1998 were eligible for inclusion in the study – regardless of offences committed, gender or race. The achieved sample was representative of English and Welsh probation caseloads when examined for age, gender, previous convictions and the offence for which the order was imposed (see Farrall 2002: ch. 3 for further details of the research methodology and sample characteristics). The general methodology builds on that developed by Burnett (see 1992, 2000, 2004).

This chapter, as well as providing an outline of the main findings, highlights the complex and interdependent relationships between the main variables of interest, namely, social context, motivation and probation supervision. The implications of some of the findings for probation work will be examined. First, however, a brief outline of some of the elements of complexity theory is necessary.

Complexity and causation

When analysis of the data commenced it quickly became apparent that the relationships between key variables were not linear. That is to say that it was not simply the case that more of X was associated with more of Y. There were, of course, instances in which these sorts of relationships existed (for example, those with more previous convictions were more likely to have reported continued offending), but in the main the relationships between important variables were far more complex. To this end, the work of David Byrne (especially 1998) was important in shaping the approach taken to the data analyses, which became influenced by theories of complexity.

One of the basic principles of complexity is that, at their very heart, lie interactions between three or more variables. Byrne (1998: 2) describes interaction (the process by which the relationship between two variables is modified by the value of a third) as a 'grudging recognition' that the impact of variables is not additive (linear) but, rather, dependent (and therefore non-linear). It is commonly held that for a system or process to exhibit complexity, it requires a minimum of three variables (Brown 1995: 9). As such, the outcome of any social process is not merely a sum of other variables but is affected by the relationships between several variables, meaning that causal processes are contingent upon earlier states and conditions. In reality, as we shall see shortly, this often means that outcomes have multiple cause, and that these causes interact with one another (Lee 1997: 22; Byrne 1998: 20). However, despite the seeming randomness of causal processes, their outcomes usually fall within a known set of boundaries. That is to say, while we will not know exactly what the outcome of a processes may be, we have a pretty good idea of the range of outcomes which are probable. As such, while social processes are chaotic, chaos is determined – in other words, it has limits.

The interaction effects of variables mean that, over time, different outcomes are produced (Price 1997: 11; Byrne 1998: 28). Bifurcation means that at Time One, if A occurs then either X or Y will occur. If A reaches a certain threshold, Y will occur; if it does not, the outcomes will be X. There is no reason why this should be limited to only two outcomes, or why bifurcation points should not be sequential. Closely related to bifurcation points is the principle of sensitivity to initial conditions (often referred to as the 'butterfly effect' – Turner 1997: xxix). This principle holds that even very small variations in an initial condition have the potential to lead to hugely differing outcomes. For example, the difference between being below a threshold compared to being above it may be very small, but the outcomes (X or Y) may themselves be substantially different from one another.

Any system may, of course, contain various 'pathways' through it. For example, at Time One there may be 100 people, of whom 50 own cars. At Time Two, of these 100 people, there may still be 50 car owners. This apparent stability may in fact hide differing pathways of car ownership over time. For example, some of our 100 people who started with cars may have sold them and, similarly, those initially without cars may have bought cars by Time Two. This very basic observation implies that unless the two groups are differentiated at the aggregate level one runs the risk of (incorrectly) assuming that there had been no change over time when in fact there had been considerable change between Times One and Two (Horsfall and Maret 1997: 184). In essence, and drawing upon Byrne's (1998: 2–28) use of complexity theories, a set of core statements can be made:

- That complex social processes have *multiple* causes.
- That these causes are not necessarily additive; in other words, the outcome is not *simply* the sum of the separate effects.

- That *small* differences in initial conditions may, over time, or following specific bifurcation points, produce big differences in eventual outcomes.
- That many outcomes, nevertheless, fall within a range of known or calculable outcomes.
- That multiple pathways exist, such that different cases can get from the similar initial states to similar end states via different trajectories.

Two examples – one drawn from Byrne and the other a criminological example – illustrate these assertions. Byrne (1998: 38–9) cites the example of an eminent interwar physician called Bradbury who was interested in what caused tuberculosis (TB) on Tyneside. The answer, as both Bradbury and Byrne point out, is (initially) very simple: tuberculosis bacteria cause TB. The problem, however, was that not everyone exposed to the TB bacteria developed TB. Bradbury's investigations suggested that three factors were important in understanding who developed TB and who did not. These were poor housing, poor diet and being Irish. The first two are fairly easily understood: the worse the conditions of one's housing and the worse one's diet, the more likely one was to develop TB. However, the third was less straightforward. Irish migrants had, at that time, not been living on Tyneside for very long and had less experience than the rest of the Tyneside population of urbanisation (about two generations less). TB, like many other bacteria, bred for resistance. Hence at that time Irish migrants were particularly susceptible to developing TB as they had had less exposure to the TB bacteria and the conditions in which it thrived. Thus the causal mechanisms for TB on Tyneside during the 1930s were complex and contingent. Good housing and good diets prevented infection; being Irish made it more likely.

The second example (this time hypothetical) concerns sentencing in criminal courts. Imagine a study designed to explain the sentences which were imposed on all those found guilty in a magistrates' court. A number of factors can be identified which might be of use in accounting for variations in sentences: previous criminal history (chiefly previous convictions and outcomes of previous disposals); current offence (intentions to harm and actual harm to victim, the efforts made by the guilty party to repair the harm they caused, the tariff and so on); the pre-sentence report and the recommendations made in it; the plea entered; the characteristics of the guilty party (demeanour, signs of distress, age, gender and so on); and the public's attitude towards crimes of that nature at the time and probably several other factors. In coming to their decision, magistrates may take into account any number of these factors.

Some will make custody more likely, others will make probation (or a community rehabilitation order, to use the new terminology) seem appropriate and still others may make community service (now a community punishment order) or a suspended sentence appear to be a sensible disposal.

These two examples illustrate the sorts of issues with which theories of complexity attempt to deal. In both there can be found a conglomeration of factors which influence the outcomes. In the TB example these were housing conditions, diet and ethnicity (or, rather, ethnicity in particular time and space dimensions). In the sentencing example, these were hypothesised to be criminal history, offence, etc. However, as shown in the TB example, these causes are non-additive. Similarly, sentencing decisions can also be hypothesised to be non-additive: unique factors, variations and contingencies may influence the outcomes of sentencing decisions in various ways, some aggravating and some mitigating. Despite this, the range of outcomes in both cases is known with some degree of certainty: people either will or will not get TB. The range of sentencing options can often be estimated both in terms of the type of sentence (custodial or non-custodial) and the severity of the sentence (length of custody or numbers of hours community sentence, for example).

Probation, motivation, context and desistance

One of the most consistent findings of the literature on the termination of criminal careers concerns the successful resolution of obstacles to reform by the would-be desister. The men and women who have successfully made the transition away from crime frequently refer to the stigma of their pasts, problems in getting work, giving up alcohol dependency, disassociating from criminal friends, poor financial circumstances and a host of other obstacles which stood between them and 'reform'. For example, Rex's (1999) probation-based sample, Burnett's (1992) prison-based sample, Cusson and Pinsonneault's (1983) and Dale's (1976) samples drawn from outside the criminal justice system and Maruna's (1997) sample of published autobiographies of desistance all reported that 'obstacles', 'impediments' or 'road-blocks' were common features of the desistance process.

The 199 probationers interviewed as part of the research reported on here were no different in this respect. Over 50 per cent (101) stated that they faced at least one such obstacle when they were first interviewed (at the start of their orders). Their probation officers (POs) were even more downbeat in their assessments – all but 18 officers said that their probationer faced an obstacle (see Table 9.1).

Table 9.1 Identified obstacles to desistance: probationers' and officers' reports[1]

Category	Probationers		Officers	
	n	%	*n*	%
No obstacles expected	98	49	18	9
Friends and family	29	15	74	37
Financial reasons	17	9	13	7
Drugs and alcohol	37	19	74	37
Social problems	13	6	54	27
Personal characteristics	18	10	60	30
Other responses	8	4	32	16
Total obstacles	*122*	*100*	*307*	*100*

Of the 101 probationers who said that they faced one or more obstacles, their own use of substances (drugs and alcohol, 19 per cent) was the most commonly cited, closely followed by their friends and family (15 per cent). Other obstacles were less frequently mentioned. Overall, few probationers cited social problems (such as their employment and housing situations) as obstacles to desistance, despite the well documented evidence that social factors play a large part in offending careers (e.g. Smith *et al.* 1991; Farrington 1997). Only one in ten probationers regarded any of their own personal attributes as obstacles.

Unlike those whom they supervised, nine out of ten POs said that the probationer faced at least one obstacle. Several officers thought that friends and/or family along with drugs and alcohol were likely to be obstacles (37 per cent). Officers also reported more obstacles relating to social problems, in particular the probationer's employment situation, than did probationers. Interestingly, there were few citations of cognitive-behavioural obstacles (such as poor thinking skills or anger management), suggesting that these were either not features of the current sample's problems, or that they were not features which were readily identified by POs.[2]

Relative to those who had not overcome the obstacles which they faced, those who had overcome their obstacles appeared more likely to have at least started to desist from involvement in crime (see Table 9.2).

Table 9.2 Desistance or persistence by obstacles (probationers' reports)[3]

	Faced no obstacles		Obstacles were resolved		Obstacles not resolved		Total	
	n	%	*n*	%	*n*	%	*n*	%
Desisters	62	82	27	69	20	51	109	71
Persisters	14	18	12	31	19	49	45	29
Total	*76*	*100*	*39*	*100*	*39*	*100*	*154*	*100*

What were the 'motors' which drove obstacle resolution? Was this the result of the good work of POs? Was it due to the motivation of some probationers to avoid further trouble? Or was it due to some other factors, or combination of factors? It was these sorts of questions to which the project sought answers. Because the aim of the project was to develop an understanding of the processes involved in influencing these outcomes rather than just the correlates of these outcomes (Pawson and Tilley 1997), it was not enough to employ 'black box' approaches to these sorts of outcomes. The keys used to 'open' the 'black box' of probation required a reliance upon both quantitative and qualitative data sources, and an emphasis on locating probation supervision in wider social and personal contexts. To this end it was assumed that, to varying degrees, all the following would influence the outcome of probation supervision:

- The work of the supervising PO.
- The motivation of the individual probationer.
- The individual probationer's social and personal circumstances.

It was further assumed, in line with Byrne (1998), that these influences would:

- interact with one another, sometimes working to support one another and sometimes working to cancel each other out; and
- be dynamic, changing both their nature and the extent to which they influenced one another and, ultimately, the outcome of supervision.

Supervision and the work of probation officers

The most logical starting point for the inquiries into what 'drove' the resolution of obstacles was the work of POs. During the follow-up interviews, both probationers and probation officers were asked, for each of the obstacles originally identified, what each of them had done to address the specific needs of the probationer with regards to the obstacles at hand. These reports, when analysed, suggested that very few of the modes of intervention employed by POs were related to whether the obstacle had been resolved – suggesting that few particular modes of intervention were any more likely to be effective than any *other mode*, and that virtually all modes were ineffective in combating the obstacles. Similarly, none of the reports of the probationer's actions were significantly associated with the 'successful' resolution of obstacles either. However, officers who reported that the probationer had *not* been motivated to address the obstacle were significantly more likely also to report that the obstacles had *not* been resolved ($p < = .000$). In other words, from the officers' and probationers' accounts of their own work and the actions of the other, it would appear that no particular modes of intervention were more effective than any other in helping probationers to overcome the obstacles they faced. Similar analyses were undertaken, this time controlling for the extent to which officers and probationers appeared to have worked together. Again these analyses suggested that the extent to which officers and probationers had worked together was not related to the resolution of obstacles.

Motivation and the orientation of individual probationers

Having the motivation to avoid further offending is perhaps one of the key factors in explaining desistance. West (1978), Shover (1983), Shover and Thompson (1992), Moffitt (1993), Sommers *et al.* (1994) and Pezzin (1995) have all pointed to a range of factors which motivated the offenders in their samples to desist. These included the desire to avoid negative consequences (such as death or serious injury); realising that legitimate financial gains outweigh criminal gains; wanting to 'lead a quieter life'; embarking upon a committed personal relationship; and so on. Burnett (1992, 1994) suggested that those ex-prisoners who reported that they *wanted* to stop offending and, importantly, felt they were *able* to stop offending were more likely to desist than those who said they were unsure if they wanted to stop offending: 'more of those who desisted stated unequivocally at both the pre-release [from prison] and the post-release [interview] that they wanted to desist' (Burnett 1966: 66).

In the current study, both probationers and officers were asked if the probationer wanted to stop offending and if they would be able to do so. These responses indicated that there were three groups of probationers:

- Some 110 probationers who said that they wanted to stop offending, and felt that they would be able to stop offending *and* whose officers agreed with these assessments (and who will be referred to as the 'Confident').

- The second group (*n* = 46) of probationers said that they wanted to and felt able to stop offending, but whose officers did *not* support this assessment – they either felt that the probationer did not want to desist, was unable to desist, or both. These cases will be referred to as the 'Optimistic'.

- The 'Pessimists' (the remaining group of probationers, *n* = 43) said that they did not want to stop, would be unable to stop, or both. In some cases, officers supported their assessments but, in others, they did not.

These groups of probationers, on further inspection, were found to have subtly different criminal pasts, as summarised in Table 9.3. While there was little difference in their age at the *start* of the orders, the Pessimists were younger when *first convicted* (being on average 17 years old) compared to the Confident (on average 20 years old) or the Optimists (aged on average 19 years when first convicted). Consequently the average length of their criminal careers varied: Confidents had the shortest careers at five years, Optimists' average career length was six years and the Pessimist had by far the longest, with an average nine-year criminal career. There were substantial differences in the average number of convictions recorded against each group: the Confident were the least frequently convicted (averaging six convictions each), with the Optimistic the next most convicted (averaging 11 convictions each) and

Table 9.3 Criminal histories at commencement of supervision

Average for each group	Confidents	Optimists	Pessimists	All
Age at start of order	25 yrs	25 yrs	26 yrs	25 yrs
Age at first conviction	20 yrs	19 yrs	17 yrs	19 yrs
Previous convictions (*n*)	6	11	19	10
Previous prob. orders (*n*)	0.5	0.6	2.4	0.9
Previous custody (*n*)	0.6	2.4	2.3	1.3
OGRS	53%	61%	68%	58%
Total	*110*	*46*	*43*	*199*

the Pessimistic the most convicted (averaging 19 convictions each). Their average number of previous probation orders also differed: the Confident and Optimistic had had little experience of either, while the Pessimistic had had more experience. When previous custodial sentences were considered, the Confident can be seen to have had very little experience, unlike either the Optimistic or the Pessimistic.

To what extent was motivation a factor in the frequency with which probationers faced obstacles and overcame them? Analyses like those described immediately above were repeated, this time controlling for motivation. These analyses suggested that there were few differences in the *nature* of the obstacles that probationers faced, but that there were differences in the rates with which each faced obstacles and resolved these. This is represented diagrammatically in Figure 9.1.

A model of desistance is starting to emerge from the analyses reported so far. Solving obstacles was related to desistance (Table 9.2), but it would appear that the mode of probation intervention was *not* associated with resolving obstacles (see above). Motivation, however, *does* appear to influence the extent to which obstacles were both faced and overcome. These relationships are presented diagrammatically in Figure 9.1 – which charts the progress of each of the three groups of probationers towards desistance.[4]

Fewer of the Confident (40 per cent) faced obstacles than either of the other groups, while almost five out of ten Optimists and eight out of ten of the Pessimists faced one or more obstacles. Of the few Pessimists who faced no obstacles, 67 per cent desisted. However, 64 per cent of those Pessimists who faced an obstacle but *overcame* it desisted, while even fewer – only 31 per cent – of those Pessimists who faced an obstacle but did *not* overcome it desisted. For the Optimists and Pessimists, solving obstacles was particularly strongly related to desistance: of the six Optimists who overcame the obstacle they faced, all but one desisted. On the other hand, of the 11 who did not overcome the obstacle they faced, five desisted and five did not (one was lost during the follow-up). Desistance rates were highest among those groups that faced no obstacles and lowest (with one exception – the Confident) among those who faced obstacles but did not overcome them. This suggests that overcoming obstacles is successively more important for each group. Most of the Confident desisted regardless of their resolving their obstacles. However, 64 per cent of the Pessimists who resolved their obstacles desisted, compared to 36 per cent of those who did *not*.

Figure 9.1 Motivation, obstacles and desistance: a summary
Note: All figures are *n* (%); probationers' reports

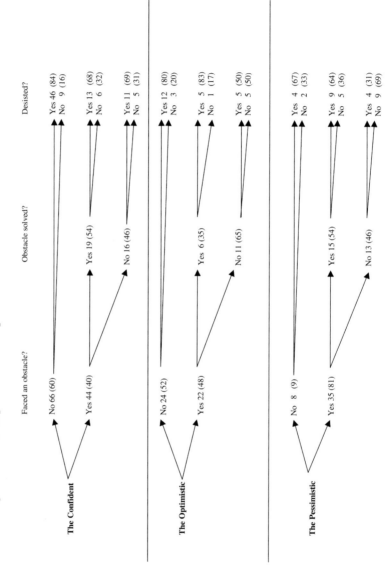

Social and personal circumstances

To the above model a further dimension can be introduced – that of social and personal circumstances. Qualitative data (see Farrall 2002) suggested that positive life changes were associated with changes in employment and family relationships. As probationers gained work, were reunited with family members or developed attachments to new partners or children, so they refrained from behaviours likely to result in offending – drug use, excessive drinking, 'aimless hanging around' or general aggressiveness. Further quantitative data, again not presented herein, suggested that those probationers who took the lead in addressing the employment and family-related obstacles they faced (itself indicative of possessing the motivation to confront and resolve problems) were also those most likely to have solved such obstacles by the time the order had been completed.

These analyses, taken together, suggest that the outcome of probation supervision (i.e. resolving obstacles to desistance) is the result of a series of interactions between motivation and social and personal contexts. Gaining employment would, from the descriptions of POs and probationers, appear to have brought about dramatic changes in the lives of the probationers. Similarly, families of formation appear to have acted as a motivating influence on probationers' desires to desist, while families of origin appear to have offered an avenue of support in achieving this change (see Farrall, 2004 for an extended discussion of these points).

When the role of probation supervision in helping probationers to achieve these changes was considered, the themes established earlier re-emerged. That is, that while officers would appear to have identified appropriate obstacles and taken what they considered to be appropriate steps to tackle these obstacles, and while most of the obstacles identified *were* indeed resolved by the end of the order, this appears more often to have been the result of the probationer's own actions and his or her own circumstances rather than as a result of the actions of the officer (see also Crow 1996: 60).

As such it is possible to develop further the model of desistance outlined in Figure 9.1. Figure 9.2 introduces to the model the issue of social and personal contexts.[5] The introduction of social and personal contexts, especially the extent to which these circumstances remained stable or either improved or worsened, has the unfortunate effect of reducing cell sizes. However, by including change in social circumstances, one is able more readily to grasp the extent to which some probationers started in a more advantageous position and the extent to which improvements in social circumstances were related to both the

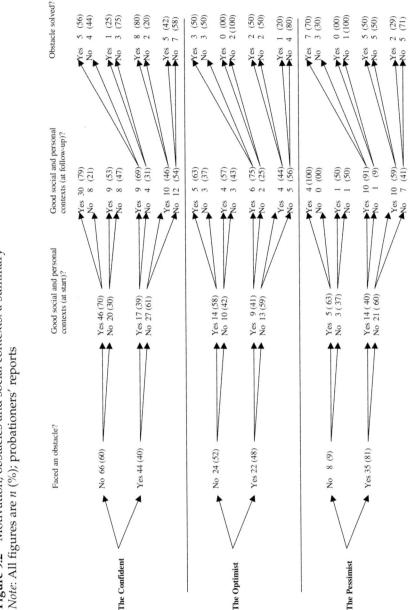

Figure 9.2 Motivation, obstacles and social contexts: a summary

Note: All figures are *n* (%); probationers' reports

presence of obstacles and the resolution of obstacles.

Consider, for example (in Figure 9.2), the Confident who faced no obstacles: of those who were living in good contexts at the start, 79 per cent were still living in good social circumstances at the follow-up. Of the Confidents who did face obstacles, more were living in poor rather than good social circumstances (61 v. 39 per cent). Living in social circumstances which were initially good, but which deteriorated, was, irrespective of motivation, more frequently associated with failing to resolve obstacles than with resolving obstacles. For example, of the four Confident probationers who were initially in good social circumstances which worsened, only one resolved the obstacles which he faced. Similarly, of those Confidents who *never* lived in good circumstances, 58 per cent did not overcome the obstacles they faced. However, of the ten Confidents who were initially in poorer circumstances but which *improved*, eight overcame the obstacles they faced.

The initial starting points (for which motivation is both important and a proxy of other important factors, such as previous criminal histories) are important in understanding both who faced obstacles and who solved their obstacles (see Figure 9.1). Solving obstacles appeared to be especially important for Optimists and Pessimists while, for the Confident, the resolution of an obstacle was less important. Similarly changes in social circumstances (which could be seen as a series of bifurcation points) influence the extent to which obstacles were resolved.

Conclusion: what matters?

There are a number of points that should be emphasised in concluding this brief overview of the project. First of all, probation supervision would appear to have had little impact upon the resolution of obstacles by probationers (although it may be important in building and encouraging motivation). This was one of the main messages of the research project, and a finding which seemed to come through 'loud and clear' from both interviews with POs and probationers themselves. Secondly, motivation and social and personal circumstances appeared to have been far more important factors in determining the extent to which obstacles were faced and resolved and hence desistance 'produced'. Again this finding was supported by data collected from both officers and probationers. It would appear, therefore, that probation is missing it's target by some degree. The full implications of these findings for probation work, the What Works agenda and other crime policies have been outlined in detail elsewhere (Farrall 2002, 2004) and it is not my intention to restate these here. What I do wish to do, however, is to reflect first upon the research methodologies used in evaluating probation and, in greater depth, upon the near total absence of cognitive behavioural obstacles uncovered during the study (see Table 9.1).

Tracking Progress on Probation was essentially a survey of probationers. Experiments, the other (and much more common) approach to assessing probation interventions, only make sense as research tools if one can reasonably assume that the processes being evaluated are linear and simple. Experiments do *not* work well if one is evaluating complex, multi-causal and contingent processes. Under such conditions it is impossible to control for everything and, as such, the use of experiments is limited (although not totally without use). However, as a body of work, the What Works literature has become not so much overly reliant, but *dependent* upon the experiment as its methodological modus operandi. This criticism strikes a cord with Kaplan's (1964) portrayal of the late-night drunk who has lost his door keys and searches for them under the nearest street light, not because this is where he believes they are, but because this is where he has most light (cited in Wacquant 1992: 28). In short, we must move away from the total reliance upon experiments as the basis of what we know about the impact of probation.

Cognitive behaviouralism has been in the vanguard of the 'rehabilitation' of rehabilitation – and for this alone we should be grateful. However, as Sue Rex has noted, even the architects of cognitive programmes emphasised the requirement that effective supervision should also attend to the social and personal problems faced by probationers (Ross and Ross 1995: 8 cited in Rex 1999: 373). Cognitive behavioural work should thus *complement* the social and economic interventions undertaken to assist probationers. However, an examination of the swath of interventions currently in vogue in probation practice suggests that cognitive behavioural programmes far outstrip those programmes which place an emphasis on social or economic assistance. For example, the second report from the Joint Prison/Probation Accreditation Panel, subtitled 'towards effective practice', emphasised cognitive 'thinking' and 'reasoning' programmes (2002: 8–10). Yet Tracking Progress on Probation found very few examples of cognitive behavioural obstacles to desistance. Indeed, during the interviews with probationers very few of them showed signs of poor thinking skills – rather the opposite; as the quotations below show, many could quite clearly see the connections between their lifestyles and their offending:

[Working] keeps me occupied and that. I've got money, don't need to make money and I don't have to go out drinking during the day. It just keeps me occupied ... Because I have work, I have got things to do. Because, before, when I committed crimes, I didn't have a job and I was just going around just to make money and that and I had time on my hands so I was drinking all the time. Now I have got a job and that, I am working all the time and I haven't got time to drink. (PR067)

I mean, obviously if I'm at work, I can't smoke [heroin]. You know, I can't go out for a drink every ten minutes or I can't have a line of coke every hour you know. So really, it's quite good because it's controlling me. (PR164).

I've cut down a lot [on drinking]. I only get really drunk one night a week. Before I would have had a few cans whilst getting ready to go out, now I don't. (PR014).

I've been promoted in my job. I have got more responsibility now, so obviously I can't smoke [cannabis] during the week – which I was before. I have to concentrate because I work on the railways. (PR039).

I've cut [drug use] right down and I know I can't do it at work, so it's only at the weekend, which basically only leaves me two evenings, Friday and Saturday evenings. You've got all week to think about it, if your wages and money is suffering. It's like anything, the reason why I stopped doing base[6] and speed was because I had one mental day and four really shit days of coming down. The first day you're coming down you think 'oh, it was a really good time', the second day, third day, fourth day 'ah, it wasn't really worth it'. This work thing is bringing it home to me as well – if I blow £60, £100 on the weekend I notice it all week long – 'why did I do that?' (PR065).

I wasn't going to move back home – I had a flat lined up, I was going to move in with somebody. It was somebody from the alcohol sessions. He'd been dry for a long time. And we got on really well. He lived 15 minutes away from where I worked, so it was all dandy – it was going to be cheap, it was all perfect. I was meant to move in there on the Saturday, and I rang him up and he was drunk. So, that was it. I couldn't afford to put myself in that situation. He was older than me – he'd gone through an awful lot more. He was further along in the alcohol line than I was – much further along. I couldn't put myself in that situation. So my only option was to go home. At first it was … like going backwards, but then, after speaking to a few people, I realised it is not going backwards, it is going sidewards. It is just putting things on hold for a little while and doing things more sensibly. (PR063)

These people – selected at random from the cases interviewed – hardly sound like they are in need of cognitive behavioural interventions. One wonders, then, why so much of the literature places such a high emphasis on cognitive behaviouralism? The officers interviewed did not report much of it; neither did the probationers and in-depth interviews with both confirmed this picture. Perhaps cognitive behaviouralism is a solution in search of a problem to solve or, to quote a colleague of mine, 'for every new solution we can create new problems'. If this is the case, we have still much to learn from the mistakes of our ancestors. As Michel Porret and Clive Emsley (2002) note in their introduction to the annual colloquium of the International Association for the History of Crime and Criminal Justice: 'in the C19th, as Bernard Schnapper has shown, "the obsession with the recidivist" undermined many practical and ideological penal reforms (the development of crime statistics, judicial policing, criminology, criminal medicine) [and] especially those that focussed on correction'.

We may now find ourselves in a situation in which the obsession with cognitive behaviouralism – and its associated experimental method-ology – is diverting our attention away from other forms of intervention which may be equally or more 'corrective'. For example, the employ-ment schemes evaluated by Sarno et al. (1999, 2000) were found to reduce reconviction rates. One of the schemes had 43 per cent of participants reconvicted within the first year compared with 56 per cent of those referred but who did not attend; those who did offend took longer to offend (cf. Farrington et al. 1986); and many of the participants reported that they felt the project had had a positive impact on their lives (Sarno et al. 2000: v). Tracking Progress on Probation also found that improving employment (and family) circumstances was strongly related to desistance and that when officers gave the probationer help, such circumstances were more frequently solved (Farrall 2002: ch. 9), sug-gesting that help with these obstacles produced benefits. This is encouraging news for probation services. While motivation and social and personal contexts appear to be the dominant forces in determining whether the obstacles facing probationers are successfully resolved, there was evidence that the work of officers could *improve* the chances of success, but note – these are *neither* cognitive behavioural problems *nor* were their solutions cognitive in their nature.

None of this is intended (nor should it be taken) to suggest that cognitive behavioural interventions are without use or relevance to modern probation work. The suggestion is, rather, that there is an imbalance in the current focus of probation work. As already mentioned, Sue Rex (1999) has reminded us that cognitive behaviouralism was intended to be implemented alongside social and economic inter-ventions. Ultimately this reinforces the arguments put forward by Bottoms and McWilliams over 20 years ago when they wrote that 'help may be more crime-reducing than treatment' (1979: 174). As such, more effort should be focused on how officers can support probationers in addressing either their existing family problems, or attempting to prepare them for events like parenthood. Similarly, more effort should be focused on getting probationers into employment (Bridges 1998). This might entail a shift in the orientation of probation work. One probationer (065), when asked what would prevent him from re-offending replied:

> Something to do with self progression. Something to show people what they are capable of doing. I thought that that was what [my officer] should be about. It's finding people's abilities and nourishing and making them work for those things. Not very consistent with going back on what they have done wrong and trying to work out why – 'cause it's all going around on what's *happened* – what you've already been punished for – why not go forward into something … For instance, you might be good at writing – push that forward, progress that, rather than saying 'well look, why did you kick that bloke's head in? Do you think we should go back into anger management courses?' when all you want to be is a writer. Does that make any sense to you at all? *Yeah, yeah. To sum it up, you're saying you should look forwards not back.* Yeah. I know that you do have to look back to a certain extent to make sure that you don't end up like that [again]. The whole order seems to be about going back and back and back. There doesn't seem to be much 'forward'.

Now, at the start of a new century and under the auspices of the newly created National Probation Service, might be an appropriate time to start thinking about how we can inject some 'forward' into probation interventions.

Notes

1 Multiple responses possible.
2 For example, of the 60 obstacles relating to personal problems identified by the POs, 28 related to the probationer's 'state of mind', depression or stress while only seven officers referred to their probationer as having 'poor temper control'. Of the 18 probationers who reported that they faced personal characteristics which would make desistance hard, only six were related to poor temper control – the rest being problems associated with changing one's lifestyle, boredom, finding crime exciting or being depressed.
3 Virtually identical results were obtained when POs' reports of whether obstacles had been resolved or not were cross-tabulated against desistance and persistence.
4 For those who faced more than one obstacle, the overall extent to which all the obstacles they faced was used to determine whether they were counted as having their 'obstacle solved'. For cases which had equal numbers of obstacles solved or unsolved, the outcome of the main obstacle was used.
5 These measures were summations of the social and personal circumstances which probationers reported were 'problems'. Those with three or more problematic circumstances were classified as not having good contexts.
6 'Freebase' – smoking pure cocaine.

References

Bank, L., Patterson, G.R. and Reid, J.B. (1987) 'Delinquency prevention through the training of parents in family management', *The Behaviour Analyst*, 10: 75–82.

Barclay, G. (1990) 'The peak age of known offending by males', *Home Office Research Bulletin*, 28: 20–3.

Bottoms, A. and McWilliams, W. (1979) 'A non-treatment paradigm for probation practice', *British Journal of Social Work*, 9 (2): 159–202.

Bridges, A. (1998) *Increasing the Employability of Offenders*. Probation Studies Unit Report 5. Oxford: Probation Studies Unit.

Brown, C. (1995) *Chaos and Catastrophe Theories*. Newbury Park, CA: Sage.

Brownlee, I.D. (1995) 'Intensive probation with young adult offenders: a short reconviction study', *British Journal of Criminology*, 35 (4): 599–612.

Burnett, R. (1992) *The Dynamics of Recidivism*. Oxford: Centre for Criminological Research.

Burnett, R. (1994) 'The odds of going straight: offenders' own predictions', in *Sentencing, Quality and Risk: Proceedings of the 10th Annual Conference on Research and Information in the Probation Service*. Birmingham: Midlands Probation Training Consortium.

Burnett, R. (1996) *Fitting Supervision to Offenders: Assessment and Allocation Decisions in the Probation Service*. Home Office Research Study 169. London: Home Office.

Burnett, R. (2000) 'Understanding criminal careers through a series of in-depth interviews', *Offender Programs Report*, 4 (1).

Burnett, R. (2004) 'To reoffend or to not reoffend? The ambivalence of offenders', in S. Maruna and R. Immarigeon (eds) *After Crime and Punishment*. Cullompton: Willan.

Byrne, D. (1998) *Complexity Theory and the Social Sciences*. London: Routledge.

Crow, I. (1996) 'Employment, training and offending', in M. Drakeford and M. Vanstone (eds) *Beyond Offending Behaviour*. Aldershot: Ashgate.

Cusson, M. and Pinsonneault, P. (1986) 'The decision to give up crime', in D.B. Cornish and R.V.G. Clarke (eds) *The Reasoning Criminal*. New York, NY: Springer-Verlag.

Dale, M.W. (1976) 'Barriers to the rehabilitation of ex-offenders', *Crime and Delinquency*, 22 (3): 322–37.

Farrall, S. (2002) *Rethinking What Works with Offenders: Probation, Social Context and Desistance from Crime*. Cullompton: Willan.

Farrall, S. (2004) 'Social capital, probation supervision and desistance from crime', in S. Maruna and R. Immarigeon (eds) *After Crime and Punishment: Ex-offender Reintegration and Desistance from Crime*. Cullompton: Willan.

Farrington, D.P. (1997) 'Human development and criminal careers', in M. Maguire *et al.* (eds) *The Oxford Handbook of Criminology* (2nd edn). Oxford: Clarendon Press.

Farrington, D.P., Gallagher, B., Morley, L., St. Ledger, R.J. and West, D.J. (1986) 'Unemployment, school leaving and crime', *British Journal of Criminology*, 26 (4): 335–56.

Folkard, M.S., Smith, D.E. and Smith, D.D. (1976) *IMPACT Intensive Matched Probation and After-care Treatment. Volume II. The Results of the Experiment*. Home Office Research Study 36. London: HMSO.

Gendreau, P. (1996) 'The principles of effective intervention with offenders', in A. Harland (ed.) *Choosing Correctional Options that Work*. London: Sage.

Guidry, L.S. (1975) 'Use of a covert punishment contingency in compulsive stealing', *Journal of Behaviour Therapy and Experimental Psychiatry*, 6: 169.

Hazaleus, S.L. and Deffenbacher, J.L. (1986) 'Relaxation and cognitive treatments of anger', *Journal of Consulting and Clinical Psychology*, 54: 222–26.

Horsfall, S. and Maret, E. (1997) 'Short-term changes in the domestic division of labor: intimations of complexity', in A. Eve *et al.* (eds) *Chaos, Complexity and Sociology*. Newbury Park, CA: Sage.

Hughes, M. (1997) 'An exploratory study of young adult black and Latino males and the factors facilitating their decisions to make positive behavioural changes', *Smith College Studies in Social Work*, 67 (3): 401–14.

Kaplan, A. (1964) *The Conduct of Inquiry: Methodology for Behavioural Science*. San Francisco, CA: Chandler.

Lawson, L.S. (1983) 'Alcoholism', in M. Hersen (ed.) *Outpatient Behaviour Therapy: A Clinical Guide*. New York, NY: Grune & Stratton.

Lee, M. (1997) 'From enlightenment to chaos: towards nonmodern social Theory', in A. Eve *et al*. (eds) *Chaos, Complexity and Sociology*. Newbury Park, CA: Sage.

Lösel, F. (1995) 'The efficacy of correctional treatment: a review and synthesis of meta-evaluations', in J. McGuire (ed.) *What Works: Reducing Reoffending*. Chichester: Wiley.

Mair, G. and Nee, C. (1992) 'Day centre reconviction rates', *British Journal of Criminology*, 32 (3): 329–39.

Martinson, R. (1974) 'What Works? Questions and answers about prison reform', *The Public Interest*, 35: 22–54.

Maruna, S. (1997) 'Going straight: desistance from crime and life narratives of reform', *The Narrative Study of Lives*, 5: 59–93.

May, C. (1999) *Explaining Reconviction Rates Following a Community Sentence: The Role of Social Factors*. Home Office Research Study 192. London: Home Office.

McDougall, C., Barnett, R.M., Ashurst, B. and Willis, B. (1987) 'Cognitive control of anger', in B.J. McGurk *et al*. (eds) *Applying Psychology to Imprisonment: Theory and Practice*. London: HMSO.

McGuire, J. and Priestly, P. (1995) 'Reviewing "What Works": past, present and future', in J. McGuire (ed.) *What Works: Reducing Reoffending*. Chichester: Wiley.

Moffitt, T. (1993) '"Life-course persistent" and "adolescent-limited" antisocial behaviour: a developmental taxonomy', *Psychological Review*, 100: 674–701.

O'Donnell, C.R., Lydgate, T. and Fo, W.S.O. (1979) 'The Buddy System: review and follow-up', *Child Behaviour Therapy*, 1: 161–9.

Pawson, R. and Tilley, N. (1997) *Realistic Evaluation*. London: Sage.

Pezzin, L.E. (1995) 'Earning prospects, matching effects and the decision to terminate a criminal career', *Journal of Quantitative Criminology*, 11 (1): 29–50.

Porret, M. and Emsley, C. (2002) 'Problematique/Introduction.' Presentation to the International Association for the History of Crime and Criminal Justice Conference, Geneva, 6–8 June.

Price, B. (1997) 'The myth of postmodern science', in A. Eve *et al*. (eds) *Chaos, Complexity and Sociology*. Newbury Park, CA: Sage.

Priestly, P., McGuire, M., Flegg, J., Hemsley, M., Welham, D. and Barnitt, R. (1984) *Social Skills in Prisons and the Community: Problem Solving for Offenders*. London: Routledge.

Radzinowicz, L. (ed.) (1958) *The Results of Probation. A Report of the Cambridge Department of Criminal Science*. London: Macmillan.

Rex, S. (1999) 'Desistance from offending: experiences of probation', *Howard Journal of Criminal Justice*, 38 (4): 366–83.

Ross, R.R. and Ross, R.D. (1995) *Thinking Straight*. Ottowa: Air Training Publications.

Sarno, C., Hearnden, I., Hedderman, C., Hough, M., Nee, C. and Herrington, V. (2000) *Working their Way out of Offending*. Home Office Research Study 218. London: Home Office.

Sarno, C., Hough, M., Nee, C. and Herrington, V. (1999) *Probation Employment Schemes in Inner London and Surrey – an Evaluation.* Home Office Research Findings 89. London: Home Office.

Schnapper, B. (1983) 'La récidive, une obsession créatrice au XIXe siècle', in *XXIe Congrès de l'Association française de Criminologie: Le Récidivisme* (Poitiers, 7–9 Octobre 1982). Paris: P.U.F., 25–64.

Shover, N. (1983) 'The later stages of ordinary property offender careers', *Social Problems*, 31 (2): 208–18.

Shover, N. and Thompson, C. (1992) 'Age, differential expectations and crime desistance', *Criminology*, 30 (1): 89–104.

Smith, D.A., Visher, C.A. and Jarjoura, G.R. (1991) 'Dimensions of delinquency', *Journal of Research on Crime and Delinquency*, 28 (1): 6–32.

Sommers, I., Baskin, D.R. and Fagan, J. (1994) 'Getting out of the life: crime desistance by female street offenders', *Deviant Behaviour*, 15 (2): 125–49.

Turner, F. (1997) 'Chaos and social science', in A. Eve *et al.* (eds) *Chaos, Complexity and Sociology.* Newbury Park, CA: Sage.

Wacquant, L. (1992) 'Towards a social praxeology: the structure and logic of Bourdieu's sociology', in P. Bourdieu and L. Wacquant (eds) *An Invitation to Reflexive Sociology.* Cambridge: Polity Press.

Wilkinson, J. (1997) 'The impact of Ilderton motor project on motor vehicle crime and offending', *British Journal of Criminology*, 37: 568–81.

Chapter 10

Community reintegration: for whom?

Jon Spencer and Jo Deakin

The What Works agenda has become a central element of probation service policy and practice over the past decade and provides the context for a 'renewed interest' in community sentences and specifically in reintegration (Johnson and Rex 2002). In this chapter we examine the concepts and definition of community reintegration and set this within the political and social context of the What Works agenda.

The What Works context

What Works is a fundamental element of the Government's community sanctions strategy. This is evidenced by the introduction of a National Probation Service with one of its immediate tasks to ensure delivery of the What Works strategy; the increase in the number of probation officers being trained;[1] and the optimistic targets set for the numbers of offenders to have completed accredited programmes by 2005 (in the region of 60,000 although likely to be substantially revised in a downwards direction). These changes are based upon What Works research, and there can be little doubt that the Labour government has understood the potential benefits of the outcomes of 'effective intervention' as argued by the research (see, for example, Gendreau and Ross 1980; Ross and Fabiano 1985; McGuire 1995; Bonta 1996; Underdown 1998; Dowden and Andrews 1999). While the immediate appeal of What Works programmes is that they will lead to a reduction in reconviction rates, a more fundamental outcome is economic.

In essence government policy is based on the assumption that meta-analysis is a reliable method and provides an accurate prediction of programme outcome (reductions in offending rates) with regard to cognitive behavioural programmes for offenders. The government anticipates that associated with this reduction in reconviction rates there will be a reduction in the 'social costs' of crime and a reduction in the prison population. The policy of What Works is, therefore, essentially decarcerative, resulting in a less expensive prison system and more economic forms of managing offenders in the community. The average annual cost of a community rehabilitation order is in the region of £1,950 and for a community punishment order £1,750 (Home Office 2002). The annual cost for an uncrowded prison place was £36,535 in 2001–2 (Home Office 2003a). Therefore the potential economic benefits that accrue to a community sanctions policy (with the exception of home detention curfews) are considerable.

However, a policy of decarceration has to meet the political test of being seen to be tough on criminals. A What Works policy that makes demands on offenders and can be couched in a discourse of punishment fits political as well as economic criteria and can thus be embraced as a positive policy option. There are, of course, sound arguments for decarceration and limiting the powers of sentencers to impose custodial sentences.[2] One possible outcome of such an approach would be a reduction in the harm caused by imprisonment; this, however, could be seen as being 'soft' on offenders and so any policy of decarceration has to be introduced more by sleight of hand rather than as a policy benefit in its own right. This Janus-faced approach to decarceration has been a feature of criminal justice policy for the past decade or so and is one reason for the continuing rise in the prison population, at a record number of 73,657 at the time of writing (June 2003; see Home Office 2003b).

The What Works agenda has therefore been introduced in order to meet a number of policy imperatives: the need to decarcerate, to achieve some positive intervention with offenders and to be seen to be tough on offenders even if they remain in the community. The associated developments in policy, management and practice in relation to What Works have occurred mainly over the past decade and are a feature of New Labour's criminal justice policy response. These developments appear to meet the underlying policy rationale, although their implementation has occurred to different degrees. The rationale of policy is primarily concerned with attempting to manage offenders, preferably in the community, with a number of enforcement sticks and carrots in place to ensure compliance. The introduction of this element of criminal justice policy has occurred in a typical New Labour fashion, where there has been a pull of power to the centre that has allowed the Home Office greater scope to be directive about the future of the National Probation Service and to monitor probation areas' compliance with policy directives and implementation strategies. This has to some extent curtailed the traditional autonomy of Chief Probation Officers and tied the hands of chairs of probation boards (Wargent 2002). It has also highlighted the political terrain yet to be resolved between the National Probation Directorate, probation areas in the shape of board chairs and chief officers and the role of the regional structure of the directorate. However, while there is a degree of political uncertainty it is clear that the What Works agenda has a certain degree of *practice* momentum. A consequence of this has been the manner in which practitioners have integrated the What Works demands into their day-to-day professional practice with offenders. This transference of the What Works strategies into practice can be seen at more than one stage of development.

Initially the first area of concern was how programmes that met the test of evaluation research would be implemented. The Joint Prison and Probation Accreditation Panel was established in order to provide a means of vetting, approving and ensuring 'theroretical consistency' in a cognitive behavioural approach to *all* programmes that probation services were to deliver. The elements of programme accreditation were defined as part of a wider strategy to prevent the development of a plethora of programmes, many of which would not have conformed to the strict tests for inclusion in the accredited programme portfolio. It also provided the Home Office with some element of control over what could be delivered. Essentially it allowed for the introduction of particular programmes. So, 'Think First' has been introduced as the generic programme for offenders. The Home Office is assured through establishing the National Probation Service that there is consistency across the country with all areas delivering the Think First programme. Consequently this allows for targets to be set, with financial incentives to encourage compliance by areas, and for the reduction in reconviction targets to be met.

Development of the What Works agenda

The What Works agenda instigated a series of changes in theoretical outlook and practical application. First, there was a need to change dramatically the culture of practice, moving away from the traditional welfare-orientated approach to work with offenders. This was partly achieved by the disconnection of training arrangements from those of social work. At the outset, the disconnection of probation and social work training was not part of the What Works strategy; it was a Conservative Party strategy, in the run-up to the 1997 General Election, to demonstrate that 'prison works' and that the government was tough on criminals. However, the New Labour government was not going to allow any hostages to fortune in their first term, especially in the policy area of crime and criminal justice. So this disconnection from social work provided New Labour with not just the ideological position that it was as tough on criminals as its predecessors but at the same time to put in place what could be perceived as a more humane and socially inclusive criminal justice strategy. The changes to the training arrangements were therefore an important element of the future direction of the probation service and also provided a change of focus for practice and inter-vention. The new training arrangements laid the groundwork for there to be a cultural shift in the practice ideology of the probation service. With the expansion in trainee numbers between 2001 and 2003 this ideological and cultural shift may occur more rapidly than initially anticipated.

Secondly, as it became clear that the delivery of accredited pro-grammes would be a core part of probation service activity, it was necessary to ensure that the assessment and management of risk be recognised as a core probation service function. These two strategic developments occurred in tandem. The development of risk prediction scales, which Raynor (2002) identifies as having its origins in Canada, has become an integral element of probation officer practice: the 'Level of Service Inventory – Revised' (or LSI-R-developed in Canada) is one key risk assessment instrument, while the Probation Studies Unit at Oxford developed the 'Assessment, Case Management and Evaluation' instrument (ACE). This focus on risk was not confined solely to probation work – it was pervasive in all areas of life – but the impression was given that the potential risk of an offender in relation to reoffending and harm could be ascertained by the use of these instruments, and that when this had been done a risk management strategy could be put in place to prevent further offending or harm by the offender to others or self (for a more detailed discussion of risk management in probation, see Kemshall 1996, 1998; Kemshall and Maguire 2001).

Thirdly, there has been the expansion of case management strategies to ensure the delivery of the What Works strategy in practice (Holt 2000). This expansion of case management has been due, in part, to the need for probation areas to prove to the National Probation Directorate (NPD) that they are properly managing punishment in the community and that there are proper levels of enforcement. Interestingly, case management was not devised as the structure within which the new What Works interventions were to be delivered. It has, rather, followed on behind, being put in place after the interventions have been established. This has led to a number of different models being implemented by different probation areas, and once again we witness the NPD having to select one model and roll this out on a national basis. Case management is also a managerial device to ensure that large numbers of cases can be managed effectively, and this is related to one of the aims of the What Works strategy – to reduce prison numbers either through the use of community sentences or through forms of early release supervision.

These are significant changes and signal a very different probation service now – one that is primarily concerned with risk assessment and management rather than offender rehabilitation and reformation. Alongside these changes, probation has also moved from being a semi-autonomous agency rooted in local government relations to a new National Probation Service (NPS) that comes with the bureaucratic infrastructure of a directorate and regional offices. The probation service about which Bill McWilliams wrote in the late 1980s is one that no longer exists (1983, 1985, 1986, 1987). There *may* be many advantages to this restructured probation service; there *may* even be a reduction of re-offending. However, we are still awaiting research that finds positive outcomes in relation to the current strategy.

The National Probation Service Directorate has, it could be argued, taken a 'leap of faith' in structuring the service around the What Works agenda. Initial findings from the Pathfinder research are mixed:

> Early interviews with those involved in these programmes … indicate some concerns, such as the fairly high drop-out rates for most of the programmes, which need further research. One aspect which seems to be common to all of these programmes is the enthusiasm of the staff for the programmes generally, the material and training. (Hollin *et al.* 2002: 41)

The issue of the number of offenders completing programmes is a theme throughout the first interim report (Hollin *et al.* 2002: 42) where it is acknowledged that there is a problem with attrition rates:

> there were high drop-out rates from programmes, particularly either before the start or in the early stages. This is linked with the issue of appropriate referrals [it] could also be a reflection of the material used, particularly at the start of a programme. The first sessions of some programmes … were felt to be too long and too

intense at such an early stage. Research is needed to focus on factors influencing drop-out, the extent to which this may be associated with aspects of the programme and whether these can be modified. The fact that some staff saw high drop-out rates as inevitable (groups are often larger than is considered appropriate on the grounds that they will get smaller in time) is also an area which could be usefully explored.

The research would seem to suggest that, while there is a certain enthusiasm for programmes by staff who are delivering them, there is also a certain reluctance on the part of offenders to be as enthusiastic as those delivering the programmes, evidenced by high drop-out rates.

The concept of community reintegration

One of the key principles behind the What Works agenda is community reintegration, although this has been somewhat marginalised in the literature. The notion of an offender being fully restored to his or her rights and rank in society is as old as the concept of rehabilitation (McWilliams and Pease 1990). Interventions are based on the assumption that the offender will be assisted to desist from offending in the future, and that this will mean that he or she is fully reintegrated into the community. Such an assumption raises at least as many questions as it answers, but it is especially notable that it is all too often seen to be concerned with particular types of dangerous offenders who only make up a relatively small proportion of persons under community supervision. Sex offences, for example, in 2000 only made up 5 per cent of all recorded violent crime (Home Office 2001) and just over 1,000 sex offenders were subject to supervision by the NPS (Home Office 2002). As the probation statistics (Home Office 2002) indicate, the bulk of offenders under supervision are involved in property crimes rather than crimes of violence. Consequently, the aim of probation intervention should be to ensure the successful reintegration of this group into the community and a reduction in their offending. However, the concentration on defining and managing 'risky' populations results in a lack of focus on reintegration, the failure to articulate the notion of reintegration in a meaningful way for offenders and a refusal to understand its complexity.

It is in relation to the articulation of the principle of community reintegration within probation work that we are most critical. The aim is narrowly defined, essentially as being related to employment or the acquisition of basic skills that will in time improve the chances of employability (Chapman and Hough 1998). This narrow focus on skills removes any concept of community or the process by which the offender requires assistance either to reintegrate or to help remove the obstacles to reintegration. There appears to be a lack of theoretical thinking in relation to what 'community reintegration' actually means both in terms of policy and practice. There is a paucity of writing on the topic within the What Works literature and this may be because, as a concept, it is one with which we would all agree and yet to define what we mean by it creates a range of problems and difficulties.

There are a number of individual traits identified as being essential to community reintegration. These essential characteristics are defined at the personal level. For example: 'a resilient temperament, positive social orientation, emotional and cognitive skills and pro-social gender definitions' (Chapman and Hough 1998: 67). There are also a number of external elements that are defined as providing a positive influence on an individual. For example: 'family cohesion and warmth, relationships which reinforce individual competence and commitments and provide a pro-social belief system, authority figures who lead by example, have high expectations of achievement and offer recognition and praise, healthy lifestyles, opportunities for involvement and participation in pro-social activities and relationships and employment, (Chapman and Hough 1998: 67).

We would argue that there are a number of problems in utilising this rather formulaic definition of community reintegration that potentially renders it as a meaningless and facile concept. Community reintegration should be a core task of the NPS and one that not only provides the opportunity for offenders to exploit their own potential but also allows for effective social inclusion. The formula set out above is naïve, assuming that offenders can access these positive aspects of emotional, family and community life. For many offenders the lived experience of day-to-day life is significantly different from this rather romanticised view of reintegration. For many it is about managing the consequences of long-term poverty, social isolation and exclusion, and personal biographies that include high levels of abuse.

Punitive strategies versus inclusionary ideals

The process of community reintegration resulting in rehabilitation can be a complex, demanding and difficult process. For many offenders communities are often conflictual, excluding and disintegrated, a stark contrast to the more romanticised notion of community often favoured by government. It is at this point when the notion of reintegration is problematised that we can see the contradiction in some criminal justice strategies. Populist exclusionary strategies, which are intended to demonstrate the government's tough approach to offenders and crime, such as anti-social behaviour orders and sex offender registration, contradict its ideological commitment to social inclusion (Deakin and Spencer 2003). For example, the anti-social behaviour order (ASBO) is designed to:

> deter anti-social behaviour and prevent the escalation of such behaviour without having to resort to criminal sanctions, although a breach does give rise to criminal proceedings and penalties. They were designed to complement existing measures to combat anti-social behaviour and are only one in a range of measures available to local authorities and the police. (Campbell 2002: 2)

The scope of these orders is extensive – they can be used to identify individuals in particular areas in an attempt to enforce a change of behaviour. The strategies for the enforced change of behaviour are through the use of the local press and the inclusion of conditions in the ASBO that are defined as being 'more general, local authority-wide conditions prohibiting behaviour which is likely to cause harassment, alarm and distress [and] can help ensure the behaviour is not simply displaced' (Campbell 2002: 6). These strategies to obtain compliance appear to be populist ones, designed to appeal to 'common sense'. The definition of anti-social behaviour is presumed to be universally understood and this definition criminalises the behaviour rather than defining it, as previously had been the case, as a form of nuisance and disruption to be dealt with through civil actions. Interestingly, however, the test of proof to secure an order is that of the civil rather than criminal court; a test that is less rigorous than that of criminal law.

The sanctions available in relation to a person subject to the ASBO can be extensive (e.g. there is the power to prohibit individuals from going to particular locations or from engaging in certain activities). Such strategies identify individuals and exclude them from being able to undertake unfettered day-to-day activities. This is argued as being appropriate as they have transgressed the boundaries of 'normal and acceptable' behaviour; therefore to proscribe their activities is an appropriate and reasonable curtailment of their liberty by the state. However, these strategies of categorising and classifying can be viewed as being practices of social exclusion, placing people who are on the boundaries of their communities even more outside them by banning them from entering certain geographical areas. These types of strategies reinforce exclusionary practices and could result in a large group of people being even further alienated from community and society.

Another form of classification and categorisation is that of the sex offenders' register. This device identifies individuals who are considered to be more 'risky', or to present a greater danger to the community, than other types of offenders. Therefore their identification and registration is a strategic device to ensure that the community feels 'safer'. The register requires a person found guilty of any sexual offence since 1997 to inform the police of his or her address and any change of address. The police are also able to apply for a community protection order that can prohibit those subject to the order entering certain areas – and such orders can last indefinitely. In 1998, as part of the Crime and Disorder Act, sex offender orders were introduced. These are similar to ASBOs inasmuch that the standard of proof is civil rather than criminal. Again we see the reduction of the elements of proof in order to facilitate the policing of an identified group of offenders. Again there are severe restrictions placed on freedom of movement and action, and these restrictions are justified on the grounds that such constraints provide greater safety and security for the potential victim population.

The purpose of community reintegration

The concept of community reintegration is one that it would be difficult to argue against. However, policy initiatives such as ASBOs and other forms of categorisation and classification such as sex offender registration are, in themselves, exclusionary. They are designed to exclude people from the community or to identify those individuals who are considered problematic. It is here that we see the policy conundrum – on the one hand there is the discourse of inclusion and reintegration, and on the other there are policy processes actively working against such a goal by being exclusionary. This begs at least one serious question in relation to the meaning of community reintegration: with policy initiatives such as these, why be concerned with the process of community reintegration? The two policy initiatives just discussed, both of them evident from the coming to power of New Labour in 1997, indicate a preference for criminal justice policies that constrain the movement of those who have at one time been either convicted of a sexual offence or who are deemed to behave in an anti-social manner. This is not to doubt that some neighbourhoods suffer from the behaviour and activities of a few disruptive people, but a range of other forms of social inequality and disadvantage plagues such neighbourhoods and anti-social behaviour is more symptomatic of these elements of disadvantage than it is of individual personality flaws. So the policy imperative appears to be to isolate and remove what are perceived as 'troublesome' elements, thus meeting the political imperative of *being seen to be doing something*. However, this highlights the policy contradiction between classification and categorisation, illustrated by ASBOs and sex offender registration and the claim to promote community reintegration for offenders. Both orders can physically exclude individuals from certain geographical areas and both emphasise the individual's offending or behaviour in such a manner as to place him or her on the boundaries of communities; in essence, the central thrust behind sex offender registration and ASBOs is exclusionary. What Works, on the other hand, claims to be socially inclusive yet community reintegration remains a somewhat nebulous final brick in the What Works strategy.

We would not wish to argue that the government has failed to acknowledge the social processes that have resulted in social exclusion and its effects: the failure of public and welfare services, the impact of a low-wage economy and the high levels of unemployment sustained throughout the 1980s. Consequently, there have been a variety of socio-economic strategies to reduce social exclusion. Alongside such policies of inclusion, however, are criminal justice policies that are designed to identify, categorise, classify and exclude those people who are defined as being either a considerable nuisance or potentially dangerous or risky. The irony is that these people are those who – generally – experience the effect of social exclusion. This raises the following question: why should community reintegration be an essential element of society's criminal justice strategy? It is to this question that we now turn.

Community reintegration and social responsibility

Most academics and criminal justice practitioners would probably agree that 'community reintegration' is a responsible social value; there would be few, if any, prepared to argue the opposite. It is clear that the idea of community reintegration generates the notion of social responsibility, the idea that we all have a responsibility to each other. Furthermore it generates an idea of recognising that there are members of our communities who have a range of problems and disadvantages, and that the resolution of these factors is to some extent the responsibility of the community. This does not take away individual responsibility, but it does provide recognition that in order for individuals to meet their responsibilities they need – and have a right to – community support and acceptance. It is this sense of 'shared' responsibility, of mutual support, that provides some of the cement that holds communities together. Politicians often invoke these sentiments in order to try to bind society together. A constant source of political anxiety is the idea that society may become more fractured, more open to disharmony and more intolerant. A call to community is often a perceived way of directing people to consider their local responsibilities. The period of Thatcherite economics of the 1980s was based upon a particular variety of individualism and was characterised by the denial of society – a denial that only exacerbated the processes of social exclusion. One of the main political concerns in relation to social order over the past one hundred years or so has been the maintenance of a society that is bound together through a set of common, and shared, values; the politics of the Thatcher period undermined this desire for consensus. The rejection of this highly individualised society has resulted in a return to the attempt to build communities underpinned by mutual tolerance. Crime has become a focus of anxiety with many assumptions made about its corrosiveness on communities, and the need to tackle the offender's behaviour in order to socialise him or her as a non-offending member of society. It is our view that the problem of crime is more complex than many politicians and some academics assume, and that a conceptualisation of 'community reintegration' as a final stage in the resocialisation of offenders is not only misguided but also demonstrates a failure to understand the dynamic between offenders and their communities.

Janet Foster (1995) argues that crime is not a problem that results in hopelessness and despair in many communities as is claimed, and that there is an understanding in many communities of the dynamics of crime and a certain degree of tolerance. There was, Foster argues, a sense in which many residents on the estate she was researching considered that they could still do something about those forms of behaviour that led to crime: 'There was still a belief that they *could* do something about the glue sniffers on the walkway, loud music causing a disturbance, and tackle racial harassment on the estate, even though generalized fears about crime sometimes made residents reticent to intervene' (Foster 1995: 580, emphasis in original).

So this estate, which was defined as being high crime in statistical terms, did not appear to 'suffer' from what politicians assume people suffer in high-crime areas. This is not to argue that crime is unimportant or has little impact on people's lives – it does. We are arguing that people in high-crime areas are still bound together by positive notions of what the community has to offer and they still draw support from the community and recognise their own individual responsibilities and duties to *their* community. Foster's work (1995) also goes on to illustrate that there is an interaction between the formal social controls, policing and probation, for example, with informal social controls of peer group networks and friendship and kinship networks, for example. Foster's research confounds the popularly held belief that forms of informal social control are absent in 'poor' communities as she was able to identify the presence of many informal means of social control.

It may be that Foster (1995) is describing a particular type of community where social ties exist and where there is 'social capital'.[3] This notion of social capital is of importance in understanding the process of both informal social control and the dynamic of reintegration. However, as Morenoff *et al.* (2001: 519) have argued, social capital is *not* due to the 'attributes of individuals but stems from the structure of social organization'. It has to be acknowledged that Foster's work is concerned with communities in the UK while that of Morenoff *et al.* is in the USA and the structure of and issues that face these communities will be significantly different. However, the idea of social capital is useful in the UK context and it also begins to point towards some understanding of the process of integration and the problematic nature of the concept.

The What Works strategy of community integration assumes that community ties are important in providing the context of a crime-free life. These ties may be formed through community interaction in the workplace as well as within the social arena, thereby accounting for the emphasis on basic skills and employment. It is assumed that the integrative processes in communities are those that bind people together and also place limits on behaviour by sanctioning unacceptable behaviour and reproducing social order through the informal means of social control such as work, family and peers. The work of Morenoff *et al.* suggests that such an approach may be, at best, naïve. For example, they note that 'disadvantaged urban neighbourhoods are places where dense webs of social ties among neighbours may impede social organization' (2001: 519).

This comment is based on the work of Wilson (1996) who noted that many 'economically disadvantaged' neighbourhoods have high levels of social integration in common and that it is this very process of integration that results in an isolation from 'mainstream' social processes. These well integrated and 'disadvantaged' communities do not exercise what might be termed positive informal social controls on behaviour (or non-criminal forms) and thus there is little sanction in being identified as a known offender. Other research cited by Morenoff *et al.* (2001) suggests that we need to consider the negative as well as the positive impacts of 'dense' forms of social integration. They argue that it may well be that dense social ties, while promoting 'social capital', also promote strong bonds between 'criminal' groups or those dealing in certain forms of illicit products, such as drugs or stolen property. So the practice of community reintegration could be seen to include crime-supporting as well as crime-reducing mechanisms. Consequently, the notion of community reintegration requires a theoretical understanding of community and how the dynamics of social ties affect rates of crime. Indeed, as Hope (1995) has argued, it may be that strong community ties are not important in developing communities that are crime free. In some cases crime reduction may rely on the construction of communities that are loosely bound together relying on privacy and denying strangers access to its resources.

Probation practice in the area of community reintegration

This more problematic understanding of how communities work, and with it the revision of the concept of community as problematic, complex and dynamic, raises at least four questions in relation to community reintegration and probation practice:

1   How should the probation service define and respond to the key elements of community reintegration in practice?

2   How can community reintegration be evaluated?

3   Can the elements of risk management and public protection be incorporated into community reintegration?

4   What are the implications for probation and more widely criminal justice policy?

In trying to answer these questions we define some key principles in order, we hope, to help define policy and practice. In relation to the first question regarding how the probation service should define and respond to the key elements of community reintegration in practice, there are a number of elements that we would define as 'key' to probation officer practice in relation to reintegration. First there is a need for the probation officer to understand the community into which the offender is reintegrating or going to live in for the first time. This requires the probation service to analyse the structure and nature of the different communities in which it works. However, it needs to go further than this as it needs to understand the nature and structure of the community in relation to individual offenders. For example, a community is more likely to be tolerant of a burglar than a sex offender, it may be more willing to accept offenders of similar ethnic backgrounds and it may have more resources for men than women. So the probation officer has to know how the community will deal with and manage diversity and how the resources in the community can be made available to particular clients. The probation officer also needs to know how and with whom to negotiate in relation to offenders and the community. The idea that probation officers can assume that just by living in a crime-free way will ensure integration may be misguided. For example, a certain type of offender, with a degree of notoriety, may live a crime-free life but experience considerable discomfort after returning to the community. Therefore, in relation to probation practice it is important that the probation officer understands how the offender's offence is going to be dealt with by the local community. For many offenders their offences will carry little stigma in relation to their own community, but on occasions it may be regarded as unacceptable and the probation officer will need to consider how to equip the offender and the community with strategies to deal with this difficult situation.

Therefore probation workers need to know how to negotiate on behalf of their clients and how to assist them in integrating into the community. They also need to understand that clients may come under considerable pressure by peers to offend; it may indeed be an accepted form of behaviour. Probation officers once gathered such detailed and personal knowledge through home visits and interaction with the 'local community' via community-based offices. This practice has now been over-ridden by the need to ensure compliance with national standards, the requirement to hit targets and the grouping of probation officers in non-community-based sites.

We would further argue that the core element of any practice agenda must be to develop and promote social capital. However, as noted above, social capital is not an unproblematic concept because in many communities in which offenders live there can be a strong degree of social capital; and it may well be that social capital can be offence-tolerant. The problem this creates in relation to the development of interventions is at least threefold. First, how do probation officers effectively intervene in an offender's life in such a way that diminishes the influence of those social networks that are crime tolerant and are a crucial component to the offender's social capital? Secondly, how can any intervention be evaluated and evidenced? Finally, how can social capital in communities be increased to generate non-crime-tolerant forms of informal social control? In many respects all these questions require the development of partnerships between agencies with resources and community residents, allowing residents to take control of how resources are allocated and spent. This is a reinforcement of the local over the central and we can see that such forms of decentralised intervention appear less than likely in the current 'law and order' political climate.

The second question is concerned with the process of evaluation. This is a key element of the What Works agenda: evaluation to demonstrate that it actually works is viewed as a core element of any intervention. Cumulatively it is expected that these evaluations will demonstrate that the What Works strategy is one that delivers reductions in reoffending and thus makes the public safer. However, the literature is very silent on exactly how community reintegration is to be evaluated. In some ways this is not surprising because, as we have argued in this chapter, the process of community reintegration is a complex and dynamic one that varies with each community and over time. This makes evaluation difficult and it is made even more problematic by the fact that terms such as community and reintegration are contested. It is our view that the issues concerning community reintegration are multilayered, requiring an understanding of the mechanisms of informal social control, the relationship of social networks to informal social control mechanisms and the place of offending in such a dynamic. For the probation service to assist in the process of reintegration into positive and non-offending social networks it will require the provision of assistance in helping clients to negotiate their own way back into the community. Such a strategy may result in individuals desisting from further offending as they become integrated into new social networks that reinforce the informal social control of a non-offending lifestyle. Probation intervention is only one element of this process and it becomes nearly impossible to evaluate how significant probation intervention is in reducing offending compared to all the other social processes experienced by an individual.

It is difficult, complex and expensive to attempt an evaluation of community reintegration at the broadest level. It is, we believe, more purposeful to take account of the individual client's experience of reintegration and use these qualitative data to evaluate how effective the probation service is in assisting in the process of community re-integration. However, there should also be an element of the evaluation that takes account of how the community responds to the process of 'reintegration' – no matter how difficult this may be – given the key role we have argued that the community plays in the reintegrative process. There should be a focus and account taken of the deficits of the local community. So a community group opposing offenders living in their midst needs dialogue with their local probation area in order to ensure that the concerns of local residents are taken into account in the reintegrative process. Consequently much of probation's involvement will be concerned with establishing partnerships that include local residents. The evaluation of these partnerships should be ongoing in relation to how the community responds to the difficulties and dilemmas that some offenders may pose.

This leads us to the third question – how risk management and public protection can be incorporated into community reintegration. This is a difficult issue to engage with on the basis that it is anticipated that the majority of communities will react against having certain types of offenders living among them. The important element is an attempt to establish trust between the community and the probation service. This will require a very real engagement with the community over its concerns, but not an approach that either identifies or names offenders. The more the community is involved in the process of reintegration the more it will be able to manage the diverse nature of the task and provide appropriate and proper support for those returning to the community. In the vast number of cases the issues will not trouble the local community; it is only in relation to the 'difficult' cases, sex offenders and so on where there will be issues of contention. These will have to be negotiated with the community sensitively and openly. Such an approach is, we feel, more likely to provide resolution of tensions between communities and offenders than episodes of vigilantism.

Finally, what are the implications for probation and criminal justice policy more widely? For probation it is clear that there will need to be a move away from an overdependence on assessing risk to finding interactive means of managing that risk with offenders and local communities. This will necessitate making connections not only with official agencies but also with local people. It will require probation officers to reconsider the meaning of rehabilitation and reintegration and to develop some of the ideas of how offenders can be actively reintegrated (see, for example, McWilliams and Pease 1990). This should help to stimulate a review of sentencing, moving away from custodial sentences, with their exclusionary realities, to community forms of sanction that require the offender and the probation officer to engage in a sequence of negotiations that are truly reintegrative. These are new directions and new practices that draw upon the probation service's long history of community engagement with a better understanding of the issues faced by those communities and the risks *some* offenders may pose. This in our view opens up a new and exciting area for policy and practice that incorporates the realities of risk and how it is managed with the need to assist offenders to live in crime-free ways.

Community reintegration for whom?

The question that we posed in the title of this chapter was community reintegration for whom? We think that this is best answered by acknowledging that a society that has no processes of community reintegration is one that is fragmented and fractured and socially divisive. Therefore an inclusionary and integrated society utilising the processes of informal social control is, in our view, likely to be more crime reductive, since there are more linkages across the society binding it together. The more extensive these linkages then the more likely people are to have broad-based social networks and circles thus making individuals more integrated and thus more likely to have connections to networks that are less tolerant of crime. Connections to non-tolerant networks are more likely to be influential in encouraging desistance from offending, especially if a programme of intervention has been completed. However, where the non-offending networks are weak or non-existent, the programme of intervention has to achieve much more without any form of community-based support. So the development of social capital should, we believe, be seen as a priority for the National Probation Service.

Reintegration then begins to work for a number of interests: first, for the offender, who can be properly rehabilitated and reintegrated into the local community where other forms of social capital that are not associated with offending and criminal lifestyles can be developed. Secondly, the community develops sustainable means of managing offenders who live in it and builds tolerance that will have associated benefits in relation to diversity, the community being able to accept different people with different backgrounds. Furthermore, this acceptance is premised on appropriate behaviour and an active con-tribution to the community. This should make communities safer and also witness a reduction in crime. This has a wider social impact in that it reintroduces toleration and management of offenders in communities without the intervention of state agencies and technocratic social control. Community reintegration is rehabilitation by another name, and rehabilitation requires that communities and the broader society accept that offenders – once having completed their sentences – can demand,

and deserve, the same rights, rank and privileges as all other members of that society. The ultimate benefit of community reintegration lies in its assistance in the process of rehabilitation, ensuring respect for the (ex)-offender as a full citizen.

Notes

1 The numbers trained under the new arrangements commencing in 1998–9 were approximately 340; by 2001 this number had increased to 1,020 and just under 1,000 in 2002, although a decrease was expected in 2003.
2 Although the current policy option seems to be to extend magistrates' powers from a maximum of six months' imprisonment to twelve months.
3 Social capital is defined in accordance with Putnam as being 'features of social organisation, such as networks, norms, and trust, that facilitate coordination and cooperation for mutual benefit' (1993: 36).

References

Bonta, J. (1996) 'Risk needs assessments and treatment', in A. Harland (ed.) *Choosing Correctional Options that Work*. London: Sage, 18–32.

Campbell, S. (2002) *A Review of Anti-social Behaviour Orders*. Home Office Research Study 236. London: Home Office.

Chapman, T. and Hough, M. (1998) *Evidence-based Practice: A Guide to Effective Practice*. London: Home Office.

Deakin, J. and Spencer, J. (2003) 'Women behind bars: explanations and implications', *Howard Journal of Criminal Justice*, 42 (2): 123–36.

Dowden, C. and Andrews, D. (1999), 'What works for female offenders: a meta-analytic review', *Crime and Delinquency*, 45 (4): 438–52.

Foster, J. (1995) 'Informal social control and community crime prevention', *British Journal of Criminology*, 35 (4): 563–83.

Gendreau, P. and Ross, R. (1980) 'Effective correctional treatment: bibliotherapy for cynics', in P. Gendreau and R. Ross (eds) *Effective Correctional Treatment*. Toronto: Butterworths.

Hollin, C., McGuire, J., Palmer, E., Bilby, C., Hatcher, R. and Holmes, A. (2002) *Introducing Pathfinder Programmes into the Probation Service: An Interim Report*. Home Office Research Study 247. London: Home Office.

Holt, P. (2000) 'Case management: context for supervision', *Vista*, 6 (2): 126–34.

Home Office (2001) *Criminal Statistics England and Wales 2000* (Cm 5312). London: Home Office.

Home Office (2002) *Probation Statistics England and Wales 2000*. London: Home Office.

Home Office (2003a) *Prison Statistics England and Wales 2001* (Cm 5743). London: HMSO.

Home Office (2003b) *Occupation of Prisons, Remand Centres, Young Offender Institutions and Police Cells England and Wales 30 June 2003.* London: Home Office.

Hope, T. (1995) 'Community crime prevention', in M. Tonry and D. Farrington (eds) *Building a Safer Society.* Chicago, IL: University of Chicago Press.

Johnson, C. and Rex, S. (2002) 'Community service: rediscovering reintegration', in D. Ward *et al.* (eds) *Probation: Working for Justice* (2nd edn). Oxford: Oxford University Press.

Kemshall, H. (1996) 'Reviewing risk: a review of research on the assessment of risk and dangerousness: implications for policy and practice in the probation service.' Unpublished report to the Home Office Research and Statistics Directorate.

Kemshall, H. (1998) *Risk in Probation Practice.* Aldershot: Ashgate.

Kemshall, H. and Maguire, M. (2001) 'Public protection, partnership and risk penality: the multi-agency risk management of sexual and violent offenders', *Punishment and Society,* 3 (2): 237–64.

McGuire, J. (ed.) (1995) *What Works: Reducing Reoffending.* Chichester: Wiley.

McWilliams, W. (1983) 'The mission to the English Police Courts 1876–1936', *Howard Journal of Criminal Justice,* 22: 129–47.

McWilliams, W. (1985) 'The mission transformed: professionalisation of probation between the wars', *Howard Journal of Criminal Justice,* 24: 257–74.

McWilliams, W. (1986) 'The English probation system and the diagnostic ideal', *Howard Journal of Criminal Justice,* 25: 241–60.

McWilliams, W. (1987) 'Probation, pragmatism and policy', *Howard Journal of Criminal Justice,* 25: 97–121.

McWilliams, W. and Pease, K. (1990) 'Probation practice and an end to punishment', *Howard Journal of Criminal Justice,* 29 (1): 14–24.

Morenoff, J.D, Sampson, R.J. and Raudenbush, S.W. (2001) 'Neighbourhood inequality, collective efficacy and the spatial dynamics of urban violence', *Criminology,* 39 (3): 517–59.

Putnam, R.D. (1993) 'The prosperous community: social capital and public affairs', *The American Prospect,* 13: 35–42.

Raynor, P. (2002) 'Community penalties: probation, punishment and what works', in M. Maguire *et al.* (eds) *The Oxford Handbook of Criminology* (3rd edn). Oxford: Oxford University Press.

Raynor, P. and Vanstone, M. (2002) *Understanding Community Penalties: Probation, Policy and Social Change.* Milton Keynes: Open University Press.

Ross, R.R. and Fabiano, E.A. (1985) *Time to Think: A Cognitive Model of Delinquency Prevention and Offender Rehabilitation.* Johnson City, TN: Institute of Social Sciences and Art.

Underdown, A. (1998) *Strategies for Effective Offender Supervision: Report to the HMIP What Works Project.* London: Home Office.

Wargent, M. (2002) 'The new governance of probation', *Howard Journal of Criminal Justice,* 41 (4): 182–200.

Wilson, W.J. (1996) *When Work Disappears: The World of the New Urban Poor.* New York, NY: Knopf.

Chapter 11

Community service as reintegration: exploring the potential

Loraine Gelsthorpe and Sue Rex

Introduction

This chapter reflects key findings from recent research on community service.[1] We draw out its rehabilitative and reintegrative potential from that research. In view of the fact that so little attention has been given to women and community service in the past, we also give particular attention to the findings regarding women. First, however, we set out the context for the research, indicating the rather chequered history of community service.

The inclusion of community punishment[2] within the UK government's What Works agenda represents a new challenge. It offers a somewhat different approach from the more traditional offending behaviour programmes to the question of how to achieve a positive impact on offenders' lives and reduce the likelihood of their future offending. The classic image of such orders is of a 'fine on time' – despite the best intentions of its architects, the Wootton Committee, in 1970, to promote community service as 'rehabilitation'. When community service was first introduced it was thought that there would be enormous 'rehabilitative' value for offenders in undertaking unpaid work for the community. The Wootton Committee argued that the idea of offenders performing work for the community would appeal to adherents of different penal philosophies:

> To some, it would be simply a more constructive and cheaper alternative to short sentences of imprisonment; by others it would be seen as introducing into the penal system a new dimension with

> an emphasis on reparation to the community; others again would regard it as a means of giving effect to the old adage that the punishment should fit the crime; while others still would stress the value of bringing offenders into close touch with those members of the community who are most in need of help and support. (Advisory Council on the Penal System 1970: 13)

This 'all weather' and 'Jack of all trades' image undoubtedly proved to be one of the main attractions of community service, but at some cost, for 'philosophical confusion' has pertained for some considerable time (Mair 1997). As McIvor (1990) has indicated, the lack of clarity over its purpose has led to a persistent uncertainty about the precise position that community service might occupy within the sentencing tariff and confusion as to the offenders to whom it should be given. (Arguably, this plays out wider uncertainties about the role of non-custodial sentences, arising from their lack of a clear conceptual framework since the loss of faith in the rehabilitative idea – Rex 1998.)

Essentially, the Wootton Committee recognised that community service would necessarily have to have a punitive element, but hoped that offenders would recognise the more positive benefits beyond this. In practice, however, the concept of punishment has predominated in thinking about community service over the last 25 years; the reintegrative and rehabilitative aspects of the work have taken second place to the punitive. Introduced in the Criminal Justice Act 1972, and piloted in six areas before its national implementation from 1975, the community service order was one element in the government's strategy to offer courts alternatives to custody in an attempt to stem the rising prison population (see Bottoms 1987). However, this was not unproblematical and research suggested that it was replacing custody in only half the cases in which it was imposed (Pease 1985). This meant that the order had little impact on attempts to reduce the prison population.

Another attempt to clarify the role of non-custodial sentences such as community service occurred in the rationale underpinning the Criminal Justice Act 1991. Section 6 of that Act applied desert-based principles to non-custodial penalties. To mark their new status as punishments in the community in their own right, they were renamed community orders and reconceptualised in terms of restrictions on liberty commensurate with the seriousness of the offence. Two other changes emphasised the point: probation orders were changed from a 'welfare'-orientated order to a sentence of the court, and combination orders were introduced. The combination order allowed probation to be combined with community service in a single sentence. Discussing community service, the government stressed its reparative and reintegrative dimensions: it provided reparation to the community and should be used in a way that strengthened, rather than weakened, offenders' links with the community (Home Office 1990). The practical effect of the 1991 Act, however, was to intensify the distinction between probation as rehabilitation and community service as punishment (for further discussion of the significance and effects of these changes, see Rex and Gelsthorpe 2002).

We would suggest here that community service has not fared particularly well in its reconceptualisation as punishment in the community. Following a peak of 11 per cent in 1993, 1994 and 1995, the proportionate use of community service for indictable offenders has settled at 9 per cent over the last few years. In 2002, for instance, the order was used for 9 per cent of males and 8 per cent of females (aged 21 and over) in England and Wales (Home Office 2002a: Table 7.10). However, there has been a marked reduction in its use for offenders with prior experience of custody and an increase in its use for those with no prior conviction; 51 per cent of those receiving community service in 2001 had no previous convictions (Home Office 2002b). Indeed, this is part of a general trend for the proportion of those starting the three main order types with no previous convictions more than doubled between 1993 and 2001 for each type of order (Home Office 2002b). From this we can see that community service has slipped quite steeply down-tariff, at a time when there is both renewed interest in rehabilitation and when there has been a dramatic decrease in the use of the fine for indictable offences (from nearly 40 to 27 per cent over the last ten years in the case of males, and from 28 to 20 per cent in the case of females aged 21 and over – see Home Office 2002a). More detailed consideration of sentencing patterns is precluded by reasons of space in this chapter, but the inference must be that community sentences – including community service – are now attracting less serious offenders, who might previously have received a fine (see Chapter 2 of this volume; Morgan 2003). Thus community sentences appear to be having little impact on the use of custody – widely recognised as being on the increase for both males and females (from 18 per cent in 1991 to 30 per cent for males aged 21 and over in 2001, and from 6 per cent in 1991 to 17 per cent for females aged 21 and over in 2001).

Rediscovering rehabilitation and reintegration in community service

Interestingly, despite the more recent punitive orientation of community service and evidence of its use as punishment, renewed interest has been given to its rehabilitative potential. A series of reconviction studies in the 1990s following various community sentences began to hint that community service might reduce recidivism. McIvor's (1992) study of community service in Scotland offered some insight into the mechanisms by which offenders' experience of undertaking community work might have a positive impact on their behaviour. One common finding from the studies of Lloyd *et al.* (1995), Raynor and Vanstone (1997) and May (1999) was that the reconviction rate for community service was a few percentage points below the rate predicted on the basis of offenders' sex, age and previous criminal histories. In May's study, this effect remained when social factors (such as drugs problems and employment) were added to the baseline prediction model. Such a finding must be treated with caution because the results could well be explained by some factor in the prior experience of the groups sentenced to community service that the predictive model failed to take into account. May's findings nevertheless led him to conclude that 'the low reconviction rate for [community service] could not be explained by the criminal histories and available social factors of offenders ... and that the sentence itself may have had a positive effect on reconviction' (1999: x).

McIvor's (1992) study offers some evidence to suggest that the *quality of the experience* of doing community service may have had an impact on offenders. She found that people who viewed their experience of community service as very worth while (because it gave them the opportunity to gain skills or because they could see that it benefited the community) had higher rates of compliance and lower rates of recidivism. Again, the findings have to be treated with caution because some background factors might incline certain individuals towards a positive view of community service and towards compliance with the requirements of the order. An interesting finding was that the differences were particularly strong in the case of individuals who were unemployed or had previous experience of social work supervision, perhaps indicating that they perceived particular benefits in performing community service work.

Killias and Ribeaud (2000) have also found a positive effect, looking at community service compared with short periods of custody. Investigating what it was about community service that might produce lower rates of rearrest and reconviction, Killias and Ribeaud found a strong statistical relationship between having served a custodial sentence rather than a community service sentence and having perceived that sentence to be 'unfair'. However, no clear relationship emerged and the researchers were not in a position to look at community service and fairness – though it is conceivable that if offenders see a sentence as 'fair' in the first place this will make them more receptive to any constructive and reintegrative elements of that sentence. Thus here we turn to our own attempts to explore the reintegrative and rehabilitative effects of community service.

Under the Crime Reduction Programme within the UK, various Pathfinder projects in community service were identified in 1999. The nomenclature is particularly meaningful if we see such projects as exploring new ways of working with offenders in order to increase the effectiveness of interventions. The Pathfinder projects concerning community service were built on practitioner-led initiatives starting in the mid-1990s. The philosophy underpinning the projects can perhaps best be described as *rehabilitative/reintegrative*. It is believed that the practical setting within which community service occurs, and the nature of the contacts with supervisors and beneficiaries which community service involves, offer learning experiences at least as powerful as approaches that tackle offending behaviour in a more didactic manner. The projects were implemented in ten probation areas across England and Wales[3] and incorporated the following elements.

Encouraging socially responsible attitudes and behaviour (pro-social modelling)

Hitherto, it has primarily been in relation to probation practice that pro-social modelling has been conceived and developed. In the probation context, it has perhaps been most fully developed in Australia through the work of Christopher Trotter. Trotter has defined pro-social modelling as 'the practice of offering praise and rewards for … pro-social expressions and actions … the probation officer becomes a positive role model acting to reinforce pro-social or non-criminal behaviour' (1993: 4). The idea is to give the offender a definite lead, in a constructive and positive way; the approach combines elements of reinforcement (through encouragement and reward) and modelling through exemplifying the desired behaviour. The aim of the Pathfinder projects was to exploit what is seen as a natural environment for promoting the development of socially responsible behaviour. The performance of tasks in a practical setting is thus seen as providing opportunities for offenders to be encouraged to practise pro-social behaviour, for example, by completing tasks, working as a team and learning from each other. Moreover, there is potential for those supervising community service to act as positive role models by showing offenders how to undertake the work and improve their performance, for example. As McIvor's (1992) research has suggested, the work itself may offer immediate tangible rewards, specifically through giving offenders a sense of achievement in doing something useful for the community. Direct contact with beneficiaries might enable offenders to see at first hand what people have gained from the work they have done. Reflecting on her earlier research, McIvor characterises the most 'rewarding' community service placements as reintegrative and entailing some reciprocity and exchange:

> In many instances, it seems, contact with the beneficiaries gave offenders an insight into other people, and an increased insight into themselves; the acquisition of skills had instilled in them greater confidence and self-esteem; and the experience of completing their community service orders placed them in a position where they could enjoy reciprocal relationships – gaining the trust, confidence and appreciation of other people and having the opportunity to give something back to them. (1998a: 55–6)

These ideas broadly rehearse Bandura's (1997) work concerning beliefs in one's personal capabilities (self-efficacy) so that the offender comes to see that he or she has a valuable contribution to make to society.

The very notion of 'pro-social modelling', of course, raises questions about the cultural values inherent within the concept (especially race and gender-related values). Given potential links between the recognition of social differences, human rights, compliance and good citizenship, it is arguable that attempts to accommodate such differences are intrinsic to the very meaning and spirit of pro-social modelling (Gelsthorpe 2001). To be treated not as a composite offender but as a fully human, socially and culturally differentiated offender, is perhaps to engender reciprocal respect and thus to lead to increased recognition of the legitimacy of probation service intervention and the criminal justice system more widely. It is partly these ideas which prompt us to make special mention of differences in findings between men and women within this chapter.

Facilitating the development of employment skills (with appropriate certification of such skills)

The other main strand in the Pathfinder projects concerns offenders' development of employability skills and their accreditation through a range of nationally recognised awards. This strand of thinking is based on earlier findings that many offenders lack the basic skills for employment, and on the statistically significant relationship between unemployment and reconviction found, for example, by May (1999). This element of the Pathfinder projects on community service thus reflects earlier efforts on the part of practitioners to link the prospect of reducing recidivism to the improvement of employment skills. There is some support for this proposition in criminal careers research (see Sampson and Laub 1993, for example), though the evidence that giving offenders employability skills will lead directly to their employment and therefore lower rates of reconviction is scant (Palmer and Hollin 1995), perhaps because offenders' own community networks can be more successful in meeting their employment needs than efforts by social workers (Haines 1990).[4] More optimistically, it is conceivable that any skills developed through community service will motivate and assist offenders in obtaining jobs through informal contacts in their local communities. Some attempts are being made in the Pathfinder projects to offer routes into further training and employment, and Sarno *et al.* (2001) report promising – if inconclusive – findings from two probation employment schemes involving practical measures to improve the employment and training prospects of 16–25-year-olds. Our challenge, in evaluating the Pathfinder projects in relation to community service, was to establish whether or not, and how, offenders experience improvements in their employment status following participating in skills accreditation.

Tackling offending-related needs

Here the aim was to use community service to help *address the problems* which contribute to offending (perhaps a lack of employment-related skills, an inability to problem solve or inadequate awareness of the point of view of other people such as potential victims).

Scope of research and research design

There are obvious inter-relations between these approaches in that employment-related skills are also an offending-related need and their acquisition is likely to prove rewarding for offenders. This makes the respective strands difficult to disentangle or to compartmentalise, either in practice or in evaluation, although we have been able to use findings from the different projects to compare the various strands. These were implemented by the probation areas involved in the research as follows:

- *Pro-social modelling:* Bedfordshire and Cambridgeshire.
- *Skills accreditation:* Norfolk and Suffolk, Gloucestershire.
- *Skills accreditation and pro-social modelling:* Northumbria and Durham.
- *Tackling offending-related needs:* Hampshire, Somerset, Leicestershire.

The key questions guiding the research were as follows:

1 Were the intended elements described above implemented in practice?

2 What impact did they have on outputs (performance and attendance) and outcomes (gains in skills, employment and training; changes in attitudes and offending behaviour)?

3 Were any such changes linked to subsequent reductions in reconviction rates?

4 What were the costs of achieving these changes?

We concentrate on the first two questions identified here and, as previously indicated, we then draw out the findings on women as a matter of interest – in view of the apparent under-utilisation of community service for women over the past decade or more, compared with probation supervision (now community rehabilitation orders). We highlight the experiences of about 150 women included in the evaluation both to provide new evidence of the impact of community service on women offenders and facilitate comparative analysis of the effects of community service on men and women. As previously indicated, the third question will be addressed in the reconviction study which will end in July 2004 (cost considerations will also be addressed in this study).

The findings on the evaluation of the community service Pathfinder projects cover 1,851 offenders who came into the projects after January 2000 and whose orders terminated by 30 November 2001. The exact sampling periods varied between areas. The evaluation drew on the following main sources of information:

- Information from probation area databases, including criminal justice characteristics, supervision records and termination details.
- OGRS[5] scores derived from the Home Office Offenders Index.
- Assessment forms and termination summaries completed by staff on individual offenders.
- Interviews with 127 members of staff ranging from assistant chief probation officer to community service supervisors and administrative staff.
- CRIME PICS II[6] administrations in the first six weeks and within the last 20 hours of community service hours.
- Community service worker (offender) questionnaires completed by offenders within the last 20 hours of community service hours, a proportion of which were administered face to face to produce additional qualitative data about these offenders' experiences of community service.
- Follow-up questionnaires for offenders on employment/training three months after completion of community service.
- Data on resources expended pre-project and during setup, and during the projects.
- Data on in-county comparison groups of 84 offenders in Norfolk and 105 in Leicestershire.
- Data on out-of-county comparison groups of 596 offenders in Lancashire and 206 in Warwickshire.[7]

Profile of offenders

Of the 1,851 offenders covered in this evaluation, 74 per cent were on community punishment orders (64 per cent serving 100 community service hours or less), and the remaining 26 per cent were on combined orders. Over a quarter (28 per cent) had been convicted of motoring offences, and just under a quarter (23 per cent) for violence They showed the following characteristics:

- In terms of *demographics*, the mean age was 27, with younger profiles in two areas (Gloucestershire and Durham) and older profiles in four (Norfolk, Suffolk, Somerset and Leicestershire). Only 8 per cent were female, with a slightly older profile than the males. Some 11 per cent were from ethnic minority groups.

- In terms of *risk* most offenders were in the low–medium band, with an average OGRS score of 47 but with higher risk profiles in Gloucestershire and Northumbria. On CRIME PICS II, offenders registered low scores on both pro-criminal attitudes and self-

perceived problems. Assessments of offenders by staff at commencement of the orders indicated high levels of motivation and support
from friends and family for completion of community service hours,
compared to other samples, for example in the STOP evaluation
(Raynor and Vanstone 1997).

- In terms of *social factors*, offenders showed a comparatively 'settled'
  profile. Only 3 per cent were in unstable accommodation (bed and
  breakfast, hostel or no fixed abode), and over half were in employment or education (though unemployment rates were high in
  Northumbria and Durham – 72 and 86 per cent, respectively). Over
  half (51 per cent) had achieved some school-leaving qualification,
  and 22 per cent were assessed by staff as having some basic skills
  problems (unsurprisingly, there was an association between these
  factors). Relatively little use of drugs was recorded (6 per cent of
  offenders reported the use of Class A drugs), and 36 per cent
  acknowledged links between their use of alcohol and offending.

Project implementation

How well the projects were implemented, of course, is critical to an
understanding of any findings relating to their impact on offenders'
lives. During the course of the research we found much evidence of
preparation and commitment within the probation areas. The interviews
with staff revealed that there was also a well developed understanding
of the project aims, despite stresses and frustrations experienced in their
implementation – often arising from perceptions of lack of prior
consultation or preparation. But we also learnt from interviews that
there were some doubts about the priority given to the projects, as
reflected in a perceived failure to increase staff resources to meet the
additional demands of the Pathfinder work. In a small number of areas,
wider reorganisation was thought to have overshadowed the community service project to the point where it impinged on project
implementation. We also learnt from interviews that the coherence of the
projects was sometimes called into question in relation to their
integration with other elements of community service and probation
practice, and some staff perceived that community service was competing with offending behaviour programmes for suitable offenders.
Notwithstanding the numerous positive comments given in interview
relating to *training* in preparation for the implementation and
functioning of the projects – that it reinforced existing ideas, gave
legitimacy to existing practice and set out expectations – its benefits were
not always obvious to staff and were sometimes seen to dissipate all too

quickly once people became immersed in practice. Structured, inter-active training was seen to work best – especially if there was a rolling programme of training to reinforce preparatory training. Staff in project areas gave examples of ways in which the Pathfinder projects had facilitated more effective *communication*, and levels of *support* within and between different groups of staff were usually described as strong.

In terms of whether or not the projects were *delivered* effectively, the targeting of offenders for the projects was seen by some staff as constrained by a tremendous variability in sentencing decisions and a lack of direct influence by community staff on decisions to place people on community service. Although the evaluation revealed considerable variation in formal documentation or procedures, portfolios and offender feedback were often seen as good measures of quality assurance. Overall, the projects were described by staff as having a range of positive effects: improved assessments of offenders (and therefore allocation to placements); better working relationships with offenders and stronger case management; and positive cultural changes within the organisations as a whole. For example, some staff felt that the focus on pro-social modelling in work with offenders had led to more recognition of the value of their own work, although others wryly wished that it would do so. The increased contact with beneficiaries brought about by the projects was also mentioned by staff in positive terms. As one supervisor put it: 'It is satisfying when a beneficiary comes to see the group and says to the group, you're doing a really good job … because it means more coming from a beneficiary than from a supervisor.'

The context for the effective implementation of the projects, then, as a critical factor when trying to discern whether or not the enhanced community service projects held any potential for offender rehabilitation and reintegration was largely positive. There was some awareness of refinements that had been made or that there were still to make in order to ensure their smooth functioning, and a small number of staff felt ill-prepared and inadequately trained, but overall staff were highly motivated to implement the projects in the intended ways.

What works?

The reconviction part of this research will not be completed until 2004, but one key element of any evaluation is, straightforwardly, successful completion (outputs). According to local probation information systems, 1,851 orders were terminated by the end of November 2001, of which 1,347 (73 per cent) were successful completions. Offenders in more stable situations, with existing jobs or education (possibly where qualifications had been obtained), and not too young or with high risk of continued offending, did better in completing in the projects. Other output and outcome measures indicated the following:

- No association was found between the length of community service hours and successful completion.

- *Employment status*: of cases where the relevant data were available, just under 15 per cent (170) of offenders experienced an improvement in their employment status while on CS. Younger offenders and those with slightly higher OGRS scores were more likely to be assessed as experiencing these improvements.

- *Compliance*: staff ratings on termination summaries indicated high levels of compliance and performance: 75 per cent of offenders were rated as achieving very good/good levels compliance, and 81 per cent very good/good levels of performance. Younger offenders with higher OGRS scores seemed to perform less well than other offenders.

- *Attitudes*: while we need to enter a note of caution regarding the interpretation of data because of commonly found differences between what people say they will do and what they actually do, intermediate outcomes can give some indication of 'what works' (the final outcomes being dependent on reconviction data). Second administrations of CRIME PICS II in this study showed highly significant reductions in pro-criminal attitudes and significant reductions in self-perceived problems.[8] In 241 cases (about 30 per cent) there was both an improvement in attitudes and a reduction in problems.

- *Measures of change*: in termination summaries, staff rated around 60 per cent of offenders as having undergone positive change and as having good prospects for future change (although this varied between the areas). The impact on employment status was seen as less marked, though views were more positive in areas where the focus of the project was skills accreditation. Staff rated nearly two thirds of offenders as having no or a low likelihood of reconviction, although this was very probably a reflection of their relatively low-risk profile at the outset.

Discussing the impact of community service on offenders in interview, a number of staff saw offenders as valuing their experiences of undertaking community service because they saw the work as useful or valued the qualification they might gain. There were also staff accounts of offenders' gaining a sense of achievement and self-confidence. The achievement of completing portfolios, and gaining relevant awards, was seen to develop offenders' self-esteem, especially for those who might have had negative experiences at school. Staff were gratified to hear about people who had gone on to further training or employment. One offender was described as being 'over the moon' having gained a placement with the council; another had contacted the CS office to report having used her qualification to gain employment. Indeed, the opportunity to gain awards for skills learnt on community service had an impact as, in the words of one community service organiser, 'a carrot' for which offenders 'would put 100 per cent effort into it and their attendance usually gets better'. Equally, pro-social modelling was described as giving offenders a 'tremendous boost' in motivating them to think about their situations.

The community service worker (offender) questionnaires provided an opportunity to explore the offender's perspective. In these question-naires offenders expressed positive views on community service as part of a sentence, with 96 per cent agreeing with the statement that it was 'better than going to prison' and 91 per cent with the statement that it was 'a chance to do something for other people'; 77 per cent of the offenders said that it was a 'fair sentence' and a 'chance to learn new skills'; and 60 per cent saw it as 'good at keeping people out of trouble'. Barely a third of the offenders saw it as an 'easy option'. Scores reflecting how offenders saw themselves as being treated were high, with an average score close to 80 per cent. On value to the offender and levels of motivation, scores were generally quite high (averaging 63 and 67 per cent, respectively); scores on value to the beneficiary were middling (averaging 54 per cent). Asked whether community service makes a difference, offenders were more likely to see the experience as having an impact on their propensity to offend (76 per cent) than on their attitudes (58 per cent) or behaviour (47 per cent).

The reconviction study will of course test any claims made here, but these intermediate gains should not be underestimated. Reflecting on what they had gained from community service in interview, offenders reported particular gains in relation to practical skills. One commented: 'I used to hate painting and decorating. I can do it now. I've got the patience to do it.' Another referred to gains in regard to social skills: 'I suppose [I've learnt] social skills because I've been mixing with people that I wouldn't normally mix with; just the volunteers around here as well as the community service people, and seeing how a place of work goes about its day.' Some offenders referred directly to the awards they were working towards on community service: 'It has made me realise that I can do more and get more out of myself', or to the pleasure gained from seeing beneficiaries, 'the Head will speak to us, a teacher will come and look, it makes you feel like you are doing something a bit more worth while'.

In follow-up questionnaires[9] (three months after completing their community service), over half (59 per cent) of the offenders reported being in full-time employment, and over a third (40 per cent) as having experienced a change in status (though there was some considerable area variation here); 84 per cent reported no further charge or court appearance since completing their community service. We also looked at the relationship between offenders' characteristics at the commencement of the community service and some of the key outcome measures in order to investigate whether certain characteristics[10] might predict change. Interestingly, we found that where there was improvement on both elements of CRIME PICS II (pro-social attitudes and self-reported problems), the only statistically significant difference was that 49 per cent of those who improved on both scales were employed or in education at the start of their orders, compared with 59 per cent of those whose scores got worse, stayed the same or improved only on one element of the scale.

In terms of improvement recorded on community service (offender) questionnaires (where an offender claimed that his or her skills had improved a lot and that he or she was less likely to offend), there were two statistically significant differences between the group that responded positively to both questions and those who did not: positive respondents were less likely to be white (86 per cent compared with 91 per cent for other groups); and they were less likely to have been employed or in education at commencement (45 per cent compared with 56 per cent for other groups). But overall the offender questionnaire revealed a positive view from offenders both of how they were treated and what they gained from community service. There was a statistically significant association between both these elements (treatment and gains) and a positive impact on their skills, attitudes and behaviour (three quarters reporting that undertaking community service made them less likely to offend). There is clearly support here for the models of change that informed the Pathfinder initiative, alongside evidence from offenders' comments in interview about the benefits of learning new skills and achieving awards, and the impact of their contact with the beneficiaries of the work. Offenders expressed some doubts, however, both in interview and in the questionnaires administered, that undertaking community service would directly lead to improved employment prospects. These are all factors that we will explore further in the reconviction study.

Finally, in terms of low or no likelihood of reconviction as assessed in the termination summary, three statistically significant differences were found between those assessed by staff as having low or no likelihood of reconviction and those assessed as having a high or medium likelihood: those offenders deemed to be low risks were more likely to be employed or in education at commencement (58 versus 43 per cent for medium/high risks); they also had lower average OGRS scores (0.37 versus 0.49); and they were more likely to be on a community punishment order as opposed to a combined order (78 versus 71 per cent).

Some general observations

Thus some interesting points emerge from these findings. Improvement registered by offenders seemed to have taken place independently of their characteristics (or perhaps where they had something to gain). Staff perceptions of offenders' prospects, on the other hand, seemed to a greater extent to be informed by assessments made on the basis of offenders' characteristics at the outset. Such findings will have to be set alongside reconviction data in due course, but for the moment there is cause for optimism.

Comparing the different Pathfinder strands is difficult until we know how reconviction rates relate to those predicted by OGRS, to other offender characteristics or to the outputs and intermediate outcomes. Nevertheless, the outcomes from the evaluation suggest that the projects focusing on skills accreditation produced the best results, although the costs evaluation indicated that the cost of pro-social-modelling was lower. A combination of skills accreditation with pro-social modelling appeared to be effective. Projects prioritising offender-related needs did not appear to produce positive outcomes overall, possibly because a lack of a strong focus hampered success.

Women and community service

A glance at statistics for England and Wales suggests that community supervision is in general a popular disposal for women currently. The numbers of women sentenced to community service or probation (now community punishment orders and community rehabilitation orders) have increased over the past ten years from 6,200 in 1991 to 9,700 in 2001 (Home Office 2002a).[11] Indeed, it is a popular, if controversial and unfounded assumption that women receive community supervision while men get prison sentences (Hedderman and Gelsthorpe 1997). But there are some interesting fluctuations. From the 1960s the number of women given community supervision increased. By 1980, women comprised 35 per cent of those sentenced to community supervision. The 1980s witnessed a reversal in this trend, however, and in 1993 they comprised only 16.5 per cent. Such fluctuations mask the general reluctance over time to sentence women to community service (Barker 1993; Hine 1993; Home Office Inspectorate of Probation 1991, 1996; McIvor 1998a, 1998b; Howard League 1999).

It is generally supposed that sentencers are unwilling to sentence women to community service because they view women as needing 'treatment' as much as punishment (Gelsthorpe and Loucks 1997), and because they are unaware of the range of placements on community service and assume that any such 'labouring' disposal would not be appropriate. It is also thought that sentencers tend not to see community service as a viable sentencing option for women because of their child-care or other caring responsibilities.[12] Although Barker (1993) found probation services in England and Wales had made available child-care facilities for mothers undertaking community service, many were reluctant to leave their children with strangers, preferring instead to make their own arrangements for the care of their children. The women's absences from community service placements often resulted from difficulties when the children were ill and the mother reluctant to leave the child with the carer, even when that person was a family member or friend.

The most recent study on women and community service in the UK concerns a small study of 37 women carried out by Goodwin and McIvor (2001) in Scotland.[13] Over 75 per cent of the women claimed positive gains from the orders – notably in respect of the work they carried out and the relationships they formed during the order. However, they also identified some difficulties, particularly a narrow range of placements in terms of the work offered (with concomitant effects on motivation to complete the orders and practical issues of cost and time where women had to travel long distances in order to do the work).

Thus it is especially important to examine the situation of women in the ten probation areas which formed the basis for our overall evaluation of community service Pathfinder projects. We should emphasise that what we report here is but the *beginning* of an analysis of this sort, however. We have identified many more questions than we are able to report on.

Women and community service: towards an evaluation

Women comprised 148 of the sample (n = 1,851) in the study. Their profile is different to that of the men in a number of ways:

- The mean age of the women was 29.2 years compared with a mean age for men of 27.1 years. Thus the women were an 'older' group than the men (only 18 per cent under 21 compared with 29 per cent of the men). Some 43 per cent of the women were aged 30 years or over compared with 31 per cent of the men.

- An even higher proportion were white than was the case with the men (95 per cent of the women were white compared with 90 per cent of the men).

- In terms of educational qualifications or employment status, women were better qualified but less likely to be working than the men. Some 36 per cent of the women were in education or work at the time of the commencement of the community service compared with 43 per cent of the men. However, 47 per cent of the women were assessed as having educational or vocational qualifications at the commencement of the community service, compared with 40 per cent of the men.

- Some 69 per cent of the women appeared to be in stable accommodation (owned or rented property) at the commencement of the community service, compared with 57 per cent of the men.

- Some 10 per cent of the women indicated use of Class A or B drugs prior to the commencement of CS compared with 19 per cent of men.

- Overall, the majority of offenders in the study did not have responsibility for dependants, but this masks differences between women and men. Indeed, 45 per cent of the women compared with 30 per cent of the men reported either sole or shared responsibility for dependants.

- One key area for this analysis concerns OGRS (Offender Group Reconviction Scale) which, as previously indicated, indentifies a risk of reconviction based on a sample of criminal careers. While the overall mean score was 0.47 (a medium-risk band), the mean score for women was 0.35 (that is, low to medium) compared with 0.48 for men (medium risk of reconviction).

- The existence or otherwise of a supportive context for change is also important, as it concerns offenders' motivations to change. Here we find that women and men experienced broadly similar levels of close personal support, at the commencement of the orders, for completing community service work (66 per cent of women compared with 62 per cent of the men were assessed to have complete or moderate support). The vast majority of offenders indicated high levels of motivation to complete the CS work at the commencement of their order. There were no major differences here either – with 67 per cent of the women and 69 per cent of the men assessed to have complete or moderate motivation.

At risk of simplification, as a group, the women were older, at lower risk of reconviction, had more educational or vocational qualifications than the men though were less likely to have been in education or employed at the commencement of community service. They were also in more stable accommodation, had more responsibility for dependants than the men and were less likely to have used Class A or B drugs at the commencement of the community service. On the whole, the women had neither more nor less personal support than the men to complete the community service, and were neither more nor less motivated to complete the community service work.

What works with women on community service compared with the men?

From the various attempts to gain a picture of change so far, in the absence of the reconviction study that is still to follow, we can draw together a number of preliminary findings:

- From offenders' own assessments of what they gained from community service, 49 per cent of the women indicated that they had improved their skills either a lot or quite a lot – compared with 35 per cent of the men.

- Some 51 per cent of the women reported that they were either very likely or quite likely to do more training (compared with 33 per cent of the men).

- Interestingly, 53 per cent of the women believed that the community service work would be likely to help them get a new job (whether the community service had involved pro-social modelling, skills accreditation or the addressing of offending-related needs). This was compared with just 39 per cent of the men who believed this. It is possible that the women's beliefs were stronger than the men's because women were better qualified in the first place.

- In terms of their perceptions of the impact of community service, 68 per cent of the women reported that the community service had helped them change the way they saw things (compared with 57 per cent of the men). However, only 34 per cent of the women thought that community service had had any impact on their actual behaviour (compared with 48 per cent of the men). Yet an equal number of female and male offenders suggested that the community service work had meant that they would be less likely to offend (77 per cent of the offenders in each case).

The contrast between women and men that emerges in the last point (women were more likely to report an impact on the way they see things, and men more likely to report an impact on their behaviour) is striking given that the same proportions reported a potential impact on offending; could this reflect different pathways to offending and desistance? Recent research on pathways into crime and what might work in terms of reducing crime has concentrated on criminogenic factors which revolve around cognitive deficits and related factors (McGuire 1995), but broader research also highlights a number of different factors which may pave the way towards crime for women – including crime as an act of desperation in light of pressing economic and social circumstances (poverty, child-care responsibilities) and low employment opportunities, for example (Rumgay 1996; Chesney-Lind 1997; Cook 1997; Mair and May 1997; Gelsthorpe 2003). However, these claims have still to be tested out, for it is important not to confuse broad and indirect pathways to crime with direct causes (Howden-Windell and Clark 1999; Gelsthorpe and Morris 2002). But more information on motivations for offending could help us understand both what facilitates and what militates against women's desistance from crime. Conceivably, changing the way women see things through community service could have as much to do with changing perceptions of their own potential self-efficacy (Bandura 1997) and self-esteem (Pollack 2000), and thus their own view of their employability, as changing problematic behaviour that leads to crime.

We have but started our analysis of women and community service, and this has been somewhat limited in the first phase of the research reported on here because of the small sample size, but we will deepen our analysis of women's experiences upon completion of the re-conviction study.

Conclusion

The evaluation thus far has highlighted the fact that the areas involved in the community service Pathfinder projects have largely managed to implement what was intended. Indeed, the findings suggest high levels of commitment, flexibility and practical creativeness involved in delivering good-quality community service projects on the ground (notwithstanding the various exigencies of organisational practice amidst major structural reform which may have impeded implementation to some extent). There were some differences in areas in terms of what appeared to work best – or have the potential for making things work in terms of impact on offending behaviour. We know that youth and risk seemed to be negative indicators for completion of the community service work, but on the other hand these factors seemed to have some positive features with regard to improved employment status (although we need to be cautious here because of the low numbers involved). Offenders themselves identified a positive impact on their attitudes and behaviour irrespective of their characteristics at commencement. When it came to women, it appears that community service offered some considerable scope to improve the circumstances which might lead to offending.

We must be cautious about the conclusions we are prepared to draw before we have a chance to analyse reconviction data, and our analysis will always be limited by the small number of women in the sample. However, there is enough here to challenge (and therefore to warrant further investigation of) the assumption that community service is not a suitable disposal for women.

At the beginning of this chapter we suggested that the application of What Works principles to community service presents new challenges. This is largely because What Works principles have been conceived with an almost exclusive focus on cognitive skills and are based on a relatively narrow range of research evidence. It is arguable that a rounded understanding of effective work with offenders might encompass the proper implementation of cognitive-behaviouralism alongside interventions aimed at helping offenders to improve their social environments (by addressing accommodation and employment difficulties, for instance), thereby buttressing the normative processes associated with taking non-offending choices (see Gaes et al. 1999; Gelsthorpe 2001 and Rex 2001 for further discussion of these points).

Hitherto, the delivery of 'What Works' has largely been as an individual-based intervention to stable groups of offenders in single settings with identified tutors. Community service, of course, does not fit this model; work groups change as new offenders are given relevant orders and as others complete their orders and leave. The probation service's use of a large army of part-time supervisors and weekend placements, alongside work placements vulnerable to the unpredictability of beneficiaries and the weather, also create challenges for programme integrity. In all these ways, community service is quite different from traditional What Works programmes. Moreover, meta-analytic studies reflect an accumulated evidence base which does not yet include community service (McGuire 2002). The application of What Works principles to community service is thus breaking new ground.

How is the challenge working out? As part of the community punishment or combined order, community service offers opportunities to influence offenders' attitudes and promote their normative development, as well as to improve their positions in the social environment in practical ways through skills training and instilling a belief that they have something useful to offer to the community. In this way, community service shifts the What Works initiative to rather broader foundations. The newly constituted Correctional Services Accreditation Panel (formerly the Joint Accreditation Panel) has accommodated this proposed marriage of ideas between What Works and community service by developing accreditation criteria for 'integrated systems' and awarding the Enhanced Community Service Scheme 'recognised' status in September 2002. Moreover, while the overall effectiveness of the community service Pathfinders is contingent upon the findings from the reconviction study on which we have now embarked, there are some encouraging signs (as described above) that the 'marriage' may be worthwhile.

What about women here? There have been many critiques of the conception and delivery of What Works principles with regard to women and other diverse groups (see, for example, Zaplin 1998; Gelsthorpe 2001; Rex 2001). In particular, those critiques have focused on the way in which What Works cognitive behavioural programmes have been devised on the basis of men's experiences and what is known about men's cognitive deficits. The findings described in this chapter thus deepen our understanding of how far the application of What Works principles in community service can affect women. In particular, the findings suggest an impact on women's psychological motivation (the way they see things) through community service, and a good proportion of the women felt that community service had enabled them to improve their skills. It is possible that an impact on *actual* behaviour has yet to come from what our sample of women said (although an equal number of women and men *thought* that they would be less likely to offend as a result of the community service). On this point, the reconviction study will hopefully enlighten us. For the moment we should hold on to a possibility to which we have already alluded; that changing the way women see things may have a significant impact on perceptions of self-efficacy and self-esteem – factors which have the potential to disrupt the problematic behaviour that leads to crime.

Notes

1 The analysis which is included in this chapter was conducted by the Institute of Criminology in conjunction with colleagues in the Probation Studies Unit at Oxford University. This is the first major evaluation of community service in England since the early 1970s, though evidence of this sort was examined in relation to Scottish Community Service schemes in the early 1990s and more recently at the beginning of the century (McIvor 1992, 2002). The evaluation included 1,851 offenders who came into ten probation areas after January 2000 and whose orders had terminated by 30 November 2001. The full reconviction study has now been commissioned, with a final report due in July 2004.

2 The Criminal Justice and Court Services Act 2000 came into force in April 2001, and renamed the community service order as the community punishment (CP) order. The combination order (involving elements of both probation and community service) was renamed as the community punishment and rehabilitation order. Although most of the offenders covered by the evaluation were on community service orders or combination orders respectively, to avoid confusion we refer to the orders by their new names. We retain 'community service' to refer to the work undertaken by offenders under a CP or a combined order.

3 The Pathfinder projects preceded 'Enhanced Community Punishment' (ECP), the National Probation Service's next initiative in the What Works programme; ECP was due to be implemented in June 2003.

4 Haines is referring to prisoners' general after-care and 'social work' needs in this context; hence the reference to social workers.

5 OGRS (Offender Group Reconviction Scale) calculates what proportion of a group of offenders with the characteristics of the sample might be expected to be reconvicted within two years.

6 CRIME PICS II has been referred to as an 'industry standard' interim outcome measure. It was originally used in the evaluation of the Straight Thinking on Probation (STOP) programme (Raynor and Vanstone 1997), and consists of two components. The first comprises 20 items to which offenders are asked to (strongly) agree or disagree, producing a crime index which summarises the extent to which attitudes support offending; possible scores range from 17 to 85. The second component consists of a problem inventory of 15 items for self-rating on a scale of four (big

problem) to one (no problem), producing a possible range of scores from 15 to 60. It therefore provides a fairly straightforward (and easily administered) route by which to collect information on offenders' attitudes and perceptions of their problems – both at the outset of the order and again towards the end of an order to assess whether or not there had been any change in the mean time.

7   There was a certain amount of missing data, as might be expected, especially at the termination stage. Also, although data derived from information systems maintained by probation areas were largely complete, the data set included varying amounts of data from other sources. Staff achieved a high level of completion for assessment forms (88 per cent), but a lower rate for termination summaries as orders were ending (68 per cent of orders successfully completed, or 50 per cent of the sample as a whole). Forms administered to offenders had slightly lower completion rates – so the data set includes two administrations of CRIME PICS II and completed community service worker questionnaires for 61 per cent of those success-fully completing their orders (i.e. 816). Finally, we carried out 267 follow-up questionnaires – from around a fifth of the offenders who had successfully completed their orders (quite an achievement for a questionnaire administered when offenders were no longer under statutory supervision). This means that we have data at termination for around 50 per cent of the sample, and we cannot be entirely certain to what extent the completers on whom we have those data are representative of either all completers or the whole sample. Where appropriate, we have compared the commencement characteristics of completers and non-completers, as well as those of completers on whom we have termination data and completers on whom we lack data.

8   The statistical significance was $p > 0.01/p > 0.05$, respectively, for the two findings (the drop in average attitude scores was significant at the higher level and the drop in average problems scores at the lower level).

9   Completed follow-up questionnaires were received from 267 offenders, a third of those who completed a community service worker (offender) questionnaire. This represents quite a high response rate from those who completed a questionnaire, though it varied considerably between the different areas.

10 These characteristics included age, sex, OGRS scores, employment, education, qualifications, accommodation, drug use, responsibility for dependants, motivation to comply, support from family or friends.

11 The number of women given a combination order, subsequently a community punishment and rehabilitation order (CPRO), in 1993 was below 100; in 2001, the number was 700 (Home Office 2002a).

12 Indeed, such concerns are regularly rehearsed in a course for senior practitioners – judges, magistrates, prison governors, senior police officers, Crown Prosecution Service prosecutors and YOT workers and the like – held biennially in Cambridge.

13   Some 326 women were identified as having completed community service orders between 1 January and 31 December 1997, but only 37 self-completion questionnaires were returned – a response rate of 11 per cent.

References

Advisory Council on the Penal System (1970) *Non-custodial and Semi-custodial Penalities* (the Wootton Report). London: HMSO.

Bandura, A. (1997) *Self-efficacy: The Exercise of Control.* New York, NY: Freeman & Co.

Barker, M. (1993) *Community Service and Women Offenders.* London: Association of Chief Officers of Probation.

Bottoms, A.E. (1987) 'Limiting prison use in England and Wales', *Howard Journal,* 26: 177–202.

Bottoms, A.E., Gelsthorpe, L. and Rex, S. (eds) *Community Penalties: Change and Challenges.* Cullompton: Willan.

Chesney-Lind, M. (ed.) (1997) *Girls, Women and Crime.* Thousand Oaks, CA: Sage.

Cook, D. (1997) *Poverty, Crime and Punishment.* London: Child Poverty Action Group.

Dowden, C. and Andrews, D. (1999) 'What Works for female offenders', *Crime and Delinquency,* 45 (4): 438–52.

Eaton, M. (1993) *Women after Prison.* Buckingham: Open University Press.

Gaes, G., Flanagan, T., Motiuk, L. and Stewart, L. (1999) 'Adult correctional treatment', in M. Tonry and J. Petersilia (eds) *Prisons.* Chicago, IL: University of Chicago Press.

Gelsthorpe, L. (2001) 'Accountability: difference and diversity in the delivery of community penalties', in A.E. Bottoms *et al.* (eds) *Community Penalties: Change and Challenges.* Cullompton: Willan.

Gelsthorpe, L. (2003) 'Female offending: a theoretical overview', in G. McIvor (ed.) *Women Who Offend: Research Highlights in Social Work 44.* London: Jessica Kingsley.

Gelsthorpe, L. and Loucks, N. (1997) 'Magistrates' views of the sentencing of women', in C. Hedderman and L. Gelsthorpe (eds) *Understanding the Sentencing of Women.* Home Office Research Study 170. London: Home Office.

Gelsthorpe, L. and Morris, A. (2002) 'Women and imprisonment in England and Wales: a penal paradox', *Criminal Justice,* 2 (3): 277–301.

Goodwin, K. and McIvor, G. (2001) *Women's Experiences of Community Service Orders.* Stirling: University of Stirling Social Work Research Centre.

Haines, K. (1990) *After-care Services for Released Prisoners: A Review of the Literature.* Cambridge: Institute of Criminology, University of Cambridge.

Hedderman, C. and Gelsthorpe, L. (eds) (1997) *Understanding the Sentencing of Women.* Home Office Research Study 170. London: Home Office.

Hine, J. (1993) 'Access for women: flexible and friendly?', in D. Whitfield and D. Scott (eds) *Paying Back: Twenty Years of Community Service*. Winchester: Waterside Press.

Home Office (2002a) *Criminal Statistics in England and Wales 2001*. London: HMSO.

Home Office (2002b) *Probation Statistics England and Wales 2001*. London: Home Office.

Home Office Inspectorate of Probation (1991) *Report on Women Offenders and Probation Service Provision. Report of a Thematic Inspection*. London: Home Office Inspectorate of Probation.

Home Office Inspectorate of Probation (1996) *A Review of Probation Service Provision for Women Offenders. Report of a Thematic Inspection*. London: Home Office Inspectorate of Probation.

Howard League (1999) 'Do women paint fences too? Women's experience of community service' (briefing paper). London: Howard League for Penal Reform.

Howden-Windell, J. and Clark, D. (1999) 'The criminogenic needs of women. A literature review' (unpublished paper). London: HM Prison Service.

Killias, A. and Ribeaud, D. (2000) 'Does community service rehabilitate better than short-term imprisonment? Results of a controlled experiment', *Howard Journal*, 39 (1): 40–57.

Lloyd, C., Mair, G. and Hough, M. (1995) *Explaining Reconviction Rates: A Critical Analysis*. Home Office Research Study 136. London: Home Office.

Mair, G. (1997) 'Community penalties and the probation service', in M. Maguire *et al.* (eds) *The Oxford Handbook of Criminology* (2nd edn). Oxford: Clarendon Press.

Mair, G. and May, C. (1997) *Offenders on Probation*. Home Office Research Study 167. London: HMSO.

May, C. (1999) *Explaining Reconviction Rates Following a Community Sentence: The Role of Social Factors*. Home Office Research Study 192. London: Home Office.

McGuire, J. (ed.) (1995) *What Works? Reducing Reoffending – Guidelines for Research and Practice*. Chichester: Wiley.

McGuire, J. (ed.) *What Works? Reducing Reoffending. Guidelines for Research and Practice*. Chichester: Wiley.

McIvor, G. (1990) *Sanctions for Serious or Persistent Offenders: A Review of the Literature*. Stirling: Social Work Research Centre, University of Stirling.

McIvor, G. (1992) *Sentenced to Serve*. Aldershot: Avebury.

McIvor, G. (1998a) 'Pro-social modeling and legitimacy: lessons from a study of community service', in S. Rex and A. Matravers (eds) *Pro-social Modelling and Legitimacy* (the Clarke Hall Day Conference). Cambridge: Institute of Criminology, University of Cambridge.

McIvor, G. (1998b) 'Jobs for the boys? Gender differences in referral to community service', *Howard Journal of Criminal Justice*, 37 (3): 280–90.

McIvor, G. (2002) 'What works with women on probation? Key findings from research with women on probation in Scotland.' Paper presented to the British Society of Criminology Conference, Keele, July.

Morgan, R. (2003) 'Thinking about the demand for probation services', *Probation Journal*, 50 (1): 7–19.

Palmer, E. and Hollin, C. (1995) *A Literature Review: The Effectiveness of Vocational and Educational Training in Reducing Recidivism. Report to the Prison Service Agency.* Leicester: Leicester University Department of Psychology.

Pollack, S. (2000) 'Reconceptualising women's agency and empowerment: challenges to self-esteem discourse and women's lawbreaking', *Women and Criminal Justice*, 12 (1): 75–89.

Prison Reform Trust (2000) *Justice for Women: The Need for Reform. The Report of the Committee on Women's Imprisonment.* London: Prison Reform Trust.

Raynor, P. and Vanstone, M. (1997) *Straight Thinking on Probation (STOP): The Mid Glamorgan Experiment.* Probation Studies Unit Report 4. Oxford: University of Oxford Centre for Criminological Research.

Rex, S. (1998) 'Community Penalties in England and Wales 1967–1998', *Overcrowded Times*, 9, 6, 1: 16–20.

Rex, S. (2001) 'Beyond cognitive-behaviouration? Reflections on the effectiveness literature', in A.E. Bottoms, L. Gelsthorpe and S. Rex (eds) *Community Penalties: Change and Challenges.* Cullompton: Willan.

Rex. S. and Gelsthorpe, L. (2002) 'The role of Community Service in Reducing Offending: Evaluating Pathfinder Projects in the UK', *Howard Journal of Criminal Justice*, 41 (4): 311–25.

Rumgay, J. (1996) 'Women offenders: towards a needs based policy', *Vista*, September: 104–15.

Sampson, R. and Laub, J. (1993) *Crime in the Making: Pathways and Turning Points through Life.* Cambridge, MA: Harvard University Press.

Sarno, C., Hearnden, I. and Hedderman, C. (2001) *Working their Way out of Offending. An Evaluation of Two Probation Schemes.* Home Office Research Study 218. London: Home Office.

Trotter, C. (1993) *The Supervision of Offenders. What Works?.* Sydney: Victorian Office of Corrections.

Zaplin, R. (ed.) (1998) *Female Offenders: Critical Perspectives and Effective Interventions.* Baltimore, MD: Aspen.

Chapter 12

What Works: a view from the chiefs

George Mair

Introduction

Given the speed and fervour with which the What Works initiative has been planned and implemented, there has been little time (or encouragement) for reflection about its meaning on the part of probation staff. Yet if those who are responsible for an initiative are not fully committed to it, the likelihood of success is diminished. Enthusiasm, drive and energy tend to be associated with practitioners involved in new developments – partly because the novelty of the development encourages such characteristics, and partly because those staff recruited for a new project are, to some extent, chosen because they appear to have such attributes. This is very often a critical – though all too often ignored – factor in the success of a new initiative. Because staff are enthused and committed and want to see their new venture succeed, new programmes often do succeed. Evaluations of new initiatives are important, but it is rare for a second evaluation to be carried out several years later when staff turnover has occurred, the novelty of the initiative has become stale and the drive to succeed has become the mundane practice of everyday work.

Staff views about What Works have not been examined in any detail, yet the significance of such views may be vital to the success of the initiative. Rumgay (2003: 49) has recently noted that 'I have yet to meet a probation officer who regards the effective practice initiative without scepticism' and, while scepticism – generally speaking – may be a useful attitude for probation staff, it may not be a helpful contribution to What Works.

This chapter will examine the views of Chief Probation Officers (CPOs) about the What Works initiative. Chief officers do not have to grapple with the practical realities of delivering accredited programmes to offenders but, although they are not at the coal-face, their views about What Works are important. Chief officers lead their respective probation areas – although they do not have the power that they had prior to the reorganisation of probation that took place on 1 April 2001 – and thus they will, to a large degree, shape the way in which What Works is seen in a probation area. If they have doubts about the initiative it is possible that these may be transmitted (albeit unconsciously) to a workforce that needs to be convinced.

The research

Robert Reiner, in his path-breaking study of Chief Constables (1991), noted that virtually nothing was known about this group of powerful individuals as research had tended to focus upon lower levels in the police. If this was the case for the police, then how much more so is it for probation? We know little about the views and attitudes of probation officers, and nothing at all about the attitudes of Chief Probation Officers who, although perhaps not perceived in the same way as Chief Constables, manage a significant criminal justice agency which has begun to take on a more public role in the last five years. The research that forms the basis of this chapter was consciously modelled upon that of Reiner and intended to do for CPOs what he did for Chief Constables – examine in some detail their views and attitudes about key issues in their respective agencies and provide information about the personal careers of respondents.[1]

The study aimed to interview all serving CPOs before 1 April 2001 (a total of 54). In the event, partly due to a delay in beginning the fieldwork which commenced in November 2000, interviewing took much longer than planned and was completed in June 2002. In all, 47 chiefs were interviewed and by the time of interview eight of these individuals were no longer chiefs. Nine CPOs were not interviewed for the following reasons:

- One felt it would be inappropriate as she had only been a chief for a short time and would not have a chief's job after 1 April 2001.
- One had left his post on extended leave as soon as he had found out that he had failed to secure a chief officer's post in the new structure.
- Two refused as a result of being 'too busy'.

- One refused, giving no reason.
- Four did not respond to repeated attempts to contact them by telephone and letter.

Interviews were loosely structured and lasted on average 120 minutes; the longest took 159 minutes, while the shortest was 73 minutes. Topics covered during the course of the interview included the career history of the CPO, the work of the probation service, management of staff, relations with other organisations and sociodemographic information. All interviews were recorded on mini-disk and transcribed.

Of the 47 CPOs interviewed, 34 were male and 13 female. Relative to other criminal justice agencies, this is a high proportion of females in top management posts, but it should be remembered that the latest figures show that more than 60 per cent of main-grade officers are female (Home Office 2002). The average age of respondents was 52, with the females a little younger than the males (49 v. 53). It had taken the CPOs an average of 19.5 years to reach the top (ignoring one respondent who had entered the service directly as a CPO from an outside career, the shortest time was 13 years while the longest was 28); female chiefs had taken 21 years on average, although this had included periods of maternity leave for some while, for male chiefs, it had taken 19 years. CPOs had been in post for just over seven years, although females were less experienced than males (4.2 v. 8.3 years). Some 20 (three females) out of 47 respondents were leaving the probation service on 31 March 2001, with 16 of these accepting what were agreed to be substantial redundancy packages. Of the remaining four, one (a female chief) decided to leave while the other three failed to secure chief officer jobs. Those leaving the service had an average of 10.25 years as CPOs, while those staying had an average of 5.2 years; of the 14 chiefs with ten or more years in post, 11 chose to take the redundancy package. In other words, a considerable amount of experience and knowledge was departing from the probation service at a time when great change was underway – and some departing CPOs questioned the wisdom of this.

There were two points in the questionnaire where What Works might have been discussed spontaneously by CPOs: one early question asked about the single most important change that had occurred in the probation service during the respondent's time in the service; a little later another question asked respondents to name three key issues that the probation service had had to face up to during the past decade (essentially the 1990s). Given the importance of What Works, a specific set of questions about it was included, asking about just how significant it was for the probation service, perceptions of the origins of the initiative and who the key players were, and responses to possible criticisms of the initiative.

The results

The significance of What Works

When chiefs were asked what had been the single most important change that had taken place in the probation service during their careers, a wide variety of responses was given, some ranging as far back as the introduction of community service in the 1970s. Most tended to focus around the structural changes that had taken place during the previous ten years or so: greater accountability, the move from a social work agency to a criminal justice/law enforcement/punishment-oriented perspective, the introduction of cash limits, greater visibility, the move to a performance-driven climate. Half a dozen respondents (two leavers and four stayers), however, were in no doubt that the most significant change was What Works:

> The What Works initiative because it will reshape the service in a way; the others were incremental, additional changes of focus or shape. This is whole-system shifting, so this will be a different order completely, I think, to anything we have ever experienced before. I know that people vote for the best record of the 1990s and they always vote for the one that was top last week, but I think this is different. This is like a Beethoven arriving in the musical firmament or the Beatles landing. Its epoch-shifting. (Male, stayer)

> I think, for me, the beginnings of the development of some sort of sense of needing evidence and research and the What Works movement. I mean I was completely grasped by that in Manchester, you know, that awakening sense that we had really … to prove what we were doing … which challenged all the old notions of the nice, autonomous probation officer, you know, doing what they felt like doing. (Female, stayer)

> the single most important change came very near the end of my career, because I think it's the stuff that's around the cognitive behaviour agenda, the agenda that Graham Smith built and pushed. There were lots of other changes, but in retrospect I think

the thing that – rightly or wrongly – significantly changed the character of the service in practice terms, is that agenda. (Male, leaver)

Interestingly, while these respondents agreed upon the fundamental significance of What Works, they offered various reasons for this: it would 'reshape the service'; it pushed to the forefront the need for evidence about the effectiveness of probation work; it challenged the traditional idea of probation officer autonomy; and it introduced the cognitive behavioural agenda.

Academic commentators have, of course, also acknowledged the importance of What Works to the probation service prior to the essays contained in this book (see, e.g. McGuire 1995; Mair 1997; Bottoms *et al.* 2001; Crow 2001; Raynor and Vanstone 2002; Chui 2003). But while only a handful of chiefs considered What Works to be the single most important change that had occurred in the probation service, one third mentioned it spontaneously as one of the three key issues that the service had had to confront in the past ten years.

However, when asked specifically about just how significant the development and implementation of the What Works initiative had been for the service, there was little doubt – it was only a question of what kind of language was used. All responses used such terms as it was massively/hugely/enormously significant, it was absolutely funda-mental, the defining issue, it was make or break for the service, it was a revolution and it was 'driving the agenda absolutely completely'. But along with such endorsements of the importance of What Works, there were notes of caution – even from the most enthusiastic:

I think it's huge. I think it's absolutely huge … it is changing the nature of probation in a very significant way. I would like to think that it doesn't get too bureaucratised, but I would like to think every member of staff thinks in terms of What Works, from an admin person right the way through to probation officers, managers and everybody else. What's the best way in which we can actually intervene in the lives of offenders in order that their offending is reduced, and if we go about it in that way and continue to try and find new pathfinders, new areas to look at, and carry on with the best and dump some of the worst based on evidence and research, then I think it is a very exciting future. But I think the issue about who delivers it is also a big issue. I mean, I think a lot of other organisations can deliver this What Works programme, and I think partnerships with other organisations, for instance, probably should be at something like 25, 30 per cent of the service rather than seven per cent or whatever it is. (Male, leaver)

It's huge. I mean I think it's probably beginning to dawn on a lot of people just how big an agenda its going to be ... I'm a big fan of it actually. I think there's a huge amount to commend it, but it also makes me nervous because it has spawned a kind of industry of specialists and of audit and inspection and service delivery, some of which has become so technical and specialised that I worry about it. I actually worry about our ability to deliver it to scale. I think I can see us delivering elements of it very successfully, but I think we are actually committing ourselves to a huge, absolutely changed agenda which we are just beginning to see the implications of just now. (Male, stayer)

Oh I think it's massively significant. I mean it's what everybody talks about and has to talk about, and it's what we are being measured against. My performance this year and the last year is measured against ... National Standards and how we're doing on What Works. My performance next year will be measured on how well I'm doing on enforcement and how well I'm getting on with my accredited programmes – how many people I get through. I mean it's that important and the whole service, at the moment, is being built around that. You know, at the same time ... the Chief Inspector's Annual Report gave us some really cautionary notes I think. Yes, What Works is important and it's the right way to be going in many ways, but if that's the only thing we talk about, and we don't talk about all the other issues that affect offenders and their ability to stay out of offending, then ... we're not seeing it. (Female, stayer)

One theme that appeared regularly in interviews was that while What Works was very important it was also a high-risk initiative. Respondents often used metaphors such as 'putting all our eggs in one basket' or 'putting all our money on one horse'. Such metaphors suggest that total loss is possible and their recurrence in interviews makes it clear that CPOs were fully aware that the price of failure could be high – indeed that it could lead to the demise of the probation service:

I think it's highly significant; I think when you put all your money on one horse it's fairly significant whether its going to get past the winning post isn't it? I mean it's not even a two-way bet, is it? (Male, leaver)

in terms of the longer term survival of the service, if the What Works commitment and investment doesn't actually show that we're having an impact on reducing crime, there is a very significant question mark over our sort of medium to longer term future. We've put a lot of eggs in the basket. (Female, stayer)

I really do think it's the big gamble and, you know, the critics say that it is putting all the eggs in one basket. The other argument, the Mephistophelean pact argument is, well, at least we've got eggs and this is the challenge – to deliver on What Works or die and we would be transformed so radically we are not recognisable. (Male, stayer)

Some chiefs worried that, by going down the What Works road, the probation service was cutting itself off from other approaches irrevocably; that too many resources were being expended on a single approach and a variety of skills would be lost; and that other aspects of probation work would suffer from neglect. Work to reduce offending behaviour was seen as a multifaceted activity and, as such, an eclectic approach had advantages:

I've never been a believer in putting all of your eggs in one basket; I've always been fairly eclectic in style … my worry about accredited programmes is failure and what will happen if they don't work. I suppose my greatest nightmare is that we will all get involved in accredited programmes and are my staff geared up for them? We've just got our first 15 through the training for pro- gramme tutors and … some of them are very enthusiastic about it, because after all, who can argue about doing things which actually work to stop people offending, that's what we're about. I suppose my concern is about the people who drop off the end. (Female, leaver)

I believe very strongly that the service must measure what it's doing at the front line, make a link with what its intervention has been with that person and learn what actually delivers the reduction of reoffending … I believe very strongly that the service needs to look at what it is doing and to be critical of it, and stop doing things that don't work, and build and strengthen things that do work. I have reservations about ... the current thinking about What Works, i.e. cognitive behavioural programmes basically. I have reservations about whether or not in the long term they will be seen to be as effective as people think they are. And one of the worries I have for the service is that it will have put all its eggs in that one basket and that in four to five years time the research and the reviewing of the information base will say that it's not working well. It will have lost some of the wider based skills that were around in just broad-based offender supervision ... So I worry about the amount of time, effort and resources that goes into a narrow approach when the strength of the organisation over the years has definitely been proved to be eclectic. (Male, leaver)

It's very significant, but it's not the only set of goal posts we have still got to keep our very close eye on ... I think achieving a much more consistent level of performance in relation to National Standards compliance is probably as important ... I wouldn't put all my eggs in one basket, that's basically what I'm saying, and keep some eggs in the National Standards basket ... I think that the other basket that I would put my eggs in is the crime and disorder partnership sort of basket ... working with the police in particular but other crime reduction partners. (Male, stayer)

One highly experienced chief who was staying on pointed to several tensions in the way in which What Works had been implemented – for so-called evidence-based practice there was little hard evidence, proven local programmes with specific target groups of offenders were being scrapped in favour of national Pathfinder programmes with different target groups, accredited programmes were inflexible but dealt with human beings – and also managed to acknowledge the personal tension in having to market What Works to sentencers when he was not personally fully committed to its agenda:

Potentially, it is very significant in the sense that we are putting all our eggs in one basket. I mean the trouble is that there is a ... gap between accepting intellectually and realistically that if you're going to treat people – whether it's a doctor treating a patient, whether it's an offender being treated by a probation officer – you need to ensure that whatever you're engaged in is somehow locked into empirical evidence of effectiveness. Now I can accept that as a principle. Where I part company with that is on the basis of very limited empirical evidence where the programmes began in prisons and then in the absence of any longitudinal studies. In terms of evidence of effectiveness it was hailed as the best thing since sliced bread and we should all do it. I think ministers made an unacceptable leap of faith from an intellectual appreciation that we should be much more disciplined and look at effective methods of engaging with offenders – as in terms of what worked – and suddenly buying in off the shelf the only product that was available called an accredited programme. Albeit with various different colours and shapes but by and large, an accredited programme. And the logic and the reasoning behind accredited programmes again appears impressive, but would you sail in a boat across the Atlantic which has been only recently designed, which hasn't been properly tested and no one would know whether it would stand the test of time and would actually make the length of the journey; you'd say hang on I'm not going to do that, I want to see evidence from pilot schemes and I would want to see an incremental approach and I want to see the evidence from longitudinal surveys and then I'll buy into it, in fact I'll become a season ticket holder. And that's where we're at at the moment, we're getting Pathfinder programmes from the Home Office which apparently stand up to scrutiny from the academics and which we're now required to undertake. And a good example of that is the Thames Valley Sex Offenders Treatment Programme. Well, actually, the sex offenders, the Thames Valley programme was designed for first time sex offenders, it was not designed for persistent sex offenders and paedophiles and yet we have been told scrap the programme we're doing which is actually for serious, persistent sex offenders which has got a very good reputation, been very effective for many years on the evidence we've gathered, but no we've had to scrap all that and now we have to take on board the Thames Valley programme which on the basis of a very limited period is now designated as the programme for dealing with sex offenders and it has got to be cascaded to act throughout all forty-two services. I feel very uneasy about the leap that has been made, I think we're travelling too fast, we want quick fix results to impress whoever, the public, the ministers, the civil servants, whatever, but human nature doesn't respond in quite the same way, it is a much more complex process. And the accredited programmes have much going for them, but also there are criticisms about their inflexibility, and for some offenders, they're not ready to take on some bits of it or they get to some parts of it and they actually want to start engaging in some pretty intensive discussion on something and they're told sorry we've only got fifteen minutes for this particular part, we've got to move on to the next module. That is no way to treat human beings, so I do have reservations even though I have to toe the party line and say yes to magistrates, these accredited programmes are going to really lock us into a disciplined framework and we're going to monitor it all effectively, it will produce results. Whether it will actually make the sort of significant differences that have been promised I don't know. (Male, stayer)

As well as those already noted, other reservations about the What Works initiative are evident in the preceding quotations: other organisations could deliver the What Works programme, thereby sidelining the probation service or even eliminating it completely; the scale of the initiative is such that it will be difficult to implement successfully; how far are probation staff fully prepared for the changes associated with What Works; and, ultimately, what will happen if the initiative is judged to have failed? Such reservations and apprehensions cannot be dismissed as the complaints of dissidents and Luddites; only time will tell whether such fears are justified or prove to be groundless.

Chiefs raised other issues too that concerned them, one of which was the political aspect of What Works. Previously, the probation service was very much in the background – both publically and politically – and, while there may have been disadvantages to such a position, there were also advantages in that the service was not subject to a great deal of political scrutiny and accountability. What Works had changed that position; considerable resources had been made available to fund the What Works initiative and, as a result, the NPS was now subject to keen political interest and could find itself at the mercy of the whims of politicians:

after Mr Howard came Mr Straw and I don't think the incoming Labour government were totally convinced by the probation service either. I think there was a period where the service had to prove itself, that it could reduce reoffending, that it had a role to play within the criminal justice system, and I think one of the catalysts for that has been the whole What Works movement, that preceded Labour coming into power but obviously gathered momentum under the new regime. I certainly think that if the probation service hadn't done all the work on What Works that our future would have been as rosy as it appears today – and I still don't think that it appears terrifically rosy. (Male, stayer) politically it's [What Works] been of tremendous importance in terms of funding and political credibility. (Male, stayer)

[What Works has] given politicians something on which they can actually bite and place their reliance on the service to deliver for the future. (Male, leaver)

it's politically important for the probation service that it delivers what it's supposed to do. Whether it will actually reduce crime or whether it will actually save the government's policy measures in four year's time, I've no idea. (Male, leaver)

Politically it's very important and my fears are that the research integrity story of What Works, where it started, is in danger of being hijacked if we're not careful by a need – a very understandable need – for government to be able to deliver … And, therefore, because it's urgent for government, it's urgent for us and we've got to do it, and we've got to get it right. (Female, stayer)

Other potential problems with What Works were noted. One especially experienced chief who was retiring, while acknowledging certain advantages, also pointed to some possible difficulties – the dependence of What Works programmes on psychologists, whether such programmes could really engage with the problems posed by young adult offenders, the boredom engendered in staff who had to deliver programmes regularly. What Works was not the only answer:

It brings with it skill development, consistency of practice and all those benefits. But it has the danger of becoming an all-consuming orthodoxy by a new priesthood – and I say that advisedly, not because I am cynical about the development, but having been in the service for 36 years there are new messiahs who have been and gone. In other words, you have seen the development of hostels, day centres and community service and other forms of initiatives which are good in themselves but are not the final solution … And I think there are all kinds of consequences from effective practice that we don't know sufficiently about. Effective practice is being driven and developed by clinical psychologists. Many of them have operated in fairly limited circumstances, i.e. in prisons and hospitals and I think those particular environments can be sterile … If you develop a model like this, which you consistently deliver, one of the comments that I am getting back now from

young probation officers is – having delivered several programmes, I am bored. Its very predictable, it's a bit like a colouring
book for young children ... so it raises issues about who is best to
deliver these programmes ... But not everything will work [and] I
think, for example of the higher velocity offenders between 17 and
21 and I think about the demands of structured programmes and
whether they sufficiently capture the immaturity, the loss of
attention, the educational deficits of some of these kids. (Male,
leaver)

A few chiefs argued that it was still too early to say exactly what the
significance of What Works was; after all, it had only been in operation
for a relatively short time. Despite its relatively recent implementation,
What Works had assumed a high profile for the probation service;
indeed, one complaint was that – given its importance – the initiative
had been pushed through far too quickly. Even if it all fell apart,
however, valuable lessons could be learnt:

If we allow ourselves to become entrenched into only doing
cognitive behavioural programmes that, you know, someone in
North America says are wonderful, then it could turn out to be a
blind alley. I have got no problem with Think First or R & R or any
of the rest of them – as long as we remember ... that they are
devices to achieve ends. So long as there is a real evidence-driven
philosophy that says we will try to make sure that we are investing
this money and these people's time wisely, and that what they are
doing makes a difference and we will be scrupulous about trying to
keep check that its being done properly and is still making a
difference and there isn't any better product available somewhere
else, which is what I take it [What Works] to mean, then I am
entirely happy with it. If it becomes, you know, people actually
marketing their products to us – and I think there are some signs
that it might be beginning to shift into that – then that would have
a lot of negative potential. (Male, leaver)

I just hope for the sake of the service that we are able to adjust what
we do in the light of research, and that we don't get stuck with what
the received wisdom is now. I mean, my understanding is that the
basis of What Works is that it is continually refreshed as new
research about effective practice is ... fed back into the system. But
systems have a way of getting stuck, getting sort of mauled up, and
I think that if that happens to the What Works initiative then we

will be so vulnerable to the next Michael Howard who might come along in five years or whatever. I think we need to remain true to the real ideals of effective practice, rather than getting stuck with – this is the way of doing it, there can be no better way. (Female, leaver)

I'm saying that if we can hold on to the What Works agenda, and genuinely – if that doesn't work – move on to something else that is found to work, I think that's healthy and positive and we can close one thing down and open something up. But my slight fear is that we're developing a sort of series of unstoppable oil tankers, because they're all being done on a national scale, and that to either introduce new tankers or stop one, is going to be very hard. (Male, stayer)

The origins of What Works

Given the significance of What Works for the probation service as well as the general historical myopia that afflicts practitioners and the short-termism and 'initiativitis' that pervades current criminal justice policy, it was considered important to ask respondents about their views of the origins of What Works: who were the key players and where had these 'unstoppable oil tankers' come from? There was one overwhelming response to this question: Sir Graham Smith, who had been Chief Probation Officer of the Inner London Probation Service and latterly (1992–2001) Her Majesty's Chief Inspector of Probation, was agreed to be the key player in the development of What Works. Two thirds of respondents mentioned Smith by name and most of the rest spoke of the Inspectorate generally as being behind the initiative.

The influence of Canadians was also noted, especially the work of Robert Ross, although several chiefs pointed out that James McGuire and Philip Priestley had long been working at developing cognitive behavioural programmes for the probation service in this country. Some respondents claimed that Graham Smith had been fully aware of the developments in Canada.

A few CPOs were seen as having been particularly influential in pushing the What Works agenda: the late David Sutton who, as CPO of Mid-Glamorgan, had set up the STOP programme, a version of Robert Ross's Reasoning and Rehabilitation programme (see Raynor and Vanstone 1997); Jenny Roberts when CPO of Hereford and Worcester had worked closely with her husband Colin (an ex-probation officer turned academic) in setting up and evaluating a programme for young offenders (Roberts 1989); and Cedric Fullwood, who as CPO of Greater Manchester had with Jenny Roberts sponsored a series of national What Works conferences in the first half of the 1990s where many probation staff heard for the first time about the work that had taken place in Canada – often directly from the Canadians themselves.

Straddling the area between Inspectorate, probation service and academia, some respondents pointed to the work carried out by Andrew Underdown. Initially, Underdown (then an Assistant Chief Probation Officer) had written a paper on the effectiveness of community supervision as a result of attending a course at the Institute of Criminology at the University of Cambridge (Underdown 1995). This paper had been taken up by Graham Smith, who arranged for Underdown to be seconded to the Inspectorate where he carried out an extensive project that paved the way directly for the What Works initiative (Underdown 1998).

Other key players mentioned were the prison service because they had gone down the cognitive behavioural programmes route in advance of the probation service; Chris Nuttall, who was head of the Home Office Research and Statistics Directorate for most of the 1990s and who had previously worked in Canada; and the Association of Chief Probation Officers (ACOP). Several respondents pointed out (perhaps ironically) that What Works was the offspring of 'nothing works' and that the originator was therefore Robert Martinson.

The chiefs' historical overview seemed to run as follows: 'nothing works' had appeared to sweep all before it but had had little appreciable impact upon day-to-day work with offenders; Canadian psychologists (along with one or two Britons) had quietly worked away at undermining 'nothing works' by literature reviews and meta-analyses and by developing programmes for offenders based upon cognitive behavioural principles; several probation services in England and Wales began to pick up on the Canadian work and develop programmes; all this work was recognised by Graham Smith who persuaded the Home Office of its significance and drove it on to a national programme. Smith, however, could not have done this successfully if the ground had not been fertile; the probation service was in trouble by the mid-1990s, the Treasury was keen on cost savings and evidence-based practice was a watchword for the Labour government that won power in 1997 (as one or two CPOs noted, it was not just probation that was in the frame – both health and teaching have had to face the challenge of What Works).

There was an acknowledgement that the probation service had been in some danger during the Michael Howard years, but just how much of a serious threat was posed to the existence of the service was unclear.

Some chiefs noted that Graham Smith and the Inspectorate had been willing to use the idea that the probation service had been in mortal danger and that What Works had been marketed as a way of saving the service. The so-called threat to the service offered an opportunity to sell the What Works agenda to government and, at the same time, demonstrate that the Inspectorate was in the forefront of probation thinking:

> I think the problem with What Works was that it was led by the Inspectorate, and I think the Inspectorate saw it as a means of convincing politicians that the service should be saved, and I think it was seen by the Inspectorate as the way the service would survive ... I think they needed to convince somebody about something, so in that sense What Works was as good as anything else. (Male, leaver)

> I think Graham rightly read the ... political disenchantment with what the service was doing. And I don't think that was about party political disenchantment, I think that went across the board ... And I think that he was the right person in the right place at the right time to affect the political context in which the service could take on that agenda ... I mean the Inspectorate in a sense ceased to be an Inspectorate and became a development agency – and thank God it did, I think. (Male, leaver)

> I think Graham Smith ... saw ... we were in a bit of a whirlpool ... potentially going down the plughole and I think he sort of, virtually ... got hold of this [What Works] as a way of tugging us into some sort of future. (Female, stayer)

the other thing I wanted to add is about the vacuum at the centre, because I think that certainly during most of the 90s there was a vacuum at the centre, there was nobody you could identify within the probation unit ... that actually was driving the future of the probation service. Now maybe that was inevitable because of the prevailing political position and the attitudes of home secretaries during that era. But I think the result was that there was a kind of administrative functioning in the probation unit that delivered what was required to keep the show on the road. But in terms of envisaging what the future might be for the service and what actually gives the future some security, there was a vacuum and I think that's where the Inspectorate and Graham Smith stepped in and just recognised unless somebody did [something], there was a problem about whether the service would have a future. Again, that's perhaps easier to see in retrospect than it was at the time, so in terms of how What Works gained the credence that it did, it seems to me that it was actually a bigger credence because it was ... the vehicle that stepped into that vacuum. (Male, leaver)

Scepticism about the role of the Inspectorate and Graham Smith can be seen in some of preceding quotations. Indeed, a few chiefs openly questioned whether the part played by HMIP in What Works had been appropriate; as far as they were concerned, the Inspectorate was there to inspect, not to define policy and implement it:

I think it has compromised the Inspectorate in their ability to inspect what is currently happening on the What Works initiative. I think a new chief inspector will have to find a way of overcoming that problem. (Male, leaver)

I know of no other Inspectorate that has actually been rolling out policy in the way [HMIP] has, and I think it's a very good thing that it's not going to be continued by them. Not because I have got anything against them doing it, but it's not their role to do it. And I think the conflicting role is bizarre ... absolutely bizarre. (Male, leaver)

Graham [was] filling a vacuum really ... and acting almost certainly entirely inappropriately. (Male, leaver)

Given the power and authority of Sir Graham Smith as Chief Inspector of Probation and his perceived role in the What Works initiative, the potential for tension with the Director of the new National Probation Service was considerable, and Smith's retirement in 2001 and replacement by Professor Rod Morgan may well have defused a power struggle. It is notable that in the foreword to his first annual report, the new Chief Inspector wrote that with the creation of the NPS, and especially the Directorate, the Inspectorate had 'to take care not to trespass on the management of the service' (HMIP 2002: 3).

Responding to criticisms of the What Works initiative

The final question specifically focused on What Works asked chiefs to respond to various criticisms of the initiative: that it was based on very little research evidence and most of that was not from UK studies; that it could lead to the complete erosion of any discretion on the part of probation officers; and that it was being introduced much too quickly for such a major initiative. Only a handful of chiefs were prepared to question such criticisms, and even then it was not so much a matter of denying them as responding to them with other points: what evidence was there to demonstrate that probation had been effective in the past; the problem with What Works is overblown claims leading to inflated expectations; there is no alternative to What Works so you have to work with that:

> I respond with the line of what have we got as an alternative ... I don't think we've got any alternative but to replace when we can the existing programmes with new programmes that we think have got a better chance of creating the right impact. I don't think we can stay where we are. We go with what we've got ... It's high risk to the extent that if we don't reduce levels of reoffending by five percent then ministers may say it's failed ... I think there is a danger of that target not being met. What we are committed to is having our best shot at it. (Male, stayer)

> like it or not, if we wanted to survive we had to be into it. The professional discretion argument has a number of threads to it – you could argue that it's professional discretion that's fucked the probation service ... I think there's a professional dignity to be derived from What Works, which has been lacking for a long time. (Male, stayer)

> I think the number one point I would make is that if you criticise it in that way you have also got to look at the other side in terms of what evidence is there in what probation officers have been doing for some time actually works and there's ... not a big body of evidence that it does work. I think if I have got one major criticism of What Works it's that the accredited programmes ... are just one part of What Works represents to me. (Male, stayer)

> applied correctly in the right way it seems to me that the What Works kind of prescriptions carry most of the key features of what good probation practice has told us over quite a long period of time ... [so] I am less resistant to what's claimed for What Works, even though the claims may be overblown. I think the problem is that people are expecting too much from it too fast, and the kind of

271

numbers that people are expecting, the politicians are expecting to come through from services, and the challenges internally to local services to deliver those numbers against programmes that aren't yet available, means that there is an incipient air of panic among services that they simply won't be able to deliver on that, and they will lose money at the end because they aren't delivering to the targets. And my fear is that in the scramble to deliver the numbers, compromises will be made on setting the programmes up right, getting the referral processes right, getting the infrastructure right, and we might create a rather unsteady fabric around it. (Male, leaver)

Even where chiefs were prepared to accept the criticisms of What Works as justified, they could still see possible advantages. What Works offered a crucial opportunity for the probation service to prove itself capable of taking on a national role, of being more influential in the criminal justice process. Probation now operated – for better or worse – in a political environment, and What Works could lead to a major culture change for the NPS:

I think by and large what you say is true … [but] the point is that the probation service is operating in a political world and it needs to take advantage of opportunities which seem better than what we've got at the moment. And the underpinning drives for What Works seem to be really important to me and worth while going for, that is we're going to have a better consistency of service, there's more evidence … that people will have a positive experience, that actually it will not only be fair but will provide them with more choices and more chances to avoid crime … it's too good an opportunity to miss both in terms of the influence on the culture of the probation service and in terms of responding to a national agenda. (Male, stayer)

that may be right academically, it may be right in terms of scholastic disciplines, but it's not the way that politics works. So if that gives us the chance to increase our influence, we've got to be in there. (Male, leaver)

I think that's fair … you know, this is a high risk strategy … I think the risk is the future of the service politically and with the Treasury if we can't come up with the goods. But in terms of the service being able to develop, reinvent itself and potentially still use this as something that can help us, sort of, you know, create and shape and fashion our own future, I wouldn't underestimate [it]. (Female, stayer)

Some argued that it was the underlying message of What Works that was important. As long as What Works helped to develop a culture of research, evaluation and learning in the probation service, any immediate problems with it would not matter:

I would agree with all of that and I'm not sure that it matters very much as long as … we are prepared to say, well we have done this stuff and it doesn't work … As long as it's kicking off a process of continuous learning and trying to improve, then all the things you said about the slight evidence base and the fact that it's not specific to a UK context or whatever, I don't think it matters because we will be acquiring more than enough of our own as long as we are prepared to learn from it. (Male, leaver)

A degree of weary resignation was evident in some chiefs who, while willing to contemplate the failure of What Works, could still see silver linings behind that possible cloud. The blame for failure would be difficult to pin on the probation service and prior to any search for scapegoats the NPS would be more unified, more disciplined and more credible as a result of What Works. A return to 'nothing works' was the last thing anyone wanted:

Well, I think that it could be risky … we are … putting the whole bundle on one horse. What happens if there is no demonstrable effect in terms of lowering reconvictions? But then I think that probably may be the case, but there are certain hopes of us not having to carry all the blame if that were to happen. For a start, if there is a reduction its very difficult to explain that sociologically and criminologically. It could be because of what we have been doing, or it could be because the economy gets better or worse, or there is a different government, a different feel, or we win the World Cup or whatever. Loads of reasons could be attached to it. And if there is an effect, a reduction in reoffending, we'll claim that along with lots of other people … If it doesn't go down, if it stays about the same, we could argue it would have got worse in all the circumstances. If it actually does get worse, we can point to the efficiency with which we have carried out the whole project and blame other things, you know, the economy, etc. And in the mean time, it will have unified the service in a way, make it more accountable, more easily manageable and more publicly credible. So if you've got a service that is working up to standard and can be relied on for certain things and can't be any longer labelled as soft, you will have achieved something. (Male, stayer)

I would respond to it by saying, well it was ever thus ... We've gone down this road ... without giving it a huge amount of serious consideration and its become the new panacea. And there are dangers attached to that. Having said all of that ... you'd also have to say I would much rather organisationally speaking, the service was doing something which was part of a national programme where staff were properly trained, where they did have a consistency of delivery, where they did have the skills to do that, where we did exercise levels of monitoring. And I think the discipline of What Works, it may not actually help reduce crime ... but there's a discipline attached to it which is actually very important for the service, because we've not had that discipline in the past. So, you know, I think it's part of the credibility argument ... Whether it really reduces reoffending, well, we'll have to wait and see, but I think I wouldn't throw it out. Because I think the danger is that we may well end up going around in a circle again; we'll suddenly discover that it doesn't actually do that, oh fuck it, we'll throw What Works out the window, we're back to 'nothing works' again. (Male, stayer)

Conclusions

There is no doubt that Chief Probation Officers recognised the significance of What Works for the probation service, and this was just as true for those who were leaving the service as those who were staying, and for those who had considerable experience as CPOs as well as those who had been chiefs for only a few years. Recognising its significance, however, did not mean that chiefs were whole-heartedly in favour of it. What Works was seen as a high-risk strategy which – if unsuccessful – could put the future of the National Probation Service into question. Many possible problems were noted about the initiative, including questions about resourcing, staff training, the inflexibility and narrow focus of What Works programmes, the marginalisation of other parts of probation work with offenders, inflated expectations, the paucity of the evidence base, the speed with which the initiative had been implemented, the role of the Inspectorate and the high targets that had been imposed.

Despite such misgivings, CPOs were still able to see positives in What Works. It had given the probation service a public profile and offered increased credibility that had been conspicuously absent in the past. It would help to change the culture of the probation service from a welfare-oriented, 'soft' organisation to one where staff were fully accountable and fully committed to being part of a criminal justice agency. It would help to unify the service nationally and lead to greater consistency in work with offenders. Even if the accredited programmes did not succeed, the basic idea behind What Works of monitoring and rigorously evaluating practice, and replacing less effective programmes with more effective ones, was a major step forward. Less optimistically, some chiefs noted that failure could be sloughed off, that you had to go with what was available and – in any case – what was the alternative?

What Works, then, as far as CPOs were concerned, came with a number of perceived problems that threatened its potential effectiveness but also carried major, long-term hopes for the future of the National Probation Service. Just how far the problems will be realised and adversely impact upon effectiveness, or the hopes will be fulfilled, will become clearer during the next few years. In the mean time, the data presented here suggest that CPOs were by no means unequivocally positive about What Works.

CPOs might not be emotionally committed to What Works and they were certainly not enthusiastic about the way in which it had been imposed but, because of its strategic importance, they were committed to doing their best to make it work in practice. If failure was the outcome, then they hoped that the idea of evidence-based practice would ensure that lessons were learnt and the probation service could move on to try something else. Expressions of real enthusiasm and energy about What Works were notable by their absence; instead, a rather weary deter-mination to struggle on in the face of obstacles was the underlying message. Two brief quotations from chiefs who were staying on encapsulate the climate of opinion: 'I would like to get out before the shit hits the fan' and 'Its going to be a difficult trip, I think.'

Note

1   I am grateful to acknowledge the support of the Economic and Social Research Council which funded the research (Award no. R000223319).

References

Bottoms, A., Gelsthorpe, L. and Rex, S. (eds) (2001) *Community Penalties: Change and Challenges*. Cullompton: Willan.

Chui, W.H. (2003) 'What works in reducing reoffending: principles and programmes', in W.H. Chui and M. Nellis (eds) *Moving Probation Forward: Evidence, Arguments and Practice*. Harlow: Pearson Longman, 56–73.

HMIP (2002) *Her Majesty's Inspectorate of Probation Annual Report 2001/2002*. London: Home Office.

Home Office (2002) *Probation Statistics England and Wales 2001*. London: Home Office.

McGuire, J. (ed.) (1995) *What Works: Reducing Reoffending*. Chichester: Wiley.

Mair, G. (1997) 'Community penalties and the probation service', in M. Maguire *et al.* (eds) *The Oxford Handbook of Criminology* (2nd edn). Oxford: Clarendon Press, 1195–232.

Raynor, P. and Vanstone, M. (1997) *Straight Thinking on Probation (STOP): The Mid-Glamorgan Experiment*. Probation Studies Unit Report 4. Oxford: Centre for Criminological Research.

Raynor, P. and Vanstone, M. (2002) *Understanding Community Penalties: Probation, Policy and Social Change*. Buckingham: Open University Press.

Reiner, R. (1991) *Chief Constables: Bobbies, Bosses or Bureaucrats?* Oxford: Oxford University Press.

Roberts, C. (1989) *Hereford and Worcester Probation Service Young Offender Project: First Evaluation Report*. Oxford: Department of Social and Administrative Studies.

Rumgay, J. (2003) 'Drug treatment and offender rehabilitation: reflections on evidence, effectiveness and exclusion', *Probation Journal*, 50 (1): 41–51.

Underdown, A. (1995) *Effectiveness of Community Supervision: Performance and Potential*. Manchester: Greater Manchester Probation Service.

Underdown, A. (1998) *Strategies for Effective Offender Supervision*. London: HMIP.

Chapter 13

Purposes matter: examining the 'ends' of probation

Gwen Robinson and Fergus McNeill

Introduction

In recent years the probation literature has been dominated by discussion around the means and methods of offender supervision. Reflecting a What Works movement which has been gathering momentum for a decade, practitioners, managers and academics have engaged enthusiastically with questions about the most effective types of intervention, in particular the 'new orthodoxy' of cognitive-behavioural methods (McGuire 1995; Vanstone 2000; Crow 2001; Raynor and Vanstone 2002). Rather less attention has been paid to the ends, objectives or aspirations of probation practice, and the fit (or otherwise) between 'official' statements of purpose and the views of those who are actually engaged in the supervision of offenders. In this chapter we argue that, in the absence of explicit statements about the intended purposes or outcomes of probation practice, questions about 'what works?' are at best problematic and at worst meaningless.

The chapter takes as its subject-matter both 'official' and 'front line' perspectives on the purposes of contemporary probation[1] in two juris-dictions: namely, England and Wales and Scotland. It begins with a brief examination of the organisational contexts of probation practice in the two jurisdictions and of how the objectives or 'rationale' of probation have changed in official discourse throughout its history. We then compare and contrast the current 'official' objectives of probation in the two jurisdictions, reflecting on the ways in which these objectives have been shaped by differing organisational contexts and policy themes. Drawing mainly on two contemporary research studies conducted by the authors, we then address the question: how do those at the front line understand the purposes of their work? The concluding discussion focuses on the complexities of public protection as an overarching purpose for probation, and on the wider implications of accepting this revision of probation's ends.

Two organisational contexts

The contexts of the systems for statutory offender supervision north and south of the border are, in many ways, in stark contrast (see Table 13.1). In England and Wales, the probation service has, in recent years, witnessed unparalleled organisational changes.[2] For most of its history, the probation service comprised a collection of local area services organised according to county or city boundaries, each managed locally by area-based probation committees. In April 2001 a National Probation Service for England and Wales came into being, and the 54 existing area services were reorganised into 42 local areas in line with police and Crown Prosecution Service areas (Home Office 1998). Probation committees have been supplanted by new probation boards and the service is now overseen by a national director who is accountable directly to the Home Secretary (Wargent 2002). Another significant recent change for the probation service has been the severing of probation from its traditional social work roots. This occurred in the mid-1990s, when the then Home Secretary repealed the need for probation officers to hold a social work qualification and new routes to probation practice were established (e.g. see Nellis 2001a). Probation officers in England and Wales, then, are no longer social workers, and the context in which they work is no longer that of a social work agency but, rather, a 'law enforcement agency' (NPS 2001).

In Scotland, by contrast, the supervision of offenders, for the time being at least, continues to come firmly within the remit of social work.[3] Having functioned independently for some four decades, the Scottish probation service was disbanded by the Social Work (Scotland) Act 1968 and integrated within generic social work departments (McIvor and Williams 1999). Subsequently, 'criminal justice social work' has been the responsibility of local authorities, despite being funded largely by the Scottish Office and, more recently, the Scottish Executive. This has permitted considerable variation in local arrangements, an issue highlighted in the consultation paper *Community Sentencing: The Tough Option* (Scottish Office 1998).[4]

Table 13.1 A summary of the different organisational contexts for 'probation services' in mainland Britain

	England and Wales	Scotland
Organisational context	National Probation Service for England and Wales	Local authorities
Agency type	Law enforcement	Social work
Leadership	Area probation boards responsible to National Director	Criminal justice managers responsible to Directors of social work and local councils
Funding	Home Office	Scottish Executive via local authorities
Inspection	Her Majesty's Inspectorate of Probation	Social Work Services Inspectorate
Status of practitioners	Employees of local probation boards	Social workers
Professional education	Diploma in Probation Studies	Diploma in Social Work

Probation's purposes: a brief history

In England and Wales, the nearest thing to an account of probation's changing goals or purposes is McWilliams' quartet of essays (1983, 1985, 1986, 1987) which purports to 'trace the history of ideas sustaining the English [sic] probation system since its beginnings' (1987: 97). McWilliams' account, which remains to be seriously challenged, describes three major phases in the development of probation from the turn of the twentieth century to the mid-1980s. The early decades of probation, McWilliams explains, witnessed a shift in its underlying purpose from the mission of 'saving souls' to the 'cure' of offenders through rehabilitative treatment. The rehabilitation of offenders constituted probation's *raison d'être* until the 1970s, after which the empirical and ideological attack on the 'rehabilitative ideal' left probation struggling to articulate a coherent rationale to explain its purpose (e.g. Bottoms and Preston 1980; Allen 1981). Probation subsequently entered a 'phase of pragmatism', during which it came to be reoriented towards the pressing need to reduce the numbers of offenders in custody. In the context of this government policy of 'penal reductionism' (e.g. see Home Office 1977), probation became, in official discourse, a significantly less ambitious project: an 'alternative to custody' rather than a 'treatment' aiming to change people (McWilliams 1987; Raynor 1997).

While acknowledging penal reductionism as a laudable policy, highly commensurate with probation's tradition of helping offenders, McWilliams lamented the loss of a 'transcendent justification' for the service's work. Clearly anticipating the arrival of the government's 'punishment in the community' strategy, which in the latter 1980s sought to bolster the utilisation and credibility of probation by defining it as a form of punishment, McWilliams argued that, in the absence of any overarching purpose, the probation service would in future be vulnerable to centrally driven changes to its role and to the tasks of probation officers (McWilliams 1987, 1989; Home Office 1988, 1990a; McWilliams and Pease 1990). Indeed, when in the mid-1990s the government's hostility to the idea of social work with offenders led the then Home Secretary to repeal the need for probation officers to hold a social work qualification,[5] the service lost any claim to an identity defined outside government policy, as one earlier commentator had forewarned (Haxby 1978: 108–9).

Meanwhile, probation in Scotland had experienced its own, rather different, changes of identity. After the disbanding of the Scottish probation service in 1969, criminal justice services were integrated within generic social work departments and offenders were placed alongside others deemed to be in need of social work services, the common duty of which was to 'promote social welfare' (Social Work (Scotland) Act 1968: s. 12). However, by the late 1970s commentators in academic and professional journals were expressing concerns about the viability of probation and after-care services when subsumed within the social welfare functions of the social work departments (Marsland 1977; Nelson 1977; Moore 1978). Subsequently, when in 1989 the Scottish Office initiated central, ring-fenced funding for most criminal justice social work services, this was interpreted by some as recognition that such services had fallen into a state of comparative neglect (Huntingford 1992; Moore and Whyte 1998). When a policy of penal reductionism was clearly expounded as 'The Way Ahead' for Scottish penal policy in the late 1980s (Rifkind 1989), criminal justice social work looked set to follow the 'alternatives to custody' model which had already taken root in England and Wales. Indeed, the first objective delineated in the new national objectives and standards (SWSG 1991a) was 'to enable a reduction in the incidence of custody … where it is used for lack of a suitable, available community based social work disposal' (s. 12.1).

In both jurisdictions by about 1990, then, probation was understood primarily as an alternative to custody.[6] But, in England and Wales, while arguably signalling limited ambitions, this reframing of probation was in fact to play a significant role in terms of stimulating the development of programmes which aimed to reduce reoffending rates and, ultimately, an empirical revival of 'rehabilitation' (e.g. Hudson 1987). For example, Raynor (1995) has explained how the series of probation-run What Works conferences which commenced in 1991 was partly attributable to the search for 'meaningful' supervision content inspired by the punishment in the community strategy (e.g. McGuire 1995; Rowson and McGuire 1991, 1996). Though probation in Scotland was not required to negotiate the ideological traverse towards punishment in the community, a focus on reducing reoffending, informed from the outset by emerging research evidence (McIvor 1990; SWSG 1991b), was none the less seen as being critical to the enhanced credibility of community penalties on which reduction in the use of custody was thought to depend (e.g. Paterson and Tombs 1998). By the end of the 1990s, optimism in England and Wales about the propensity of probation intervention to impact on reoffending rates was such that the reduction of reoffending had been articulated as an official objective of the probation service (Home Office 1999).

However, in England and Wales, this academic and professional revival of optimism concerning rehabilitative interventions occurred in the broader context of a punitive turn in penal policy. When, in 1993, the then Home Secretary infamously announced that 'prison works', it was clear that penal policy had moved on from the penal reductionist stance which had informed the Criminal Justice Act 1991 (see also Nellis 2001b; Home Office 1996: para. 1.12). Although frequently conflicting with the 'just deserts' framework put in place by the 1991 Act, 'populist punitiveness' came to dominate official responses to questions about sentencing and punishment (Bottoms 1995) and the probation service found itself under attack for perpetuating an approach which was perceived as being 'soft on crime' and too closely aligned with the interests of the offender. It was in this context that the principle of 'public protection', initially introduced via the white paper, *Crime, Justice and Protecting the Public* (Home Office 1990b), came to dominate in the criminal justice and penal fields (e.g. see Garland 1996, 2001; Nellis 1995, 2001c).

A growing national emphasis on public protection coincided with the introduction of significantly higher-risk populations of offenders to probation caseloads. In both jurisdictions, legislative changes in the early 1990s required prisoners serving sentences in excess of four years to undertake compulsory community supervision on release (Criminal Justice Act 1991; Prisoners and Criminal Proceedings (Scotland) Act 1993). In England and Wales, this prompted the development of joint strategies and close working relationships between the probation services and other 'public protection agencies' – most notably the police – in respect of high-risk and potentially dangerous offenders (HMIP 1998; Nash 1999; Maguire *et al.* 2001).

In Scotland, advances in both the rhetoric and the practice of public protection were similarly rapid. Although it did not appear as an objective in the original standards (SWSG 1991a), by the time of the publication of *The Tough Option* (Scottish Office 1998) the then minister responsible was declaring both that 'Our paramount aim is public safety' (s. 1.2) and that the pursuit of reductions in the use of custody 'must be consistent with the wider objective of promoting public and community safety' (s. 1.2.3). Revisions to the Scottish standards on throughcare services (SWSG 1996) and court reports (SWSG 2000), as well as other central reports and guidance (SWSI 1997, 1998) both presage and reflect this shift in emphasis.[7]

The 'official' purposes of contemporary probation

It has already been made clear that probation systems north and south of the border have been subject to 'official' statements of objectives and priorities for a number of years. More generally, both systems of probation operate in accordance with a framework of primary and secondary legislation which sets out statutory objectives for supervision. In this section we focus on the contemporary 'official' objectives of the two systems as set out in a number of contemporary documents.[8]

The clearest point of convergence in respect of the objectives of probation in the two jurisdictions is with regard to *public protection*, which in both cases receives top billing. For example, the first of the three priorities mentioned in the current Scottish statement of *National Priorities* for criminal justice social work is to make a 'contribution to increased community safety and public protection' (Justice Department 2001: 3). In England and Wales, the Criminal Justice and Court Services Act 2000 (CJCSA) unambiguously places 'protection of the public' at the head of the official objectives of the new National Probation Service.

However, the mirroring of official purposes in the two jurisdictions appears both to begin and end with public protection. In Scotland, unlike England and Wales, we find that the rise of public protection as an official purpose has been associated with a continuing, if somewhat more qualified, commitment to 'anti-custodialism' (Nellis 1995). This is reflected in the second of the *National Priorities*, which is to 'Reduce the use of unnecessary custody by providing effective community disposals' (Justice Department 2001: 3). The strategic framework for the new National Probation Service, by contrast, contains no such aspiration (NPS 2001). This state of affairs reflects not only the decline of the policy of penal reductionism in the wake of the Criminal Justice Act 1991 and the rise of a more punitive mood[9] but also the recent repositioning of probation alongside prisons in a 'field of corrections' (Nellis 1999, 2001b). This latter development is exemplified by the recent *Prisons – Probation Review* and the subsequent publication of a policy framework setting out common objectives for the two services (Home Office 1998).

In England and Wales, it is 'reducing reoffending' which has been articulated as the second primary aim of probation. Thus, for example, the Home Secretary's Foreword to the *Correctional Policy Framework* explains that 'We have put the focus firmly on outcomes – reducing re-offending and improving public protection. Success will be measured in those terms. The achievement of this common aim … must be a first consideration for everyone engaged in delivering correctional policy, and not an afterthought' (Home Office 1999: 1).

The foregrounding of this aim reflects the Home Office's appropriation of the effective practice or What Works movement to which we have already referred (e.g. Home Office 1998). Indeed, where 'rehabilitation' is articulated as an aim in official documentation south of the border, it is 'rehabilitation-as-treatment' or 'correctionalism' which is inferred: that is, the reduction of reoffending risk via the application of accredited, 'rehabilitative' programmes of intervention (e.g. see NPS 2001: 7).

The articulation of the concept of rehabilitation differs somewhat in Scotland. Despite its hardening of the rhetoric around community penalties, *The Tough Option* made clear the link between crime and social exclusion, recognising that 'Criminal justice social work services are often dealing with the consequences of exclusion and it follows that … offenders … should be able to access services and resources which can assist in their reintegration' (Scottish Office 1998: s. 2.2.1).

The same theme underpins the third of the *National Priorities*, which is to 'Promote the social inclusion of offenders through rehabilitation, so reducing the level of offending' (Justice Department 2001: 3). In this context, rehabilitation is cast as the means of progressing towards two compatible and interdependent ends: not only the reduction of reoffending but also the social inclusion of offenders.[10] This reading of rehabilitation remains entirely consistent with the social welfare philosophy underlying the Social Work (Scotland) Act 1968 which placed offenders alongside others in need of such services. South of the border, by contrast, there is nothing to indicate that the promotion of offenders' welfare or social inclusion is regarded as a laudable end in its own right.

Related to this last observation is the more punitive tone of probation in England and Wales. For example, the vision for probation outlined in *A New Choreography* 'has in it a concept of the proper punishment of offenders'. This is explained as follows: 'Under NPS supervision, offenders and the public will "know" that they have been punished through the demands made on their time, the nature of their expected engagement and behaviour and because compliance has been secured or breach action taken' (NPS 2001: 7).

Here the promise of enforcement is invoked to support the notion of probation-as-punishment and it seems fair to form the same conclusion in respect of the service's newly acquired 'soundbite': enforcement, rehabilitation and public protection (NPS 2001), albeit that the ordering of these three core objectives does not accord with the primacy given to public protection and rehabilitation elsewhere. While both 'punishment' and 'enforcement' are held up as legitimate objectives of probation practice in the strategic framework of the NPS, neither is present in the Scottish *National Priorities* document.

Researching 'front line' perspectives

It is perhaps surprising that, in a penal professional field which has, in the last two decades or so, proved so vulnerable to changes in official ideologies, little research attention has been paid to the responses of practitioners (and, indeed, managers) to such change. There are, however, one or two exceptions. For example, an English study by Humphrey and Pease (1992) indicated that probation officers tended to frame their practice in terms of the then 'official' objective of providing alternatives to custody. This was clear from the fact that the vast majority of those interviewed defined effectiveness in terms of increasing probation's 'market shares', thereby diverting greater numbers of offenders from custodial sentences. Interestingly, however, a number of interviewees viewed the 'slowing of criminal careers' as a legitimate objective and lamented the absence of official interest in such outcome measures. This finding adds weight to the hypothesis that the 'rehabilitative ideal' was not in fact wholly abandoned within the service south of the border following its banishment from official discourse (Pease 1980; McWilliams 1987; Smith 1987; Raynor 1996).

More recent studies on both sides of the border point to an increasing emphasis on outcomes. For example, no doubt reflecting the acceleration of a What Works agenda, Brown (1998) found that stopping offending was the ultimate goal of the probation officers she interviewed in one English area service. In Scotland, McIvor and Barry (1998a) found that addressing offending and related attitudes and problems, as well as getting the probationer through the order, were the most common objectives for probation supervision identified by social workers. Their study of community-based throughcare (McIvor and Barry 1998b) similarly found that avoiding or addressing offending featured as an objective in three fifths of the cases they reviewed. A further study of front-line perspectives on effective probation practice also suggested that, while Scottish workers had varied views about how best to define and measure effectiveness, they prioritised reducing reoffending, changing probationers' attitudes, increasing victim empathy *and* alleviating probationers' needs (McNeill 2000).

In order to explore whether and how the most recent developments in official discourses which we have described in both jurisdictions might be reflected in contemporary 'front line' discourses, we next present some related findings from two independent studies conducted by the authors.

Two contemporary studies

England and Wales

The findings reported here derive from a research study conducted in two probation service areas towards the end of 1999 (Robinson 2001, 2002). Twenty-nine staff members of all grades (including 15 main-grade officers) took part in in-depth, semi-structured interviews. Although the interviews covered a number of subject areas, the findings reported here relate to the last part of the interviews, in which individuals were asked, first, what they thought the probation service was expected to achieve, at that point in time; and, secondly, to reflect on the legitimacy of these expectations.

As we have seen, the official purposes or objectives of probation in

England and Wales have been rearticulated very recently, principally by means of the CJCSA 2000 and the strategic document *A New Choreography* (NPS 2001). That these documents announced ideological changes which had in fact evolved over a period of time is evident in that, although the research reported here was carried out in 1999 prior to the publication of either of the key documents, those interviewed – almost without exception – identified one or more of the 'official' purposes or objectives of probation when asked to say what they thought the probation service was currently expected to achieve. That is, interviewees tended to recognise at least one element of what we might term the 'official ideological trinity' of public protection, rehabilitation (defined as reducing reoffending) and enforcement.

Most of those interviewed identified one or both of 'public protection' and 'reducing reoffending' as being outcomes expected of the probation service, and there was a high degree of identification with these 'core purposes'. In other words, not only were contributing to public protection and reducing reoffending cited by the majority of interviewees of all grades as the main perceived expectations but also, importantly, these were regarded as legitimate – albeit not necessarily easily achievable – objectives, both for the service as a whole and for them as individuals.

In contrast, 'enforcement' was mentioned by only a small minority of interviewees and tended to be perceived in less positive terms. This was not because enforcement was associated with the notion of probation-as-punishment but, rather, because a preoccupation with enforcing orders on the part of the service's masters was thought to signal a lack of concern with broader or more meaningful outcomes. For example, consider the following extract:

Interviewer: So what would you say are the expectations of the service at the moment?

Practitioner: Oh, that's an interesting one, isn't it? [laughs] We're expected to achieve that after three unacceptable failures to report, they're returned to court for breach.

Interviewer: What about more broadly than that?

Practitioner: I don't think there's any concern really, is there? Just in people being breached.

Two core purposes... or one?
Reflecting the findings of previous research (see above), 'reducing reoffending' tended to be regarded as a 'traditional' objective of

probation practice. As one practitioner commented: 'Well I think the general expectation is what it always has been: what are we in the job for if not to reduce offending?' Comments such as this clearly add weight to the argument that, within the probation service, the 'rehabilitative ideal' survived its official demise and continued to be a personal objective for practitioners throughout the period in which 'nothing works' was the dominant view (Martinson 1974; Folkard *et al.* 1976; Raynor and Vanstone 2002: ch. 4). There was, however, an acknowledgement among interviewees that this objective had only recently been afforded a new 'official' legitimacy. This was viewed as extremely important in terms of enhancing the service's credibility and legitimacy in the eyes of external audiences:

In sort of '96 '97 when I think I first *really* started getting enthusiastic about [effective practice] I think colleagues in ACOP [the Association of Chief Officers of Probation] equally felt that there was the *basis* for something that would aid the credibility of the probation service; give staff a sense that what they were doing *mattered* and made a difference; boosted our confidence with courts and satisfied the Home Office and ministers that we were doing the right things. (Senior manager)

I think it is reassuring to think that ... we can actually reduce reoffending, and therefore we have a purpose, we fit within the criminal justice system. (Senior practitioner)

The objective of reducing reoffending, then, was strongly linked with perceptions of credibility and legitimacy for the probation service.

The pursuit of public protection, too, was seen by many to be linked with credibility and the projection of a positive image. As one senior manager explained: 'I think the willingness of probation staff to work on a multi-agency basis to manage risk is very impressive and I think will continue to grow and bring us increased credibility and so I feel very positive about that.' In common with a number of other interviewees, this senior manager tended to equate the notion of public protection with the practice of managing high-risk or potentially dangerous offenders. This way of talking and thinking about public protection reflected the fact that both the area services studied had in the last 18 months established specialist 'public protection teams' comprising a small number of experienced practitioners, whose remit was to supervise those offenders assessed as posing the highest risks to the community (see also Robinson 2002). On the other hand, however, a number of comments made in the course of the interviews pointed to another, broader understanding of public protection: that is, as an *overarching* objective of probation practice, common both to specialist work with high-risk offenders (a.k.a. 'public protection practice') and more generally in the context of 'mainstream' practice. This 'generic' perception of public protection was conveyed by one interviewee as follows: 'We're told by the Home Secretary – and I believe we do operate – that the client is not the offender our client is the *public* now; it's all about identifying risk and protecting the public' (senior practitioner).

This reorientation towards victims and potential victims of crime was regarded as an unavoidable one on the part of the probation service; an 'inevitable manoeuvre' reflecting a broader political shift which had, in the early 1990s, explicitly placed the interests of victims and the wider public at the heart of the system of criminal justice. The perceived inevitability of having public protection as an explicit aim clearly went some way towards explaining its perceived legitimacy, albeit that there was some acknowledgement of this 'shift' being easier for some than for others: 'I think there *are* people who've struggled with it, with the transition from the social work ethos to the public protection ethos, and I think those people are not happy and for them it *does* feel different' (Senior practitioner).

Despite this perception, the transition towards a public protection stance tended to be understood by interviewees in more subtle and relatively unproblematic terms: for example, one practitioner described it as a 'different way of looking' at familiar problems. Public protection was also seen as compatible with the more 'traditional' aim of reducing reoffending; indeed, the comments of several interviewees pointed towards a perception of public protection as lending legitimacy to the notion of offender rehabilitation. For example:

> I mean, what's being promoted is the probation service as a public protection agency. And how do you protect the public? You protect the public by managing the risk that offenders pose and by reducing offending. (Senior manager)

> I think, the aim is to reduce reoffending and in so doing to protect the public, and that's what we're here for. (Practitioner)

> [We're expected to bring about] a reduction in reoffending, thereby better to protect the public. Because that's the thrust of where we're going. (Practitioner)

For these and other interviewees, then, the reduction of reoffending was framed not so much as an aim or end in its own right but, rather, as a *means* towards the more generic end of protecting the public. The implication here is that, while in England and Wales we are clearly witnessing a revival or relegitimation of rehabilitation in the probation context, rehabilitation itself has not been reinstated as a 'transcendent justification' for the service's work (e.g. McWilliams and Pease 1990). Rather, by virtue of their promise to impact on reoffending rates, rehabilitative programmes are being understood as one of a number of legitimate routes towards effective public protection. Put another way, we may in fact be witnessing the rise of public protection to the status of a 'meta-narrative' or overarching purpose for the National Probation Service (Lyotard 1984).

Scotland

The preliminary findings reported here come from an ongoing study being conducted in two Scottish sites. This section draws on in-depth, focused interviews with all the staff engaged in the delivery of criminal justice social work services in 'Oldtown' – a large town served by criminal justice staff working as a sub-team of a large generic social-work team. Interviews were conducted in autumn 2001 with nine workers, one senior social worker and the senior manger responsible for criminal justice services across the council area. Though the interviews covered a wide range of themes, questions of purpose represented a substantial area of discussion.

Though the *National Priorities* document (Justice Department 2001) was issued a few months before the interviews took place, none of those interviewed referred to it directly in their discussions of policy or of purposes. None the less, in the discussion of probation's purposes there was clear and consistent evidence that public protection was regarded as a legitimate policy purpose by all those interviewed. As in England and Wales, this may attest to an ideological evolution of purpose presaging the explicit shift in policy.

More specifically, almost all those interviewed described their own views of purposes in a manner consistent with the following 'formula': reduce reoffending *by* assisting people *so as to* protect the community *and* enhance its welfare. The following exchange was fairly typical:

Interviewer: How do you understand the purpose of it all, criminal justice social work, what's it for?

Practitioner: ... It is about protecting the community and trying to reduce the offending or the impact of offending on the community. And I think that – I mean, that doesn't mean that I don't still believe that people should be respected and valued ... that my clients deserve [to be] valued, but I think they also have to – there is a bit there that you have to challenge that offending behaviour and you have to, you have to allow them to see that they have to take responsibility for it ...

However, despite this consensus about public protection as a legitimate purpose, perhaps even a 'paramount' purpose (Scottish Office 1998), closer examination of the workers' views about the interpretation and operationalisation of public protection revealed interesting variations. Concerning the interpretation of public protection, two main positions emerged when workers were questioned more closely. Some workers clearly regarded assisting individuals as an *intrinsic* good, an end in itself, albeit one the pursuit of which should also serve to protect the interests of the wider public:

Interviewer: Are you [providing assistance] for the individual in front of you, for their benefit, or are you doing it for the benefit of the community ...?

Practitioner: I'd say both really. I mean, obviously for the individual that's in front of you at that point in time, but if you manage to change that person that's sitting in front of you, *at the end of the day* you're helping the community.

Interviewer: Uh-hu, which is more important though ...?

Practitioner: The punter in front of me, I'm afraid!

Interviewer: ... Why is that?

Practitioner: Oh – because that's just the way I feel I face my work. It's the person I've got sitting there, that person who needs help at that point in time. And that's just the way I am ... I know *in the long run* it is helping the bigger, the wider community ... (*emphasis added*)

Other workers, by contrast, were clear that the provision of assistance was an *instrumental* good, a means to the end of reducing offending and thus protecting the public:

Interviewer: ... Do you provide assistance ... as an end in itself because, as you say, people are worth while?

Practitioner: No, no, I'm clear ... as a criminal justice social worker that fundamentally I do not accept people offending, you know, and they would have to sort of move towards that and try to reduce their offending behaviour.

Although it might be tempting to designate the first interpretation as a 'traditional' social work or welfare response and the second as representative of a more criminal justice-oriented perspective, it was clear that none of the workers, including those who adopted the latter view, owned punishment as an objective. Indeed the only worker who mentioned punishment, despite being one who viewed assisting offenders as a means and not an end in itself, did so to disavow it:

I don't and never have seen it as a sort of punishment ... maybe [because of the] grounding of social work I have ... clearly that has influenced my work on a personal level and it obviously influences my value stands and the way I see things and how I probably *fit and shape* things to suit that as I go on about my daily business. (Practitioner, emphasis added)

The business of fitting and shaping things, of operationalising purposes, related to three main ways in which the welfare or social work tradition continued to find expression, despite the paramountcy afforded to public protection. First, as is already obvious, workers argued that helping communities *requires* helping offenders and used this to lend renewed legitimacy to 'welfare' activities:

Community protection [is] a valid part or objective. But ... criminal justice social work – one of the reasons I want it to stay in social work – also has another element to it which is to do with assisting individuals. In the context of criminal justice social work obviously you are assisting them *not only in their own right* but also to reduce the likelihood of them offending again. But arguably that's in their interests as well as of course the potential victims' interest ... because assisting the individual does assist society. I suppose I would argue for assisting the individual further than is immediately necessary to protect society, but even that could be viewed as a kind of reinforcing, or reducing the likelihood that in the future he or she will get back into trouble. (Senior manager, emphasis added)

The second means by which the welfare tradition found expression lay in the way in which workers characterised the social work relationship as the vehicle for change:

> You're working with people … who would chose not to be your client – you have to engage them … You have to … meet them half way … and say – 'Right, okay, we'll deal with that [welfare issue] but don't forget this [offending behaviour] is why you're here … I'll tackle that [welfare issue] because if I tackle that with you it might let you see that I'm being more amenable to you and therefore you might be more inclined to buy into my agenda [reducing offending]'. (Practitioner)

Thirdly, workers stressed the broader social contexts of offending behaviour and of their efforts to bring about change:

> I think you've got to look at the broader picture … the education, the housing, the whole shebang, not just people who are out offending … I think really that – you know, you can't just get somebody to stop offending, you've got to help them change their whole lifestyle and that's really what I would set out to, task myself out to do. (Practitioner)

These ways of linking public protection and social welfare concerns – through highlighting mutual social interests, social work relationships as vehicles of change and the social contexts of change efforts – perhaps reflect the Scottish policy in suggesting a broader concept of re-habilitation connected with social inclusion agendas. However, they also illustrate how, at the front line, ideological change can be negotiated, mediated and managed in practice by individual penal professionals finding differing ways to reinscribe existing purposes and practices within evolving ideologies. Like their counterparts in England and Wales, the Scottish workers related the necessity for such manoeuvres to the perceived legitimacy of criminal justice social work in the eyes of its external audiences in the justice system and in society at large. This is not to say that the changes involved were merely shifts in the rhetoric of what might be termed a 'penal-professional apologetics', adapting to relegitimate traditional services and practices in changing social contexts. That the changes involved were also reflected in practice was most clearly evidenced in the workers' discussions of cases. Perhaps unsurprisingly in this regard, it was apparent that the ways in which public protection came to be interpreted and operationalised in practice were primarily governing by risk, and in particular, risk of harm. Workers and others moved more clearly towards public protection as a superordinate or governing purpose and, correspondingly, towards assisting individuals *primarily* as an instrumental rather than an intrinsic good, in cases where the risk of serious harm to the public was seen as significant. It might be safe to assume that it is in such cases that front-line workers become most preoccupied with the 'gaze' of the external audience.

Discussion

We have seen that the 'official' purposes of probation in the two jurisdictions have not remained static. This is principally because neither system exists in an ideological vacuum; rather, in common with other public services, each has been required to adapt to changing criminal justice and social policy agendas and, perhaps to a lesser extent, to the findings of research into the effectiveness of their efforts. To date, more dramatic changes have been evident in probation in England and Wales. While Scotland's policy agendas, and thus the identity of criminal justice social work, have remained relatively stable over time, a more volatile policy context south of the border has engaged probation in something of a permanent revolution. None the less, the systems of probation in England and Wales and in Scotland have, in recent decades, been characterised by *both* continuity and change in respect of their 'official' purposes.

We have also seen that recent developments in respect of the purposes or objectives of probation north and south of the border have in many ways continued to mark them out as separate systems with contrasting concerns and priorities. This state of affairs reflects not only relatively independent policy contexts but also the different organisational contexts for statutory offender supervision, which have diverged increasingly since the probation service in England and Wales lost its claim to a social work identity. However, recent developments in official discourse appear at the same time to signal a degree of convergence in respect of purpose; most notably we have witnessed the emergence of 'public protection' as a principal objective of probation in both juris-dictions. Beyond this 'official' discourse, public protection also appears to be emerging as a 'meta-narrative' for probation at the front line.

Indeed, we have shown that there is, in both jurisdictions, a high degree of what Derber (1982) has characterised as 'ideological co-optation' in respect of public protection as a core purpose. That is, workers are tending to identify with this recently instated official objective, rather than denying, ignoring or rebelling against it.

Why is it that we appear to be seeing the emergence of public protection as a 'core purpose' or meta-narrative in two jurisdictions which, on a number of levels, are very different? We saw that, in England and Wales, at least some of the enthusiasm for public protection reflected the perceived *inevitability* of the service's adoption of a more victim-centred approach. Indeed, the comments of interviewees in this respect very much echoed Nellis's prescient observation that: 'the placing of offenders' needs and interests *above*, as opposed to *alongside*, the rights of victims and the requirements of public safety lacks moral justification and, in the 1990s, political credibility' (1995: 26).

A second explanation for the popularity of public protection as a meta-narrative for probation is that it appears to offer probation services, loosely defined, the coherent identity they have been accused of lacking for some time. Here, then, an acceptance of public protection as a legitimate purpose appears to be linked with a perceived injection of credibility for the service after quite a long period of uncertainty and criticism (Nash 2000).[11]

In both jurisdictions, however, a large measure of the 'ideological co-optation' which we observed in respect of public protection appeared to be related to its perceived compatibility with other objectives to which interviewees subscribed. In other words, public protection appeared to constitute a sort of 'ideological umbrella' under which a variety of other objectives or aims could be subsumed. We saw, further, that in both jurisdictions certain 'traditional' objectives and methods were perceived not only as compatible with but also as being afforded a new legitimacy alongside, or in the context of, public protection. For example, in England and Wales, interviewees tended to frame rehabilitative inter-ventions and the reduction of reoffending in the context of the 'more general' quest for public protection, lending support to Garland's (1997: 6) observation that:

> Probation staff now emphasise that 'rehabilitation' is necessary for the protection of the public. It is future victims who are now 'rescued' by rehabilitative work, rather than the offenders themselves ... [Rehabilitation is increasingly being] represented as an instrument of risk management, inculcating self-controls, reducing danger, enhancing the security of the public.

In Scotland, interviewees appeared to understand public protection as lending legitimacy to 'welfare' activities and, perhaps partly because of a broader vision of rehabilitation and inclusion in policy statements, they insisted on identifying commonalities of interest between offenders and communities.

As a narrative for probation practice, then, public protection is unusually elastic, and it is arguably this elasticity which accounts for much of its appeal to practitioners and their managers.[12] Thus, while in the official discourse of probation in England and Wales public protection is accompanied by objectives of reducing reoffending and enforcement, in Scotland we find it dovetailing just as neatly with the 'softer' objectives of social inclusion and anti-custodialism in the context of criminal justice social work.

However, the elasticity of public protection creates problems as well as apparent 'solutions' for probation. One potential problem with public protection's elasticity is that it stretches as a paramount purpose across a range of criminal justice agencies, thus depriving probation of any claim to a distinctive ideological identity. While enhancing the 'seamlessness' of the system might be seen simply as the welcome development of a more 'rational' criminal justice, it has been argued that too much ideological uniformity across criminal justice agencies and the related diminution of probation's historical claims to offer a unique contribution should provoke a degree of unease (Nellis 1999a). This might be less of a problem if probation's distinctiveness within the justice system could rest on its techniques and approaches to achieving the 'systemic' end of public protection. However, developments in England and Wales (most notably the establishment of a Joint Accreditation Panel (Mair 2000) and the recent appointment of the former Director General of the Prison Service as Commissioner for Correctional Services) suggest that any claims to such distinctiveness might be false. In the absence of a distinctive ideological identity or a unique repertoire of skills and approaches, the justification for the existence of community-based penalties (at least as we might currently recognise them) seems to rest on a purely technical debate about the relative efficacy of different sanctions in delivering protection. Within this context in England and Wales, the What Works initiative, for better or worse, assumes central significance, becoming the bet on which probation has staked its future.

That this represents a high-risk strategy emerges from the concerns of front-line workers in both jurisdictions about the consequences of failing to live up to the (implicit) promise to protect, whether through risk management strategies or 'effective' rehabilitative programmes (Robinson 2002). This is not simply an issue about whether such programmes can produce compelling evidence of their effectiveness in protecting the public; rather, it concerns a more fundamental paradox at the heart of public protection, at least where it performs legitimating functions for probation. This rests on the fact that legitimation through the offer of protection seeks to address the public's fear of crime while at the same time depending upon it. In turn, the form of reassurance that agencies provide serves to confirm the existence of a threat, the potency of which can only be partly mitigated, even by the best policies and practices. Thus when research evidence of *general* effectiveness is set against inevitable but spectacular 'failures' to protect in *specific* high-profile cases, the credibility of agencies of protection must suffer, increasing public anxiety and diminishing public trust. Particularly when set against a backdrop of populist punitiveness, this dynamic has the potential to drive both policy-makers and perhaps the leaders of these agencies in the direction of ever more coercive, constraining and incapacitating methods of protection (see also Rutherford 1998) in order to sustain popular, political and fiscal support for their activities.

As a 'meta-narrative' for probation, then, public protection arguably threatens to bring a range of punitive, exclusionary and ultimately unpalatable tasks and/or methods into probation's repertoire. The possibility of such a 'punitive drift' is made possible because, as a rationale for action, public protection lacks an ethical dimension (Nellis 1999; Harding 2000). In other words, in the context of an overarching purpose of public protection, virtually any form of sanction for wrongdoing may be rendered legitimate or 'effective'. Within this broader narrative, rehabilitative measures are merely one of many possible means to an end, carrying no peculiar moral merit. Moreover, judgements *between* differing methods of rehabilitation – from, for example, the brutal aversive therapy of the Ludovico method[13] to the provision of enhanced opportunities for social inclusion – lose any moral dimension, reducing to questions of technical effectiveness.

A related point is that, in forefronting the risks to potential victims, protectionism tends to be associated with defensive decision-making, which may threaten offenders' rights to liberty, or the least necessary restrictions (Tuddenham 2000; Hudson 2001). If, as we have argued, public protection discourses are now influencing and shaping practice not just with the most 'risky' but with the whole range of offenders, then the parameters of this potential skewing of the rights of offenders and of the public are widening.[14]

This analysis of the strengths and weaknesses of public protection as a 'meta-narrative' for probation leads us to concur with Harding's conclusion that 'Beyond public protection, the probation service stands in need of a more transcendent justification for its activities' (2000: 16). Though public protection is arguably a necessary part of probation's ideology, it can be neither sufficient nor superordinate. As Nellis commented in response to the *Prisons – Probation Review* (Home Office 1998):

> It takes one facet of the Probation Service's purposes – public protection – and promotes it as the purpose above all others. This is no more ethically sophisticated than the claims once made by the service itself that the rehabilitation/welfare of the offender was a purpose-cum-principle above all others in criminal justice. Neither claim is sustainable. (1999a: 315)

Though Nellis has been both a fierce and a fair critic of social work's contribution to probation (1995), it seems particularly telling, in the light of the comparative analysis offered here, that the prospects for a more distinctive and balanced probation ideology – pursuing anti-custodialism, social inclusion and public protection within local services and communities – seem, for the moment at least, much brighter in Scotland than in England and Wales. If there is some encouragement for those with significant doubts about contemporary developments in probation south of the border, perhaps it may come from the evidence offered here that probation professionals are far from being the passive vessels of 'official' discourses. The brief exploration above of the subtle and nuanced processes through which professional workers construct their purposes exposes the role that personal and professional agency continues to play, even in increasingly structured and structuring penal organisations (Giddens 1984). Though this agency may frustrate the What Works initiative and other managerialist attempts to standardise practice in line with policy, it may also protect probation's longer-term future, by preserving a degree of diversity of purpose and approach. Thus, just as rehabilitation survived as a purpose and practice at the front line during the era of 'nothing works' (Vanstone 2000), so during the 'public protection' era, other purposes of probation work, though lost or marginalised in the official rhetoric, might endure in probation practice.

Notes

1 In this chapter we use the term 'probation' not to refer to a particular disposal of the courts but as shorthand for the penal-professional field occupied by the National Probation Service in England and Wales and by criminal justice social work services in Scotland.

2 For further discussion of the current organisation of the probation service in England and Wales, and the background to the recent changes, see Bottoms *et al.* (2001).

3 This situation now looks set to change. Between the drafting of this chapter (early 2003) and its going to print, proposals for significant organisational changes emerged in Scotland. The Scottish Labour Party's manifesto for the Scottish parliamentary election campaign in May 2003 promised 'We will set up a single agency – the Correctional Service for Scotland – staffed by professionals and covering prison and community based sentences to maximise the impact of punishment, rehabilitation and protection offered by our justice system' ('On your side', available at: http://www.scottishlabour.org.uk/manifesto/). The partnership agreement between Scottish Labour and the Scottish Liberal Democrats, published following the elections, moderated this position slightly: 'We will publish proposals for consultation for a single agency to deliver custodial and non-custodial sentences in Scotland with the aim of reducing reoffending rates' ('A partnership for a better Scotland, available at: http://www.scotland.gov.uk/library5/government/pfbs.pdf). COSLA (the Convention of Scottish Local Authorities) and ADSW (the Association of Directors of Social Work) responded to the Labour manifesto commitment by pledging to fight 'tooth and nail' against the proposed measures, arguing that there was no justification for change and no evidence that it would work to cut reoffending (*The Scotsman* 9 May 2003). At the time of writing (August 2003), all that can be reported is that the debate continues.

4 In pursuit of greater consistency of provision and economies of scale, the criminal justice services provided by Scotland's 32 local authorities have since been reorganised into 11 'groupings'; however, they remain local authority social work services.

5 The break with social work and the onset of new training arrangements for probation officers was not a wholly unpopular move (e.g. Nellis 1995).

6 In England and Wales, probation's new and comparatively modest rationale was endorsed in the first Home Office *Statement of National Objectives and Priorities* (SNOP) (Home Office 1984).

7 Most recently, Part One of the Criminal Justice (Scotland) Bill, currently before the Scottish Parliament, concerns itself with 'Protection of the public at large', including measures to establish a Risk Management Authority and an order for lifelong restriction.

8 In respect of the newly inaugurated National Probation Service for England and Wales, we pay particular attention to *A New Choreography* (NPS 2001), a

lengthy strategic document which builds on both *The Correctional Policy Framework* (Home Office 1999) and the recently revised legislative framework of the Criminal Justice and Court Services Act 2000. In Scotland, the founding legislation for criminal justice social work, the Social Work (Scotland) Act 1968, has remained in place for over three decades. The Scottish document most nearly equivalent to *A New Choreography* is the rather less imaginatively titled *Criminal Justice Social Work Services National Priorities for 2001–2002 and Onwards* (Justice Department 2001). Comparison of these sources is arguably problematic since the Scottish document reflects neither the glossy presentation nor the comparative detail of *A New Choreography*; indeed, it runs to only three pages. Its content is none the less revealing and important. In common with *A New Choreography*, the *National Priorities* sit within a broader policy framework; however, in Scotland there is no direct equivalent to *The Correctional Policy Framework*. Rather, *A Safer Scotland: Tackling Crime and its Causes* (Scottish Office 1999) offers an account of government policy across a range of crime prevention, community safety and criminal justice themes. *The Tough Option* (Scottish Office 1998) remains the most recent detailed statement about community penalties.

9 When in 1993 the Conservative Home Secretary announced that 'prison works', it was clear that penal policy had moved on from the penal reductionist stance which had informed the Criminal Justice Act 1991 (see also Home Office 1996: para. 1.12).

10 Social inclusion is also a strong theme of *A Safer Scotland* (Scottish Office 1999). However, while the document refers repeatedly to underlying needs and problems of both children and adults who offend, the language of social inclusion, perhaps unsurprisingly, is more consistently deployed in the discussions of early intervention, crime prevention and community safety.

11 Indeed, it is worth noting that in recent years the probation service has won significant praise for its engagement with the public protection agenda (e.g. HMIP 1998).

12 The elasticity of public protection also accounts for its endurance as a penal narrative in England and Wales throughout the 1990s – a period commonly acknowledged to be a turbulent decade in criminal justice policy (Faulkner 1996; Garland 1996). Initially introduced in England and Wales in a liberal, 'rational' moment in government thinking (Home Office 1990b), the principle of public protection was initially used to justify the focusing of the state's limited resources on those offenders thought to pose the greatest risks to the public. However, when 'populist punitiveness' (Bottoms 1995) held sway, as under the Conservatives in the mid-1990s, the same principle was used to legitimate an increasingly punitive stance towards offending *in general*, and to bring an increasing number of offenders into categories requiring increased levels of control and surveillance (e.g. Home Office 1996).

13 The Ludovico method is described in Anthony Burgess's novel, *A Clockwork Orange*, and is depicted, in all its brutality, in Stanley Kubrick's film of the same title.

14 This 'generalisation' of public protectionism to entire populations of offenders should perhaps be of particular concern in the light of evidence that the relative 'seriousness' of probation caseloads is decreasing, in England and Wales at least (see Chapter 2 of this volume; Morgan 2003).

References

Allen, F. (1981) *The Decline of the Rehabilitative Ideal.* New Haven: Yale University Press.

Bottoms, A.E. (1995) 'The philosophy and politics of punishment and sentencing', in C. Clarkson and R. Morgan (eds) *The Politics of Sentencing Reform.* Oxford: Clarendon Press.

Bottoms, A., Gelsthorpe, L. and Rex, S. (eds) (2001) *Community Penalties: Change and Challenges.* Cullompton: Willan.

Bottoms, A.E. and Preston, R.H. (eds) (1980) *The Coming Penal Crisis.* Edinburgh: Scottish Academic Press.

Brown, I. (1998) 'Successful probation practice', in D. Faulkner and A. Gibbs (eds) *New Politics, New Probation? Proceedings of the Probation Studies Unit Second Colloquium.* Probation Studies Unit Report 6. Oxford: Centre for Criminological Research.

Crow, I. (2001) *The Treatment and Rehabilitation of Offenders.* London: Sage.

Derber, C. (1982) 'Managing professionals: ideological proletarianization and mental labor', in C. Derber (ed.) *Professionals as Workers: Mental Labor in Advanced Capitalism.* Boston, MA: G.K. Hall.

Faulkner, D. (1996) *Darkness and Light.* London: Howard League for Penal Reform.

Feeley, M. and Simon, J. (1992) 'The new penology: notes on the emerging strategy of corrections and its implications', *Criminology*, 30: 449–74.

Folkard, M.S., Smith, D.E. and Smith, D.D. (1976) *IMPACT Intensive Matched Probation and After-care Treatment. Volume II. The Results of the Experiment.* Home Office Research Study 36. London: HMSO.

Garland, D. (1995) 'Penal modernism and postmodernism', in T.G. Blomberg and S. Cohen (eds) *Punishment and Social Control.* New York: Aldine de Gruyter.

Garland, D. (1996) 'The limits of the sovereign state: strategies of crime control in contemporary society', *British Journal of Criminology*, 36 (4): 445–71.

Garland, D. (1997) 'Probation and the reconfiguration of crime control', in R. Burnett (ed.) *The Probation Service: Responding to Change. Proceedings of the Probation Studies Unit First Colloquium.* Probation Studies Unit Report 3. Oxford: University of Oxford Centre for Criminological Research.

Garland, D. (2001) *The Culture of Control.* Oxford: Oxford University Press.

Giddens, A. (1984) *The Constitution of Society*. Cambridge: Polity Press.

Harding, J. (2000) 'A community justice dimension to effective probation practice', *Howard Journal of Criminal Justice*, 39 (2): 132–49.

Haxby, D. (1978) *Probation: A Changing Service*. London: Constable.

HM Inspectorate of Probation (1998) *Exercising Constant Vigilance: The Role of the Probation Service in Protecting the Public from Sex Offenders*. London: Home Office.

Home Office (1977) *A Review of Criminal Justice Policy 1976*. London: HMSO.

Home Office (1984) *Probation Service in England and Wales: Statement of National Objectives and Priorities*. London: Home Office.

Home Office (1988) *Punishment, Custody and the Community* (Cm 424). London: HMSO.

Home Office (1990a) *Supervision and Punishment in the Community: A Framework for Action* (Cm 966). London: HMSO.

Home Office (1990b) *Crime, Justice and Protecting the Public* (Cm 965). London: HMSO.

Home Office (1996) *Protecting the Public* (Cm 3190). London: HMSO.

Home Office (1998) *Joining Forces to Protect the Public: Prisons – Probation*. London: Home Office.

Home Office (1999) *The Correctional Policy Framework*. London: Home Office.

Howe, D. (1991) 'Knowledge, power, and the shape of social work practice', in M. Davies (ed.) *The Sociology of Social Work*. London: Routledge.

Hudson, B. (1987) *Justice through Punishment*. London: Macmillan.

Hudson, B. (2001) 'Human rights, public safety and the probation service: defending justice in the risk society', *Howard Journal of Criminal Justice*, 40 (2): 103–13.

Humphrey, C. and Pease, K. (1992) 'Effectiveness measurement in probation: a view from the troops', *Howard Journal of Criminal Justice*, 31 (1): 31–52.

Huntingford, T. (1992) 'The introduction of 100% central government funding for social work with offenders', *Local Government Policy Making*, 19: 36–43.

Justice Department (2001) *Criminal Justice Social Work Services: National Priorities for 2001–2002 and Onwards*. Edinburgh: Scottish Executive.

Lyotard, J.-F. (1984) *The Postmodern Condition: A Report on Knowledge*. Manchester: Manchester University Press.

Maguire, M., Kemshall, H., Noaks, L. and Wincup, E. (2001) *Risk Management of Sexual and Violent Offenders: The Work of Public Protection Panels*. Police Research Series Paper 139. London: Home Office.

Mair, G. (2000) 'Reflections: credible accreditation? *Probation Journal*, 47 (4): 268–71.

Marsland, M. (1977) 'The decline of probation in Scotland', *Social Work Today*, 8 (23): 17–18.

Martinson, R. (1974) 'What works? Questions and answers about prison reform', *The Public Interest*, March: 22–54.

McGuire, J. (ed.) (1995) *What Works: Reducing Reoffending*. Chichester: Wiley.

McIvor, G. (1990) *Sanctions for Serious and Persistent Offenders: A Review of the Literature*. Stirling: University of Stirling Social Work Research Centre.

McIvor G. and Barry (1998a) *Social Work and Criminal Justice. Volume 6. Probation*. Edinburgh: Scottish Office Central Research Unit.

McIvor G. and Barry (1998b) *Social Work and Criminal Justice. Volume 7. Community Based Throughcare*. Edinburgh: Scottish Office Central Research Unit.

McIvor, G. and Williams, B. (1999) 'Community-based disposals', in P. Duff and N. Hutton (eds) *Criminal Justice in Scotland*. Aldershot: Ashgate/Dartmouth, 198–227.

McNeill, F. (2000) 'Defining effective probation: frontline perspectives', *Howard Journal of Criminal Justice*, 39 (4): 382–97.

McWilliams, W. (1983) 'The mission to the English police courts 1876–1936', *Howard Journal of Criminal Justice*, 22: 129–47.

McWilliams, W. (1985) 'The mission transformed: professionalisation of probation between the wars', *Howard Journal of Criminal Justice*, 24 (4): 257–74.

McWilliams, W. (1986) 'The English probation system and the diagnostic ideal', *Howard Journal of Criminal Justice*, 25 (4): 241–60.

McWilliams, W. (1987) 'Probation, pragmatism and policy', *Howard Journal of Criminal Justice*, 26 (2): 97–121.

McWilliams, W. (1989) 'An expressive model for evaluating probation practice', *Probation Journal*, 36 (2): 58–64.

McWilliams, W. and Pease, K. (1990) 'Probation practice and an end to punishment', *Howard Journal of Criminal Justice*, 29 (1): 14–24.

Moore, G. (1978) 'Crisis in Scotland', *Howard Journal*, 17 (1): 32–40.

Moore, G. and Whyte, B. (1998) *Moore and Wood's Social Work and Criminal Law in Scotland* (3rd edn). Edinburgh: Mercat Press.

Morgan, R. (2003) 'Thinking about the demand for probation services', *Probation Journal*, 50 (1): 7–19.

Nash, M. (1999) *Police, Probation and Protecting the Public*. London: Blackstone.

Nash, M. (2000) 'Deconstructing the probation service: the Trojan Horse of public protection', *International Journal of the Sociology of Law*, 28: 201–13.

National Probation Service (2001) *A New Choreography*. London: Home Office.

Nellis, M. (1995) 'Probation values for the 1990s', *Howard Journal of Criminal Justice*, 34 (1): 19–44.

Nellis, M. (1999a) 'Towards "the field of corrections": modernizing the probation service in the late 1990s', *Social Policy and Administration*, 33 (3): 302–23.

Nellis, M. (1999b) 'Probation, politics and the English language', *Vista*, 4 (3): 233–40.

Nellis, M. (2001a) 'The new probation training in England and Wales: realising the potential', *Social Work Education*, 20 (4): 415–32.

Nellis, M. (2001b) 'Community penalties in historical perspective', in A. Bottoms *et al.* (eds) *Community Penalties: Change and Challenges.* Cullompton: Willan.

Nelson, S. (1977) 'Why Scotland's after-care is lagging', *Community Care*, 14 (12): 87.

Paterson, F. and Tombs, J. (1998) *Social Work and Criminal Justice. Volume 1. The Impact of Policy.* Edinburgh: Scottish Office Central Research Unit.

Pease, K. (1980) 'The future of the community treatment of offenders in Britain', in A.E. Bottoms and R.H. Preston (eds) *The Coming Penal Crisis.* Edinburgh: Scottish Academic Press.

Raynor, P. (1995) '"What works": probation and forms of justice', in D. Ward and M. Lacey (eds) *Probation: Working for Justice.* London: Whiting and Birch.

Raynor, P. (1996) 'Evaluating probation: the rehabilitation of effectiveness', in T. May and A.A. Vass (eds) *Working With Offenders: Issues, Contexts and Outcomes.* London: Sage.

Raynor, P. (1997) 'Evaluating probation: a moving target', in G. Mair (ed.) *Evaluating the Effectiveness of Community Penalties.* Aldershot: Avebury.

Raynor, P. and Vanstone, M. (2002) *Understanding Community Penalties: Probation, Change and Social Context.* Buckingham: Open University Press.

Rifkind, M. (1989) 'Penal Policy: the Way Ahead', *The Howard Journal of Criminal Justice,* 28 (2): 81–90.

Robinson, G. (2001) 'Probation, risk and governance.' Unpublished PhD thesis, University of Wales, Swansea.

Robinson, G. (2002) 'Exploring risk management in the probation service: contemporary developments in England and Wales', *Punishment and Society,* 4 (1): 5–25.

Rowson, B. and McGuire, J. (1991) *What Works: Effective Methods to Reduce Re-offending. Conference Proceedings, 18–19 April 1991.* Manchester: What Works Planning Group.

Rowson, B. and McGuire, J. (1996) *What Works: Making it Happen. Conference Proceedings, 7–9 August 1994.* Manchester: What Works Planning Group.

Rutherford, A. (1998) 'Criminal policy and the eliminative ideal', in C.J. Finer and M. Nellis (eds) *Crime and Social Exclusion.* Oxford: Blackwell.

Scottish Office (1998) *Community Sentencing: The Tough Option – Review of Criminal Justice Social Work Services.* Edinburgh: Scottish Office.

Scottish Office (1999) *A Safer Scotland: Tackling Crime and its Causes.* Edinburgh: The Scottish Office.

Smith, D. (1987) 'The limits of positivism in social work research', *British Journal of Social Work,* 17: 401–16.

Social Work Services Group (1991a) *National Objectives and Standards for Social Work Services in the Criminal Justice System.* Edinburgh: Scottish Office Social Work Services Group.

Social Work Services Group (1991b) *Social Work Supervision: Towards Effective Policy and Practice – a Supplement to the National Objectives and Standards for*

Social Work Services in the Criminal Justice System. Edinburgh: Social Work Services Group.

Social Work Services Group (1996) *Part 2. Service Standards: Throughcare.* Edinburgh: Social Work Services Group.

Social Work Services Group (2000) *National Standards for Social Enquiry and Related Reports and Court Based Social Work Services.* Edinburgh: Social Work Services Group.

Social Work Services Inspectorate (1997) *A Commitment to Protect – Supervising Sex Offenders: Proposals for More Effective Practice.* Edinburgh: The Stationery Office.

Social Work Services Inspectorate (1998) *Management and Assessment of Risk in Social Work Services.* Edinburgh: Scottish Office.

Tuddenham, R. (2000) 'Beyond defensible decision-making: towards reflexive assessment of risk and dangerousness', *Probation Journal*, 47 (3): 173–83.

Vanstone, M. (2000) 'Cognitive-behavioural work with offenders in the UK: a history of influential endeavour', *Howard Journal of Criminal Justice*, 39 (2): 171–83.

Wargent, M. (2002) 'The new governance of probation', *The Howard Journal of Criminal Justice*, 41 (2): 182–200.

Chapter 14

Getting personal: developments in policy and practice in Scotland

Gill McIvor

Introduction

This chapter discusses the development of 'evidence based' social work practice with offenders in Scotland, contrasting this with policy and practice development elsewhere in the UK. Even prior to political devolution, Scotland's unique legislative framework and organisational structures enabled it to maintain a distinctive approach to penal policy and offered it a degree of protection from the increasingly punitive neoliberal rhetoric that has shaped the work of the probation services in England and Wales. Recent developments in Scotland – such as the introduction of programme accreditation and the identification of Pathfinders – closely parallel similar developments elsewhere in the UK. Where they appear to differ is in their broader interpretation of the What Works? principles to encompass a greater emphasis upon social inclusion and social justice and their attempts to decentralise 'ownership' of effective practice.

It is argued that recent policy developments in Scotland are supported by research findings that caution against an over-reliance on a programmatic approach to the supervision of offenders in the community. While offenders may benefit to varying degrees from structured interventions aimed at changing their attitudes and behaviour, such benefits are likely to be limited and shortlived if attention is not similarly paid to their wider social and personal needs. Greater emphasis correspondingly needs to be placed upon social inclusion and upon putting 'people' back into the equation by recognising the importance of the supervisory relationship in enhancing offenders' motivation not to reoffend.

Criminal justice social work in Scotland: a brief historical overview

Since the late 1960s there has been no separate probation service in Scotland. Instead, responsibility for the supervision of offenders in the community rests with local authority social work departments. This arrangement has pertained since 1969 when the existing probation service was merged with other welfare services to create generic social work departments. The primary strength of the new arrangement was seen as its emphasis upon the commonality of skills and values which underpinned all areas of social work practice. At a practical level, however, social work with offenders was accorded low priority in comparison with other areas of practice such as child protection work. Over time the courts began to lose confidence in the quality of supervision afforded to offenders on probation orders and the numbers of orders made on an annual basis steadily declined (McIvor 1994).

The decline in the use of probation ran contrary to central government policy at that time which was concerned to minimise the use of short custodial sentences by encouraging the courts to make greater use of probation orders and community service orders (Rifkind 1989). While financial expediency clearly influenced the desire to impact positively upon Scotland's traditionally high prison population, the policy also recognised the relative ineffectiveness of custodial sentences with respect to subsequent recidivism and the damaging consequences of imprisonment for offenders and their families. To ensure that sufficient resources were available to meet the demand for community service orders by the courts, the Scottish Office assumed full responsibility for the funding of community service schemes in Scotland in 1989, though responsibility for the management and operation of schemes still rested with the local authority social work departments.

National Objectives and Standards for community service were introduced in 1989 (Social Work Services Group 1989). They were followed two years later by the introduction of 100 per cent central government funding and national objectives and standards for other statutory social work services to the criminal justice system – social inquiry reports and court services, probation and throughcare (Social Work Services Group 1991). The most significant practical consequence of the new funding mechanism was the creation of specialist arrangements for the management and delivery of criminal justice social work services. In most parts of the country these services were provided by teams of social workers with a specialist remit or, in rural areas, by specialist workers located within generic teams.

The primary objectives of supervision identified in the National Standards were 'to help offenders tackle their offending behaviour, assist them to live socially responsible lives within the law and, whenever appropriate, further their social integration through the involvement and support of their families, friends and other resources in their community' (Social Work Services Group 1991: para. 12.7).

The National Standards were, however, essentially a procedural document offering little guidance as to how, in practice, the principal objectives of the policy could be achieved. There was clearly a danger that considerable energy could be devoted to meeting national standards without there being an attendant increase in the quality and effectiveness of social work practice. That said, 100 per cent funding and National Objectives and Standards appeared to have provided a much-needed impetus to social work services in the criminal justice system, not least by enabling the creation of a dedicated workforce and ensuring, through inspection and local quality control mechanisms, that minimum standards of practice were being met.

Challenges to the development of effective practice were sub-sequently presented by local government reorganisation in 1996 which saw the existing two-tier structure of regional and district local govern-ment replaced by single-tier unitary authorities. This had the effect of vesting responsibility for social work services with 32 local authorities rather than with nine mainland and three islands authorities as had hitherto been the case. It quickly became apparent that under the new arrangements small authorities were unable to achieve the economies of scale that had previously been possible, nor could they efficiently and effectively deliver the growing range of disposals and services that were introduced during the latter part of the 1990s. In 1998 a consultation document set out options for the provision of social work criminal justice services: the status quo, a centralised service or the creation of 'groupings' of local authorities with shared responsibility for delivering social work services to the criminal justice system (Scottish Office 1998a). In the absence of broadly based support for either the status quo or the centralisation of services, the 'tough options groupings' were created in April 2002, though with little centralised guidance from the Scottish Executive as to how they should be managed. Against this backdrop of organisational flux spanning more than 30 years, it has been argued that many of the debates about effective practice that shaped the focus and practice of probation services in England and Wales over that period largely bypassed Scotland. As Whyte (2002: 1–2) has observed:

In truth many of these debates by-passed Scotland possibly because the country was set on developing its own distinctive policy direction, characteristic of a re-emerging national identity which subsequently has found expression in the re-establishment of a Scottish Parliament with autonomous responsibility for criminal and youth justice policy and provision.

That is not to suggest that Scotland has remained untouched by developments in the rest of the UK and beyond. As we shall see, there is in Scotland as much concern with 'evidence based' policy and practice as there is elsewhere in the UK. However, its separate legislative framework and, latterly, the devolution of responsibility for justice policy to the Scottish Parliament have placed a distinctively Scottish stamp on recent policy developments which sets them apart from the centralised, administrative approaches exemplified by the National Probation Directorate in England and Wales.

Towards 'evidence based' practice

Over the last decade or so increasing efforts have been made to identify 'what works' in reducing recidivism. More recent qualitative literature reviews and meta-analyses have refuted Martinson's (1974) much misquoted conclusion that 'nothing works' by suggesting that some approaches to the supervision of offenders are more likely than others to bring about reductions in offending behaviour (e.g. McGuire 1995; Chapman and Hough 1998). In particular, it has been argued that structured techniques involving the use of cognitive-behavioural methods have been more consistently shown to be associated with reductions in recidivism (e.g. Vennard *et al.* 1997). This may in part be because interventions of this type are, indeed, more effective. However, it may also be because cognitive behavioural methods are, by their very nature, more amenable to evaluation than other less structured approaches. They are also more likely to be employed by psychologists who, as a profession, are more rigorous in evaluating their work. Whatever the merits of cognitive-behavioural interventions, it could be argued that the emphasis placed upon them has had the effect of narrowing the focus of offender supervision in an unhelpful way, by diverting attention from the social and economic context in which offending occurs. Cognitive-behavioural interventions with offenders are rarely conducive to the development of practice that is aimed at empowerment, enhancing social justice and promoting inclusion in society.

In England and Wales, however, this is the direction in which probation work with offenders is being pushed. An increased emphasis upon 'evidence based' practice has been fuelled by a political climate that demands that probation services demonstrate their effectiveness in reducing crime. This is being taken forward by the Effective Practice Initiative spearheaded by Her Majesty's Inspectorate of Probation in England and Wales. This initiative has been accompanied by the introduction of a new (non-social work) qualification for probation officers, the increased centralisation of probation services through the creation of a National Probation Directorate, a renaming of existing community-based disposals to reflect their more punitive elements and the setting of performance targets (including those related to recidivism) that the Home Office expects probation services to meet. Pathfinder projects based on the What Works literature have been established, a joint system of accreditation of prison and probation programmes has been introduced and targets have been set for the number of offenders who will take part in accredited programmes.

One effect of these developments has been to depersonalise probation practice both for offenders and for probation staff. Although the critical role of the supervisor as case manager is recognised in relevant documents (e.g. Chapman and Hough 1998), the primary emphasis upon programmes effectively removes the personal qualities and skills of the probation officer from the equation. At the same time, the personal attributes of offenders are redefined in terms of 'responsivity'. This is despite the growing literature that points to the central importance of the relationship between offenders and their supervising officers in encouraging the former to change. For example, Barry (2000) and others (e.g. Beaumont and Mistry 1996; Mair and May 1997) have shown how offenders value having a non-judgemental listener who can help them access relevant practical resources, while Rex (1999) and Trotter (2000) point to the importance of pro-social modelling as a powerful tool for helping motivate offenders to change. As Rex (1999) observes, supervising officers are often unaware of the personal influence they can exercise over, and the loyalty they may instil in, those they supervise on orders.

In Scotland, too, there has been an evolving concern with ensuring that social work with offenders is 'evidenced based'. However, there has been more emphasis placed upon encouraging a 'bottom up' approach to the development of effective practice and engendering a sense of common ownership of the effective practice agenda. The Getting Best Results Steering Group was established in Scotland late in 1998 'to provide leadership, direction and co-ordination in the development of effective practice in the community supervision of offenders in Scotland' (Scottish Executive 2001a: 1). Its membership consists of representatives from central and local government (the Association of Directors of Social Work and the Convention of Scottish Local Authorities), the voluntary sector, the Scottish Prison Service and the research community, and its broad aim is 'to identify and disseminate best practice, knowledge and information from the increasing amounts of international research concerned with identifying those interventions which have the greatest impact on offending behaviour' (Scottish Executive 2001a: 1).

The Getting Best Results Steering Group has been responsible for creating a framework for promoting the development of effective practice in a number of ways. Within that broad framework, subgroups have been tasked with taking forward specific areas of work and a Pathfinder initiative has been established to examine what can be learnt from attempts to introduce effective practice in different organisational contexts.

Quality assurance

The first major piece of work initiated by the steering group was the development of a quality assurance system for criminal justice social work. A need for a consistent approach to quality assurance was highlighted and the challenge was to identify a system that could be used across all local authorities and voluntary agencies while being consistent with wider quality assurance systems in these organisations. It was agreed that a quality assurance system would be developed based upon the model that was being used by a large voluntary organisation – NCH. A subgroup of Getting Best Results was tasked with adapting the system for use in local authorities and the resulting system is being piloted through the Pathfinder initiative.

Accreditation

One of the subgroups that were formed focused upon the development of a system to accredit social work practice with offenders in Scotland. The accreditation subgroup was set up to 'devise a formal accreditation system for the content and delivery of community supervision programmes' (Scottish Executive 2001b). The subgroup was not intended to act as the accreditation panel itself but to develop the framework within which an accreditation panel should operate. It adopted a definition of a 'programme' which included a planned series of interventions, delivered in a certain time frame, which could be demonstrated to change positively attitudes, beliefs, behaviour and social circumstances to reduce offending.

The subgroup concluded that the main criteria for the accreditation of programmes were a clear model of change; targeting of participants and dynamic risk factors; the use of effective methods of intervention; the ability to motivate and engage participants; a focus on skills acquisition; programme length and intensity linked to seriousness of the offending; integration with the overall service; and inbuilt evaluation and monitoring. Linked to the above, site accreditation would be based on a quality assurance system. Key criteria would include staff support, management, recruitment and training; a delivery process based on an internal verification system; adequate case management and recording; and clear systems for monitoring and evaluation (Scottish Executive 2001b).

Although a separate panel already existed for the accreditation of prisoner programmes (SPS 2002), the subgroup recommended the setting up of an independent accreditation panel to accredit both programmes and sites in the community, although it is intended that the two panels will eventually combine. The accreditation panel was established at the beginning of 2003. Its role is to set standards, promote excellence in programmes dealing with offenders and to accredit and encourage effective approaches. Unlike the Joint Accreditation Panel for England and Wales, whose composition has been criticised by Mair (2000) for its over-reliance upon those who are wedded to cognitive behavioural methods, the Scottish panel is composed of members with experience/knowledge of community supervision programmes, the principles of effective practice and/or accreditation. A key underpinning principle of the system that is being developed is that it should support criminal justice social work staff in their day-to-day work by offering support and assistance in identifying the most effective forms of intervention. It is also hoped that local authorities and voluntary organisations will present locally developed programmes for accreditation and not only 'off the peg' programmes developed elsewhere. This means that the 'evidence' underpinning these programmes is more likely to have a clear grounding in practice than be based wholly on theory.

National standards

Another subgroup of the Getting Best Results Steering Group was tasked with revisiting the national objectives and standards for social work services to the criminal justice system that were first introduced in 1991. National standards were viewed as having made a vital contribution to service development by tackling some of the weakness of services – including their inconsistent quality – and helping to secure a framework of contact within which effective work might be undertaken. However, experience had shown that very detailed and prescriptive standards could quickly be overtaken by legislative changes, practice innovation, research findings or wider policy development. Also, they could appear insufficiently flexible to accommodate individual changes in needs and risks over time.

In view of this, the subgroup was asked to develop an approach to standard setting that would not become out-dated so quickly, and focused more consistently on objectives, effectiveness and outcomes. It proposed an approach which changes emphasis from the 'silos' of detailed individual standards for each area of service (probation, CSO, SERs, etc.) to a thematic or cross-cutting approach which would apply in common across all service areas, with brief annexes to address any unique expectations relating to a specific service. The new approach will identify overarching objectives and principles for all areas of service and common standards for assessment (which will apply to most forms of supervision, to inform content and intensity as well as to SERs and parole reports); the content of supervision; case management (including planning and review); discipline and enforcement; and monitoring and evaluation (to ensure a focus on outcomes) (Scottish Executive 2001a).

Monitoring and evaluation

A subgroup of the Getting Best Results Steering Group was established to develop a framework for monitoring and evaluation of criminal justice social work services. The group produced a paper outlining possible options for a national framework, identifying the principal outcomes of interventions as those relating to reductions in the serious-ness and frequency of reoffending. However it also identified a list of secondary outcome measures pertaining to changes in offenders' attitudes and behaviour and to improvements in their personal and social circumstances. A briefing paper on monitoring and evaluation has been produced to introduce practitioners to basic concepts and approaches (Scottish Executive 2002a) and a reference document on monitoring and evaluation is being developed based upon the *Evaluation Handbook* that has been developed for use by probation services in England and Wales (Merrington and Hine 2000).

Pathfinders

A central feature of the Getting Best Results initiative has been the identification of 'Pathfinder providers' to lead the way in developing more effective programmes and procedures for the supervision and rehabilitation of offenders. Three Pathfinders were launched in July 2000. One is a partnership between four local authorities in the north of Scotland; the second is a partnership between Glasgow city social work department and two voluntary organisations (NCH and APEX); and the third involves a single local authority – Dumfries and Galloway, in the south of the country. The intention is that the experiences of the Pathfinders will inform the development of services in other parts of the country.

The Pathfinder initiative illustrates the divergent approach to What Works? that has been taken in Scotland, in comparison to England and Wales. In England and Wales the Effective Practice initiative spearheaded by the National Probation Directorate and the Probation Inspectorate is focusing upon the implementation of specific programmes of intervention. In Scotland, by contrast, the Getting Best Results Pathfinders are being assisted to implement effective practice throughout the organisation, to introduce systems of quality assurance, to ensure that staff have the necessary training to meet needs identified at the local level and to monitor and evaluate the services that they provide. Rather than focusing upon the design and delivery of programmes that tackle offending behaviour in isolation, the aim of the Scottish Pathfinders is to promote a culture of change in organisations as a whole. The experiences of the Pathfinders will be drawn upon to identify barriers to institutional change and to learn how these can be overcome.

Training and development

The Scottish Executive has taken forward a number of initiatives aimed at providing advanced specialist training and support to criminal justice social work staff. In 1994 the Universities of Edinburgh and Stirling were awarded a contract to provide an MSc in Advanced Social Work Studies in Criminal Justice which combined an academic masters degree with the CCETSW advanced award in social work practice or management. A post-qualifying award in criminal justice social work has now also been introduced. A Criminal Justice Social Work Development Centre was established at the Universities of Edinburgh and Stirling in January

2001, with funding provided by the Scottish Executive. Its aim is to bridge the gap between current research knowledge and practice development in the fields of criminal and youth justice social work.

The Criminal Justice Development Centre has a remit *inter alia* to promote evidence-based policy and practice by promoting and testing models of best practice and management; preparing and issuing briefings on best practice; providing advice to assist local authorities and others to monitor and evaluate practice and management; assisting service providers to apply the lessons of research to their particular circumstances; and establishing and maintaining a database of research and information about good practice and management from throughout the UK and beyond.

The development centre operates as an independent national resource working in partnership with service providers, statutory and voluntary, government agencies and other stakeholders to promote the development of good practice across the criminal and youth justice systems. It is intended that the centre will provide a means of ensuring that the most up-to-date knowledge and advice about 'what works' in reducing offending is available in Scotland to assist agencies in planning, designing and evaluating research-led provision and to meet the future challenges of programme accreditation. Practitioner involvement in the identification and promotion of effective practice has been taken forward through the establishment of 'champion groups' who are initially focusing upon work with sex offenders, female offenders, youth justice and throughcare.

Specific initiatives in Scotland

The preceding developments have been aimed at taking forward effective work with offenders on a broad front. While they are rooted to a large extent in the What Works? literature, they are also cognisant of the need to adopt a more holistic approach to the supervision of offenders and to encourage and support 'grass roots' initiatives that are developed in response to locally identified needs. In this way they have, thus far, avoided the more mechanistic features that characterise similar developments in England and Wales. That they have succeeded in doing so may be because work with offenders has retained its basis within generic social work departments and within a broader policy framework that is committed to enhancing social justice.

Scotland has, for these reasons, managed to retain the more personalised approach to offender supervision that has arguably been eroded in England and Wales, although multi-professional teamwork and the redefinition of traditional professional roles are likely to be an increasing feature of social work services to the criminal justice system in the coming decade. The final part of this chapter examines two areas in which the importance of personal relationships has been recognised and ascribed prominence: intervention with women who offend and with drug users in the criminal justice system. The latter is of particular interest in that it effectively shifts the locus of the relationship from the social worker (who now assumes the role of case manager) to the sentencer.

A better way? Responding to women who offend

One of the most striking penal phenomena in Scotland during the last decade has been the steady increase in the numbers of women given sentences of imprisonment and in the daily average population of sentenced female offenders. In this respect Scotland is similar to other parts of the UK (Home Office 2002) and, indeed, to most other western jurisdictions (Cook and Davies 1999).

Following the introduction of 100 per cent funding for social work services to the criminal justice system in 1991 the number of community-based social work disposals (that is, probation and community service orders) made in respect of women increased from 1,236 in 1990 to 1,364 in 1996. However, the number of orders imposed upon men increased much more dramatically, from 7,771 orders in 1990 to 10,650 orders in 1996. A 10 per cent increase in the number of women given orders was paralleled by a 30 per cent increase in the number of orders imposed on men. To the extent that the new funding arrangements and the national objectives and standards could be deemed responsible for this increase, they would appear to have had a primary effect, at least initially, on increasing the use of community-based social work disposals with men. The increase in the number of women made subject to probation and community service orders was, in addition, matched by an increase in the number of women imprisoned during this period, from 737 in 1990 to 875 in 1996 (Scottish Office 1998b). A decrease in the proportionate use of community-based social work disposals and an almost identical increase in the proportionate use of imprisonment suggested that probation and community service were often being used instead of fines. This was despite the intention of government policy that probation and community service should function as alternatives to short sentences of imprisonment.

Towards the end of the last decade, women who offend began to attract increasing attention from policy-makers and practitioners for a number of reasons. First, there has been an increase in recent years in the number of young women appearing before the courts, largely attributable to an increased incidence of drug misuse (primarily heroin) among young women. Secondly, as the number of women charged with offences has increased, academics and practitioners begun to question the appropriateness of existing sentences and associated interventions for women who offend.

Thirdly, and perhaps most influentially, a series of seven suicides in 30 months at Scotland's only female prison (Cornton Vale) resulted in a wide-ranging review of the use of imprisonment and non-custodial sentences for female offenders. The number and timing of the deaths were all the more shocking because there had only been one previous suicide – some nine years previously – since the opening of Cornton Vale. Although no single reason for the suicides emerged from the subsequent fatal accident inquiries, it appeared that a history of drug abuse and withdrawal problems shortly after being incarcerated was a common experience among the women who died.

The resultant review – undertaken by the Inspectorates of Social Work and Prisons and entitled *A Safer Way* – concluded that 'the backgrounds of women in prison are characterised by experiences of abuse, drug misuse, poor educational attainment, poverty, psychological distress and self harm' (Social Work and Prisons Inspectorates 1998: 13). It also produced a number of recommendations aimed at keeping women, where possible, out of prison and at improving the conditions for those who were, by necessity, detained. These included the development of bail provision for women; the development of a unitary fine system; the increased use of supervised attendance orders for women who default on payment of their fines; and the development of an interagency project aimed at developing services for women offenders in Glasgow (since the majority of women in Cornton Vale are from Glasgow and the west of Scotland).

The primary thrust of *A Safer Way* was towards achieving a reduction in the imprisonment of women – at the remand stage, at the sentencing stage and following default on the payment of a fine. However, the published statistics showed that, far from there being a reduction in the custodial sentencing of women following the publication of *A Safer Way*, the number of prison sentences imposed on female offenders and the daily female prison population actually *increased* in 1999. There was a 21 per cent increase in the number of convictions resulting in a custodial sentence for women aged under 21, and a 12 per cent increase in the use of custody for women aged 21–30. By comparison, there was a 5 per cent rise in the use of imprisonment for men in the 21–30 age group, a 1 per cent decrease among men under 21 years of age and a 5 per cent decrease among men over 30 years of age (Scottish Executive 2000a). The number of male young offenders received into custody under direct sentence receptions in 1999 was the lowest level experienced since 1991. However, female young offender direct sentence receptions in 1999 were at their highest level of the decade (Scottish Executive 2000b). Over the ten-year period 1990–9, the average daily female prison population increased by 55 per cent – which is more than double the growth experienced in the male prison population (which increased by 27 per cent) over the same period (Scottish Executive 2000a).

One of the recommendations of *A Safer Way* was the establishment of an interagency forum to develop services for female offenders in Glasgow. The forum was set up in August 1998 with its membership consisting of all the key agencies dealing with women who offend. This included criminal justice agencies as well as organisations employed in areas of health, housing, employment and drugs rehabilitation. The second annual report of the forum was published in February 2001 (Inter-agency Forum on Women's Offending 2001). It contained a total of 13 recommendations aimed at providing women with access to a range of services and support to address the social and personal problems that contribute to their offending. These included exploring the possibility of establishing a daily court for women, providing additional resources to enable women to address their drug use, building upon and expanding existing diversion strategies at all stages in the system and the creation of 'time out' centres to provide a wide range of residentially or non-residentially based support services for women.

The work of the Glasgow interagency forum was subsequently taken forward by a ministerial group charged with turning the forum's proposals into practical measures. The ministerial group was established in December 2000 and reported in 2002, by which time a further two women had committed suicide in Cornton Vale (Scottish Executive 2002). The number of female sentenced receptions into prison in Scotland had also continued to rise as had the average daily female prison population, which showed an increase of more than 17 per cent over the previous year (Scottish Executive 2002b).

The ministerial group's report, entitled *A Better Way*, concluded that the existing system for dealing with women who offend was not working effectively. Instead, it recommended that greater emphasis should be placed upon alleviating the social circumstances that lead some women to offend, intervening early to ensure that women's needs can be met without recourse to imprisonment, promoting the use of the full range of community disposals (including the 'time out' centre advocated by *A Safer Way*) and shifting the penal culture away from punishment and towards rehabilitation and 'treatment':[1]

> We believe that the broader range of community penalties now available, supported by the Time Out centre and a specialist care management service for women in Glasgow, offers an integrated approach which, with the co-operation of the courts, can reduce significantly the number of women who receive custodial sentences. The message here is that we need to establish services which can give focus to and can energise the work with women offenders, and which can establish a service with which women clients can identify, and whose relevance they can recognise. *These should focus on women's needs to create relationships as an influential aspect of programmes which work with women.* The process can reduce stigma and isolation and increase confidence and self esteem, improve social skills, alter criminal attitudes and behaviour and so engage with these women. (Scottish Executive 2002c: 38, emphasis added)

Significantly, *A Better Way* recognised the importance of avoiding the simplistic assumption that the What Works? principles and the pro-grammes derived from them can appropriately be applied to women. The principles which are driving social work practice with offenders throughout the UK and beyond are based upon research into the effectiveness of interventions with young men and their applicability to women remains largely unexplored. For this reason social workers in Scotland (and, no doubt, in much of the rest of the UK) are operating in something of a theoretical and empirical vacuum in their supervision of women who offend. Increasingly, however, practitioners are acknowledging that different approaches from those adopted with men ma y be necessary if women on supervision are to be engaged effectively in the process of change. Growing interest is being paid by both prac-titioners and policy-makers to the development of gender-specific programmes. These programmes should be better able than existing male-oriented programmes to address women's needs in a safe and non-threatening environment that is conducive to the development of the reciprocal relationships which appear to be central to women's growth and change (Bloom and Covington 1998; Covington and Bloom 1999).

Dealing with offenders who misuse drugs

The importance of personal relationships in encouraging and sustaining change has also been reflected in Scotland in recent criminal justice responses to offenders who are dependent upon or who have a propensity to misuse drugs. Drug treatment and testing orders (DTTOs) – which are aimed at providing courts with a further community-based option to deal more effectively with some serious drug misusers who commit crimes to fund their habit – were introduced in the UK through provisions in the Crime and Disorder Act 1998. Under the relevant legislation, courts can require an offender to undergo treatment for his or her drug misuse, subject to the offender's consent to such an order being made.

DTTOs were first introduced in the UK in three pilot schemes in Croydon, Liverpool and Gloucestershire (Turnbull *et al.* 2000). The first Scottish scheme was established in Glasgow in October 1999 when orders became available to the Glasgow Sheriff, Stipendiary Magistrate and (subsequently) High Courts. A second pilot area began in Fife in July 2000 when DTTOs were made available to Cupar, Dunfermline and Kirkcaldy Sheriff Courts. Following an encouraging evaluation, which suggested that DTTOs had a marked impact, at least in the short term, on drug use and associated offending (Eley, Gallop *et al.* 2002), the Scottish Executive agreed to a phased roll-out of DTTOs to other Scottish courts. At the time of writing, funding for the establishment of DTTO schemes had been provided to 14 other local authorities in Scotland.

DTTOs differ from existing provisions in so far as the role of the supervising officer is limited, mandatory drug-testing is an integral component of the order and the courts have powers to review orders on a regular basis. Importantly, DTTOs involve the adoption of a new role for sentencers, requiring them to have regular – usually monthly – contact with offenders on orders via review hearings. In this capacity, the role of the sentencer is to motivate, encourage and sanction the offender for progress or lack thereof. DTTOs thus differ from traditional community-based sentences in that sentencers have active overview of the progress and outcomes of their sentencing decisions. This contrasts with, for example, a probation order (now community rehabilitation order in England and Wales) where the offender will only be brought back before the court in the event of the order being breached.

The evaluation of the pilot DTTO schemes in Scotland found that the majority of review hearings were characterised by direct interaction between the sentencer and the offender and were encouraging on the sentencer's side and responsive and co-operative on the part of the offender (Eley, Gallop *et al.* 2002). Among those review hearings that were observed by the researchers, it was found that the majority of offenders appeared before the same sentencer on each occasion. Continuity of sentencer appears to be an important element of this type of order; Goldkamp (2000), for example, has suggested that the frequent rotation of judges rather than the use of a core judge had reduced the effectiveness of some drug courts in the USA.

DTTOs share many similarities with drug courts. The latter likewise aim to reduce drug misuse and associated offending by offering treatment-based options outside the traditional court setting. Although there are wide differences in the manner in which drug courts operate (Nolan 2001), Gebelein (2000) has suggested that they are, in general, characterised by the integration of substance abuse treatment with criminal justice processing; the use of a non-adversarial approach; the 'fast-tracking' of participants into treatment; the provision of a con-tinuum of treatment, rehabilitation and related services; frequent testing for illicit drugs (and, usually in the USA, alcohol); a co-ordinated strategy between judge, prosecution, defence and treatment providers to secure offender compliance; ongoing judicial review of and interaction with each participant; integral monitoring and evaluation; continuing interdisciplinary education; and partnerships with public agencies and community-based organisations.

The impetus for the establishment of drug courts in North America came in part from a growing acknowledgement of the link between drug misuse and crime coupled with increasing evidence of the efficacy of drug treatment, including treatment that is compelled rather than undertaken on a voluntary basis (e.g. Hough 1994; Gebelein 2000). As a recent review by the Scottish Consortium for Crime and Criminal Justice concluded:

> while the long term answers to the 'drug problem' lie in wider social and economic change, the criminal justice system does have a key role to play in developing a more effective strategy. In small but significant ways, criminal justice practices can improve the prospects of problematic drug and alcohol users who are now caught in the revolving door of court, prison and the street ... To do this requires a far reaching change in priorities and the develop-ment of a penal policy which gives precedence to the three principles already mentioned: the reduction of harm, the pro-

motion of community safety, and the integration of problem drug users into productive life. (2002: 53)

Local and national evaluations of drug courts in the USA have been broadly encouraging. Belenko (1998, 2001), in reviewing drug court evaluations, concluded that they achieved better completion rates than traditional courts and brought about reductions in drug use and recidivism while offenders were participating in the programme. Williams (1999), however, in a process evaluation of the West Yorkshire Drug Court, questioned whether abstinence – the usual goal of US drug court programmes – was an appropriate initial goal of treatment in the UK context. Drug courts are now also operational in a range of other jurisdictions, including Australia, Canada and Ireland (Walker 2001).

Drug courts were initially established in the USA by sentencers who were frustrated at the limited range and effectiveness of existing measures for dealing with those whose offending was related to the misuse of drugs. A similar disillusionment with existing sentencing options prompted the introduction of DTTOs. It also lay behind the subsequent establishment, in February 2001, of a working party tasked by the then Deputy Justice Minister with producing proposals for the introduction of a drug court within existing legislation in Glasgow Sheriff Court. Scotland's first drug court was introduced on a pilot basis in Glasgow Sheriff Court in October 2001. Its objectives are to reduce the level of drug-related offending behaviour, to reduce or eliminate offenders' dependence on or propensity to use drugs and to examine the viability and usefulness of a drug court in Scotland using existing legislation (Glasgow Sheriff Court 2001). A second pilot drug court was subsequently established in Fife (sitting in Kirkcaldy and Dunfermline Sheriff Courts), making its first drug court order in September 2002.

The importance of the sentencer in reviewing drug court orders was highlighted in a process evaluation of the first six months' operation of the Glasgow Drug Court. Eley, Malloch *et al.* (2002) found that direct dialogue between the sheriff and the offender accounted for a high proportion of the review hearings (37 per cent overall), which generally concluded with the sheriff setting a target to be achieved by the offender by the next review. Importantly, the duration of the sheriff–offender dialogue and the proportion of the review hearing it accounted for increased with subsequent reviews. There was also a tendency for the sheriff in later reviews to comment upon the improved physical appearance of the offender. The concept of drug use as a relapsing condition was emphasised strongly in shrieval dialogue with offenders on drug court orders. As one sheriff observed:

> I go out of my way to say to them that we understand that this will not be a process in which there are no setbacks, that we understand that it is a relapsing condition and what we're expecting is not miracles. We expect commitment and we expect honesty but we don't expect miracles.

DTTOs and drug courts differ from traditional community penalties in that the possibility of relapse is explicitly recognised and will not, in itself, necessarily result in the termination of the order. In the case of drug courts in other jurisdictions, including the USA, the ability to sanction continued drug use while maintaining the offender in treatment is usually achieved through the imposition of graduated penalties, such as short community service orders and periods of imprisonment. Similar measures are planned for Scotland, contained in a Criminal Justice Bill which, at the time of writing, had just received royal assent.

Despite a sometimes sceptical and even hostile media, the Scottish Executive has remained supportive of the concept of drug courts. For example, on the six-month anniversary of the Glasgow Drug Court the then Deputy Justice Minister observed that it was:

> encouraging to see the early results from the Glasgow drug court. The potential success this unique course of justice can deliver can have a dramatic impact on reducing crime in the city as well as diverting suitable cases away from custody to rehabilitation with the aim of breaking the cycle of crime and drug dependency. (Scottish Executive 2002d)

Drug courts are the first specialist courts to have been established in Scotland, aimed at dealing more appropriately with those convicted of particular types of offending but it is likely that further specialist courts – such as domestic violence courts – will be developed. Some of the key features of the drug courts were incorporated into a pilot youth court, which became operational in June 2003. This pilot is one of a number of initiatives that have been proposed by the Scottish Executive to respond more effectively to the 'problem' of youth crime. A Youth Court Feasibility Group reported to the Deputy First Minister Jim Wallace at the end of December 2002 (Scottish Executive 2002e). It concluded that the establishment of a pilot youth court was feasible under existing primary legislation.

The pilot youth court will target persistent young offenders in the 16–17 year-old age groups with the flexibility to deal with 15-year-olds in certain circumstances. A fast-track process will aim to ensure that young offenders are brought to court quickly. The pilot youth court will also be characterised by having a group of designated sheriffs who will provide supervision of every young offender made the subject of a youth court order. The court will also have access to a range of disposals specifically designed for this younger group of offenders. This will include a broader and more intensive range of community programmes than currently exist, services that can tackle the social problems which might lead these young people to reoffend and enhanced intervention programmes specifically targeted at the young offender age group. In certain respects, therefore, the youth court will share certain similarities with the drug courts though the Executive is also keen to ensure that it is not perceived to be a 'soft option'.

Conclusions

Scotland's unique legislative system and, latterly, the existence of a devolved Scottish Parliament, have ensured that it has retained a distinctive approach to criminal justice and penal policy. Although there is some evidence that policy initiatives have in part been predicated upon a desire to be seen to 'get tough' on offenders there is, equally, a concern to address wider issues of social justice and enhancing social inclusion. There is also, as in the other parts of the UK, an increasing preoccupation with managing the risk posed by a relatively small number of serious violent and sexual offenders through the use of increasingly lengthy prison sentences and extended periods of supervision in the community. However, there also appears to be a commitment to impacting positively upon Scotland's unacceptably high prison population through the more widespread use of non-custodial options. This has been evidenced, for example, in a recent Justice 1 Committee review of alternatives to custody (aimed at exploring how the courts might be encouraged to make greater use of them) and in its opposition to proposals for the building of three new private prisons following an estates review (Scottish Parliament 2003). Identifying and implementing What Works will remain a central feature of criminal justice social work policy and practice in Scotland as elsewhere in the UK for the foreseeable future. But a monolithic approach based around narrowly conceived programmes – as has typified the case in England and Wales – is not the only way to proceed. Scotland, too, has taken an evidence-based path but this has not led to a programme-centric approach. Early developments in Scotland, as reported in this chapter, indicate that a more holistic approach may be equally – if not more – effective. Indeed, as the initiatives described in this chapter indicate, there is still reason to be optimistic that policy and practice will resist being driven by the narrow empiricist agenda that has typified recent developments in England and Wales.

Note

1   While a shift in emphasis away from punishment is to be welcomed, there is also a danger that a greater emphasis upon rehabilitation and treatment will increase rather than decrease the incarcerating tendencies of the courts. In particular, sentencers may need to be persuaded that they are not doing women a 'favour' by remanding them in custody or sentencing them to a period of imprisonment to give them a 'respite' from their use of drugs.

References

Barry (2000) 'The mentor/monitor debate in criminal justice: "what works" for offenders', *British Journal of Social Work*, 30: 575–95.

Beaumont, B. and Mistry, T. (1996) 'Doing a good job under duress', *Probation Journal*, 43 (4): 200–4.

Belenko, S. (1998) *Research on Drug Courts: A Critical Review*. New York, NY: National Center on Addiction and Substance Abuse at Columbia University.

Belenko, S. (2001) *Research on Drug Courts: A Critical Review 2000 Update*. New York, NY: The National Center on Addiction and Substance Abuse at Columbia University.

Bloom, B. and Covington, S. (1998) 'Gender-specific programming for female offenders: what is it and why is it important?' Paper presented at the annual meeting of the American Society of Criminology, Washington, DC.

Chapman, T. and Hough, M. (1998) *Evidence Based Practice: A Guide to Effective Practice*. London: The Home Office.

Cook, S. and Davies, S. (eds) (1999) *Harsh Punishment: International Experiences of Women's Imprisonment*. Boston, MA: Northeastern University Press.

Covington, S. and Bloom, B. (1999) 'Gender-responsive programming and evaluation for women in the criminal justice system: a shift from What Works to what is the work?' Paper presented at the annual meeting of the American Society of Criminology, Toronto, Canada.

Eley, S., Gallop, K., McIvor, G., Morgan, K. and Yates, R. (2002) *Drug Treatment and Testing Orders: Evaluation of the Scottish Pilots*. Edinburgh: Scottish Executive Social Research.

Eley, S., Malloch, M., McIvor, G., Yates, R. and Brown, A. (2002) *Glasgow's Pilot*

Drug Court in Action: The First Six Months. Edinburgh: Scottish Executive Social Research.

Gebelein, R.S. (2000) 'The rebirth of rehabilitation: promise and perils of drug courts', in *Sentencing and Corrections: Issues for the 21st Century*. Washington, DC: NIJ.

Glasgow Sheriff Court (2001) *Glasgow Drug Court Reference Manual* (1st edn). Glasgow: Glasgow Sheriff Court.

Goldkamp, J.S. (2000) 'What do we know about the impact of drug courts: moving research from "Do they work?" to "When and how they work"', in *Testimony to the Senate Judiciary Committee on Youth Violence*. Philadelphia, PA: Crime and Justice Research Institute.

Home Office (2002) *Statistics on Women and the Criminal Justice System: A Home Office Publication under Section 95 of the Criminal Justice Act 1991*. London: Home Office.

Hough, M. (1994) *Problem Drug Use and Criminal Justice: A Review of the Literature*. London: South Bank University.

Inter-agency Forum on Women's Offending (2001) *Second Year Report*. Edinburgh: Scottish Executive Justice Department.

Mair, G. (2000) 'Credible accreditation?', *Probation Journal*, 47 (4): 268–71.

Mair, G. and May, C. (1997) *Offenders on Probation*. Home Office Research Study 167. London: Home Office.

Martinson, R. (1974) 'What works? Questions and answers about prison reform', *The Public Interest*, 35: 22–54.

McGuire, J. (ed.) (1995) *What Works: Reducing Reoffending – Guidelines from Research and Practice*. Chichester: Wiley.

McIvor, G. (1994) 'Social work and criminal justice in Scotland: developments in policy and practice', *British Journal of Social Work*, 24: 430–48.

Merrington, S. and Hine, J. (2001) *A Handbook for Evaluating Probation Work with Offenders*. London: Home Office.

Nolan, J.L. (2001) *Reinventing Justice: The American Drug Court Movement*. Princeton NJ: Princeton University Press.

Rex, S. (1999) 'Desistance from offending: experiences of probation', *Howard Journal*, 38 (4): 366–83.

Rifkind, M. (1989) 'Penal policy: the way ahead', *Howard Journal*, 28: 81–90.

Scottish Consortium on Crime and Criminal Justice (2000) *Rethinking Criminal Justice in Scotland*. Edinburgh: SCCCJ.

Scottish Consortium on Crime and Criminal Justice (2002) *Making Sense of Drugs and Crime: Drugs, Crime and Penal Policy*. Edinburgh: SCCCJ.

Scottish Executive (2000a) *Criminal Proceedings in Scottish Courts 1999*. Edinburgh: Scottish Executive National Statistics.

Scottish Executive (2000b) *Prison Statistics Scotland 1999*. Edinburgh: Scottish Executive National Statistics.

Scottish Executive (2001a) *Getting Best Results Newsletter – Issue One*. Edinburgh: Scottish Executive.

Scottish Executive (2001b) *Getting Best Results Newsletter – Issue Two: Accreditation Special*. Edinburgh: Scottish Executive.

Scottish Executive (2001c) *Report of a Working Group for Piloting a Drug Court in Glasgow*. Edinburgh: Scottish Executive.

Scottish Executive (2002a) *Getting Best Results – Guidance Note on Monitoring and Evaluation of Programmes for Offenders*. Edinburgh: Scottish Executive.

Scottish Executive (2002b) *Prison Statistics Scotland 2001*. Edinburgh: Scottish Executive National Statistics.

Scottish Executive (2002c) *A Better Way: The Report of the Ministerial Group on Women's Offending*. Edinburgh: Scottish Executive.

Scottish Executive (2002d) 'Drug courts judged a success', *Scottish Executive Justice Department News Release*, 039: 14 May.

Scottish Executive (2002e) *Youth Court Feasibility Project Group Report*. Edinburgh: Scottish Executive.

Scottish Office (1998a) *Community Sentencing: The Tough Option: Review of Criminal Justice Social Work Services*. Edinburgh: Scottish Office Home Department.

Scottish Office (1998b) *Criminal Proceedings in Scottish Courts 1996*. Edinburgh: Scottish Office.

Scottish Parliament (2003) *Justice/Committee 3rd Report: Alternatives to Custody Volume 1* (SP Paper 826), available at: http://www.scottish.parliament.uk/S1/official_report/cttee/just1.htm

Social Work Services Group (1989) *National Standards and Objectives for the Operation of Community Service by Offenders Schemes in Scotland*. Edinburgh: The Scottish Office.

Social Work Services Group (1991) *National Objectives and Standards for Social Work Services in the Criminal Justice System*. Edinburgh: Scottish Office.

Social Work Services and Prisons Inspectorates for Scotland (1998) *Women Offenders – a Safer Way: A Review of Community Disposals and the Use of Custody for Women Offenders in Scotland*. Edinburgh: Scottish Office.

SPS (2002) *SPS Prisoner Programmes Accreditation Services Annual Report 2000 – 2001*. Edinburgh: Scottish Prison Service.

Trotter, C. (2000) 'Social work education, pro-social orientation and effective probation practice', *Probation Journal*, 47 (4): 256–61.

Turnbull, P.J., McSweeney, T., Webster, R., Edmunds, M. and Hough, M. (2000) *Drug Treatment and Testing Orders: Final Evaluation Report*. Home Office Research Study 212. London: Home Office.

Vennard, J., Sugg, D. and Hedderman, C. (1997) *Changing Offenders' Attitudes and Behaviour: What Works? Part 1. The Use of Cognitive-behavioural Approaches with Offenders – Messages from the Research*. Home Office Research Study 171. London: Home Office.

Walker, J. (2001) *International Experience of Drug Courts*. Edinburgh: Scottish Executive Central Research Unit.

Whyte, B. (2001) *Responding to Youth and Adult Crime: Future Directions*. CJSW Briefing Paper 1. Edinburgh: Criminal Justice Social Work Development Centre for Scotland.

Williams, K. (1999) *Process Evaluation of the West Yorkshire Drug Court/STEP Programme*. Farrel-Dixon Associates.

Chapter 15

What Works[1] and the globalisation of punishment talk

Anne Worrall

Pluralitas non est ponenda sine necessitate. (William of Ockham, 1280–1349)

It is language that betrays all. (Dutton and Xu 1998: 310)

For those in the business of trying to keep as many offenders as possible out of prison for as long as possible, while also protecting the public, the last decade of the twentieth century was dominated by the doctrine of What Works (Vanstone 2000). The Anglophone world of probation and community corrections has been preoccupied with a model of focused, accountable, standardised intervention in the lives of offenders, based on the actuarial concept of risk assessment, the science of cognitive behavioural psychology, the morality of individual responsibility and the politics of restorative justice. At the same time, that world has seen a dramatic rise in the prison population and a blurring of the boundary between freedom and custody. Offenders increasingly receive sentencing packages that involve time spent under supervision both inside and outside prison, and technology now makes it possible for many of the restrictions of imprisonment to be visited on offenders in their own homes and communities. In addition, practitioners are often overloaded with the bureaucratic demands of 'programme integrity' and evaluation, finding themselves with less and less time to consider the underlying values and philosophy of their work and thus making themselves vulnerable to the vagaries of crisis-driven law and order policy. The globalisation of punishment talk has provided comforting *prêt à manger* solutions in the form of an international trade in penal ideas: restorative justice, family group conferencing and mandatory sentencing are but a few examples of ideas that have been imported and exported through the Anglophone world. What Works is another – the fast food of punishment in the community. Little account, it seems, need be taken of regional, let alone local differences of demography, culture or economy.

So how do we make sense of these developments in the context of the globalisation of crime and punishment discourses? How do we take advantage of the insights offered by global knowledge while at the same time taking account of national, regional and local differences? How can we learn from each other without being forced into adopting a bland and simplistic language which we *think* we all recognise but which may, in reality, mean very little to any of us?

The idea for this chapter stems from work undertaken in 1998 (Worrall 2000) and followed up in 2002–3 in Western Australia, looking at the ways in which community corrections personnel have interpreted the What Works agenda. Much of the work being undertaken in the state capital, Perth, would indeed be recognisable by What Works workers anywhere in the world, but I was intrigued by the adaptations of What Works principles in other areas, especially for work in Aboriginal communities. I consider myself to be a critical friend of the What Works agenda, having seen many good things happen in its name but also sensing that an element of criticism is overdue. This chapter aims to do three things. First, it gives an overview of the globalisation of punishment discourse, with particular reference to community-based penalties. Secondly, it considers the specific case of Western Australia as a study in the adaptation/subversion of the What Works agenda to local (in this case, Aboriginal) needs.[2] Thirdly, it raises questions about the future of What Works as a global discourse and suggests an agenda for its adaptation if it is to survive into the twenty-first century.

The globalisation of punishment talk

Weiss and South (1998) identify the 'great developments' that have affected imprisonment worldwide: the rise of neoconservative politics and neoliberal economics in North America and western Europe, with attendant economic decline and class polarisation; the introduction of the market economy in China; the collapse of the Soviet Union and other east European regimes; the return to civilian rule in most of Latin America; and, finally, the fall of apartheid in South Africa. From these major social and economic shifts emerge global similarities in penal discourse or, as I would argue, the construction of a global trading language of penology. From our own nation-state viewpoints we (mis)recognise the increasing politicisation of crime, policies of inclusion and exclusion resulting from economic decline and the fear of the 'Other' (that is, the global over-representation of indigenous peoples, foreigners and ethnic minorities in prison), less eligibility, managerialism, selective incapacitation, privatisation and the toughening of penal regimes. Too often overlooked are the very different social, economic and cultural backgrounds from which these apparent similarities are emerging and too readily accepted are simplistic comparisons. In order to talk to one another, we have to find a trading language but, as Dutton and Xu (1998: 297) argue, in finding that language we lose the 'etymological trail that informs the meaning of the original word ... Translation obliterates the shadowy etymology which links words to their past meaning'.

Nowhere is this more apparent than in the 'orientalist' misappropriation of the term *restorative justice* (Blagg 1997). Orientalist discourses, Blagg argues, 'are powerful acts of representation that permit Western/European cultures to contain, homogenize and consume "other" cultures' (1997: 483). Referring to the widely disseminated 'Wagga model' of police-dominated conferencing for young offenders, Blagg demonstrates how an already-distorted version of traditional New Zealand Maori justice has been imposed on Australian Aboriginal youths who have a totally different cultural heritage, as though 'all of these cultures manifest similar mechanisms for adherence to accepted standards of behaviour and that all societies maintain a similar balance between social structures and emotions such as shame' (1997: 487). Reintegrative shaming, as Blagg elaborates, assumes that one belongs to a community in the first place and that that community operates within a 'shaming paradigm of social control' (1997: 487). Contrary to Braithwaite's (1997) claim, Blagg argues that 'shaming' does not have a universal social meaning and has a very different derivation – or, to use Dutton and Xu's term, 'etymological trail' – within Australian Aboriginal culture. Findlay turns this point into a more general one: 'If consensus is flawed, respect is absent. If the community [identified] is little more than a model structure created for the purposes of the reintegration exercise, strategies for re-integration may become just another dimension in the apparatus of repression and marginalisation' (1999: 198).

What Works in Western Australia: a case study

O'Malley (2002) has suggested that actuarial justice has not taken a hold in Australia generally. He acknowledges that the situation is more ambiguous in Western Australia (WA) and the Northern Territory (NT) but is dismissive of their bizarre mandatory sentencing legislation, saying that 'this has either been disowned or the subject of hostile attack by all other state and federal governments and judicatures' (2002: 212). Morgan (2002) rightly feels that it is of more significance and deserves more attention, since mandatory sentencing does not exist in a vacuum. It has its own 'etymological trail' which leads back very clearly (in the case of WA) to the importation of actuarial justice in the early and mid-1990s. In 1992, an ill-fated and short-lived Crime (Serious and Repeat Offenders) Act aimed at 'hard core young offenders in high-speed pursuits in stolen vehicles' was explicitly based on notions of selective incapacitation (Morgan *et al.* 2001). The mandatory minimum sentence of 12 months' imprisonment for 'third strike' home burglary was introduced in 1996 because WA shared with the USA and the UK an exasperation at the inability of the criminal justice system to prevent the recidivism of persistent property offenders. It was followed by attempts to introduce a sentencing matrix to fetter the discretion of the judiciary. Both provisions are the subject of much heated debate in the state (and the sentencing matrix has yet to be implemented) but mandatory sentencing continues to impact significantly on sentencing practice while, according to Morgan, having little or no impact on the crime rate. The greatest impact has been on young (as young as 10 and 11 years old) non-urban Aboriginal males. A staggering 80 per cent of all 'three strikes' cases have been drawn from 4 per cent of the state's population (Morgan 2002). Similar legislation in the Northern Territory has now been repealed, leaving WA the pariah state in this respect:

> From whatever perspective they are examined, mandatory detention laws in WA and the NT are bad law ... I applaud the NT government for acknowledging this and repealing the provisions. Once more, I call for the WA government to repeal its mandatory detention provisions ... and to ensure compliance ... with Australia's Human Rights obligations ... (Aboriginal and Torres Strait Islander Social Justice Commissioner 2002: 130)

It is with this background of punitive sentencing – purporting to reflect community concern – that community-based intervention has had to contend. Yet, as elsewhere, studies of public opinion have suggested that there is more support for community corrections programmes than the media chooses to convey (Indermaur 1990 cited in Israel and Dawes 2002; Roberts *et al*. 2003). Western Australia's criminal justice policy is very close to that of England and Wales, although the term 'probation service' was abandoned over ten years ago in favour of 'community corrections'. Western Australia's Sentencing Act 1995 bears many similarities to the Criminal Justice Act 1991 of England and Wales. Imprisonment is to be imposed only where the seriousness of the offence or the protection of the community requires it. Despite this, prison receivals (receptions) have continued to rise (from just over 3,700 in 1996 to 6,556 in 2001) (Fernandez and Loh 2002).[3] The Department (then Ministry) of Justice, responsible for both the Prison Service and Community Based Services, underwent a major 'refocus' based on the concept of restorative justice, and the What Works agenda was adopted as the driving force behind rehabilitative work with offenders both inside and outside prison.

WA has embraced actuarial justice to a greater extent than have other Australian states. For example, Daley and Lane (1999) have outlined the development of the actuarially based 'online' risk assessment method-ology used in Western Australia, and Israel and Dawes (2002) provide further evidence of the commitment of Daley (then General Manager for Community Based Services) to the measurable objectives and evaluation of programmes (see also Howells and Day 1999). But such apparent similarities with the UK and the USA are misleading if viewed in the absence of WA's – and indeed Australia's – greatest criminal justice problem, namely, the excessive imprisonment of its indigenous people (Harding *et al*. 1995). Overall in Australia, indigenous prisoners account for 20 per cent of the average prison population, compared with 2 per cent in the population as a whole (Australian Bureau of Statistics 2002). But the proportion in WA is nearer 33 per cent overall (and 40 per cent of all receptions), 40 per cent for women (over 50 per cent of receptions) and nearer 60 per cent for juveniles (Fernandez and Loh 2002). Western Australia has the highest indigenous imprisonment rate in all Australia at 3,036 prisoners per 100,000 adult indigenous population, compared with 1,829 overall in Australia – 20 and 15 times, respectively, the rate of non-indigenous imprisonment (ABS 2002). It is a problem that presents the greatest possible challenge to community corrections. It also demon-strates the shortcomings of an ideological adherence to What Works. What works in the centre of Perth is certainly not what works in the regions. At a more fundamental level, as previously argued (Blagg 1997), notions of reintegrative shaming and restorative justice are wholly inappropriate to members of a civilisation that has been all but destroyed by British colonialism (see also Broadhurst 2002). Rather than separating out crime problems into discrete and apparently unrelated components (for example, domestic violence, alcohol abuse, petrol sniffing), Blagg later argues (1998: 10) that we should see such issues as 'aspects of a collective suffering' requiring an understanding akin to that shown to the survivors of disaster or trauma.

One Arm Point is a real place; it is also a symbolic place. It 'stands in for' all those geographical, social, economic and cultural places where What Works might not work. At One Arm Point the earth is bright red, the bush is bright green, the sky is bright blue, the sea is bright turquoise – and the temperature rarely falls below 25 degrees centigrade. The community of about 300 people is joined to the nearest town, Broome, some 200km away by an unsealed road open only to 4WD vehicles. The community council has prohibited alcohol but some of the men smuggle it in from Broome anyway. When they are drunk, some of the men become very violent, most frequently towards the women. Aboriginal women are 45 times as likely to be victims of what we would call domestic violence (a term not accepted by many Aboriginal communities) than are non-Aboriginal women (Ferrante et al. 1996). Although Aboriginal people make up less than 3% of the population of Western Australia, just under half of all cases of 'family violence' (the preferred term) reported to the police involve Aboriginal families. This, many would argue, is the legacy of colonialism that stripped indigenous Australians of their land and their dignity in ways too various and complex to discuss here. As Margaret Smallwood says, 'This violence is not our way':

The patriarchal attitudes of colonial Australia replaced Aboriginal kinship laws and the resultant breakdown in the Aboriginal society generated violence within the family unit (1996: 131)

One Arm Point is in the far north of a state the size of Western Europe with a population of less than two million, over one million of whom live in metropolitan Perth, 2,300km to the south. The remainder are scattered across the 'country' in small towns and hundreds of Aboriginal communities. The Community Corrections Centre at Broome, with two sub-offices covers a region twice the size of the UK with 12 community corrections officers. Home visits are carried out on expeditions, which may involve camping,

> travelling in a 4WD vehicle with a satellite phone and last on average two weeks. Offenders have to be found, for they have no sense of diaried time, yet, according to local community corrections officers, probation orders are more highly respected by the offender, their family and friends, than seems to be the case in the metropolitan area. (Worrall 2000: 244)

So what are the particular challenges of working with offenders in WA? In metropolitan Perth they are similar to those in many large urban centres with relatively small minority ethnic populations. The Sex Offender Treatment Unit was set up in 1987 as a prison-based service but developed community-based programmes in 1990. The programmes would be recognisable to anyone working in the area in the UK, Canada and the USA and there is a 'culturally relevant' adaptation of the programme for use with Aboriginal sex offenders. The latter includes greater use of audio-visual materials about Aboriginals, a greater emphasis on the interaction of alcohol, violence and inappropriate sexual behaviour, awareness of issues arising out of tribal law and awareness of cultural differences with respect to sexual propriety and impropriety.

Similarly, the Intensive Intervention Centre, established in 1997, shares the philosophy and many of the features of probation centres in England and Wales, including routine urinanalysis. The pattern of assessment and treatment of high-risk offenders and the delivery and evaluation of the COGS programme (Chance of Going Straight) of offending behaviour modules contain all the elements of similarly named programmes here and in North America. Some Aboriginal offenders attend, but those considered sufficiently high risk are usually imprisoned.

But this is where the similarity ends and where the local adaptations of What Works begin. The Aboriginal Family Supervision programme had its beginnings in a survey of Aboriginal families in the northern suburbs of Perth in 1995 and 1996. Concerns emerged that families wanted to be dealt with as families rather than as either individual offenders or as a homogeneous 'Aboriginal' group. Families believed that they could identify significant members who were decision-makers and authority figures. They had a concern about loss of authority among family and community elders and their inability to affect the behaviour of their younger members. As a result, a mentoring project was set up in two suburbs and one separate large town in 1996. Aboriginal co-ordinators were appointed and co-operation was also obtained from the metropolitan Council of Elders. The scheme has experienced many problems, especially in relation to the recruitment of appropriate and acceptable mentors. For example, a very high proportion of Aboriginal people have some kind of police record which is something of an impediment to their appointment as mentors. On the other hand, there is a reluctance among potentially suitable mentors to expose themselves to this kind of vetting – a feeling that white people have an audacity to scrutinise them while, at the same time, being dependent on their co-operation for the scheme to work. Because of the complex skin groupings in Aboriginal societies, it is also important that mentors are acceptable to the families of the young offenders. Such problems and negotiations go well beyond issues of 'cultural sensitivity' and expose the heart of colonial relationships.

If the What Works approach to offending has to be compromised in dealings with urban Aboriginal communities, then it becomes transformed beyond recognition when imposed on communities in the 'country':

> You can't transfer ideas of working with offenders from Perth to communities. Many Aboriginal offenders can barely speak English. They can't analyse and conceptualise offending in abstract terms, or respond immediately to the cognitive behavioural method. It's too confrontational but also the links between offending and the consequences in terms of punishment are too complex. Punishment has to be swift and relevant. White justice takes too long.

When I submitted the first draft of the article that eventually appeared in *Probation Journal* (Worrall 2000), I wanted to include this quotation from an experienced Aboriginal worker. But the editorial board explained that they would be uncomfortable printing it because they felt it displayed 'internal racism'. My immediate reaction was to be angry that the board presumed to make such a judgement. In my view, they had misrecognised racism because they had failed to appreciate the cultural context and meaning of the communication. But my second reaction was to be angry with myself for failing to take the trouble to explain that context – at least to the best of my limited understanding and experience. To say that 'many Aboriginal offenders can barely speak English' is to acknowledge that there are over 300 language groups in Aboriginal communities and to accept that speaking English is not only not a priority but is inextricably linked with postcolonial attitudes to white authority and 'introduced law'. The comment that they 'can't analyse or conceptualise offending *in abstract terms*' would perhaps be better expressed as 'in white men's terms'. Rather than perceiving this as a deficit, the speaker was identifying it as part of a 'culture of resistance' to 'white ways' (Broadhurst 2002: 265). The concept of a 'social contract', which underpins the existence of British criminal justice, has no meaning for dispossessed peoples who, prior to 1967, were classified for research purposes under the Department of Fisheries, Flora, Fauna and Aborigines.[4] To say that cognitive behavioural approaches are too confrontational and complicated is to acknowledge that the legacy of colonialism has left some Aboriginal people with an inability to handle verbal confrontation – a legacy of enforced passivity in dealing with real or perceived white authority figures. To say that punishment has to be swift and relevant is to recognise the (admittedly highly controversial) existence of 'customary law', which may include a traditional and formalised use of physical punishment, unacceptable to 'introduced law'. Customary law has been described thus by Damian McLean, an Aboriginal community adviser:

> It is severe. It is immediate. They [offenders] are then reconciled with their immediate and extended family and everyone accepts it. They then look outside the group for a reason for the behaviour, such as through sorcery, because it's hard to bring someone back into the group if you believe they have wilfully or maliciously [committed crime]. (Pedley 2002)

This combination of severe and immediate punishment, social reconciliation and 'the externalising of malice' (Pedley 2002) may not sit comfortably with cognitive behavioural approaches.

A further problem with the What Works agenda is its individualised focus, which, ironically, may neglect the strength of the complex obligations within Aboriginal communities. Community obligations over-ride individual preferences to an extent which may not be understood by those who argue that offenders need to make better individual choices, resist peer pressure and so on. I spoke to Aboriginal community corrections officers who were personally exercised by the conflict they experienced between community and professional obligations. For example, should they give a home to a community member who is in breach of an order or on the run from the police? In every case, there appeared to be no question but that community obligations should take precedence, even if that meant losing their job. If this is true for professional workers, how can it not be true for offenders themselves? According to McLean, 'the biggest offence under customary law is to not support your own kin, regardless of the issue' (Pedley 2002). It is probably naïve to suggest that such a strong sense of community obligation should perhaps be nurtured rather than undermined but, to an outsider such as me, these problems appear to be more than 'local difficulties' which can be overcome by 'cultural sensitivity'.

In my previous article (Worrall 2000) I described two projects in which Community Based Services have used a community development model of working with offenders – a model which, it could be argued, lies at the opposite end of the rehabilitative spectrum from the What Works approach. I am repeating those descriptions here because they are integral to my argument but I then describe two further developments which reach even closer to the heart of 'what matters' in work with Aboriginal peoples. Sadly (or perhaps not?), neither of these later initiatives involves community corrections workers, though one is being led by an Aboriginal former community corrections worker.

The first project is the use of contracts between the Department/Ministry of Justice and several of the larger Aboriginal communities (Daley and Lane 1999). (In the Kimberley there are more than 100 communities but fewer than 20 with populations of more than 80 people.) Under these contracts, the communities manage their own offenders, with support from Community Based Services. A major role of the services is to visit the communities regularly to provide support and training and to maintain a constant dialogue on local issues and development. A number of these communities are subject to periods of internal volatility, and leadership changes make it essential continually to promote the value of the partnerships. Until some five years ago, the communities appointed honorary community corrections officers who liaised with statutory workers in the region. But this system did not work well because of the kind of issues identified earlier in relation to mentoring, so the community council now makes its own decisions about who should supervise offenders in the community. The small number of supervisors I spoke to at one community were committed to their role but spoke of difficulties in dealing with breaches of orders (especially people not fulfilling their community work orders) and minor corruption, such as a woman community work organiser being selected to supervise her own husband on an order, choosing the best work for him and ignoring his non-compliance.

The second project in the Central Desert region illustrates a number of dilemmas and challenges to white justice. In the early 1990s serious concerns emerged about the high proportion of Aboriginal offenders imprisoned in the Central Desert region for solvent abuse, primarily petrol sniffing. At one point, up to 40 per cent of prison admissions were for petrol sniffing by Aboriginal people. Ironically, this is not a criminal offence in WA but is prohibited under Aboriginal by-laws. Through the Aboriginal Communities Act 1979, the state government gave the communities the right to decide whether or not to adopt the by-laws. In 1993 a Commonwealth (central government) grant was given to develop a programme to divert such offenders from prison and also to involve Aboriginal communities more in the management of their own offenders. By mid-1995 there was a dramatic reduction in the number of Aboriginal admissions to prison for sniffing, possession or distribution of petrol, as a result of a number of community initiatives:

1 The establishment of a diversion hostel.
2 The establishment of a skills-oriented youth centre.
3 Increased support by Community Corrections in the use of non-custodial sentences.
4 The replacement of petrol with Avgas (a form of diesel) in Aboriginal communities.

Sadly, but perhaps inevitably, the offending figures have crept up again, largely as a result of imported (and over-priced) illicit petrol from other states and the removal of the WA state subsidy on Avgas, but this environmental solution[5] to a specific form of offending, *which is illegal only in a specific environment*, seems to be of great significance to my argument that 'successful interventions do not seem to travel well' (Pitts 1992: 144) and that we need to exercise the greatest of caution in developing global discourses about the treatment of offenders.

In evaluating the solvent abuse project, the Ministry of Justice argued that there were certain lessons to be learnt that could be of use to other programmes and these lessons bear similarities to Findlay's 'potentials for integrated crime control' (1999: 217):

1 The community must be supportive of the programme's rationale, directions and pace at which it is implemented.
2 The development of trust and respect cannot be accelerated to suit bureaucratic timetables.
3 Textbook models of community development and programme design will not work. This project has been in continuous evolution and some of its best achievements were not part of the programme's original aims. It has largely evolved by trial and error, which makes evaluation extremely difficult, but even the evaluation report has acknowledged that its flexibility has been amongst its greatest strengths. (WA Ministry of Justice 1996)

A further example of Aboriginal-led crime prevention is to be found in recent research undertaken by the Crime Research Centre at the University of Western Australia into 'night patrols' across Australia (Blagg and Valuri 2003). Night patrols perform policing activities, but without formal police powers, in remote communities. Often dominated by the older women in the community, they provide practical crime prevention services such as transport home for young people, diversion of intoxicated people away from the criminal justice system and into safe 'sobering up' shelters, intervention to prevent violence and liaison with safe houses and women's refuges. Night patrols are seen to have 'cultural authority' and to reflect the community's sense of moral responsibility for its own people in trouble.

More controversial, but potentially more far-reaching, has been the setting up by the government of Western Australia of the terms of reference (known as the 'Reference') of an inquiry into Aboriginal customary law and the extent to which it should be recognised and taken into account within the legal system (Blagg et al. 2002). Based at the Crime Research Centre and led by a female Aboriginal project manager (a former community corrections officer), the inquiry is set to last for three years and to face some extraordinarily difficult discussions. One example of the kind of moral dilemmas posed by customary law is a case that became highly publicised in 2001. A young Aboriginal man who killed his friend was speared 12 times in the thigh in a traditional punishment ceremony, formally witnessed by non-Aboriginal police. Severely injured, he then had to face 'white law' and was eventually given a five-and-a-half year prison sentence for manslaughter, with the customary law punishment being accepted in mitigation and no charges being laid against those who carried it out (Pedley 2002).

W(h)ither What Works(?)

If the What Works agenda is to be more than just the *fin de siècle* 'phase' in the treatment of offenders, then it needs to demonstrate that it has within it the seeds of its own development and adaptation to changing social, political and economic circumstances. Pretending to be a universal constant amid those changes is, as they say, not an option. The What Works agenda in Western Australia cannot survive by ignoring the Customary Law Reference. In order to survive, What Works has to address three key questions:

1 What works for whom, when, where and why? (The question of *practice wisdom*.)
2 Whose interests does the What Works agenda serve? (The question of *political awareness*.)
3 Within what models of social order and control does the What Works agenda wish to operate? (The question of *social justice*.)

The question of *practice wisdom* involves national and international comparative research in order to learn about approaches and programmes that are successful with particular types of offenders, in particular locations at particular times. Some will be cognitive behavioural programmes that lend themselves to conventional forms of evaluation. But many more will have grown out of locally identified needs and resources, not the least of which will be enthusiastic and skilful individual workers. Not all will immediately reduce recidivism in any measurable way, but all will be aiming to influence offenders' attitudes, behaviour and circumstances, making them 'stop and think' before offending next time and thus offering the greatest hope of long-term protection for the public. In this search for practice wisdom there is also a need to explore what *doesn't* work. It is part of the received wisdom of What Works that intervention which focuses only on insight-giving or the therapeutic relationship and which does not include a problem-solving dimension is not successful with offenders. But what is less well publicised is that there is plenty of research on other things that don't work (Trotter 1999). These include approaches which focus on blame and punishment, those where the goals are set only by the worker rather than collaboratively, lack of clarity on the part of the worker about his or her role and authority, pessimism and a negative attitude by the worker and, finally, failing to see the offender in his or her family and social context.

Practice wisdom also needs to address the question of enforcement. In England and Wales, the probation service has been consistently criticised for its failure rigorously to enforce the keeping of appointments. National standards now require officers to commence breach proceedings after only one unacceptable failure to keep an appointment but even some of the greatest advocates of government policy are beginning to question the wisdom of such measures. In a recent article, Hedderman and Hearnden argue: 'Punishing non-compliance is something we should reserve for those who have shown themselves to be unwilling to comply despite efforts to assist them to do so ... Also, there is as yet no evidence that stricter enforcement results in lower reconviction rates' (2000: 128). It is an accepted tenet of working with offenders that 'change is a process' that takes time – motivational interviewing is now a recognised What Works skill (Chapman and Hough 1998). Yet this runs increasingly contrary to Home Office policy,[6] being replaced by what Bale satirically calls EBSST – 'Exceptionally Brief Simple Solution Therapy':

> Offenders [are] ... rapidly forced to confront their offending behaviour, speedily acknowledge their distorted thinking, instantly renounce all habit-forming substances and pledge undying commitment to an all-encompassing relapse prevention plan (2000: 130).

The question of *political awareness* involves asking why the simple phrase What Works has become so invested with meaning? Or is it precisely because it *lacks* meaning that it has become so ubiquitous? There are at least four interest groups whose purposes might be served by the What Works agenda and whether those interests are to be viewed positively or negatively will depend entirely on one's standpoint:

1 The interests of *governance* are served to the extent that the What Works agenda demonstrates to a sceptical public that community sentences can be tough, demanding and based on scientific premises which can be tested and evaluated.

2 The interests of *management* are served to the extent that the agenda demonstrates accountability – showing that resources are being used efficiently, effectively and, above all, economically – and giving managers confidence that they know exactly what their workers are doing and why.

3 The interests of *professionalism* are served to the extent that the agenda reassures individual workers that they are doing something worth while with the minimum of risk to their own status – that the areas in which they have to exercise their own judgement are limited and consequently so is the potential for error, thus reducing the otherwise stressful nature of the job.

4 Finally, the interests of *restorative justice* are served to the extent that the offender, victim and, possibly, the wider community believe that the agenda delivers on its promises. Whatever the content of any particular intervention, it can be argued that What Works aims to instil in the offender a sense of responsibility towards the community

in general and empathy for the victim in particular. But in return, the offender has the right to expect to be *reintegrated* into that community and unless that right is respected, What Works becomes little more than a sophisticated form of the stocks – as indeed it is for many sex offenders who, no matter what programmes they have co-operated with, remain irredeemable and non-reintegratable in the eyes of the community (Worrall 1997).

Forget about Socratic dialogue; what about Ockham's razor?

So what of *social justice*? As Raynor argues, 'effective programmes have their place within a model of organic justice, which aims at compatibility with social justice and communal solidarity' (2002: 180).

When she first told me that the 'Enhanced Thinking Skills' course was being delivered to women in prison through Socratic dialogue, I thought the psychologist was being uncharacteristically humorous, so I laughed. But she wasn't; she was deadly serious. Socratic dialogue was the method whereby the philosopher gently but persistently questioned his eager voluntary pupils, pretending to know nothing himself but all the while skilfully directing them to discover the answers they sought through their own intellectual endeavour. That anyone can be so disingenuous as to use this phrase within the coercive context of an offending behaviour programme in a prison leaves one speechless. But if we are in the business of wrenching bleeding chunks of philosophy from their contexts, then I would like to suggest that Ockham's razor may have something to commend it. Ockham's razor, translated from the Latin (see the opening of this chapter), states that 'entities should not be multiplied unnecessarily'. A more useful translation is: 'when you have two competing theories which make exactly the same predictions, the one that is simpler is (probably) better.' It is quite possible that, all other things being equal, people choose to offend because they are cognitively deficient and have distorted perceptions of the world. But all other things are never equal and until we address some of the more straight-forward factors that may contribute towards crime – like poverty, lack of education, poor health, poor housing, child neglect and abuse and unemployment – there seems little point in complicating matters. There are at least two staggering demographic statistics about Aboriginal people in Australia. The first is that their life expectancy at birth is almost 20 years less (and worsening) than for non-Aboriginal people – 56 for men and 63 for women, compared with 77 and 82, respectively, for non-Aboriginal men and women. The second statistic is that their infant mortality rate is 14 per 1,000 births compared with 5 per 1,000 births for all Australian people (Australian Bureau of Statistics 2001; Neill 2002). The suicide rate for young Aboriginal men (and not just in custody) has also been described as 'among the highest recorded in international literature' (Neill 2002: 216). In this context, the suggestion that they may have cognitive deficits seems, at best, supremely irrelevant and, at worst, cynically irresponsible.

But to end on a more positive note ...

Watching the video of the work of the Yuendumu Women's Night Patrol (see Blagg and Valuri 2003), no one could fail to be moved by the sight of several elderly and none-too-agile grandmothers, kitted out in 'Night Patrol' uniform, walking purposefully round a remote community in the Northern Territory in the middle of the night, descending on a group of belligerent drunken men, tipping their 'grog' into the ground, dragging them into a van and packing them off to a sobering-up shelter for the night. As a result, the children in the community got a good night's sleep and turned up for school alert enough to learn something and – who knows? – perhaps to 'stop and think' before sniffing petrol in a few years' time – which is really what matters.

Notes

1 In its early days, the phrase What Works was accompanied by a question mark which (as I read it) befitted the tentative and investigative nature of its claims. The question mark has since been dropped and the claims have become more assertive. At the same time, however, the definition of the phrase has become broader and it is now more of an 'umbrella' term, used to cover a wide variety of so-called 'evidence-based' activities (see Chapman and Hough 1998). I use the phrase 'the What Works agenda' to describe the combination of ideology, policy and practice.

2 My aim in this chapter is to provide illustration of individuals and communities which are blatantly unamenable to What Works intervention, yet who find themselves evaluated within, and required to measure up to, the complex demands of that agenda. I am not claiming for myself any expertise in the politics of Aboriginal Australia, nor do I claim in any way to be 'speaking for' Aboriginal communities and those who work with them. In addition to brief visits to relevant projects, I have been dependent on – and am very grateful to – Aboriginal and non-Aboriginal staff in the Department of Justice, WA, and the Crime Research Centre at the University of Western Australia for information and inspiring discussion. In particular, I am indebted to Harry Blagg, Neil Morgan, Frank Morgan, David Indermaur, Giulietta Valuri and Cheri Yavu Kama Harathunian. Any misperceptions or errors of fact are mine alone.

3   The WA government made much play of a decline in the average daily prison population (and especially of Aboriginal people) in 2001, claiming that it demonstrated the commitment of courts to finding alternatives. That decline has now levelled out and shows signs of rising again. In any case, as these figures show, the decline seems to have been due to a reduction in the length of sentences rather than in the 'throughput' of prisoners, though this is open to debate and the achievement of any reduction at all in the present penal climate is to be applauded.

4   For this information and many other insights, I am indebted to Cheri Yavu Kama Harathunian.

5   For a thought-provoking discussion of the relationship between situational and cognitive approaches to crime prevention, see Smith (2000).

6   As a member of the Parole Board of England and Wales, I and my colleagues spend a great deal of time deliberating before we release approximately 10 long-term prisoners a day on parole, only to replace them immediately with between 25 and 50 'recalls', for non-compliance with licences.

References

Aboriginal and Torres Strait Islanders Social Justice Commissioner (2002) *Social Justice Report 2001*. Sydney: Human Rights and Equal Opportunity Commission.

Australian Bureau of Statistics (2001) *Deaths Australia* (Cat. No. 3302.0). Canberra: ABS.

Australian Bureau of Statistics (2002) *Prisoners in Australia* (Cat. No. 4517.0). Canberra: ABS .

Bale, D. (2000) 'Pure fiction: an infallible guide to national standards', *Probation Journal*, 47 (2): 129–31.

Blagg, H. (1997) 'A just measure of shame: Aboriginal youth and conferencing in Australia', *British Journal of Criminology*, 37 (4): 481–501.

Blagg, H. (1998) 'Restorative visions and restorative justice practices: conferencing, ceremony and reconciliation in Australia', *Current Issues in Criminal Justice*, 10 (1): 5–14.

Blagg, H., Morgan, N. and Yavu Kama Harathunian, C. (2002) 'Aboriginal customary law in Western Australia', *Reform*, 80: 11–14.

Blagg, H. and Valuri, G. (2003) *An Overview of Night Patrol Services in Australia*. Canberra: Commonwealth Attorney-General's Department.

Braithwaite, J. (1997) 'Conferencing and plurality: reply to Blagg', *British Journal of Criminology*, 37 (4): 502–6.

Broadhurst, R. (2002) 'Crime and indigenous people', in A. Graycar and P. Grabosky (eds) *The Cambridge Handbook of Australian Criminology*. Cambridge: Cambridge University Press.

Chapman, T. and Hough, M. (1998) *Evidence Based Practice*. London: Home Office.

Daley, D. and Lane, R. (1999) 'Actuarially based "on-line" risk assessment in Western Australia', *Probation Journal*, 46 (3): 164–70.

Dutton, M. and Xu, Z. (1998) 'Facing difference: relations, change and the prison sector in contemporary China', in R.P. Weiss and N. South (eds) *Comparing Prison Systems*. Amsterdam: Gordon & Breach.

Fernandez, J. and Loh, N. (2002) *Crime and Justice Statistics for Western Australia 2001*. Perth: University of Western Australia Crime Research Centre.

Ferrante, A., Morgan, F., Indermaur, D. and Harding, R.W. (1996) *Measuring the Extent of Domestic Violence*. Perth: Hawkins Press.

Findlay, M. (1999) *The Globalisation of Crime*. Cambridge: Cambridge University Press.

Harding, R.W. *et al.* (1995) *Aboriginal Contact with the Criminal Justice System*. Perth: Hawkins Press.

Hedderman, C. and Hearnden, I. (2000) 'The missing link: effective enforcement and effective supervision', *Probation Journal*, 47 (2): 126–12.

Howells, K. and Day, A. (1999) 'The rehabilitation of offenders: international perspectives applied to Australian correctional systems', *Trends and Issues*, 112. Canberra: Australian Institute of Criminology.

Indermaur, D. (1990) *Perceptions of Crime Seriousness and Sentencing*. Canberra: Criminology Research Council.

Israel, M. and Dawes, J. (2002) 'Something from nothing: shifting credibility in community correctional programmes in Australia', *Criminal Justice*, 2 (1): 5–25.

Morgan, N. (2002) 'Going overboard? Debates and developments in mandatory sentencing 2000–2002', *Criminal Law Journal*, 26 (5): 293–311.

Morgan, N., Blagg, H. and Williams, V. (2001) *Mandatory Sentencing in Western Australia and the Impact on Aboriginal Youth*. Perth: Crime Research Centre, UWA.

Neill, R. (2002) *White Out: How Politics is Killing Black Australia*. Crows Nest, NSW: Allen & Unwin.

O'Malley, P. (2002) 'Globalising risk? Distinguishing styles of "neo-liberal" criminal justice in Australia and the USA', *Criminal Justice*, 2 (2): 205–22.

Pedley, D. (2002) 'Law of two lands', *The West Australian*, 31 August.

Pitts, J. (1992) 'The end of an era', *Howard Journal of Criminal Justice*, 31 (2): 133–49.

Raynor, P. (2002) 'What works: have we moved on?', in D. Ward *et al.* (eds) *Probation: Working for Justice* (2nd edn). Oxford: Oxford University Press.

Roberts, J.V., Stalans, L.J., Indermaur, D. and Hough, M. (2003) *Penal Populism and Public Opinion: Lessons from Five Countries*. Oxford: Oxford University Press.

Smallwood, M. (1996) 'This violence is not our way: an Aboriginal perspective on domestic violence', in R. Thorpe and J. Irwin (eds) *Women and Violence – Working for a Change*. Sydney: Hale & Iremonger.

Smith, D.J. (2000) 'Changing situations and changing people', in A. von Hirsch *et al.* (eds) *Ethical and Social Perspectives on Situational Crime Prevention*. Oxford: Hart Publishing.

Trotter, C. (1999) *Working with Involuntary Clients*. London: Sage.

Vanstone, M. (2000) 'Cognitive-behavioural work with offenders in the UK: a history of influential endeavour', *Howard Journal of Criminal Justice*, 39 (2): 171–83.

W.A. Ministry of Justice (1996) *Aboriginal Offender Management Initiatives: Joint Workshop, Alice Springs*. Perth: Conference Briefing Papers.

Weiss, R.P. and South, N. (eds) (1998) *Comparing Prison Systems*. Amsterdam: Gordon & Breach.

Worrall, A. (1997) *Punishment in the Community: The Future of Criminal Justice*. Harlow: Longman.

Worrall, A. (2000) 'What works at One Arm Point? A study in the transportation of a penal concept', *Probation Journal*, 47 (4): 243–9.

Index